Genocide

Key Themes

Edited by
DONALD BLOXHAM
and
A. DIRK MOSES

OXFORD
UNIVERSITY PRESS

OXFORD
UNIVERSITY PRESS

Great Clarendon Street, Oxford, OX2 6DP,
United Kingdom

Oxford University Press is a department of the University of Oxford.
It furthers the University's objective of excellence in research, scholarship,
and education by publishing worldwide. Oxford is a registered trade mark of
Oxford University Press in the UK and in certain other countries

First Edition published in 2022

Impression: 1

Published in the United States of America by Oxford University Press
198 Madison Avenue, New York, NY 10016, United States of America

British Library Cataloguing in Publication Data
Data available

Library of Congress Control Number: 2021948410

ISBN 978-0-19-286526-7

Printed and bound by
CPI Group (UK) Ltd, Croydon, CR0 4YY

Acknowledgements

Donald Bloxham thanks the Leverhulme Trust; he worked on this book during a period of leave from his regular university duties facilitated by receipt of a Leverhulme Major Research Fellowship (MRF-2016-164).

Contents

List of Contributors

Alex J. Bellamy is Professor of Peace and Conflict Studies and Director of the Asia Pacific Centre for the Responsibility to Protect at the University of Queensland, Australia. He is also Fellow of the Academy of Social Sciences in Australia. His publications include *World Peace (And How we Can Achieve it)* (Oxford University Press, 2019), *Responsibility to Protect: Principle to Practice*, with Edward C. Luck (Polity, 2019), and *East Asia's Other Miracle: Explaining the Decline of Mass Atrocities* (Oxford University Press, 2017). His most recent book is *Syria Betrayed: Civilian Suffering and the Failure of International Diplomacy* (Columbia University Press, 2021).

Donald Bloxham is Richard Pares Professor of History at the University of Edinburgh. He has written widely on genocide and its punishment. Among his publications are *Genocide on Trial: War Crimes Trials and the Formation of Holocaust History and Memory* (Oxford University Press, 2001); *The Great Game of Genocide: Imperialism, Nationalism and the Destruction of the Ottoman Armenians* (Oxford University Press, 2005); *The Final Solution: A Genocide* (Oxford University Press, 2009); and (as co-editor in both cases) *The Oxford Handbook of Genocide Studies* (Oxford University Press, 2010) and *Political Violence in Twentieth Century Europe* (Cambridge University Press, 2011).

Matthias Häussler studied Philosophy, Sociology, and Political Science at Goethe University Frankfurt, where he earned his doctorate in Philosophy in 2006 with a thesis on Hegel's conception of religion, published as *Der Religionsbegriff in Hegels Phänomenologie des Geistes* (Karl Alber, 2008 and 2015). In 2004, he became a faculty member of the Department of Sociology of the University of Siegen. Between 2009 and 2013, he conducted a research project funded by the German Research Foundation (DFG) on colonial rule, war, and genocide in German South West Africa (1904–8), leading to extended stays in Namibia, Botswana, and South Africa. Among his publications is *The Herero Genocide. War, Emotion and Extreme Violence in Colonial*

Namibia (Berghahn Books, 2021). In 2014, he was a visiting scholar at the Hamburg Institute for Social Research and in 2017–18 at the University of California, Berkeley. He is now based at the Institute for Diaspora Research and Genocide Studies at the Ruhr University Bochum, preparing a critical edition of Lothar von Trotha's diaries and papers. In addition to his research, he is on the advisory board of the *Journal of Namibian Studies*.

Rebecca Jinks is Lecturer in Modern History at Royal Holloway, University of London. A historian of comparative genocide and humanitarianism, she published *Representing Genocide: The Holocaust as Paradigm?* with Bloomsbury in 2016. She is currently working on a project encompassing gender, humanitarianism, and the reintegration of female survivors in the aftermath of the Armenian and Yezidi genocides, the first article from which was published in the *American Historical Review* in 2018 as '"Marks Hard to Erase": The Troubles Reclamation of "Absorbed" Armenian Women, 1919–1927'. Together with Dan Stone, she is also compiling *Genocide: A Documentary Reader*, an extensive collection of primary documentation from fifteen global case studies of genocide, to be published by Bloomsbury in 2023.

Elisa von Joeden-Forgey is the Endowed Chair in Holocaust and Genocide Studies at Keene State College in Keene, New Hampshire (US). Formerly she was the Dr. Marsha Raticoff Grossman Associate Professor of Holocaust and Genocide Studies at Stockton University in New Jersey, where she also directed the master's program in Holocaust and Genocide Studies and founded the world's first academic, graduate-level Genocide Prevention Certificate Program. She is former President of Genocide Watch and former First Vice President of the International Association of Genocide Scholars. She received her MA and PhD in History from the University of Pennsylvania and her BA from Columbia University. She teaches undergraduate and graduate courses on the Holocaust, comparative genocide, gender, sexual violence, war, human rights, imperialism, and genocide prevention at several universities, and has lectured and published widely on these topics. Her most recent publication is *The Cultural History of Genocide, Vol. 5: The Era of Total War* (Bloomsbury, 2020).

Rachel Kerr is Professor of War and Society in the Department of War Studies, King's College London. Her research focuses on transitional and post-conflict justice and memory and international law and war. Her publications include: *Reconciliation After War: Transitional Justice in Historical Perspective* (edited with James Gow and Henry Redwood, Routledge, 2020), the *Routledge Handbook of War, Law and Technology* (edited with James Gow, Ernst Dijxhoorn, and Guglielmo Verdirame, Routledge, 2017), *Prosecuting War Crimes: Lessons and Legacies of Twenty Years of the International Criminal Tribunal for the Former Yugoslavia* (edited with James Gow and Zoran Pajic, Routledge, 2014), *The Military on Trial: The British Army in Iraq* (Wolf Legal Publishers, 2008), *Peace and Justice: Seeking Accountability After War*, co-authored with Eirin Mobekk (Polity, 2007), and *The International Criminal Tribunal for the Former Yugoslavia: Law, Diplomacy and Politics* (Oxford University Press, 2004).

Jonathan Leader Maynard is a Lecturer in International Politics in the Department of Political Economy at King's College London. His core research focuses on the role of ideology in political violence, mass atrocities, and armed conflict, and his first book, *Ideology and Mass Killing: The Radicalized Security Politics of Genocides and Deadly Atrocities*, will be published by Oxford University Press in 2022. He is also the co-editor, with Mark L. Haas, of the *Routledge Handbook of Ideology and International Relations*, also forthcoming in 2022. He has published in scholarly journals including the *Journal of Peace Research, Ethics, the British Journal of Political Science, Terrorism and Political Violence*, and *Genocide Studies and Prevention*.

Mark Levene is Emeritus Fellow in the History Department, University of Southampton and founder of Rescue!History, http://www.rescue-history.org.uk/. His writing ranges across issues of genocide, the nation-state, and 'minority' relations, as well as environmental and peace issues, especially focusing on anthropogenic climate change. The most recent two volumes in his 'Genocide in the Age of the Nation-State' series: *The Crisis of Genocide: The European Rimlands, 1912–1953* (Oxford University Press, 2013) won the Institute for the Study of Genocide biennial Lemkin award in 2015. He was also lead-editor of *History at the End of the World?: History, Climate Change and the Possibility of Closure* (Humanities-Ebooks, 2010). Currently he is working on a study of genocide in the Cold War era intended to complete his modern genocide history.

Deborah Mayersen is Senior Lecturer in International and Political Studies at the University of New South Wales Canberra at the Australian Defence Force Academy. Deborah's research expertise is in the field of Genocide Studies, including the Armenian genocide, the Rwandan genocide, and genocide prevention. Her publications include *On the Path to Genocide: Armenia and Rwanda Reexamined* (Berghahn Books, 2014), and the edited volumes *A Cultural History of Genocide in the Modern World* (Bloomsbury, 2021), *The United Nations and Genocide* (Palgrave Macmillan, 2016), and *Genocide and Mass Atrocities in Asia: Legacies and Prevention*, with Annie Pohlman (Routledge, 2013).

Stephen McLoughlin is an Assistant Professor at the Centre for Trust, Peace and Social Relations at Coventry University. His research interests include mass atrocity prevention, the role of the UN in conceptualizing and carrying out mass atrocity prevention, the causes of genocide and mass atrocities, and the Responsibility to Protect (R2P). He is the author of *The Structural Prevention of Mass Atrocities* (Routledge, 2014) and *Rethinking Humanitarian Intervention*, with Alex Bellamy (Palgrave 2018).

A. Dirk Moses is Frank Porter Graham Distinguished Professor of Global Human Rights History at the University of North Carolina, Chapel Hill. His latest book is *The Problems of Genocide: Permanent Security and the Language of Transgression* (Cambridge University Press, 2021). He edits the *Journal of Genocide Research*.

Michelle Moyd is Ruth N. Halls Associate Professor of History at Indiana University Bloomington. Her research areas include the history of East African soldiering and warfare, the global history of the First World War, and German colonialism in Africa. Her book *Violent Intermediaries: African Soldiers, Conquest, and Everyday Colonialism in German East Africa* was published by Ohio University Press in 2014. She is also the co-author, with Yuliya Komska and David Gramling, of *Linguistic Disobedience: Restoring Power to Civic Language* (Palgrave, 2018).

Hollie Nyseth Nzitatira (also known as Hollie Nyseth Brehm) is an Assistant Professor of Sociology at the Ohio State University. Her scholarship examines why genocide occurs and how countries rebuild in the aftermath, with recent publications appearing in *Criminology*, *Social Forces*, and *Social Problems*. She is the recipient of the 2017 International Association of Genocide Scholars Prize and the 2018 American Society of Criminology Ruth Shonle Cavan Award, which are the highest awards given to early-career scholars in each association. She is currently the Principal Investigator of two grants from the US National Science Foundation and serves on a US atrocity prevention task force.

Devin O. Pendas is Professor of History at Boston College. His research focuses on the history of war crimes trials, international law, and transitional justice in global context. His publications include: *Democracy, Nazi Trials, and Transitional Justice in Germany, 1945–1950* (Cambridge, 2020), *The Frankfurt Auschwitz Trial, 1963–1965: Genocide, History, and the Limits of the Law* (Cambridge, 2006), and the edited volumes *Beyond the Racial State: New Perspectives on Nazi Germany*, with Mark Roseman and Richard Wetzel (Cambridge, 2017) and *Political Trials in Theory and History*, with Jens Meierhenrich (Cambridge, 2017).

Dan Stone is Professor of Modern History and Director of the Holocaust Research Institute at Royal Holloway, University of London. He is the author of some ninety scholarly articles and sixteen single-authored or edited books, including: *Histories of the Holocaust* (Oxford University Press, 2010); *The Liberation of the Camps: The End of the Holocaust and its Aftermath* (Yale University Press, 2015); *Concentration Camps: A Very Short Introduction* (Oxford University Press, 2019); and *Fascism, Nazism and the Holocaust: Challenging Histories* (Routledge, 2021). His forthcoming books, *Fate Unknown: Tracing the Missing after the Holocaust and World War II* (Oxford University Press) and *The Holocaust: An Unfinished History* (Penguin) will appear in 2022. He is currently co-editing (with Mark Roseman) volume 1 of the *Cambridge History of the Holocaust*.

Andreas Stucki specializes in Iberian and Caribbean history. He is currently the Ludwig and Margarethe Quidde Fellow, German Historical Institute in Rome. Prior to this he was a Lecturer and Associate Researcher at the History Department of the University of Bern. From 2017 to 2018, he was a visiting scholar at the History

Department of the University of Sydney, and from 2015 to 2016 at the Department of Iberian and Latin American Cultures at Stanford University. He has published a book on the forced resettlement of civilians in the Cuban Wars of Independence (1868–98) in German with Hamburger Edition (2012), which was translated into Spanish as *Las Guerras de Cuba: Violencia y campos de concentración* (2017). Further publications include articles in the *Journal of Imperial and Commonwealth History*, the *Journal of Genocide Research*, and the *Journal of Spanish Cultural Studies* as well as contributions to edited collections. His most recent monograph *Violence and Gender in Africa's Iberian Colonies* was published by Palgrave Macmillan in 2019.

Lorenzo Veracini teaches history and politics at the Swinburne University of Technology, Melbourne. His research focuses on the comparative history of colonial systems. He has authored *Israel and Settler Society* (Pluto Press, 2006), *Settler Colonialism: A Theoretical Overview* (Palgrave, 2010), *The Settler Colonial Present* (Palgrave, 2015), and *The World Turned Inside Out* (Verso, 2021). He co-edited *The Routledge Handbook of the History of Settler Colonialism* (2016), manages the settler colonial studies blog, and is founding editor of *Settler Colonial Studies*.

Anton Weiss-Wendt is a Research Professor at the Norwegian Center for Holocaust and Minority Studies in Oslo. He works mainly in the field of Holocaust and Genocide Studies. He is the author and/or editor of twelve books, including *Murder Without Hatred: Estonians and the Holocaust* (Syracuse University Press, 2009); *The Soviet Union and the Gutting of the UN Genocide Convention* (University of Wisconsin Press, 2017); *A Rhetorical Crime: Genocide in the Geopolitical Discourse of the Cold War* (Rutgers University Press, 2018); the two-volume *Documents on the Genocide Convention from the American, British, and Russian Archives* (Bloomsbury, 2018); *Putin's Russia and the Falsification of History: Reasserting Control over the Past* (Bloomsbury, 2020); and *The Future of the Soviet Past: The Politics of History in Putin's Russia* (together with Nanci Adler, Indiana University Press, 2021).

Introduction

Donald Bloxham and A. Dirk Moses

The growth of Genocide Studies shows no sign of abating. The established journals *Holocaust and Genocide Studies* (founded 1986, publishing mainly on the Holocaust) and the *Journal of Genocide Research* (founded 1999 after life as a newsletter) have been joined by *Genocide Studies and Prevention* and *Genocide Studies International* (founded as the same journal in 2006). Other academic journals of International Relations, International Law, and Peace and Conflict Studies also regularly publish on the subject. Handbooks, textbooks, anthologies, and multi-volume editions likewise proliferate.[1] Meanwhile, presses increasingly host book series on genocide, often with associated themes like warfare and the Holocaust.[2] The depth of this scholarship means that genocide is now included as an organizing category in general historical surveys.[3]

At the same time, cognate or alternative concepts have emerged to challenge 'genocide', like the new serials *Violence: An International Journal*, the *State Crime Journal*, the *Journal of Perpetrator Research*, and the *Journal of Mass Violence Research*. The *Cambridge World History of Violence*

---

[1] Particularly popular for teaching are Jens Meierhenrich, *Genocide: A Reader* (Oxford: Oxford University Press, 2014), and Adam Jones, *Genocide: A Comprehensive Introduction*, 3rd ed. (Abingdon: Routledge, 2017).

[2] Berghahn Books, 'War and Genocide', 'Palgrave Studies in the History of Genocide', 'The Routledge Series in Genocide and Crimes against Humanity'; Bloomsbury, 'Holocaust and Genocide Studies'.

[3] See Mark Levene, 'Genocide', in J. R. McNeill and Kenneth Pomeranz (eds.), *The Cambridge World History*, 7 Vols. (Cambridge: Cambridge University Press, 2015), 7: 420–44.

and books in 'massacre studies' consciously eschew genocide.[4] Political scientists routinely distinguish between genocide and politicide, each driven by a distinct logic.[5] The same applies to those who work on civil war and ethnic violence without utilizing genocide.[6] Neither have social scientists and historians researching political violence, especially in the Middle East, made genocide their category of choice, at least until the *Daesh* attacks on Yazidis.[7] For the same reason, some publishing houses prefer alternative concepts, like crimes against humanity and human rights, to name their book series on mass violence.[8] For its part, the United Nations (UN) bundles genocide, crimes against humanity, war crimes, and ethnic cleansing under the relatively new concept of 'mass atrocity crimes' to promote prevention strategies.[9] Still others prefer notions like 'extremely violent societies' and 'demographic surgery'.[10] Conversely, one of the editors of this volume (Donald Bloxham) is completing a study of worldwide political

---

[4] Phillip Dwyer and Joy Damousi (gen. eds.), *Cambridge History of Violence*, 4 Vols. (Cambridge: Cambridge University Press, 2020); Philip Dwyer and Lyndall Ryan (eds.), *Theatres of Violence Massacre, Mass Killing and Atrocity throughout History* (New York and Oxford: Berghahn Books, 2012).

[5] Gary Uzonyi, 'Civil War Victory and the Onset of Genocide and Politicide', *International Interactions* 41:2 (2015), 365–91; Gary Uzonyi and Victor Asai, 'Discrimination, Genocide, and Politicide', *Political Research Quarterly* 73:2 (2020), 352–65.

[6] Stathis Kalyvas, *The Logic of Violence in Civil War* (Cambridge: Cambridge University Press, 2006); Stuart J. Kaufman, *Modern Hatreds: The Symbolic Politics of Ethnic War* (Ithaca and New York: Cornell University Press, 2001).

[7] See the work of Lisa Wedeen and Wendy Pearlman; also Laura Robson, *The Politics of Mass Violence in the Middle East* (Oxford: Oxford University Press, 2020).

[8] Princeton University Press, 'Human Rights and Crimes against Humanity'; Rowman and Littlefield, 'Studies in Genocide: Religion, History, and Human Rights'. See also Donald Bloxham's and Mark Levene's Oxford University Press monograph series 'Zones of Violence'.

[9] United Nations, *Framework of Analysis for Atrocity Crimes: A Tool for Prevention* (2014), https://www.un.org/en/genocideprevention/documents/about-us/Doc. 3_Framework%20of%20Analysis%20for%20Atrocity%20Crimes_EN.pdf.

[10] Susanne Karstedt, 'Contextualizing Mass Atrocity Crimes: The Dynamics of "Extremely Violent Societies"', *European Journal of Criminology* 9:5 (2012), 455–71; Antonio Ferrara, 'Beyond Genocide and Ethnic Cleansing: Demographic Surgery as a New Way to Understand Mass Violence', *Journal of Genocide Research* 17:1 (2014): 1–20.

violence since 1945 that considers a range of political logics that can each produce genocide but also other forms of extreme violence; the focus is on the causal factors rather than any strict typology of outcomes.[11]

In response to this conceptual pluralism, the *Journal of Genocide Research*, for example, has extended its remit. It now publishes articles that push against the 'limits of the genocide lens' in three ways: first, by publishing special issues on the violence of decolonization (the Dutch 'police actions' in Indonesia) and in postcolonial states (the Biafra and East Pakistan secessionist conflicts) that are routinely excluded from the canonical list of modern genocides; second, by entertaining creative appropriations of the concept, hitherto indexed to the Holocaust archetype, such as the 'slow genocide of settler colonialism' and 'ecocide'; and, third, by including mass violence against civilians in general, for example, in the Syrian civil war.[12] Combining these trends is the émigré Syrian intellectual, Yassin al-Haj Saleh, who has coined the term 'genocracy', by which he means replacement of rule by a demos (the citizenry) by a genos (a race or kin) in which certain population groups are criminalized as terrorists. Rather than establishing rigid typologies, he discerns regressive trends that join 'mass extermination and fascism' as 'a structural product of an international system that has made the War on Terror its grand narrative, and made state violence the antidote'.[13]

To take stock of Genocide Studies in all its growing diversity requires more than a case-study approach, then. As a concept and

[11] Provisional details: Donald Bloxham, *Logics of Violence: The World since 1945*.

[12] Scott Straus, 'The Limits of a Genocide Lens: Violence against Rwandans in the 1990s', *Journal of Genocide Research* 21:4 (2019), 504–24; Pauline Wakeham, 'The Slow Violence of Settler Colonialism: Genocide, Attrition, and the Long Emergency of Invasion', *Journal of Genocide Research* (2021), https://doi.org/10.1080/14623528.2021.1885571; special issue on 'Ecocide', edited by Martin Cook and Damien Short, *Journal of Genocide Research* 23:2 (2021); forum on 'Mass Violence against Civilians in the Syrian Civil War', edited by U🞓ur Ümit Üngör (2021), https://doi.org/10.1080/14623528.2021.1979907. Disclaimer: Dirk Moses is the journal's senior editor. NOTE THAT U🞓ur is scrambled in the proofs!

[13] Yassin al-Haj Saleh, 'Terror, Genocide, and the "Genocratic" Turn', *Al-Jumhuriya*, 19 September 2019, https://www.aljumhuriya.net/en/content/terror-genocide-and-%E2%80%9Cgenocratic%E2%80%9D-turn.

legal category about identity-based violence against civilians, genocide organizes perceptions of violence into typologies and even hierarchies.[14] Conceptual self-awareness is thus required to delineate
genocide's porous and contested boundaries, so we decided that
entry-level scholarship on the subject should be thematically driven.
Each chapter surveys existing scholarship in a particular domain—
imperial violence, for instance—while highlighting problems and
making suggestions about avenues for research. Six of the thirteen
chapters are substantially revised versions of those from our *Oxford
Handbook of Genocide Studies* in 2010; the other seven were commis-
sioned for this volume.[15]

What Is Genocide?

The volume propounds no definition of genocide. We doubt that we
could have established one on which the two editors, let alone all
contributors agreed. Even had we achieved that feat, the definition
would have been but one of many contenders in the field. One of us
(Dirk Moses) has recently argued that the genocide concept conceals
more state violence than it reveals, and should be discarded.[16] However, since 'genocide' is now so widely used as an heuristic tool for
historians and social scientists, we left it to our authors to use as they
see fit. In doing so, we give no priority to the claims of lawyers, courts,
or legal theorists to arbitrate its utility. The UN Convention on the
Prevention and Punishment of Genocide (UNGC) of 1948, the jurisprudential exegesis of that document, and accumulated case-law, are
vital for anyone else seeking to make a case that the perpetrators of
some occurrence ought to be prosecuted for genocide in relevant
courts. (Though prosecutions for 'crimes against humanity' may well
be easier and the punishment no smaller, because crimes against

[14] Symptomatic is Nicole Rafter, *The Crime of All Crimes: Toward a Criminology of
Genocide* (New York: NYU Press, 2016).

[15] Donald Bloxham and A. Dirk Moses (eds.), *Oxford Handbook of Genocide Studies*
(Oxford: Oxford University Press, 2010).

[16] A. Dirk Moses, *The Problems of Genocide: Permanent Security and the Language of
Transgression* (Cambridge: Cambridge University Press, 2021).

humanity are not necessarily less morally weighty than genocide.[17])
However, those legal concerns need not be binding for those of us
concerned with analysing events in the *past*, not least because there is a
great difference between the question of whether such-and-such a
person is guilty under international law of the crime of genocide and
arguing about whether such-and-such an event constituted genocide.

Moreover, it is unclear that 'recognizing', i.e. labelling, some event
as genocide in the *present* has any particular legal ramifications for
intervention. On the purely practical level, what is the likelihood of
China being meaningfully sanctioned for the genocide that many
scholars and activists claim it is perpetrating against Uyghurs in
Xinjiang?[18] The same can be said of Myanmar regarding its campaign against Rohingya residents in 2017, given Chinese patronage of
its military dominated regime. These are but some of the critical
considerations involved in what one of us calls the 'diplomacy of
genocide'—the *realpolitik* of claiming and disputing genocide for geopolitical advantage—that makes the quest for prevention and justice a
normative but largely impotent aspiration.[19] Then there is the question of the legal principle—the matter of what the UNGC actually
says about intervention.

The assumption that recognition did legally impel action, based on
the wording of UNGC Article I, concerning prevention of genocide,
and Article VIII, concerning 'prevention and suppression' of genocide, helps to explain the reluctance of key actors to deploy the
'g-word' when it was appropriate in Rwanda in 1994. However, the
alternative reading, that the UNGC is merely exhortative rather than
binding about the responsibility to intervene, that is, 'suppress',
explains why the George Bush Jnr administration was prepared in

---

[17] Alexander R. J. Murray, 'Does International Criminal Law Still Require a
"Crime of Crimes"? A Comparative Review of Genocide and Crimes against
Humanity', *Goettingen Journal of International Law* 3:2 (2011), 589–615.

[18] Joanne Smith Finley, 'Why Scholars and Activists Increasingly Fear a
Uyghur Genocide in Xinjiang', *Journal of Genocide Research* (2020), 1–23, https://
doi.org/10.1080/14623528.2020.1848109.

[19] A. Dirk Moses, 'The Diplomacy of Genocide', in Chris Reus-Smit, et al.
(eds.), *Oxford Handbook of History and International Relations* (Oxford: Oxford University Press, 2022).

2004 to use the term to describe the situation in Darfur.[20] Putting aside the politics of recognition or non-recognition, and likewise questions about the wisdom and practicalities of intervention in this or that instance of ongoing atrocity, the fact is that the UNGC is susceptible to conflicting readings. In practice genocide can be (has been) declared without intervention following, and the fact that intervention can occur (has occurred, for instance, in the Former Yugoslavia) without genocide being officially declared, should lead genocide scholars and activists to fixate less than we tend to do about the arbitration of the term's use.

Fixations nonetheless remain. For better or for worse—and speaking purely for ourselves we volume editors increasingly think it is for the worse—'genocide' continues for many to denote the 'crime of crimes'. The word has great moral force as a mobilizing slogan and has become a mark of distinction, however gruesome. The quest for this particular 'cachet' can translate to a desire to 'prove' that such and such an event was/is genocide. It can encourage zealous advocacy rather than scholarship that is committed to letting the chips of conclusion fall where they may in light of conceptual analysis and inference from the available evidence.

A potentially distortive tendency has been that of holding on to the coattails of the handful of historical cases that are widely agreed to be genocides. The study of those cases has significantly shaped conceptions of what genocide is and 'ought' to look like, and has produced a large proportion of the empirical scholarship across all candidate cases of genocide. In a previous work we wrote: 'If the Holocaust is taken as an "ideal type" genocide, scholars and advocates of particular cases often seek to fit theirs within a "Holocaust paradigm" at the expense of careful contextualisation'.[21] One of the genocides that is sometimes fitted into a Holocaust paradigm is the Rwandan genocide of 1994, but Rwanda has also become a 'paradigm case' of its own, as

[20] Jerry Fowler, 'A New Chapter of Irony: The Legal Definition of Genocide and the Implications of Powell's Determination', in Samuel Totten and Eric Markusen (eds.), *Genocide in Darfur: Investigating the Atrocities in the Sudan* (New York: Routledge 2006), 127–39, esp. 136.

[21] 'Editors' Introduction', Bloxham and Moses, *Oxford Handbook of Genocide Research*, 4.

Clémence Pinaud points out, in just the spirit in which we made our observation, in her recent work *War and Genocide in South Sudan*.[22] Pinaud's study is one of several to illustrate that coattailing and shoe-horning can be fruitfully resisted.

Modifications in how we think about genocide do not in themselves obviate the political issues around the g-word's applicability, however. Each conceptual modification of 'genocide' still implies something about what would be excluded under the modified conceptualization. To be sure, scholarly modifiers tend to be less keen to spell out the exclusions, especially when their own modifications are expansionary, but conceptual expansion cannot be infinite or 'genocide' will lose analytical power. One major reason for reticence in some quarters about clarifying one's conceptual delimitation of genocide is that genocide scholars are especially sensitive to the charge of genocide *denial*—a charge that, like the label genocide itself, fuses cognitive and moral criteria.

Clearly in some instances the label of denier is appropriate in the sense intended, but there are also very many good faith arguments to be had about empirics in this or that case and conceptual elasticity as regards the g-word, which is precisely what is intimated by our describing genocide as a contested concept. Different people understand different things by it and many are capable of providing good reasons for their particular understanding. Only time will tell whether the g-word will continue to maintain its hold in the political arena, and whether the loose, inter-disciplinary field of Genocide Studies retains such coherence as it has. As to the present volume, we can plausibly say that all its chapters apply to genocide, albeit perhaps, depending upon definition, not only to genocide. Some may even change what readers think about genocide.

The Chapters

Each chapter deals with multiple instances of genocide and related crimes in relation to a particular domain. Many of the chapters are

---

[22] Clémence Pinaud, *War and Genocide in South Sudan* (Ithaca, NY: Cornell University Press, 2021), 227.

grouped in thematic clusters. Chapter 1 by Dirk Moses advances a revisionist account of the genocide concept to show how and why it is not fit for purpose to identify and criminalize mass atrocity crimes. Chapters 2 and 3 are concerned with identifying the conditions for genocide with practical purposes in mind. Chapter 2, 'Predicting Genocide', by Hollie Nyseth Brehm, approaches its subject-matter via an overview of global forecasting efforts, then by considering the social science that underpins predictive models. Brehm then considers specific recent developments in forecasting genocide, with a focus on sub-state dynamics of violence and trigger moments. Chapter 3, 'The Absence of Genocide in the Presence of Risk: When Genocide does not Occur', by Deborah Mayerson and Stephen McLoughlin, addresses a shortcoming in so much theorizing about genocide, namely the 'no-variance'[23] character of this thought. In other words, theories of causation have often been based on the study of (select) instances where genocide transpired to the exclusion of instances where genocide was a reasonably strong possibility but did not occur. The authors criticize what they call the 'root cause paradigm': 'By identifying causation through working backwards from major incidents of genocide', they conclude, 'this approach led to a strong focus on risk factors, and a neglect of factors that promote resilience.' The authors then outline the characteristics of an alternative 'Risk and Resilience' model.

Elisa von Joeden-Forgey's essay, 'Gender and Genocide', is the fourth chapter. It is continuous with its two predecessors in that it addresses elements of prediction. Certain gendered forms of violence, while intrinsically important, are also 'early warning signs' of more expansive violence against groups that are not principally conceived in gendered terms—for example the 'ethnic', 'religious', or 'national' groups identified in the UNGC. At the same time, irrespective of the 'sort' of group targeted for genocide—and ultimately such groups are products of perpetrators' perceptions rather than being ontologically objective demographic units, whatever the UNGC's framers may have thought—genocidal violence invariably continues to have a

---

[23] As Scott Straus calls it in his review article, 'Second-Generation Comparative Research on Genocide', *World Politics* 59:3 (2007), 476–501.

gendered quality throughout. This violence can tell us a great deal about the conscious thinking and purposes of the perpetrators but also about functional and symbolic aspects of which the perpetrators may not be conscious. Victims are of course appallingly affected at all levels, both during and after the event.

Chapters 5–8 do not present fully-fledged theories of genocide, but, rather, consider particular causal elements that are not mutually exclusive and are common to many cases. It is difficult to conceptualize genocide, or many other complex, especially collective, human activities, without reference to ideology. As noted by Scott Straus in an influential review article, particular sorts of ideology were especially prominent in the theorizing of what he called the first wave of genocide scholars.[24] After surveying existing thought, Chapter 5, by Jonathan Leader Maynard, is something of a manifesto for a new generation of scholarship on the topic 'Ideology and Genocide'. It urges us to go beyond thinking about types of ideologies, especially relatively extraordinary, obviously extreme ones, to thinking about the circumstances in which a whole range of ideologies can legitimate genocide. It breaks down the false polarity of ideology on the one hand and pragmatism or material concerns on the other. Finally, in studying the manifold, often subtle mechanisms by which ideology can influence action it discards the false choice between ideologies as rigid constant features in the minds of 'true believer' genocidaires or mere rationales for actions impelled by other causes.

The next three chapters consider other culprits. Anton Weiss-Wendt's 'The State and Genocide' makes a forthright case for what the author calls the intricate linkage between genocide and the modern state. 'Empire and Genocide' by Matthias Häussler, Andreas Stucki, and Lorenzo Veracini makes a new contribution to the increasingly populated subfield denoted by the chapter title. The authors distinguish settler colonialism from other imperial formations. Under settler colonialism, power, including the power for extreme violence, radiates centripetally, from the periphery. Under other imperial forms, power is centrifugal. Finally, the chapter considers the capacity of empire in certain modalities to constrain violence as

[24] Ibid.

well as to unleash it in not infrequently genocidal form. Michelle Moyd's chapter 'War and Genocide' brings a decolonizing perspective to bear on the relationship between the two entities. Or better, relationships, since she considers war in its function of creating conditions for genocide; war and genocide as similar processes, indistinguishable from one another; and genocide as a particular kind of war. Her final contribution is to consider undeclared forms of war in notionally peaceful societies, in order, in her words, 'to better identify the processes by which states or other violent actors render people's lives precarious, a condition that can lead to genocidal outcomes'.

Chapter 9, 'Memory and Genocide', by Dan Stone and Rebecca Jinks, provides a conceptual bridge between the chapters before and after it. Memory is a form of response to genocide, a way in which genocide is 'processed' in post-genocidal societies. By the same token the topic of memory can also be a matter of causation, because memories of the crime can foster its repetition.

Chapters 10–12 deal more exclusively with responses to genocide, specifically institutional responses at the international and national levels. The first of these three essays, Alex Bellamy's and Stephen McLoughlin's 'Armed Intervention in Genocide', is concerned with stopping processes already in train, especially by military action from outside the state in which the genocide is perpetrated. The second, 'Genocide and the Politics of Punishment', by Donald Bloxham and Devin O. Pendas, investigates the international politics of prosecuting perpetrators of genocide and like crimes with particular reference to the popular claim that the 'end of impunity' for such malefactors has a deterrent effect on would-be perpetrators. The third essay, Rachel Kerr's 'Genocide and the Limits of Transitional Justice', is concerned with judicial and non-judicial mechanisms introduced by international bodies and individual states in the aftermath of mass atrocities, including genocide. It contemplates the efficacy of these institutions in contributing to the fulfilment of sometimes conflicting goals, including democratization, justice, and peace.

Mark Levene's concluding essay, Chapter 13, is at once a study of causation and response that considers genocide and related atrocities at the nexus of national political economy and global power structures. It refers particularly to the related problems of resource conflicts, environmental degradation, and anthropogenic climate change.

Working from scientific predictions and already-observable patterns of violence, this chapter contemplates, in the words of its sub-title, 'Prospects for Genocide and its Avoidance in the Twenty-First Century'. The vision Levene outlines is horrific and utterly plausible, and constitutes a rallying-cry to everyone in and beyond Genocide Studies who was brought to the study of mass violence out of more than purely academic interest.

1

Fit for Purpose?

The Concept of Genocide and Civilian Destruction

A. Dirk Moses

Introduction

The academic 'pioneers of genocide studies' rediscovered Raphael
Lemkin in founding an academic field in the 1980s. The book in
which he introduced the new notion of 'genocide', *Axis Rule in Occupied
Europe* (1944), became the field's founding document. The Polish-
Jewish émigré jurist, the pioneers thought, was the first to identify
the destruction of nations as a recurrent historical pattern, and to
propose an international law to criminalize this 'odious scourge'.[1] So
they followed in his footsteps by redeeming his memory, honouring his
achievement and, above all, trying to prevent genocide. In reconstructing the intellectual origins of his famous concept, they retold
Lemkin's story. Written as an epic battle against cynical *realpolitik* and
jealous rivals, their hagiographies celebrated Lemkin's triumph in the
United Nations Convention on the Punishment and Prevention of
Genocide in 1948. After the disappointment of the Nuremberg Trials,
in which 'genocide' hardly figured, the Convention (UNCG) meant
that Lemkin's neologism had vanquished the rival contenders of war

[1] Raphael Lemkin, *Axis Rule in Occupied Europe: Laws of Occupation, Analysis of
Government, Proposals for Redress* (Washington, DC: Carnegie Endowment for Inter-
national Peace, 1944); Steven Leonard Jacobs and Samuel Totten (eds.), *Pioneers of
Genocide Studies* (New Brunswick, NJ: Transaction Publishers, 2002).

crimes, crimes against humanity, and crimes against peace as the 'crime of crimes'.[2]

With the UNGC, the field of Genocide Studies felt equipped to go forth and slay the 'Holocaust monster', as one of them put it.[3] That the monster continued to wreak havoc in numerous conflicts since 1948 has vexed and confounded the field. Its members have attributed this civilian destruction to the monstrous dictators of failed states, and to feckless Western leaders who have not prevented their genocidal designs. The field did not consider the proposition that the concept of genocide may not be fit for purpose, namely accounting for the sources of mass violence against civilians so that remedies can be devised.

This chapter explains not only why 'genocide' fails to satisfactorily name the varieties of violence against mass civilians but also how it enables them. For Lemkin and the UNGC criminalized the intentional destruction solely of national, ethnic, racial, and religious groups at the expense of other categories of civilians. While the latter are covered by various international crimes, only genocide towers above them as the supreme crime in international opinion. What is more, according to the UNGC, violence perpetrated in the name of national security and military necessity is not genocidal, which requires the targeting of the denoted groups 'as such', meaning on the grounds of their identity alone. Thus Genocide Studies omitted the Nigeria-Biafra War of 1967–70 and the US conduct in the Vietnam War from its canon, and never included the largest mass casualty event of the twentieth century, the famines of Mao's Great Leap Forward between 1958 and 1962 that killed up to 45 million Chinese citizens. Today, the Myanmar and Chinese governments

---

[2] Michael Ignatieff, 'The Hunger Artist: The Unsung Hero of Modern Humanitarianism', *The New Republic*, 16 September 2018, 46–51; Agnieszka Bieńczyk-Missala and Sławomir Dębski (eds.), *Rafał Lemkin: A Hero of Humankind* (Warsaw: Polish Institute of International Affairs, 2010); Samantha Power, *'A Problem from Hell': America and the Age of Genocide* (New York: Basic Books, 2002); William Korey, *An Epitaph for Raphael Lemkin* (New York: Blaustein Institute for the Advancement of Human Rights, 2002); John Cooper, *Raphael Lemkin and the Struggle for the Genocide Convention* (Basingstoke: Palgrave Macmillan, 2008).

[3] Robert Melson, 'My Journey in the Study of Genocide', in Totten and Jacobs, *Pioneers of Genocide Studies*, 142.

contend that their expulsion of Rohingya and incarceration of Uighurs respectively are security measures, and it is likely that they succeed in doing so. For security and military violence are the bedrocks of national sovereignty, especially when state existence is question. The UNGC was designed to ensure that this right of self-preservation was not hindered by international law.

In accounting for these exclusions, this chapter first returns to Lemkin and his context to demonstrate how his intervention radically constricted fuller understanding of mass criminality. From the 1920s to the 1940s, international lawyers were debating civilian destruction in broad terms in relation to aerial warfare and blockades. Lemkin ignored these discussions in fixating on ethnic categories.

Secondly, this chapter shows how the new legal idea of genocide was shaped in their own interests by agents with actual power: nation-states. If international lawyers today tend to indict perpetrators for war crimes and crimes and humanity instead of genocide, it is because the latter is so difficult to prove. That is no accident.

Lemkin's Favoured Groups

This restricted outcome was not implicit in Lemkin's claim that his basic premise was general civilian immunity. He began his justification of the genocide concept in promising terms when he declared that the distinction between civilians and combatants was elemental to the crime. Genocide was:

> the antithesis of the Rousseau-Portalis Doctrine, which may be regarded as implicit in the Hague Regulations. This doctrine holds that war is directed against sovereigns and armies, not against subjects and civilians. In its modern application in civilized society, the doctrine means that war is conducted against states and armed forces and not against populations.[4]

Here Lemkin declared that criminality was defined as warfare waged against populations rather than armies. Today, customary international humanitarian law refers to the 'principle of distinction'

[4] Lemkin, *Axis Rule in Occupied Europe*, 80.

(or discrimination).[5] But instead of following his premise about the civilian immunity, Lemkin fixated on ethnic or national groups as victims of massive hate crimes. Consequently, he did not develop a framework that also included the targeting of entire peoples as military objectives in armed conflict despite the fact that his predecessors and mentors were already thinking about prosecuting war criminals, defending minorities, and restricting aerial bombardment of civilians. They posed the questions and provided answers that he distorted for his new term.

The denouement of the First World War set the interwar international legal agenda. The victorious Allies' Commission on Responsibility of the Authors of the War and on Enforcement of Penalties, established in 1919 to investigate Central Powers' breaches of international law identified two major transgressions: provoking the war and violating 'the laws and customs of war and the laws of humanity', namely German 'systematic terrorism' against civilians and of course the Ottoman massacres and deportation of Armenians.[6] The concern for civilians continued in international conversations about the novel technology of the imprecise bombing from aircraft in the Hague Draft Rules on Air Warfare of 1923. Article 22 prohibited 'Aerial bombardment for the purpose of terrorizing the civilian population, of destroying or damaging private property not of military character, or of injuring non-combatants'.[7]

---

[5] International Committee of the Red Cross, 'Rule 1. The parties to the conflict must at all times distinguish between civilians and combatants. Attacks may only be directed against combatants. Attacks must not be directed against civilians'. Customary IHL, 'Rule 1. The Principle of Distinction between Civilians and Combatants', https://ihl-databases.icrc.org/customary-ihl/eng/docs/v1_cha_chapter1_rule1.

[6] 'Report of the Commission on Responsibility of the Authors of the War and Enforcement of Penalties', in *Violation of the Laws and Customs of War, Reports of Majority and Dissenting Reports of American and Japanese Members of the Commission of Responsibilities*, Conference of Paris, 1919 (Oxford: Clarendon Press, 1919).

[7] Hague Rules of Air Warfare *American Journal of International Law* 17, supplement (1923); Heinz Markus Hanke, 'The 1923 Hague Rules of Air Warfare: A Contribution to the Development of International Law Protecting Civilians from Air Attack', *International Review of the Red Cross* 33:292 (1993), 17.

Prominent jurists also invoked what they called 'racial massacres' in general and 'the Armenian massacres' in particular. These crimes were so grave as to justify violating the principle of state sovereignty in the interests of 'restoring the moral order which must reign in the whole of humanity', as the Romanian jurist Vespasian V. Pella (1897–1952) put it in 1925 in purporting to declare a *jus cogens* legal principle.[8] The French judge Henri Donnedieu de Vabres (1880–1952) wrote about 'attacks on humanity that might be perpetrated in a country under the influence of race hatred', while his Spanish colleague Quintiliano Saldaña (1878–1938) referred to 'acts of savagery, such as major political or racial massacres' regarding 'the massacres of Christian-Armenians and Russian Jews'.[9] Lemkin's mentor and collaborator in the late 1920s and early 1930s, the Polish vice president of the International Association of Penal Law, Emil Stanisław Rappaport (1877–1965), suggested that propaganda inciting warfare be categorized as 'a new international crime' to protect 'a *new international good—of the safety of culture and the world civilization*'. Such a law 'imposes itself on the public conscience'.[10]

These common nineteenth-century and early twentieth-century phrasings about religiously or racially motivated mass atrocities increased in circulation in the 1920s due to the Armenian experience during the war. The Russian émigré diplomat and jurist André Mandelstam (1869–1949) was a particularly prominent advocate for Armenians, eventually arguing for minority protection via the new term of 'human rights'.[11] The League of Nations minority protection regime comprised treaties between the victorious Allies and fourteen

[8] Vespasian V. Pella, *La Criminalité Collective des États et le Droit Pénal de l'Avenir* (Bucarest: Imprimerie de l'État, 1925), 145–6.

[9] Cited in John Quigley, *The Genocide Convention: An International Law Analysis* (Aldershot: Ashgate, 2006), 3. Quintiliano Saldaña, 'La Justice pénale internationale', *Recueil des cours* 10 (1925), 369; Saldaña, 'La Défense Sociale Universelle', *Revue Internationale de Sociologie* (March–April 1925), 145–74.

[10] E. S. Rappaport, 'Presente au sujet de le propaganda de la guerre d'agression', in *Conférence internationale d'unification du droit pénal (Varsovie, 1er–5 novembre 1927)* (Paris: Recueil Sirey, 1929), 40. Emphasis in original.

[11] André Mandelstam, *Le Sort de l'Empire Ottoman* (Lausanne and Paris: Librarie Payot et Cie, 1917), ix–xi; André Mandelstam, *Das Armenische Problem im Lichte des Völker-und Menschenrechts* (Berlin: Stilke, 1931); André Mandelstam, 'Der

states either established after the war or ones rewarded with new territory—though not Italy, France, and Germany—thereby acquiring large minority populations, like Greece. Although the treaties empowered the League to supervise the provisions, little was done for minorities, which could send petitions to the League but not place complaints on the official agenda. Nonetheless, their existence rankled the elites of the affected states, which blamed minorities for conspiring with international enemies to compromise their hard-won sovereignty and territorial integrity.[12] In 1929, Mandelstam drafted a 'declaration on the international rights of man', adapted by the *Institute de droit international,* whose six articles ascribed to states the duty to protect various individual rights, including those mentioned in the minorities treaties, like the freedom of religion and to use one's language in public instruction.[13] To their regret, the League of Nations declined to adopt this initiative when it was put its assembly in the early 1930s.[14]

A number of other issues concerned the League and leading international lawyers like Rappaport, Pella, and de Vabres: establishing an international criminal court and universal jurisdiction, outlawing inter-state aggression and incitement to war, defining and criminalizing terrorism, and instituting the category of 'international crimes'. Pella and de Vabres were giants in the field, drafting the first version of the UN Genocide Convention with Lemkin in 1947, while de Vabres served as a Nuremberg judge. Lemkin became involved in the

---

internationale Schutz der Menschenrechte und die New-Yorker Erklärung des Instituts für Völkerrecht', *Zeitschrift für ausländisches öffentliches Recht und Völkerrecht* 2 (1931), 335–77.

[12] Carole Fink, *Defending the Rights of Others: The Great Powers, the Jews, and International Minority Protection, 1878–1938* (Cambridge: Cambridge University Press, 2004). Poland eventually renounced its treaty in 1934.

[13] Andre Mandelstam, 'La protection des minorites', *Recueil des Cours de Academie de droit international* 1 (1923), 368–519; Mandelstam, *Le Sort de l'Empire Ottoman,* 444.

[14] Paul Gordon Lauren, *The Evolution of International Human Rights Visions Seen,* 2nd ed. (Philadelphia: University of Pennsylvania Press, 2003), 130–1; Helmut Philipp Aust, 'From Diplomat to Academic Activist: André Mandelstam and the History of Human Rights', *European Journal of International Law* 25:4 (2015), 1105–21.

International Association of Penal Law via Rappaport, and he read
and cited Pella's work. Neither man is mentioned in his
autobiography.

At its 1927 meeting, the International Association of Penal Law
resolved to contrive the category of 'international crimes (*delictum juris
gentium*)' that presented a 'common danger' to all states, like piracy,
slavery, pornography, the drugs trade, counterfeiting money, disrupting international communication, and spreading diseases.[15] Two
years later, Pella mentioned the categories of 'savagery' and 'vandalism' during the League of Nations deliberations about an anti-
counterfeiting convention, distinguishing them from the non-violent
but equally terroristic effect of forging currency.[16] Having placed
international crimes on the agenda in 1927, the association spent
subsequent years deliberating about their definition and codification.
The notion of 'terrorism' for such general dangers was discussed in the
early 1930s. Lemkin argued at the 1931 meeting that the creation of a
'common danger' to human communications (postal, telegraphic,
transport, etc.) was its salient attribute.[17] He continued this line of
argument two years later in his well-known submissions to the association's Madrid conference.[18] Given rising antisemitism in Europe,

[15] For the construction of these as 'international crimes', see Paul Knepper, *The
Invention of International Crime: A Global Issue in the Making, 1881–1914* (Basingstoke:
Palgrave Macmillan, 2010).

[16] League of Nations, Proceedings of the International Conference for the
Adoption of a Convention for the Suppression of Counterfeiting Currency, Gen-
eva, 9th April to 20th April 1929 (Series of League of Nations Publications, II:
Economic and Financial, 1929), 53; Lewis, *The Birth of the New Justice*, 188.

[17] 'Rapport de M. Lemkin', in *Actes de la IV Conférence pour l'Unification du Droit
Penal* (Paris: A. Pedone, 1933), 65; Claudia Kraft, 'Völkermord als *delictum iuris
gentium*: Raphael Lemkins Vorarbeiten für eine Genozidkonvention in der
Zwischenkriegszeit', *Simon Dubnow Institute Yearbook* 4 (2005), 79–98; Daniel Marc
Segesser and Miriam Gessler, 'Raphael Lemkin and the International Debate on
the Punishment of War Crimes (1919–1948)', *Journal of Genocide Research* 7:4 (2005),
453–68; Mark Lewis, *The Birth of the New Justice: The Internationalization of Crime and
Punishment, 1919–1950* (Oxford: Oxford University Press, 2014), 123.

[18] His supplementary report, discussed below, is the more quoted text because
it elaborates his insertion of barbarism and vandalism into the list of international
crimes. The original is Raphael Lemkin, 'Rapport et projet de textes' (sometimes
titled 'Terrorisme' or 'Le terorisme') in Luis Jimenez de Asua, Vespasien Pella, and

including Poland, it is no surprise that Lemkin combined the common vocabulary used by Pella with Rappaport's new 'international good' to protect minorities threatened by fascist regimes. In his 1933 formulation, Lemkin defined vandalism as 'the evil destruction of works of art and culture', that is, 'great' art of international significance.[19] 'Acts of barbarism' effectively reprised the violations listed in the 1919 Commission on Responsibility: 'massacres, pogroms, collective cruelties against women and children, treatment of people that violates their dignity and humiliates them'.[20] If there was little new in this proposal, it also offered no explanation for state excesses other than 'hatred', a force he presumably identified with antisemitism and Pan-Germanism. He said very little about the former after a public controversy with a Polish writer in the late 1920s, however, likely not wanting to draw attention to the Jewish sources of his thought and motivation in a pervasive antisemitic environment.[21]

Neither were his legal proposals as original as commonly supposed. Lemkin took the notions of barbarism, vandalism, the protection of culture, and international crimes from his contemporaries. Before them, the Commission on Responsibility report, like the Hague Draft Rules on Air Warfare, also referred to terrorizing civilians. Lemkin was adapting—and simplifying and racializing—familiar themes.

What is more, Lemkin's ethnic ontology of the human (see below) and related preoccupation with racial hatred led him to ignore other

---

Manuel Lopez-Rey Arroyo (eds.), *Acte de la V-me Conférence pour l'Unification du Droit Penal (Madrid, 19–20 October 1933)* (Paris: A. Pedone, 1935), 48–56. The supplement is called *'Les actes constituant un danger general (interétatique) consideres comme delites des droit des gens': Expilications additionelles au Rapport spécial présentè à la V-me Conférence pour l'Unification du Droit Penal à Madrid (14–20.X.1933)* (Paris: A. Pedone, 1935). The English translation by James T. Fussell, 'Acts Constituting a General (Transnational) Danger considered as Crimes under International Law', appears at http://www.preventgenocide.org/lemkin/madrid1933-english.htm.

[19] Lemkin, 'Rapport et projet de textes', 54.

[20] Ibid., 55.

[21] See James Loeffler, 'The First Genocide: Antisemitism and Universalism in Raphael Lemkin's Thought', *Jewish Quarterly Review* 112:1 (2022).

sinister developments that threatened to terrorize civilians. By the mid-1930s, fears of rivals' capacity to deliver a 'knock-out blow' in pre-emptive bomber strikes on cities haunted military and civilian authorities.[22] Like Lemkin, the American jurist, John Bassett Moore (1860–1947), who chaired the Hague Commission in December 1922 considering international legal regulation of radio and aircraft, affirmed that, since the Middle Ages, civilization rested in part on distinguishing between combatants and civilians in warfare. Unlike Lemkin, he lamented that the Great War and advent of modern weapons had eroded this basic principle.[23] The reasons for this erosion were explicated and supported by the American lawyer and air force pilot, Frank Quindry, in 1931:

> Considering the economic structure of a nation during a modern war and the conscriptive systems which will probably be employed by all nations, it is difficult to determine whether the civilian who helps supply the fighting forces is any less dangerous to the success of the opposing army than the soldier who operates the mechanical instruments of destruction.[24]

For many military thinkers, civilians were dangerous 'offenders' and thus military objectives. However squeamish some leaders were about strategic bombing of cities, and thus civilians, because the civilized norm prohibited 'terrorizing the civilian population' as policy objective, the collective guilt argument would be too tempting to resist in the next world war.[25]

---

[22] Brett Holman, *The Next War in the Air: Britain's Fear of the Bomber, 1908–1941* (Farnham: Ashgate, 2014); James S. Corum, 'Airpower Thought in Continental Europe between the Wars', in Phillip S. Meilinger (ed.), *The Paths of Heaven: The Evolution of Airpower Theory* (Maxwell Air Force Base: Air University Press, 1997), 151–81.

[23] John Bassett Moore, *International Law and Some Current Illusions and Other Essays* (New York; Macmillan, 1924), viii–ix, 3–6, 200–1.

[24] Frank E. Quindry, 'Aerial Bombardment of Civilian and Military Objectives', *Journal of Air Law and Commerce* 2:4 (1931), 494–5.

[25] Article 22, The Hague Rules of Air Warfare, 1923, https://wwi.lib.byu.edu/index.php/The_Hague_Rules_of_Air_Warfare.

Unlike Lemkin, some international lawyers confronted this reasoning head on. Representative was James W. Garner (1871–1938), a prodigious commentator on legal issues pertaining to international armed conflict. Reflecting on the Hague Draft Rules on Air Warfare in 1924, he observed that the bombing of civilians, civilian infrastructure, private property, and historical monuments during the First World War 'aroused a feeling of horror against which the conscience of mankind everywhere revolted'.[26] Already then, he had discerned that 'terrorization of the civilian inhabitant' was strategic bombing's aim, and that, far from demoralizing the enemy, by 'their very barbarity is rather more likely to intensify the hatred of the people against whom they are directed'. Thus, while he recognized that workers in arms manufacture could be legitimately targeted, he feared the logic of escalating reprisal would 'cause war to degenerate into a struggle of reciprocal barbarism'.[27]

This important debate about civilian immunity, so portentous for the next world war and the nuclear age, bypassed Lemkin completely. He did not respond to the obvious implications of the practices of total war during the First World War—the bombing of cities and blockades that led to the starvation of hundreds of thousands—that military thinkers like German general, Erich Ludendorff (1865–1937) systematized.[28] During the next world war, 600,000 civilians would die from aerial bombing, and another million would be maimed, while European cities lay in ruins. Some 400,000 Japanese perished from US bombing.[29] Death by starvation due to sieges, like the German siege of Leningrad (September 1941 to January 1942), also resulted in hundreds of thousands more civilian deaths, and were not

---

[26] James W. Garner, 'Proposed Rules for the Regulation of Aerial Warfare', *American Journal of International Law* 18:1 (1924), 64.

[27] Ibid., 65. See generally Thomas Hippler, *Bombing the People: Giulio Douhet and the Foundations of Air-Power Strategy, 1884–1939* (Cambridge: Cambridge University Press, 2013).

[28] Erich Ludendorff, *Der totale Krieg* (Munich: Ludendorrfs Verlag, 1935); Richard Overy, *The Bombing War: Europe, 1939–1945* (London: Penguin, 2013), i.

[29] Ian Patterson, *Guernica and Total War* (Cambridge, MA: Harvard University Press, 2007); Yuki Tanaka and Marilyn Young (eds.), *Bombing Civilians: A Twentieth-Century History* (New York: New Press, 2009).

regarded as war crimes by the American judges after the war because they did not violate the Hague Convention of 1907.[30]

Lemkin's ignoring of these developments is not surprising given that the British and French had vehemently resisted the efforts of neutral countries and the Red Cross in 1921 to limit the right of blockade that the British had used to great effect against Germany during the First World War. Like the airwar theorists, defenders of blockades argued that civilian starvation was more humane than trench warfare; if it led to an earlier cessation of hostilities, the price was worthwhile. They also argued that blockade was a legitimate sanction for the League of Nations to apply to recalcitrant states. It was thus an instrument of enforcing international law and agreements rather than representing a perfidious means of civilian destruction that should be criminalized.[31] The Western powers were thus happy to elide the distinction between combatants and civilians in enforcing international rules that suited them. On the eve of the Second World War, the future architect of the British welfare state, William Beveridge (1879–1963), pressed home this point in arguing that 'totalitarian warfare' implicated the entire population, which was thus targetable. Besides, he continued, any starvation was attributable to how the blockaded state distributed food rather than to the blockading state.[32]

Likewise, that the Hague Rules on Air War which Moore's commission proposed in 1923 were not ratified by states, especially Britain and the US, is a turning point in international law not mentioned in the same breath as the failure of League of Nations organizations to criminalize the destruction of their minorities: certainly not by

[30] United Nations War Crimes Commission, *Law Reports of the Trials of War Criminals*, Vol. XII, *The German High Command Trials* (London: HMSO, 1949), 84, 563; David Marcus, 'Famine Crimes in International Law', *American Journal of International Law* 97:2 (2003), 245–81.

[31] Nicholas Mulder and Boyd van Dijk, 'Why Did Starvation Not Become the Paradigmatic War Crime in International Law?', in Kevin Jon Heller and Ingo Venzke (eds.), *Contingency and the Course of International Law* (Oxford: Oxford University Press, 2021), 370–90.

[32] William Beveridge, *Blockade and the Civilian Population* (Oxford: Clarendon Press, 1939), 26–7, 31. Thanks to Boyd van Dijk for drawing my attention to this book.

Lemkin.[33] He regarded these powers as progressive forces in history, and was thus blinded to the illiberal permanent security measures in which they enjoyed a comparative advantage: aerial warfare and naval blockades that were driven by the same logic of military necessity—killing enemy civilians until the enemy state surrendered. Defenders of this logic distinguished it from genocide by referring to the greater good of 'civilization' (or anti-totalitarianism).

Until *Axis Rule*, Lemkin also missed another signal development in illiberal permanent security: the fascist mode of conducting war in the 1930s: the Japanese invasion of China, the Italian invasion of Abyssinia in 1935, and the Spanish Civil War. These were effectively wars of extermination that targeted the enemy population as a whole with aerial bombing, murderous mistreatment of prisoners, and, in the Japanese and Italian cases, extensive settlement projects that aimed to replace the local populations by deportation and starvation measures. The Japanese forced resettlements in northern China cost the lives of 2.3 million locals, while up to 10 million Asian civilians died at the hands of Japanese imperial ambitions. The Italians built concentration camps, bombed villages, and used poison gas against civilians, killing or causing the death by starvation of over 10 per cent of the population of 800,000. German military elites carefully observed these campaigns in developing their own radical conception of annihilatory warfare that disregarded both international treaties and the Geneva and Hague Conventions. They were particularly interested in Italian fascist settlement projects in North Africa.[34]

Lemkin had nothing to say about these dramatic projects that were so devastating to civilians, but it was not as if others ignored them. When Germany invaded Poland in 1939, Roosevelt warned belligerents not to bombard 'from the air of civilian populations or of

---

[33] Hanke, 'The 1923 Hague Rules of Air Warfare'. Some states initially adhered to the Rules voluntarily, but this restraint soon disappeared as the Second World War dragged on.

[34] Sven Reichardt, 'National Socialist Assessments of Global Fascist Warfare (1935–1938)', and Amedeo Osti Guerrazzi, 'Cultures of Total Annihilation? The German, Italian, and Japanese Armies During the Second World War', in Miguel Alonso, Alan Kramer, and Javier Rodrigo (eds.), *Fascist Warfare, 1922–1945* (Basingstoke: Palgrave Macmillan, 2019), 51–72, 119–42.

unfortified cities', because such 'ruthless bombing' in the recent past was a 'form of barbarism' and had 'profoundly shocked the conscience of humanity'.[35] By contrast, Lemkin was more interested in intra-state violence against minorities and state terrorism. Why?

Zionism and Small Nations

Lemkin was raised in an Ashkenazi Jewish religious and cultural environment imbued with a deep, ritualized memory culture of collective persecution and physical destruction as a routine and ongoing threat to Jewish survival. This consciousness was likely impressed upon the young Lemkin who—he recounts in his autobiography—heard about nearby pogroms as a boy.[36] Lemkin's youthful Zionism thus should come as no surprise. James Loeffler's important research has uncovered Lemkin's articles in the Polish-Jewish press in the 1920s that indicate avid support for a Jewish state in Palestine, some even expressed with robust organic-blood metaphors, along with impassioned pleas for Zionist political unity. 'A state consists of three factors', he wrote in 1927: 'Land, people, and political sovereignty', entailing 'colonization work' in Palestine.[37]

Lemkin's conception of humanity as comprising distinct nationalities emerged from a broadly Herderian tradition of occidental thought. Herder also depicted nations as groups of people with unique blends of cultural characteristics and a corresponding *Volk*-'spirit'. In this regard, his thinking resembled that of the slightly older Lithuanian Zionist and lawyer, Jacob Robinson (1889–1977), made a case for Jewish national—not just religious—identity in terms of language and culture.[38] Robinson thought it necessary for Jews to de-assimilate by

---

[35] Quoted in Sahr Conway-Lanz, 'The Ethics of Bombing Civilians After World War II: The Persistence of Norms Against Targeting Civilians in the Korean War', *Asia-Pacific Journal* 12:1 (2014), 2.

[36] Raphael Lemkin, *Totally Unofficial: The Autobiography of Raphael Lemkin*, ed. Donna-Lee Frieze (New Haven: Yale University Press, 2013), 17.

[37] James Loeffler, 'Becoming Cleopatra: The Forgotten Jewish Politics of Raphael Lemkin', *Journal of Genocide Research* 19:3 (2017), 340–60.

[38] Omry Kaplan-Feuereisen and Richard Mann, 'At the Service of the Jewish Nation: Jacob Robinson and International Law', *Osteuropa* 58:8–10 (2008), 157–70.

relinquishing the 'disease of multilingualism' and reviving the Hebrew language for national renewal. Again, far from advocating tribal particularism, he was echoing a common view that nations contributed to what he called 'universal human values'.[39] After their nationalization, Jews would contribute to the universal human values of world civilization which he conceived as a concatenation of national cultures: 'The Jewish Torah, Indian Buddhism, Greek philosophy and art, Roman law, Arabic Islam, Roman Catholic theocracy, Italian humanism, German Reformation, the French Revolution—all of these created universal human values from within particular boundaries though the power of nationhood'.[40] For Zionists like Robinson and Lemkin, Zionism was also a form of internationalism because it worked with the upholder of international law—the British Empire—to create a Jewish national home in Palestine that would allow Jews to re-enter history and contribute to human civilization.[41]

We do not know if Lemkin read Robinson in the 1920s, but he clearly imbibed the same message about 'national spirits' constituting the building blocks of humanity, as well as Robinson's hostility to multinational subjectivities.[42] Lemkin's conception of humanity as comprising distinct ethno-linguistic nationalities was, therefore, entirely consistent with his demonstrable Zionist commitment to the project of Jewish statehood in Palestine. He taught at a Jewish seminary in Warsaw during the 1930s and raised funds to support Zionist undertakings in Palestine. Like other Zionists at the time, he seems to have regarded the Zionist project in Palestine as a national redemption that would also offer a safe haven for Jews in an increasingly dangerous Europe.

These commitments are not apparent in his highly stylized autobiography, *Totally Unofficial*, which casts his life as an apolitical quest to

---

[39] Yaakov Robinzon, *Yediat amenu: Demografyah ve-natsiologyah* (Berlin, 1923), 133, quoted in James Loeffler, ' "The Famous Trinity of 1917": Zionist Internationalism in Historical Perspective', *Simon Dubnow Yearbook* 15 (2016): 11.

[40] Ibid., 10–11.

[41] James Loeffler, *Rooted Cosmopolitans: Jews and Human Rights in the Twentieth Century* (New Haven: Yale University Press, 2018).

[42] Loeffler, 'Becoming Cleopatra', 343.

criminalize genocide in international law from his earliest days.[43]
Lemkin also claimed his crusade was motivated by the impunity of
genocidal perpetrators, whether in Russian pogroms against Jews or
the Ottoman destruction of Ottoman Armenians during the First
World War. In fact, he celebrated the killing of perpetrators by
young Jewish and Armenian men in the late 1920s because of the
purity of their victim-centric motives.[44] He downplayed his Zionism
by implying that his Jewish engagement took an alternative form of
Jewish politics, namely the non-nationalist Jewish autonomy movement popular in Poland and Lithuania, and the idiom of criminal and
international law, which exemplified a common concern for small
nations. Autonomism is associated with the Russian-Jewish historian
Simon Dubnow (1860–1941), who summarized the project thus:
'protecting its [the Jewish nation's] national individuality and safe-
guarding its autonomous development in all states everywhere in the
Diaspora'.[45] Lemkin claims he paid homage to Dubnow on his flight
from Poland. Whether true or not, Lemkin may have mentioned the
story to fashion a non-Zionist lineage for his ethno-national
imaginary.

Lemkin hitched his cart to the ideal of 'small nations' expressed by
Central European politicians and intellectuals. This ideal was consistent with his Zionism and with the more general conception of humanity as a tapestry of nations, preferably each with their own state. As a
Pole and a Jew, Lemkin could sympathize with the Czechoslovak
aversion to German aspirations in East-Central Europe. Lemkin
traced Pan-Germanism's enduring imperative to dominate the land

[43] Lemkin, *Totally Unofficial*.

[44] Ibid., 19–22; Philippe Sands, *East-West Street: On the Origins of 'Crimes against
Humanity' and 'Genocide'* (New York: Knopf, 2017), 149–52; Peter Balakian, 'Raphael Lemkin, Cultural Destruction, and the Armenian Genocide', *Holocaust and
Genocide Studies* 27:1 (2013), 57–89. Rafail Lemkin, 'Dos gerikht far di "sheyne
farbrekhens"' ['The Judgement of the "Beautiful Crime"'], *Haynt*, 28 October
1927, cited in Loeffler, 'Becoming Cleopatra', 347–8.

[45] Simon Dubnow, *Nationalism and History: Essays on Old and New Judaism*, ed. and
intro. Koppel S. Pinson (Philadelphia: Jewish Publication Society of America,
1958), 97.

between Germany and Russia to medieval German colonization in the region. Germany was the 'classical country of genocide practices', he wrote in an unpublished world history of genocide after the Second World War.[46]

Mobilizing support for his new concept in international law required enlisting the representatives of small nations whose leaders understood themselves as cultural nations seeking to found or consolidate a new state. If genocide was the destruction of nations, and nations were cultural entities, then attacking bearers of culture and its symbols was genocide. That is why the cultural dimension of genocide included the intention to 'cripple' as well as to 'destroy' a people. This notion appeared in the form 'cultural genocide' in a draft convention in 1947 when UN committees were debating the definition of genocide.[47]

And yet, a biological assumption in Lemkin's thinking was there from the outset and flowed into his conception of nationhood. In 1934, he wrote about the biological propensity of criminals and the virtues of 'criminal biology' in relation to the 1932 Polish Penal Code, whose author was one of his former university teachers. To be sure, as a liberal, he also stressed the social factors causing criminality, and advocated that law seek the resocialization of offenders; on that basis, he criticized the Nazi criminal law reform for its deterrent rather than rehabilitative intent.[48] And yet, the shared belief in the biological-hereditary basis of anti-social conditions like 'work shyness' is impossible to overlook. Ten years later, he warned of the Nazi aim to change the 'balance of biological forces' between Germany and 'captive nations', and of the 'biological structure' of nations, while emphasizing how the Nazis (also) conceived of nations in biological terms.[49]

[46] Raphael Lemkin, 'Genocide as a Crime under International Law', *American Journal of International Law* 41:1 (1947), 151.

[47] Ibid., 147.

[48] Rafał Lemkin, 'O wprowadzenie ekspertyzy kriminalo-biologicznej do procesu karnego' ['On the Introduction of Criminal-Biological Expertise in the Criminal Trial'], *Głos Prawa Lwów* 11:3 (1934), 137–44; Lemkin, 'Reforma prawa karnego w Niemczech', *Wiadomości Literackie* 30 (1934), 7.

[49] Lemkin, *Axis Rule in Occupied Europe*, xi, 80–1.

Lemkin's Invention

By 1943, Lemkin was writing *Axis Rule* to intervene in the transatlantic discussion about international law and Nazis crimes. The debate centred on the Hague Conventions of 1899 and 1907, and whether it could cover the extent and radicality of the Nazi occupation of Europe. Lemkin proposed to augment this law with his 'generic notion' of genocide to denote the 'destruction of nations' by joining the ancient Greek word of *genos* (i.e. tribe, nation, or race) and the Latin *caedere* (to kill).[50] He did so by combining the aforementioned conception of discrete national cultures with the small nations ideology mobilized by the Allies against German expansionism in the First World War and now by exiled governments like the Poles and Czechoslovaks. Lemkin wrote:

> Among the basic features which have marked progress in civilization are respect for and appreciation of the national characteristics and qualities contributed to world culture by different nations— characteristics and qualities which, as illustrated in the contributions made by nations weak in defense and poor in economic resources, are not to be measured in terms of national power and wealth.[51]

In doing so in *Axis Rule*, Lemkin was simultaneously invoking the Fourth Hague Convention (1907) to show how the Nazis violated international law while arguing that this law was inadequate.[52] Genocide had not been foreseen by its formulators, he wrote: the Hague regime covered individuals rather than peoples. Thus, while Hague law pertained to many Nazi policies and practices, it did not anticipate the Nazis' 'various ingenious measures for weakening or destroying political, social, and cultural elements in national groups'. Accordingly, he wanted to intervene in the Allies' debate about

---

[50] Ibid., 79.

[51] Ibid., 91.

[52] Not for nothing does *Axis Rule* abound with references to the Hague Regulations and its Martens Clause. Referring to the SS, he wrote that 'Such crimes are directed not only against municipal law of the occupied countries, but also against international law and the laws of humanity': Ibid., 23.

prosecuting Axis war criminals by dealing with the 'entire problem of genocide ... as a whole'.[53]

Axis Rule, then, aimed to supplement rather than replace existing law: that is why the book is generally about Axis violations of the laws of occupation: each chapter analyses a domain of occupation that violated Hague law.[54] And that is why it contains a *single chapter* introducing his proposed innovation to this law: genocide as a 'new technique of occupation'. Lemkin stressed that it was a new crime only by criminalizing practices of national destruction that were partially covered by current international law. A new law against genocide combined relevant dimensions of the Hague Regulations with new ones Lemkin identified—like 'subsidizing children begotten by members of the armed forces of the occupant and born of women nationals of the occupied area'. Genocide was thus 'a composite of different acts of persecution or destruction'.[55] Specifically, he suggested that the Hague Convention should be amended by adding the following kinds of measures:

> every action infringing upon the life, liberty, health, corporal integrity, economic existence, and the honor of the inhabitants when committed because they belong to a national, religious, or racial group; and in the second, every policy aiming at the destruction or the aggrandizement of one such group to the prejudice or detriment of another.[56]

Lemkin imported the elements of the Axis genocidal plan from both Jewish and non-Jewish émigré sources. He adumbrated eight 'techniques' of destruction[57]:

> *Political* techniques refer to the cessation of self-government and local rule, and their replacement by that of the occupier. 'Every reminder of former national character was obliterated'.

> *Social* techniques entail attacking the intelligentsia, 'because this group largely provides the national leadership and organizes resistance against

---

[53] Ibid., 92.

[54] E.g. ibid., 12–14, 77.

[55] Ibid., 92.

[56] Ibid., 93.

[57] This discussion of the eight techniques is taken from ibid., 82–90.

Nazification'. The point of such attacks is to 'weaken the national, spiritual resources'.

Cultural techniques ban the use of native language in education, and inculcate youth with propaganda.

Economic techniques shift economic resources from the occupied to the occupier. Peoples the Germans regarded as of 'related blood', like those of Luxembourg and Alsace-Lorraine, were given incentives to recognize this kinship.

Biological techniques decrease the birth rate of occupied countries. 'Thus in incorporated Poland marriages between Poles are forbidden without special permission of the Governor ... of the district; the latter, as a matter of principle, does not permit marriages between Poles'.

Physical techniques mean the rationing of food, endangering of health, and mass killing in order to accomplish the 'physical debilitation and even annihilation of national groups in occupied countries'.

Religious techniques try to disrupt the national and religious influences of the occupied people.

Moral techniques are policies 'to weaken the spiritual resistance of the national group'. This technique of moral debasement entails diverting the 'mental energy of the group' from 'moral and national thinking' to 'base instincts'.

Genocidal techniques thus covered the gamut of occupation policies, ranging from 'aggrandizement of one such group to the prejudice or detriment of another' to mass murder. Lemkin's elaboration of his definition seemed ambiguous about the purpose of deportation: to expel or to destroy a population. 'Genocide has two phases', he wrote: 'one, destruction of the national pattern of the oppressed group: the other, the imposition of the national pattern of the oppressor. This imposition, in turn, may be made upon the oppressed population which is allowed to remain, or upon the territory alone, after removal of the population and the colonization of the area by the oppressor's own nationals.'[58] However, although biological survival was implied by this definition, it was undercut by his insistence that terms

---

[58] Ibid., 79.

like 'denationalization' or 'Germanization'—the imposition of the conqueror's 'national pattern' on the conquered people—were unsatisfactory because 'they treat mainly the cultural, economic, and social aspects of genocide, leaving out the biological aspects, such as causing the physical decline and even destruction of the population involved'.[59]

The 'biological essence of a nation' (or 'national-biological power'[60]) was elemental, because 'such a nation cannot rise again to resist an aggressor' if it is destroyed. Repeatedly, Lemkin stressed the demographic calculations of the Nazis: they 'aimed at winning the peace even though the war itself is lost' by destroying, disintegrating, and weakening an 'enemy nation'. In this way, the occupier was 'in a position to deal with . . . other peoples from the vantage point of biological superiority'.[61] Plainly, Lemkin thought biological attacks were an irreducible component of genocide, which was to resemble the Holocaust in this key respect.

The Genocide Convention

A month after the Nuremberg Trials finished in October 1946, the UN General Assembly (UNGA) passed a resolution calling for a genocide convention. It defined genocide as 'denial of existence of entire human groups', including political groups.[62] The UN then spent the next eighteen months in tortuous negotiations about a precise definition, particularly regarding political groups and 'cultural genocide'. Ultimately, the UN committees excluded both from the final definition, which was passed by the UNGA in December 1948.

---

[59] Ibid., 80.

[60] Raphael Lemkin, 'Genocide as a Crime under International Law', *American Journal of International Law* 41:1 (1947), 147.

[61] Lemkin, *Axis Rule in Occupied Europe*, 81, xi. 'The Germans hoped to control permanently a depopulated Europe, and ultimately, in partnership with Japan . . . to dominate the world. Thus genocide became a basic element of geopolitics': Raphael Lemkin, 'Genocide: A New International Crime—Punishment and Prevention', *Revue Internationale de Droit Pénal* 17 (1946): 364.

[62] The Crime of Genocide [1946] UNGA 66; A/RES/96 (I) (11 December 1946), http://www.worldlii.org/int/other/UNGA/1946/.

These debates were prefigured by key exclusions from two draft conventions. The first exclusion distinguished genocidal and military logics. The commentary of the Secretariat's Draft by the committee of experts that drafted it (Pella, Lemkin, and de Vabres) readily admitted that civilian populations were affected by modern warfare in 'more or less severe losses', but distinguished between such circumstances and genocide by arguing that in the latter 'one of the belligerents aims at exterminating the population of enemy territory and systematically destroys what are not genuine military objectives'. Military objectives, by contrast, aimed at imposing the victor's will on the loser, whose existence was not imperilled. In other words, killing masses of civilians was not illegal if motivated by military goals: victory, not destruction.[63] In this argument, collateral damage caused as part of war was legitimate even if as extensive as genocidal violence.

The Secretariat Draft of 1947 thus stated that acts that 'may result in the total or partial destruction of a group of human beings' are excluded if not intended to destroy 'a group of human beings'. Consequently, much Allied policy and practice in the recent war and postwar period were conveniently omitted from coverage: 'international or civil war, isolated acts of violence not aimed at the destruction of a group of human beings, the policy of compulsory assimilation of a national element, mass displacements of population'.[64]

In the second exclusion, the Secretariat Draft also took 'mass displacements of populations' off the table. This exclusion was motivated less by the partitions of India and Palestine, whose massive population expulsions began in the second half of 1947, than by the expulsion of millions of Germans from Central and Eastern Europe that the Allies had countenanced towards the end of war. Real-time events inevitably impinged on the debate. Responding to the refugee crisis occasioned by the flight and expulsion of Palestinians from their towns and villages by Zionist forces in 1948, the Syrian representative moved an amendment to include 'Imposing measures intended to oblige members of a group to abandon their homes in order to escape

[63] Ibid.
[64] Ibid., 231.

the threat of subsequent ill-treatment'. Yugoslavia supported the move by referring to German demographic warfare: 'the Nazis had dispersed a Slav majority from a certain part of Yugoslavia in order to establish a German majority there. That action was tantamount to the deliberate destruction of a group. Genocide could be committed by forcing members of a group to abandon their homes'. This argument did not carry the day. Led by the Soviet representative, who was not motivated to draw attention to his state's expulsion of Germans, most members of the Sixth Committee voted down the amendment. 'Transfers of population did not necessarily mean the physical destruction of a group', declared the Belgian representative, stating the emerging consensus.[65]

Other exclusions were debated in UN committees. The partition of India made its way into the debate in relation to cultural genocide, which was in the draft. It had been included on Lemkin's insistence and immediately raised hackles. The British were vehemently opposed to the 1946 UNGA resolution and the Secretariat Draft, which they tried to side-track and thwart at every turn. An internal memo condemned the Secretariat Draft as a 'highly political and provocative document' that confused minority protection (despite the draft's own distinction between cultural genocide and minority protection as well as forced assimilation) and for going far beyond group destruction to the kinds of persecution Lemkin included in *Axis Rule*: 'subjection of individuals to conditions of life likely to result in debilitation; confiscation of property; prohibition of the use of a national language, and destruction of books or historical and religious monuments'.[66] Such measures were extraneous to genocide properly understood, and could threaten British interests: 'Were it adapted, it might well serve to re-open recent political issues solutions of which have been condoned on grounds of expediency as for instance the expulsion of Germans from Poland'. Regarding cultural genocide in particular, the memo continued, 'it might quite plausibly be argued that, were the Convention in force, His Majesty's Government would

---

[65] A/C.6/SR.81, in ibid., 1479, 1490, 1492, 1495.

[66] UK National Archives, Draft Cabinet Office brief for UK Delegation to the Sixth Session of the Economic and Social Council on Genocide (7 January 1948 for Cabinet on 12 January), 3.

34 *A. Dirk Moses*

be guilty of genocide in several cases, against e.g. Germans in the British Zone, the Jews in Palestine, or even perhaps certain colonial peoples'.[67]

The Americans did not seek to block the Convention negotiations, as they feared 'a loss of moral leadership on this question'.[68] Instead, they sought to restrict its definition as much as possible. Cultural genocide could not be included because, they argued, genocide was 'the heinous crime' of 'mass extermination', namely the 'physical elimination of the group'. It should not be confused with the protection of minorities.[69] So confident were Department of State officials of the Convention's restricted application that they were 'not particularly concerned about the question of lynchings'.[70]

Other countries saw it differently. Pakistan was worried about the remaining Muslim population in India who far-right Hindus denounced as a 'fifth column': 'In India, thirty-five million Muslims were currently living under conditions of terror. Their existence as a separate cultural group was threatened. Although the use of Urdu, a language of Muslim origin, had not been prohibited by law, it was under heavy attack. Muslim cultural and religous [sic] monuments had been burned down or destroyed'.[71] The extensive debate on cultural genocide played out along the same logic as that about population expulsion: it was not genocide if not physical destruction akin to the Holocaust. The notion was struck from the final convention text and is not a legal concept, although protections of heritage and other aspects of culture made their way into other legal instruments.

[67] Ibid., 4–5.

[68] National Archives Records Administration (NARA), Department of State telegram to John Maktos, 13 April 1948, RG 59, Box 2186.

[69] NARA, RG 59, Box 2186, 'US Commentary of the Secretariat Draft Convention on Genocide', 10 September 1947, 2; 'Position on Genocide Convention in ECSOC Drafting Committee,' 10 April 1948, 2, in ibid.; Durwald V. Sandifer memo to Ernest Gross, 'Trip to New York on Genocide', 14 April 1948, 2, in ibid.

[70] NARA, RG 59, Box 2189, Durwald V. Sandifer memo to Ernest Gross, 'Cultural Genocide', 22 April 1948, 1.

[71] A/C.6/SR.63, in Hirad Abtahi and Philippa Webb (eds.), *The Genocide Convention: The Travaux Préparatoires*, 2 Vols. (Leiden: Brill, 2009), 1298.

Genocide was also depoliticized. In the first place, state representatives followed their interwar predecessors in determining that terrorism was not a political offence: suspects could only be extraditable from another country if the crime was non-political. This reasoning was now transferred to genocide.[72] Second, after intense lobbying and debate, political groups were removed from the Convention. Third, political motivations suffered the same fate. Ultimately, genocide was defined narrowly to exclude the possibility that states could be be prosecuted for repressing domestic political opposition: anti-communists for communist states, and communists for most Latin American states in particular.

The question of political groups revealed the incipient cleavages of the Cold War and imperatives of state security that concerned all states. The inclusion of political groups in two draft conventions threatened to derail negotiations and the Convention itself. The Soviets were stung by accusations of genocide levelled by emigré Baltic organizations who complained about the takeover of their countries after the war.[73] Their proposition closely mirrored that of Lemkin and the World Jewish Congress (WJC), namely that genocide 'is organically bound up with fascism-nazism and other similar race theories which preach national and racial hatred, the domination of the so-called higher races and the extermination of the so-called lower races'. This was what the Soviet representative called the 'scientific definition of genocide'.[74] Conveniently, the Soviet attack on social groups, like Kulaks in the 1930s, would thereby not be classifiable as genocide. But not for love of the Soviet Union did the Uruguayan

[72] Article VII of the Convention on the Punishment and Prevention of Genocide holds that 'Genocide and the other acts enumerated in article III shall not be considered as political crimes for the purpose of extradition'. For several US memos assenting to this proposition, see National Records Administration, Maryland, RG 353, Box 100, Committee on International Social Policy, 'Draft Convention for the Punishment and Prevention of Genocide, Commentary by the Government of the United States', 8 September 1947, 9.

[73] Beth Van Schaack, 'The Crime of Political Genocide: Repairing the Genocide Convention's Blind Spot', *Yale Law Journal* 106 (1997), 2259–91; Weiss-Wendt, *The Soviet Union and the Gutting of the UN Genocide Convention*, 58.

[74] A/C.6/215/Rev.1, in Abtahi and Webb, *The Genocide Convention*, 1969; A/C.6/SR.74 in Abtahi and Webb, *The Genocide Convention*, 1399.

representative support it when he agreed that 'The concept of genocide was, indeed, the outcome of the Nazi theories of race superiority
which were at the basis of the Hitlerian ideology'.[75]

The exclusion of political groups from the list of protected groups
would make it easier for unstable states to put down domestic dissent,
as some of them plainly admitted. Venezuela said that states would
not ratify a convention that included political groups:

> fearing the possibility of being called before an international tribunal to
> answer charges made against them, even if those charges were without
> foundation. Subversive elements might make use of the convention to
> weaken attempts of their own Government to suppress them. He
> realized that certain countries where civic spirit was highly developed
> and the political struggle fought through electoral laws, would favour
> the inclusion of political groups. But there were countries where the
> population was still developing and where political struggle was very
> violent.[76]

The Dominican Republic and Egypt agreed that the inclusion of
political groups 'would bring the United Nations into the domestic
political struggle of every country and would make it difficult for many
countries to adhere to the convention'.[77] Brazil advanced the most
self-serving argument, asserting that genocide:

> was unknown in the countries of Latin America, since in those countries
> there did not exist that deep-rooted hatred which in due course led to
> genocide. . . . In those countries political movements were always short-
> lived whereas the crime of genocide was by its very nature dependent
> on a profound concentration of racial or religious hatred. Such hatred
> could never grow out of the political movements current in Latin
> America.[78]

Like the Iranian representative, the Brazilian representative also
equated genocide with racial hatred in order to depoliticize it. Racial
destruction, the Iranian said echoing Lemkin, was 'more heinous in
the light of the conscience of humanity, since it was directed against

---

[75] A/C.6/SR.74, in Abtahi and Webb, *The Genocide Convention*, 1401.

[76] A/C.6/SR.69, in ibid., 1356.

[77] Ibid.

[78] Ibid., 1353–4.

human beings whom chance alone had grouped together'. The Brazilian added that 'A crime committed for political motives did not contain a moral element, it was free from the intention of destroying the opposing group. Today's enemies became the friends of tomorrow'.[79] This improbable unanimity of communists and anti-communists was based on a shared desire to be able to destroy one another's domestic opponents with impunity.

The WJC also sought to remove the reference to political groups, now rejecting Lemkin's broad ideas about genocide that were reflected in the Secretariat Draft. Sensing that the Convention was in danger, and hopeful that it would help protect Jewish communities in Pakistan, the Middle East, and Eastern Europe, the Congress wrote to the UN Economic and Social Council in July 1947 to urge the deletion of the political groups clause:

> Throughout history most attacks were directed against racial, religious and national groups. Genocide as a crime is connected intimately with these victim-groups. The inclusion of the political groups might be a useful addition to civilized international life. However it acts already as an undue burden and it might keep governments from entering into the Convention. Governments will never be sincere in admitting that the inclusion of political groups is the main reason for their reluctance and they might use escapism and delay. As a people who suffered unbelievable losses we appeal to the governments of the world that the Genocide Convention should not be used for political fights among nations but rather for establishing civilized standards of international life.[80]

Lemkin communicated the same argument to US Department of State officials. In one conversation with them, he was reported as arguing 'that in the Latin American countries, there were many revolutions and that extermination of opposing groups was resorted to as a result thereof. The Latinos do not want to admit that publicly. However, they may vote against the Convention or attempt to prevent its approval by the General Assembly'.[81] In the event, Latin American states did publicly admit their security concerns. Political expediency

---

[79] Ibid., 1355.

[80] AJA/WJC, B84-06, Genocide 1947.

[81] NARA, RG 59, Box 2186, Department of State, Memorandum of Conversation, 16 July 1948, 1.

thus demanded jettisoning political groups. Exterminating 'opposing groups' would not be genocide, concluded Lemkin and the WJC.

In opposition, Ecuador and Bolivia supported the retention of political groups by the same logic, only reversing the signs in a prescient manner: 'if the convention did not extend its protection to political groups', they said, 'those who committed the crime of genocide might use the pretext of the political opinions of a racial or religious group to persecute and destroy it, without becoming liable to international sanctions'.[82] The American Catholic Association for International Peace went further in their representations to the US Department of State: political logics were not just a pretext for, but the driving force of all persecution: 'Practically all persecutions in the past had some, if not a total, political basis', they argued.[83] The American diplomats tended to concur, if only to squeeze the Soviets for its domestic repression. With the British, they argued that the Nazis and Spanish fascists had also tried to destroy social and political groups and that the Cold War temperature would increase ideological rather than racial tension.[84] But these counterarguments did not carry the day: the Sixth Committee voted to exclude political groups.

The dispute was as heated regarding the question of listing specific motives in addition to the basic intention to destroy groups 'on grounds of national or racial origin, religious belief or political opinion of its members', as the Ad Hoc Committee Draft put it. Again, the Soviet Union led the opposition, arguing that:

> Crimes committed for political motives belonged to a special type of crime and had nothing in common with crimes of genocide, the very name of which, derived as it was from the word *genus*—race, tribe, referred to the destruction of nations or races as such for reasons of racial or national persecution, and not for political opinions of those groups.[85]

---

[82] A/C.6/SR.74, in Abtahi and Webb, *The Genocide Convention*, 1393.

[83] NARA, RG 59, Box 2186, Statement of the Ethics and Juridical Institutions Committee, Catholic Association for International Peace, 'The Genocide Convention,' August 1948, 2.

[84] Cf. Kurt Glaser and Stefan T. Possony, *Victims of Politics: The State of Human Rights* (New York: Columbia University Press, 1979), 8–9.

[85] E/AC.25/SR.24, in Abtahi and Webb, *The Genocide Convention*, 1016.

The Soviet Union and its supporters were happy to list motives but to omit political ones for the obvious reasons. Besides, they disavowed censorship of free speech. As the Salvadorian representative put it, 'If the rebellious group were destroyed, it would be because of its activities, and not because of its political views'.[86]

The debate became mired in the question of extradition, because the custom was that those accused of political crimes were not liable to extradition. Thus Article 8 of the Secretariat Draft stated that 'genocide cannot be considered as a political crime and shall give cause for extradition'.[87] The Soviet representative expressed the emerging postwar consensus that depoliticized genocide by pointing to victims' lack of agency: 'genocide was the mass destruction of innocent groups and could never ... be considered as a political crime'. In response, the British recognized that it 'was inherently political in that its commission could usually be traced to political motives'. For that reason, the convention text should 'state that, for purposes of extradition, it should be considered as nonpolitical'.[88]

The British also noted that listing motives would allow perpetrators 'to claim that they had not committed that crime "on grounds of" one of the motives listed in the article', an option that suited many countries. New Zealand's representative ended the debate when he pointed out that without listed motives 'bombing may be called a crime of genocide', because 'Modern war was total, and there might be bombing which might destroy whole groups'.[89] The British were quickly convinced and the deadlock broken by Venezuela's compromise suggestion to replace a list of motives with the simple phrase 'as such'. It was intended, and widely interpreted to include, motives without listing any in particular. Since political groups had been excluded from the definition, destroying groups 'as such' meant destroying its members simply by virtue of membership of them, in other words, because of their identity.[90]

---

[86] A/C.6/SR.77, in ibid., 1435.

[87] A/AC.10/42, in ibid., 118.

[88] A/C.6/SR.94, in ibid., 1630–1.

[89] A/C.6/SR.75, in ibid., 1415, 1418.

[90] Ibid., 1416–17, A/C.6/SR.76 in ibid., 1425–7, A/C.6/SR.77 in ibid., 1435. See, generally, A. W. Brian Simpson, 'Britain and the Genocide Convention', *British Yearbook of International Law* 73:1 (2002), 4–64.

The Professor of International Law at the University of Edinburgh, J. L. Brierly (1881–1955) immediately understood the implications of these restrictions. To the readers of a weekly BBC magazine in 1949, he wrote that the intended destruction of the listed groups 'as such' had a 'limiting effect': this qualification meant excluding 'many, probably most, of the famous massacres and persecutions of history'. In historical reality, the facts of perpetrator motives 'have been more obscure [than the Nazis'] and more mixed'. To qualify as genocide, the victim population would have to be targeted 'because they were Jews or Slavs, or members of some particular group of human beings whose elimination had been resolved on'—and not 'enemies in war or rebels against a government'. Accordingly, 'putting a whole enemy population, men, women, and children, to the sword' would not necessarily be genocide. The Convention, he concluded pessimistically, promised more than it delivered: 'nothing important has happened at all' with its passing by the UN.[91] In fact, repressing political opposition and destroying entire peoples in warfare was now all the easier because the genocide threshold increasingly functioned to screen out military necessity and liberal permanent security practices.

Conclusion

Genocide was defined as narrowly as possible to exclude the possibility that the states of the UN could be affected by the Convention in the treatment of domestic political opposition: anti-communists for communist states, and communists for most Latin American states in particular. Nor did they want the UN interfering in their attempts to assimilate ethnic minorities in the manner of the interwar minority treaties.[92] The thirteen Nuremberg Trials between 1945 and 1949 and UN debates showed that Germany was seen as the archetypal

---

[91] J. L. Brierly, 'The Genocide Convention', *The Listener*, 10 March 1949.

[92] Adam Weiss-Wendt, *The Soviet Union and the Gutting of the UN Genocide Convention* (Madison: University of Wisconsin Press, 2017). Israel's ambivalence about the Convention was characteristic of states generally. See Rotem Giladi, 'Not Our Salvation: Israel, the Genocide Convention, and the World Court 1950–1951', *Diplomacy & Statecraft* 26:3 (2015), 473–93.

genocidal society that had diverged from the healthy Western, and international, norm.[93] Case law on genocide by the Ad Hoc International Criminal Tribunals for Rwanda and the Former Yugoslavia has continued this narrow understanding of genocide.

As a consequence of this threshold, genocide is extremely difficult to prosecute in international criminal proceedings. The attacks on civilians in Darfur in Sudan were held by a UN investigative committee of inquiry not to be genocidal although they closely resemble the Armenian genocide. Instead, the UN committee concluded that the Sudanese government was guilty of crimes against humanity and for racial persecution, which was greeted with sighs of relief in Khartoum and by African leaders.[94] Like the international community, they regarded genocide to be a graver transgression than crimes against humanity despite the report's disavowal of any such hierarchy. This *de facto* hierarchy of criminality, atop which sits a 'crime of crimes' against identity, a hate crime driven by non-political imperatives, lessens the significance of other catastrophic forms of mass violence like war crimes, crimes against humanity, and the 'collateral damage' of missile strikes.

A frank concession of the genocide keyword's limitations is the need to couple it with 'extermination' in a world history of human destruction 'from Sparta to Darfur' or abandoning it for 'political violence' and 'reigns of terror'.[95] To all intents and purposes, prominent advocates of humanitarian intervention have abandoned or supplemented the genocide concept because its impossibly high threshold of proof deters lawyers, while its stigma inhibits states from using the term lest

---

[93] Kim Christian Priemel, *The Betrayal: The Nuremberg Trials and German Divergence* (Oxford: Oxford University Press, 2016).

[94] Report of the International Commission of Inquiry on Darfur to the United Nations Secretary-General, Pursuant to Security Council Resolution 1564 of 18 September 2004 (Geneva, 25 January 2005).

[95] Ben Kiernan, *Blood and Soil: A World History of Genocide and Extermination from Sparta to Darfur* (New Haven: Yale University Press, 2007); Donald Bloxham and Robert Gerwarth (eds.), *Political Violence in Twentieth- Century Europe* (Cambridge: Cambridge University Press, 2011); Patricia Marchak, *Reigns of Terror* (Montreal and Kingston: McGill-Queens University Press, 2003).

they be accused of genocide or compelled to prevent it.[96] Others propose 'demographic surgery' or simply 'mass killing' as broader, alternative concepts.[97] Sharing these reservations about genocide, some commentators propose 'atrocity crimes' to cover the infractions listed under genocide, crimes against humanity, and war crimes.[98] In doing so, they followed the Rome Statute of the International Criminal Court, which bundles genocide, war crimes, crimes against humanity, and crimes against peace under the rubric of 'most serious crimes of concern to the international community as a whole'.[99]

The United Nations Office of the Special Adviser on the Prevention of Genocide has effectively institutionalized this approach by stating its 'duty to prevent and halt genocide and mass atrocities'.[100] The Office's 'Framework of Analysis for Atrocity Crimes' released in 2014, elaborated this point by positing a new category of 'atrocity crime' to refer to genocide, crimes against humanity, war crimes, and ethnic cleansing. Because of the genocide concept's narrow national-ethnic-racial definition of a targeted group excludes so many other categories of people, the framework has atrocity crimes cover the more general 'protected groups, populations or individuals' included in crimes against humanity and war crimes. In doing so, the framework runs counter to the monumentalization of genocide in popular discourse:

> Atrocity crimes are considered to be the most serious crimes against humankind. Their status as international crimes is based on the belief that the acts associated with them affect the core dignity of human

[96] Gareth Evans, 'Crimes Against Humanity: Overcoming Indifference', *Journal of Genocide Research* 8:3 (2006), 325–39.

[97] Antonio Ferrara, 'Beyond Genocide and Ethnic Cleansing: Demographic Surgery as a New Way to Understand Mass Violence', *Journal of Genocide Research* 17:1 (2015), 1–20.

[98] David Scheffer, 'Genocide and Atrocity Crimes', *Genocide Studies and Prevention* 1:3 (2006), 229–50; William A. Schabas, 'Crimes Against Humanity as a Paradigm for International Atrocity Crimes', *Middle East Critique* 20:3 (2011), 253–69.

[99] Rome Statute of the International Criminal Court, Article 5(1), https://www.icc-cpi.int/nr/rdonlyres/ea9aeff7-5752-4f84-be94-0a655eb30e16/0/rome_statute_english.pdf.

[100] Office of The Special Adviser on The Prevention of Genocide, 'The Responsibility to Protect', https://www.un.org/en/genocideprevention/.

beings, in particular the persons that should be most protected by States, both in times of peace and in times of war.[101]

This innovation by scholars and diplomats working at the coalface of international politics represents a major critique of the legal architecture to protect civilians and combatants that culminated in the UNGC and Four Geneva Conventions after the Second World War. It implies that the hierarchy of these various crimes is inimical to their prevention, and that large-scale atrocity is their common denominator. It raises the basic question: is the concept and law of genocide fit for purpose?

Acknowledgement

This chapter draws on A. Dirk Moses, *The Problems of Genocide: Permanent Security and the Language of Transgression* (Cambridge: Cambridge University Press, 2021).

Select Bibliography

Clavero, Bartolomé, *Genocide or Ethnocide, 1933–2007: How to Mark, Unmake and Remake Law with Words* (Milan: Giuffrè Editore, 2008).

Irvin-Erickson, Douglas, *Raphaël Lemkin and the Concept of Genocide* (Philadelphia: University of Pennsylvania Press, 2017).

Lemkin, Raphael, *Axis Rule in Occupied Europe: Laws of Occupation, Analysis of Government, Proposals for Redress* (Washington, DC: Carnegie Endowment for International Peace, 1944).

Lemkin, Raphael, *Totally Unofficial: The Autobiography of Raphael Lemkin*, ed. Donna-Lee Frieze (New Haven: Yale University Press, 2013).

Lewis, Mark A., *The Birth of the New Justice: The Internationalization of Crime and Punishment, 1919–1950* (Oxford: Oxford University Press, 2014).

Lingen, von Kerstin, *'Crimes Against Humanity': Eine Ideengeschichte der Zivilisierung von Gewalt 1864–1945* (Paderborn: Ferdinand Schöningh, 2019).

Loeffler, James, 'Becoming Cleopatra: The Forgotten Jewish Politics of Raphael Lemkin', *Journal of Genocide Research* 19:3 (2017), 340–60.

Loeffler, James, *Rooted Cosmopolitans: Jews and Human Rights in the Twentieth Century* (New Haven: Yale University Press, 2018).

---

[101] United Nations, Framework for Analysis of Atrocity Crimes, 2014, https://www.un.org/en/genocideprevention/documents/about-us/Doc.3_Framework%20of%20Analysis%20for%20Atrocity%20Crimes_EN.pdf.

Moses, A. Dirk, *The Problems of Genocide: Permanent Security and the Language of Transgression* (Cambridge: Cambridge University Press, 2020).

Sands, Philippe, *East-West Street: On the Origins of 'Crimes against Humanity' and 'Genocide'* (New York: Knopf, 2017).

Schabas, William A., *Genocide in International Law*, 2nd ed. (Cambridge: Cambridge University Press, 2009).

Shaw, Martin, *What is Genocide?*, 2nd ed. (Cambridge: Polity, 2015).

Stiller, Alexa, 'The Mass Murder of the European Jews and the Concept of "Genocide" in the Nuremberg Trials: Reassessing Raphaël Lemkin's Impact', *Genocide Studies and Prevention* 13:1 (2019), 144–72, https://scholarcommons.usf.edu/gsp/vol13/iss1/14/.

Vrdoljak, Ana Filipa, 'Human Rights and Genocide: The Work of Lauterpacht and Lemkin in Modern International Law', *European Journal of International Law* 20:4 (2010), 1163–94.

2

Predicting Genocide

Hollie Nyseth Nzitatira

Introduction

On 6 April 1994, unknown assailants shot down the plane carrying the President of Rwanda, triggering a genocide that would claim the lives of up to a million Tutsi citizens and Hutu moderates. At the very same time that the plane crashed on the outskirts of Rwanda's capital, genocide was occurring in Bosnia-Herzegovina. Precisely two years prior to the assassination of Rwanda's President, Bosnian Serb and Yugoslav forces had begun a siege on the city of Sarajevo. Up to 100,000 people were subsequently killed in a civil war and a genocide that targeted Bosnian Muslims in Srebrenica and elsewhere throughout the country.

Many lives were lost in these two genocides—alongside widespread sexualized violence, displacement, property damage, and irrevocable harm to cultures. These losses served as a stark indicator that, decades after the Nazi Holocaust, the countries of the world had altogether failed to prevent genocide. Consequently, the persistent nature of this horrific violence, alongside the development of new research methods, ushered in a new goal: the prediction of genocide.

This chapter provides a review of research and programmes related to genocide prevention efforts. I begin by clarifying what prediction entails and defining key terms. Next, I provide a synthesized review of the factors that are associated with the onset of genocide, including general risk factors and more proximate triggering factors and related escalatory dynamics. I then address how researchers and practitioners use these factors to create early warning systems, followed by a brief overview of existing early warning efforts. Finally, I conclude by addressing the limitations of existing prediction endeavours and suggest that such approaches must move beyond a focus on the state in order to achieve more refined predictions.

Understanding Prediction: Origins and Definitions

Prediction uses past knowledge to assess the probability of a future event.[1] The first efforts to predict violence sought to identify the factors associated with war,[2] especially the possibility of nuclear war between the US and the Soviet Union.[3] Peace researchers have since attempted to predict many other types of violence and conflict worldwide, including but not limited to human rights violations, state repression, protests, and regime change.[4] Since the 1990s, this list has also included genocide.

To be sure, genocide can never be predicted with 100 per cent accuracy. Social situations are extremely complex, and anticipating humans' behaviour is far from easy. Prevention efforts thus employ probabilistic causation, or the idea that a cause raises the *probability* of an effect. For instance, smoking (a cause) raises the probability of lung cancer (an effect). But, smoking does not always cause lung cancer, nor is lung cancer only caused by smoking.

---

[1] Quantitative methods differentiate between statistical probability, likelihood, and odds. In this chapter, I use all three terms generally to refer to the possibility that a future event may occur.

[2] Lewis Fry Richardson, *Arms and Insecurity: A Mathematical Study of the Causes and Origins of War* (Pittsburg: Boxwood Press, 1960); Pitirim Aleksandrovich Sorokin, *Social and Cultural Dynamics: Fluctuation of Social Relationships, War, and Revolution*, vol. 3 (New York: Bedminster Press, 1962).

[3] Paul N. Edwards, *The Closed World: Computers and the Politics of Discourse in Cold War America* (Cambridge, MA: MIT Press, 1997).

[4] Håvard Hegre, Nils W. Metternich, Håvard Mokleiv Nygård, and Julian Wucherpfennig, 'Introduction: Forecasting in Peace Research', *Journal of Peace Research* 54:2 (2017), 113–24; Hannes Mueller and Christopher Rauh, 'Reading Between the Lines: Prediction of Political Violence Using Newspaper Text', *American Political Science Review* 112:2 (2018), 358–75; Drew Bowlsby, Erica Chenoweth, Cullen Hendrix, and Jonathan D. Moyer, 'The Future is a Moving Target: Predicting Political Instability', *British Journal of Political Science* [online] (2019), https://doi.org10.1017/S0007123418000443.

Bearing this important caveat in mind, research on the causes of genocide generally falls into two groups: 1) analyses of risk factors,[5] or structural factors and related situations that influence whether genocide is likely to occur, and 2) analyses of triggering factors (triggers) and escalatory factors, or specific events and processes that more directly influence the onset of genocide and/or the escalation of violence. For instance, genocide is more likely to occur in a situation where there is an authoritarian government. But, a particular event— such as the Rwandan President's plane being shot down in 1994— more immediately influences the onset of violence.

These two types of research[6] can be mapped onto models of the onset of genocide. Models are representations of a system that allow for investigation into the properties of the system that can, in turn, assist in predicting future outcomes. In line with the distinction between risk factors and triggering/escalatory factors, researchers have classified models of the onset of genocide into two categories: risk assessment models and early warning models. Risk assessment models typically address a country's structural conditions that affect the possibility genocide could occur, while early warning models are said to focus on more proximate dynamics that escalate or trigger violence.[7]

In this chapter, I consider research on risk factors and triggers, as well as the translation of this research to risk assessment models and early warning models. Both risk factors and triggering factors are essential to predicting genocide, and researchers can conceptualize

[5] Risk factors are also termed priming factors. See Alex Laban Hinton, *Why Did They Kill?: Cambodia in the Shadow of Genocide* (Berkeley: University of California Press, 2005).

[6] Some people engage in research on the causes of genocide in order to test and improve theories, though a primary goal of much research is to enable policymakers to create evidence-based policies regarding responses to potential genocide.

[7] Birger Heldt, 'Risks, Early Warning and Management of Atrocities and Genocide: Lessons from Statistical Research', *Politorbis*, 2:47 (2009), 65–70; Barbara Harff, 'Detection: The History and Politics of Early Warning', in Adam Lupel and Ernesto Verdeja (eds.), *Responding to Genocide: The Politics of International Action* (Boulder: Lynne Rienner, 2013), 85–110; Ernesto Verdeja, 'Predicting Genocide and Mass Atrocities', *Genocide Studies and Prevention: An International Journal* 9:3 (2016), 13–32.

and analyse them as two linked processes.[8] Because of this, risk assessment models and early warning models often each include long-standing structural factors *and* more immediate triggering factors despite their supposed different foci. I thus refer to risk assessment and early warning models broadly as prediction or forecasting efforts and consider these efforts in tandem.[9]

To begin, I turn towards the factors that researchers have found to be associated with the onset of genocide and provide an overview of the methods used to translate knowledge about these factors into the actual prediction of genocide. As many research studies and forecasting efforts employ slightly different definitions of genocide or even focus on distinct types of violence (e.g. mass killings), I refer to genocide as acts committed with intent to destroy a national, ethnic, racial, religious, or political group. This definition combines the international legal definition of genocide with politicide (genocide against political groups), and I employ other terms in line with authors' respective definitions. In the following, I first review the more general risk factors of genocide, followed by an assessment of the triggers, escalatory factors, and other signposts that genocide may be imminent.

Step 1: Risk Factors

Studies predicting genocide generally begin by addressing the structural factors associated with the onset of genocide. During the 1970s and 1980s, historians, political scientists, sociologists, and other scholars trained in related disciplines conducted case studies of

[8] Benjamin E. Goldsmith, Charles R. Butcher, Dimitri Semenovich, and Arcot Sowmya, 'Forecasting the Onset of Genocide and Politicide: Annual Out-of-Sample Forecasts on a Global Dataset, 1988–2003', *Journal of Peace Research* 50:4 (2013), 437–52.

[9] Hegre and co-authors define forecasting as 'predictions about unrealized outcomes given model estimates from realized data'. Hegre, 'Introduction: Forecasting in Peace Research'. They suggest that prediction refers to the assessment of the probability of an outcome (based on model estimates) that may or may not be applied to future outcomes. Here, I refer to both prediction and forecasting more broadly as the use of existing information to predict the likelihood or probability of a future event.

genocide to understand why genocide occurred.[10] This collective body of work—too large to review here—was vital precisely because it traced the unique histories of numerous genocides.

In-depth case studies laid the foundation for large-scale quantitative analyses of genocides that emerged during the late 1980s and early 1990s. These studies—called large-N[11] studies—typically involve datasets of country-years in which each line represents a year within a country. Then, variables within the dataset are measured at the country-year level. For example, a row of data for 'Rwanda 1963' might include various information about Rwanda in 1963—such as the gross domestic product (GDP) per capita, the population, or the type of government—in separate columns. Country-years became a common unit of measurement because most data about countries are measured annually. For example, GDP per capita is rarely measured daily, as structural conditions can be relatively slow to change over time. Furthermore, country-years are a typical unit of measurement because many theories assume that genocide is committed by governments, an assumption that I address later in this chapter.

Once a dataset of country-years is compiled, a researcher can use quantitative methods to analyse it. There are a variety of tools available to work with large-N datasets, but quantitative methods generally hold variables constant such that the researcher can identify the independent effect of each variable in question. Put another way, in a model that examines how the type of government, GDP per capita, and the presence of a civil war are associated with the onset of genocide, a researcher can see how the type of government impacts the onset of genocide independent of GDP per capita and the presence of civil war. These methods can also examine interaction effects, or how a variable may influence another variable's association with

---

[10] Much of the research focused on predicting genocide stems from political science. This is largely due to the discipline's emphasis on quantitative methods, though as I address throughout this chapter, multiple methods and interdisciplinary work are vital for genocide prediction.

[11] 'N' refers to the population, while 'n' refers to a sample in quantitative analysis. Thus, these large-N studies make use of population-level data, or data on all known genocides rather than a subsample.

genocide (e.g. how the presence of a civil war might impact the association between the type of government and genocide). Though there are regularly at least some associations between any given variable and genocide, researchers employing such models seek to identify *statistically significant* associations, which broadly means the association is unlikely to have occurred due to random chance.[12]

Large-scale quantitative studies of genocide date back to the early 1990s, when Fein disproved the then-common idea that genocide is more prevalent in ethnically diverse countries. Instead, she concluded that genocides are more likely in countries that 1) have previously experienced genocide, 2) have authoritarian governments, 3) implement discrimination, and 4) experience other upheaval, like war.[13] Krain extended this study by employing a more sophisticated analysis[14] to confirm Fein's conclusion that ethnic heterogeneity does not cause genocide.[15] He also found that war and autocratic governments are significant risk factors of genocide, emphasizing the importance of civil war and arguing that it creates an opening in the political opportunity structure of a country, including the government.[16]

---

[12] Ward, Greenhill, and Bakke illustrate that efforts to assess predictive capacity are better than assessing significance, which is done by assessing something known as a p value. See Michael D. Ward, Brian D. Greenhill, and Kristin M. Bakke, 'The Perils of Policy by P-Value: Predicting Civil Conflicts', *Journal of Peace Research*, 47:4 (2010), 363–75.

[13] Helen Fein, 'Accounting for Genocide after 1945: Theories and Some Findings', *International Journal on Group Rights* 1 (1993), 79–106. See also Leo Kuper, *Genocide: Its Political Use in the Twentieth Century* (New Haven: Yale University Press, 1981).

[14] Specifically, Fein's analysis was a bivariate analysis, which meant she examined a series of relationships between two variables (e.g. the relationship between civil war and genocide, the relationship between discrimination and genocide). Krain and most others now employ multivariate analyses that examine the relationship between many different variables at the same time and thus allow the researcher to examine the effect of one variable independent of others, as previously described.

[15] Matthew Krain, 'State-Sponsored Mass Murder: The Onset and Severity of Genocides and Politicides', *Journal of Conflict Resolution* 41:3 (1997), 331–60.

[16] See also Rudolph Rummel, *Death by Government* (New Brunswick: Transaction Publishers, 1994).

Almost a decade later, Harff explored why certain instances of regime collapse led to genocide between 1955 and 1997.[17] She arrived at a six-factor model that assessed the 'conditional probability that a genocide will begin one year after state failure'.[18] This model included four risk factors aligned with Fein's findings (prior genocide, autocracies, exclusionary ideologies, and upheaval) and two additional ones: contention regarding the ethnicity of those in power and low trade openness. In 2012, Harff added state-led discrimination as a seventh factor.[19]

Many studies have further tested the risk factors associated with the onset of genocide. This robust body of research has involved large-N studies, in-depth case studies, and comparative case studies that leverage differences and similarities across situations. Some of this research has been theoretically motivated, though other efforts have emphasized identifying concrete variables that help predict genocide with less of a focus on the mechanism behind such prediction. Taken together, this work has identified five major sets of risk factors associated with the onset of genocide: 1) political upheaval and threat, 2) state structure and capacity, 3) ideology and social divisions, 4) conflict and human rights history, and 5) international factors.[20] I will describe research on each of these categories in turn.

---

[17] Barbara Harff, 'No Lessons Learned from the Holocaust? Assessing Risks of Genocide and Political Mass Murder since 1955', *American Political Science Review* 97:1 (2003), 57–73; see also Barbara Harff, 'Systematic Early Warning of Humanitarian Emergencies', *Journal of Peace Research* 3:5 (1998), 551–79.

[18] Harff, 'No Lessons Learned', 65. But see Chad Hazlett, 'New Lessons Learned? Improving Genocide and Politicide Forecasting', [online] (2011), whttps://www.ushmm.org/m/pdfs/20111102-hazlett-early-_warning-lessons-learned.pdf.

[19] In 2015, Harff and Gurr reassessed the Harff model and found that the role of economic interconnectedness was not a significant predictor of genocide. See updates on http://www.GPANet.org.

[20] Researchers measure these factors in various ways, and often measurement of a specific variable (known as operationalization) influences results. For instance, the presence of upheaval could be measured as a scale of upheaval (ranging, for instance, from 1–10), as a simple variable that assigns a country a 1 if there is upheaval or a 0 otherwise, etc. Here, I review general findings rather than focus on specific operationalization. Note also that alternate groupings of factors have been suggested. See, for instance, James Waller, *Confronting Evil: Engaging Our Responsibility to Prevent Genocide* (New York: Oxford University Press, 2016).

***Political Upheaval and Threat*.** Political upheaval[21] and threat to those in power are the strongest risk factors of genocide. In other words, researchers can say, with a high degree of certainty, that political upheaval and threat typically have the largest effect on the probability that genocide will occur.[22] Many studies have found that civil war is particularly important for predicting the onset of genocide.[23] For civil wars that do not end in regime change, this association is likely linked to the threat felt by political leaders who, in turn, seek to solidify their power by removing perceived threats. Alternatively, for civil wars that end in regime change, this association is likely due to the fact that new leaders—possibly those with revolutionary aims to remake or otherwise transform society—rise to power.[24] In fact, civil wars that end with a clear victor, as opposed to a negotiated settlement, more commonly see a prevailing party engage in genocide and mass killing, likely because the victor does not fear

[21] Upheaval involves 'an abrupt change in the political community caused by the formation of a state or regime through violent conflict, redrawing of state boundaries, or defeat in international war'. Harff, 'No Lessons Learned', 62.

[22] Harff, 'No Lessons Learned'.

[23] Krain, 'State-Sponsored Mass Murder'; Hollie Nyseth Brehm, 'Re-examining Risk Factors of Genocide', *Journal of Genocide Research* 19:1 (2017), 61–87; Ted Robert Gurr, 'Preventing Genocides and Mass Atrocities: Evidence from Conflict Analysis', in Barbara Harff and Ted Robert Gurr (eds.), *Preventing Mass Atrocities: Policies and Practices* (London: Routledge, 2018); Angela D. Nichols, 'The Origins of Genocide in Civil War', *Trames* 22:1 (2018), 89–101.

[24] Nyseth Brehm, 'Re-Examining Risk Factors'. Valentino, Puth, and Blach-Lindsay argue that mass killing is more prominent in conflicts where guerrilla armies oppose governments. Benjamin Valentino, Paul Huth, and Dylan Balch-Lindsay, '"Draining the Sea": Mass Killing and Guerrilla Warfare', *International Organization* 58 (2004), 375–407. Yet, Krcmaric finds that mass killing is more probable during conventional wars than during guerilla wars. Daniel Krcmaric, 'Varieties of Civil War and Mass Killing: Reassessing the Relationship between Guerrilla Warfare and Civilian Victimization', *Journal of Peace Research* 55:1 (2018), 18–31. Note that Valentino and co-authors, as well as Krcmaric, focus on the state-sponsored mass killing of civilians belonging to any groups, albeit with different numeric thresholds. This focus is broader than the definition of genocide as conceptualized in this chapter, and these specific relationships should be tested with regard to genocide as well.

armed resistance.[25] Put another way, those in power may more readily choose to eliminate segments of the population due to a lack of controls from competing groups.

Coups and revolutions are two other common forms of upheaval that have similar effects on genocide depending on their success.[26] As with civil wars, successful coups and revolutions can pave the way for repressive leaders, while unsuccessful ones can threaten existing leaders—leaders who may turn to genocide as a strategic response to a perceived threat.[27] A variety of other events can cause threat and strain to those in power and/or open the political opportunity structure of regimes,[28] including but not limited to assassinations,[29] election cycles,[30] riots,[31] strikes,[32] and movements against the state.[33]

State Structure and Capacity. Factors related to the state— namely its structure and capacity—have long been tied to genocide. In terms of state structure, early research on twentieth-century genocides generally suggested that autocratic regimes are more likely to commit genocide or kill their own people.[34] Numerous studies have since solidified the mechanism behind these findings by demonstrating that a lack of controls on those in power is particularly associated with

---

[25] Gary Uzonyi, 'Civil War Victory and the Onset of Genocide and Politicide', *International Interactions* 41:2 (2015), 365–91.

[26] Nicholas Rost, 'Will It Happen Again? On the Possibility of Forecasting the Risk of Genocide', *Journal of Genocide Research* 15:1 (2013), 41–67; Nyseth Brehm, 'Re-Examining Risk Factors'.

[27] Benjamin A. Valentino, *Final Solutions: Mass Killing and Genocide in the 20th Century* (Ithaca: Cornell University Press, 2005); Manus Midlarsky, *The Killing Trap: Genocide in the 20th Century* (New York: Cambridge University Press, 2005).

[28] Krain, 'State-Sponsored Mass Murder'.

[29] Rost, 'Will It Happen Again?'.

[30] Goldsmith et al., 'Forecasting the Onset of Genocide and Politicide'.

[31] Rost, 'Will It Happen Again?'.

[32] Gary Uzonyi, 'Domestic Unrest, Genocide and Politicide', *Political Studies* 64:2 (2016), 315–34.

[33] Erica Chenoweth, Evan Perkoski, and Sooyeon Kang, 'State Repression and Nonviolent Resistance', *Journal of Conflict Resolution* 61:9 (2017), 1950–69; Nyseth Brehm, 'Re-Examining Risk Factors'.

[34] Hannah Arendt, *The Origins of Totalitarianism* (New York: Meridien, 1959); Rummel, *Death by Government*.

genocide.[35] Indeed, for genocides committed by state actors, it stands to reason that leaders may be more likely to harm citizens when they may not face repercussions or restrictions.

Nevertheless, other studies have further complicated this picture by arguing that mixed political regimes (i.e. those that are not democracies or autocracies) have a greater risk of genocide.[36] Mann goes further to suggest that democratizing countries are more likely to commit genocide and related mass violence due to the imperative to define 'the people', which inevitably excludes some of the populace in the pursuit of defining who belongs.[37] This mirrors earlier scholarship on settler genocides as well.[38]

Others connect the onset of genocide to state capacity—measured as military personnel, military spending, or GDP, among other variables—though this association is notably weaker than the association between state structure and genocide.[39] Generally, states that

---

[35] Michael Colaresi and Sabine C. Carey, 'To Kill or to Protect: Security Forces, Domestic Institutions, and Genocide', *Journal of Conflict Resolution* 52:1 (2008), 39–67; Hazlett, 'New Lessons Learned?'; Nyseth Brehm, 'Re-Examining Risk Factors'; Scott Gates and Aysegul Aydin, 'Rulers as Mass Murderers: Political Institutions and Human Insecurity', in Stephen M. Saideman and Marie-Joëlle J. Zahar (eds.), *Intra-State Conflict, Governments and Security* (New York: Routledge, 2008), 92–115.

[36] Goldsmith et al., 'Forecasting the Onset of Genocide and Politicide'; Charles H. Anderton and John R. Carter, 'A New Look at Weak State Conditions and Genocide Risk', *Peace Economics, Peace Science and Public Policy* 21:1 (2015), 1–36. Revolutionary leaders are also associated with higher odds of mass killing (see Nam Kyu Kim, 'Revolutionary Leaders and Mass Killing', *Journal of Conflict Resolution* 62:2 [2018], 289–317).

[37] Michael Mann, *The Dark Side of Democracy: Explaining Ethnic Cleansing* (Cambridge: Cambridge University Press, 2005). See also Joan Esteban, Massimo Morelli, and Dominic Rohner, 'Strategic Mass Killings', *Journal of Political Economy* 123:5 (2015), 1087–132.

[38] See, for instance, A. Dirk Moses (ed.), *Genocide and Settler Society: Frontier Violence and Stolen Indigenous Children in Australian History* (New York: Berghahn Books, 2005). Colonial genocides are excluded from predictive efforts due in part to a lack of data and are thus unfortunately largely excluded from this review.

[39] New research has suggested that researchers should treat militaries as actors in their own right. In this vein, Wilson highlights threats to militaries in particular. Chris Wilson, 'Military Anxiety and Genocide: Explaining Campaigns of Annihilation and Their Absence', *Journal of Genocide Research* 21:2 (2019), 178–200.

have greater capacity may have a greater ability to fulfil their will, which could include genocide.[40] Indeed, strong state capacity has been linked to several prominent genocides, such as those in Germany and Rwanda. However, major economic shocks (like recessions) that influence state capacity are generally not found to be associated with the onset of genocide, and the presence of economic resources has mixed effects.[41] Furthermore, new states, as well as states with low income per capita, have greater risk of genocide.[42] These findings illustrate that weak states are likewise at risk of genocide, as has been seen in the genocides in Sudan or Burundi. Different constellations of factors likely align to influence whether strong or weak states experience genocide, and more in-depth case studies of the *other* risk factors that co-occur in these strong or weak states will help clarify the impact of state capacity.

Ideology and Social Divisions. Ideologies, or the distinctive political worldviews of individuals, groups, and organizations, are also associated with the onset of genocide.[43] Ideologies result in the exclusion of individuals from the 'universe of obligation',[44] which can influence violence against members of excluded groups. More broadly, political leaders can use ideologies to persecute people whom they define as antithetical to a stated purpose (e.g. national success[45]), especially when these purposes are tied to a country's 'founding narratives'.[46] Yet, incorporating ideology into quantitative

---

[40] Colaresi and Carey, 'To Kill or to Protect'. Many forecasting models similarly include the infant mortality rate. Though there is not a theoretical linkage between infant mortality rate and genocide, this statistic might proxy a state's ability to take care of its most vulnerable population—children—and may also capture economic capacity.

[41] Chyanda M. Querido, 'State-Sponsored Mass Killing in African Wars— Greed or Grievance?', *International Advances in Economic Research* 15:3 (2009), 351–61.

[42] Anderton and Carter, 'A New Look at Weak State Conditions and Genocide Risk'.

[43] Jonathan Leader Maynard, 'Ideology and Armed Conflict', *Journal of Peace Research*, [online] (2019), https://doi.org/10.1177/0022343319826629.

[44] Fein, *Genocide: A Sociological Perspective*, 36.

[45] Eric Weitz, *A Century of Genocide: Utopias of Race and Nation* (Princeton: Princeton University Press, 2003).

[46] Scott Straus, *Making and Unmaking Nations: War, Leadership, and Genocide in Modern Africa* (Ithaca: Cornell University Press, 2015).

models used in prediction is difficult due to difficulties in measuring ideology, which in turn highlights the limits of quantification. To date, multiple studies have resorted to a simple dummy variable (i.e. 1=present, 0=absent) that captures whether those in charge of the country exhibit an ideology that excludes a segment of the population.[47] These studies have generally found that exclusionary ideologies are associated with the onset of genocide, supporting rich qualitative research with similar findings.[48]

As ideologies can influence actions in various ways, models also regularly incorporate whether or not an ideology has manifested in discrimination.[49] Economic and political discrimination are associated with the onset of genocide,[50] and this discrimination indicates that those with power are actively[51] excluding certain segments of the population.[52] Notably, however, more diverse societies—often measured by ethno-linguistic variation among the population—do not typically have higher odds of genocide or related mass violence. Instead of focusing on sheer diversity, researchers have emphasized discrimination of excluded groups and political manipulation of group difference,[53] as well as how diversity of the population may matter once political instability begins.

Conflict and Human Rights History. A country's particular human rights and conflict histories are also commonly included in predictive models. As noted above, both Fein and Harff argue that

[47] Harff, 'No Lessons Learned'; Nyseth Brehm, 'Re-Examining Risk Factors'.

[48] Eric D. Weitz, *A Century of Genocide: Utopias of Race and Nation* (Princeton: Princeton University Press, 2003). See also Leader Maynard, 'Ideology and Armed Conflict'.

[49] See e.g. Goldsmith et al., 'Forecasting the Onset of Genocide and Politicide'.

[50] Hazlett, 'New Lessons Learned?'; Nyseth Brehm, 'Reassessing Risk Factors of Genocide'.

[51] Discrimination can certainly be structural in nature as well.

[52] Many studies include political groups in the definition of genocide, as noted above. However, Uzonyi and Asal suggest that discrimination is associated with the odds of genocide but not with the odds of politicide. Gary Uzonyi and Victor Asal, 'Discrimination, Genocide, and Politicide', *Political Research Quarterly*, [online] (2019), https://doi.org/10.1177/1065912919828827.

[53] Subnational analyses of risk, discussed in more detail below, are particularly useful for measuring horizontal inequalities.

countries that have experienced genocides[54] in the past are more likely to experience genocide in the future.[55] This may be due to the presence of impunity, though prior genocide may also have other lasting societal impacts, such as effects on social divisions or state capacity.

Since prior human rights violations are predictive of future human rights violations,[56] many researchers expand beyond prior genocide to argue that other forms of past conflict, human rights abuses, or repression are associated with the possibility of genocide.[57] A government that is intent on killing its civilians may begin by restricting their rights, as has been seen in numerous examples throughout history.[58] Though this risk factor is similar to social divisions, *prior* discrimination and related repression may be particularly indicative of a long-standing will to exclude a population or of longstanding impunity. Researchers have also linked low-level violence against civilians to future atrocities of larger magnitude.[59]

International Factors. Finally, as countries do not exist in a vacuum, interactions between states are also linked to the onset of genocide. For instance, trade promotes engagement in the international system, and it may also influence the adoption of norms against violence. Accordingly, some studies and related forecasting

[54] Prior episodes of other forms of violence, like civil war, are tied to the onset of genocide as well, as noted above with the discussion of how conflicts end. The impact of prior violence likely manifests in complex ways that are not neatly captured by a measure of prior violence, however. For instance, countries that experienced civil wars may have polarization between those in power or weaker institutions than countries that have not experienced civil wars.

[55] Fein, *Genocide: A Sociological Perspective*; Harff, 'No Lessons Learned'.

[56] Steven C. Poe and C. Neal Tate, 'Repression of Human Rights to Personal Integrity in the 1980s: A Global Analysis', *American Political Science Review*, 88:4 (1994), 853–72.

[57] Goldsmith et al., 'Forecasting the Onset of Genocide and Politicide'; Rost, 'Will It Happen Again?'.

[58] To be certain, intent can also evolve over time, and governments and others that engage in genocide may not harbour genocidal intent for a long period of time prior to engaging in violence.

[59] Charles H. Anderton and Edward V. Ryan, 'Habituation to Atrocity: Low-Level Violence Against Civilians as a Predictor of High-Level Attacks', *Journal of Genocide Research*, 18:4 (2016), 539–62.

efforts include trade openness[60] or similar indicators of economic interconnectedness, such as membership in the World Trade Organization (WTO)[61] or the presence of oil or other resources.[62] Political[63] interconnectedness may likewise provide global checks and balances, though thus far quantitative studies have not found a definitive link between membership in international governmental and nongovernmental organizations and the onset of genocide. Qualitative studies have traced important links between international dynamics and genocide,[64] though some of these studies have found that ties to powerful countries may actually provide countries cover when they perpetrate genocide. For instance, Sudan arguably benefitted from China's oil investment and also received protection from China when the UN Security Council considered action in Darfur.[65]

Beyond political and economic interconnectedness, there is some evidence that international rivalry is also associated with the likelihood of genocide. Specifically, countries embroiled in inter-state rivalries generally experience increased militarization and/or conflict, which in turn may influence the onset of genocide.[66] Defeat in international war is similarly included in Harff's notion of political upheaval that was previously covered. Finally, researchers have found that conflict in neighbouring countries is associated with higher odds of genocide.[67] The precise mechanism for this association is unclear, though

---

[60] Harff, 'No Lessons Learned'. As noted earlier, however, Harff re-tested this variable and did not find a statistically significant effect. Indeed, studies including this variable typically do not find a significant relationship between trade openness and genocide.

[61] The Political Instability Task Force models, addressed in more detail below, include WTO/GATT membership.

[62] Colaresi and Carey, 'To Kill or to Protect'.

[63] Though many people differentiate between political and economic factors, these factors are notably intertwined.

[64] For one of many examples, see Donald Bloxham, *The Great Game of Genocide: Imperialism, Nationalism, and the Destruction of the Ottoman Armenians* (New York: Oxford University Press, 2007).

[65] David H. Shin, 'China and the Conflict in Darfur', *Brown Journal of World Affairs* 16:1 (2009), 85–100.

[66] Gary Uzonyi, 'Interstate Rivalry, Genocide, and Politicide', *Journal of Peace Research* 55:4 (2018), 476–90.

[67] Goldsmith et al., 'Forecasting the Onset of Genocide and Politicide'.

researchers have suggested that radicalized domestic politics, increased availability of arms, increased displacement, and amplified threat could all be at play.[68]

In sum, the risk factors associated with genocide generally fall within the following categories: 1) political upheaval and threat, 2) state structure and capacity, 3) ideology and social divisions, 4) conflict and human rights history, and 5) international factors. These classifications of risk factors are not mutually exclusive (e.g. an international factor may also serve as a threat). Risk factors also occur simultaneously, meaning that researchers focus on how multiple risk factors intersect to produce situations where genocide may occur.

Yet, simply knowing that certain causes are often associated with an event is not enough for prediction. In fact, quantitative studies can have statistically significant results but can fare quite poorly when it comes to forecasting the future,[69] as the presence of a significant association does not necessarily mean that a variable has strong predictive power. Consequently, to use risk factors for predictive purposes, researchers have to take another step geared towards the future.

One of the most common next steps is to assess something known as the Receiver Operator Characteristic (ROC) curve, which provides information about a model's predictive capabilities. The ROC curve plots the relationship between the rate of false positives (the number of incorrectly predicted onsets of genocide divided by the total number of cases where genocide did not happen) and the rate of true positives (the number of correctly predicted genocides divided by the total number of cases where genocide did happen).[70] A second, stricter option is to assess something known as out-of-sample forecasts. While

---

[68] E.g. most of the factors cited in this paragraph could be seen as threats to those in power. Further, several other factors are generally included in forecasting models but have been less commonly studied. First, forecasting models often include a dummy variable (again, 1 or 0) to indicate the post-Cold War era guided by the assumption that the world is simply different following the Cold War. Population is generally included as well, and more populated countries have a greater risk of genocide.

[69] Ward, Greenhill, and Bakke, 'The Perils of Policy by P-Value'.

[70] This is then measured on a scale from 0 to 1, and numbers closer to 1 indicate better predictive ability. See ibid. for more.

the ROC curve allows a researcher to assess how a model predicts outcomes within the same data (called in-sample forecasting), out-of-sample forecasts predict outcomes in new data. Essentially, part of the dataset is used to predict other data that are excluded from the models (e.g. years 1965–85 predict events in years 1986–95), which is a more difficult feat than in-sample forecasting.[71]

Even with one or both of these steps, predictions are never certain. Models are only as good as the data that researchers use, and even then, human behaviour is sometimes unpredictable. Researchers thus continually strive to balance false negatives and false positives in their models. While the analysis of risk factors is an important step towards attaining this goal, the second step of prediction—assessing triggering and escalatory factors—further enhances forecasting efforts.

Step 2: Triggers and Escalatory Factors

Once researchers and practitioners have identified the risk factors of genocide, including countries that may be at risk, the second step involves examining the factors more immediately associated with—and indicative of—the onset of genocide. Indeed, the risk factors reviewed thus far paint a picture of the general situations in which genocide may occur, but they do not provide information about the precise events that unfold prior to its onset. Risk factors thus cannot be used to predict genocide alone because they do not account for its timing. As such (and as previously noted), many researchers differentiate between risk assessment and early warning models, suggesting that the former is tied to broader structural factors and the latter is tied to more proximate causes, typically termed triggering or escalatory factors. Both general risk factors and triggering/escalatory factors are necessary to understand the possibility of genocide, however, so these factors must be considered in tandem.

Despite this, researchers have paid more attention to the risk factors of genocide, and systematic analyses of the triggers of genocide are relatively rare.[72] A trigger is an event or process that (1) precedes the

---

[71] See ibid. for a common way to do this (called K-fold cross validation).

[72] This may be due to a general view that triggers are more unpredictable and varied.

onset of the genocide, (2) represents a significant change in the status quo in the country or countries where the violence occurs, (3) is not itself part of the genocide, and (4) has a direct, proximate causal connection to the onset of the genocide.[73] Using this definition, Valentino analysed the triggers of thirty-two state-sponsored mass killings.[74] He concluded that anti-government protests, strikes, coups, and initial major attacks by rebels are among the most common triggers. Straus similarly examined the triggers of eighteen atrocity events, finding that threats to the political elite—such as battlefield advances, assassinations, coups, or protests—are among the most prominent triggers of mass atrocity. [75]

As these analyses make clear, there is overlap between what researchers deem to be 'triggers' and structural risk factors, as many triggers cited above are often included in models of risk factors. For instance, shocks to the political system (e.g. coups, revolutions, assassinations, upcoming elections) and, to a lesser degree, the economic system (e.g. economic declines, discovery of minerals) are often found in risk assessment models but can also be triggering events depending on their proximity to violence. As such, more detailed studies of triggers are needed. Research must also ascertain how structural factors influence which events serve as triggers in the first place. For instance, perhaps some factors—like assassination attempts or advances by non-state militias—are only triggers for certain types of governments or when a civil war is occurring.

An even smaller body of research addresses what Mayersen[76] calls 'escalatory factors'. Although escalatory factors are similar to triggers

---

[73] James D. Fearon and David D. Laitin, 'Integrating Qualitative and Quantitative Methods', in Janet Box-Steffensmeier, Henry E. Brady, and David Collier's (eds.), *The Oxford Handbook of Political Methodology* (Oxford: Oxford University Press, 2008), 756–78.

[74] Ben Valentino, Internal memo prepared for the Political Instability Task Force.

[75] Straus examines genocides as well as other forms of widespread and systematic violence against civilians. Scott Straus, 'Triggers of Mass Atrocities', *Politics and Governance* 3:3 (2015), 5–15.

[76] Deborah Mayersen, 'On the Timing of Genocide', *Genocide Studies and Prevention* 5:1 (2010), 20–38. Due to the difficulty of capturing escalatory factors in yearly data, some researchers have also urged for models to go below the country-year, such as bi-annual or quarterly forecasts.

in terms of increasing the chances of violence, they are not the ultimate 'trigger' of the violence. Rather, an escalatory factor is any factor that contributes to the escalation of violence in the months (or possibly years) prior to the onset of genocide. As such, risk factors set the stage for violence, escalatory factors cause more rapid increases in the likelihood of genocide (and thus are often not captured in quantitative analyses of annual data), and triggers are the ultimate events that spark the onset of genocide.

To illustrate, Mayersen draws upon case studies of the 1915 genocide in Armenia and the 1994 genocide in Rwanda to propose a model of the escalation of genocide. This model includes 1) the presence of an outgroup, 2) significant internal strife, 3) the perception of the outgroup as posing a significant threat to the dominant power, 4) a response to the threat (which is often violent), 5) a process of retreat and/or escalation of this response, 6) the emergence of a genocidal ideology among the dominant power, 7) an extensive propaganda campaign, and 8) genocide. Although demarcating the difference between risk factors and escalatory factors in this model is not clear cut, the latter stages—especially the response to a perceived threat and the development of a propaganda campaign—constitute escalatory factors because they accelerated the situation and, as such, the risk of genocide.[77] In each case, a final event then triggered step eight.

Finally, some researchers and practitioners have identified signposts that genocide may be imminent. Signposts are distinct from triggers or escalatory factors in that they can signify genocide is likely to occur but are not necessarily causes themselves. For instance, prior to many genocides, political elites stockpile weapons. These weapons are associated with violence, but the decision to collect weapons may serve as a sign of processes that are unfolding rather than as a specific cause of the genocide itself. It follows that such signs are often not tied to a particular causal logic but rather may indicate that violence is becoming much more likely.

---

[77] See also Verdeja, 'Predicting Genocide and Mass Atrocities'. Due to the difficulty of capturing escalatory factors in yearly data, some researchers have urged for models to go below the country-year, such as bi-annual or quarterly forecasts.

Many of these signposts are included in existing early warning efforts (covered more in the following section), though few models have attempted to *systematically* identify them. Rather, knowledge about signposts generally derives from rich case studies that have documented the events and processes that unfolded prior to the onset of specific genocides.

For example, possible signposts include the presence of hate media and the stockpiling of weapons, as noted above.[78] Speeches and other rhetoric—especially against minority groups—may also serve as a signpost of genocide.[79] To be certain, these outward 'signs' of internal processes that lead to genocide may also have a causal dimension. Indeed, speeches and rhetoric may illustrate the presence of an exclusionary ideology, but they may also simultaneously mobilize public opinion and even action.

Public commemorations of perceived grievances, including grievances that place blame on a certain segment of society for past hardships, could likewise indicate impending violence. For instance, shortly after Milošević became President of Serbia, he gave a speech coinciding with the 600th anniversary of the Battle of Kosovo, a military defeat of the medieval Serbian kingdom by the Ottoman Empire.[80] The speech emboldened Serb nationalists who expressed grievances against the Muslim 'Turks'[81] and suggested that violence might be necessary to secure Serb interests, ultimately serving as a signal of impending violence while simultaneously contributing to the escalation of violence against Bosnian Muslims.

Public mobilization against minority groups may similarly serve as a signpost of violence, as illustrated by the well-known example of *Kristallnacht*. Rapid increases in repression against certain groups—or

[78] Ibid.

[79] See also Gerard Saucier and Laura Akers, 'Democidal Thinking: Patterns in the Mindset Behind Organized Mass Killing', *Genocide Studies and Prevention* 12:1 (2018), 8.

[80] Netherlands Institute for War Documentation (NIOD), 'Part 1: The Yugoslavia Problem and the Role of the West 1991–1994', in *Srebrenica: A 'Safe Area'* (2002). Sabrina P. Ramet, *The Three Yugoslavias: State-Building and Legitimation, 1918–2005* (Bloomington: Indiana University Press, 2006).

[81] This term suggested they were outsiders associated with the Ottoman Empire's prior rule.

human rights violations more broadly—may indicate looming violence as well.[82] Furthermore, elite leaders of minority groups are often targeted prior to the onset of genocide. Terming this form of violence *elitocide*, Gratz argues its prominence in Bosnia, where key political leaders, educational elites, and religious leaders were arrested, tortured, and even killed well before the onset of violence in 1992, possibly as a way to target group culture.[83]

The recognition of these and other signposts requires an in-depth familiarity with situations on the ground. This familiarity must stem from rich qualitative methods geared towards understanding the localized context, such as interviews and ethnographies. Indeed, although much research used to predict genocide has emphasized quantitative methods—generally in pursuit of generalizability and sometimes due to a misguided notion that statistics are more objective than qualitative methods—contextualized knowledge is paramount in determining if genocide will occur in specific spaces. Researchers and practitioners should thus take risk factors, triggers and escalatory factors, and signposts of genocide—as informed by both large-N studies and in-depth qualitative studies—into account as they seek to predict genocide. Next, I turn to how the various research methods discussed above translate into actual prediction efforts, followed by a brief discussion of the future of genocide prediction.

Predictive Bodies

Governments, organizations, policymakers, researchers, and many others draw upon the research summarized thus far to create risk assessment and early warning models, generally conceptualized here as forecasting or prediction efforts. These endeavours are varied and are undertaken by governmental and nongovernmental organizations alike. Though there is not space to review all predictive bodies,

---

[82] Verdeja, 'Predicting Genocide and Mass Atrocities'. Again, these signs may also contribute to subsequent violence as well.

[83] Dennis Gratz, 'Elitocide in Bosnia and Herzegovina and its Impact on the Contemporary Understanding of the Crime of Genocide', *Nationalities Papers* 39:3 (2011), 409–24.

I briefly consider forecasting efforts that are currently underway at international, regional, and national levels.

At the international level, the Secretary-General of the United Nations (UN) initiated an Action Plan to Prevent Genocide on the tenth anniversary of the 1994 genocide in Rwanda. This involved appointing the first Special Adviser on the Prevention of Genocide, whose mandate includes collecting information on situations that might lead to genocide, acting as an early warning mechanism for the Secretary-General and the UN Security Council, and enhancing the UN's capacity to analyse information related to genocide.

The Special Adviser on the Prevention of Genocide works with the UN Office on Genocide Prevention and the Responsibility to Protect, which monitors possible situations of genocide worldwide. In 2008, this office added a second Special Adviser—the Special Adviser for the Responsibility to Protect—following a 2005 World Summit that ascertained that all countries have a moral obligation to protect people from genocide, war crimes, ethnic cleansing, and crimes against humanity.[84] While each Special Adviser operates pursuant to a distinct mandate, they cooperate with regard to an early warning framework informed by the research summarized above. This frame-work includes ten risk factors specific to genocide[85] as well as select indicators, defined as different manifestations of the risk factors. The risk factors include: 1) armed conflict and political, economic, and social instability, 2) past or present violations of human rights and humanitarian law, 3) weak state structures (though, as noted above, genocides also occur in strong states), 4) motives and incentives (e.g. exclusionary ideologies and perceived threats), 5) capacity to commit atrocity crimes (e.g. arms, international support), 6) intergroup tensions/discrimination, 7) signs of intent to destroy a group in whole or in part, 8) the absence of mitigating factors (e.g. lack of international ties, though as noted above, international ties may also be aggravating

[84] This norm suggests that when a country fails to meet its obligation, the international community has the responsibility to act to protect those populations, including the use of force in the event peaceful means are unsuccessful.

[85] The framework also includes information meant to predict war crimes and crimes against humanity.

factors), 9) enabling circumstances and preparatory actions, and 10) triggers.[86]

Using this framework, the Office, its Special Advisers, and its other staff monitor situations worldwide and work with regional and national bodies to develop prevention mechanisms. Indeed, several regional governmental and nongovernmental bodies—such as the African Union, the Organization for Security and Cooperation in Europe (OSCE), and the European Union (EU)—maintain dedicated early warning offices. The Organization of the American States' Department of Sustainable Democracy and the Special Missions and the Economic Community of West African States likewise engage in forecasting endeavours.

At the national level, the US Political Instability Task Force (PITF), formerly known as the State Failure Task Force, is a particularly prominent government forecasting project. The US government created the PITF in the wake of the 1994 genocide in Rwanda to forecast multiple forms of instability, including genocide. Harff's research formed the basis of much of the early PITF modelling on genocide. Today, the PITF no longer specifically forecasts genocide as a form of political instability.[87] Rather, it forecasts mass killings, defined as situations where actions of the state result in the deaths of at least 1,000 non-combatants from a discrete group over a sustained period of violence over a two-year period.[88] More recently, the US Department of State also created the Atrocities Prevention Board. This board sponsors regular meetings of high-level government officials with the goal of sharing information, identifying possible atrocities, and harmonizing prediction and prevention efforts across the US government.

---

[86] Moses argues, however, that this framework may identify many situations as 'pre-genocidal' based on a view of genocide in ideal typical terms. For more, see Dirk Moses, 2006, 'Why the Discipline of Genocide Studies Has Trouble Explaining Why Genocides End', http://howgenocidesend.ssrc.org/Moses/.

[87] Harff, 'No Lessons Learned'. Notably, until 2018, Barbara Harff and Ted Gurr continued to forecast genocide and politicide on their own. These forecasts were located at http://www.gpanet.org/content/barbara-harffs-risk-assessment.

[88] Available from the author.

Many other governments have created early warning mechanisms.[89] For instance, Kenya, Tanzania, Uganda, and South Sudan each created national committees meant to engage in early warning efforts. The Commission for International Humanitarian Law of Costa Rica (CCDIH) and the Office of the Ombudsman of Ecuador also seek to predict and prevent genocide.[90] Other countries are presently in the midst of creating national early warning mechanisms as well.[91]

National nongovernmental organizations also engage in forecasting efforts. Genocide Watch, founded by Gregory Stanton, uses a ten-stage model[92] of analysis to predict genocide. Though the ten stages are not linear and are processes themselves, the first few stages are tied to classifying and dehumanizing groups while the latter stages include exterminating a group and, eventually, denying the genocide. Genocide Watch regularly uses these stages to publish a list of countries at risk of genocide, politicide, and what they deem 'other genocide-like crimes'.[93] Similarly, the US Holocaust Memorial Museum launched the Early Warning Project in 2015. This project engages in forecasting efforts as well as crowdsourcing via a public opinion poll and an annual survey.

Numerous other nongovernmental organizations around the world engage in early warning efforts. The International Crisis Group creates a monthly list of countries it deems at high risk of violence, including genocide.[94] In one of many other examples, the Canadian

---

[89] For a full review, see Samantha Capicotto and Rob Scharf, 'National Mechanisms for the Prevention of Atrocity Crimes', *Genocide Studies and Prevention* 11:3 (2018), 6–19.

[90] Auschwitz Institute, http://www.auschwitzinstitute.org/wp-content/uploads/2016/01/2018-National-Mechanisms-Booklet-web-1.pdf.

[91] Most of these state-level bodies undertake risk assessment to some degree, though the level of research and engagement varies greatly. Though not a government-led initiative, Australia has also become well-known for predicting genocide due to the efforts of Ben Goldsmith and his team at the Australian National University. See Benjamin E. Goldsmith and Charles Butcher, 'Genocide Forecasting: Past Accuracy and New Forecasts to 2020', *Journal of Genocide Research*, 20:1 (2018), 90–107.

[92] Notably, the model originally had eight stages.

[93] This list has three levels: genocide watch, genocide warning, and genocide emergency.

[94] Verdeja, 'Predicting Genocide and Mass Atrocities'.

Sentinel Project evaluates countries at risk of genocide based on Genocide Watch's Stages of Genocide and a data visualization programme known as the Conflict Tracking System. The Global Centre for the Responsibility to Protect, the Integrated Crisis Early Warning System, and many other nongovernmental organizations undertake similar efforts as well.

These and other early warning bodies are consistently creating lists of countries at risk of genocide, which is arguably an achievement in itself. However, researchers, policymakers, and other members of organizations must also engage in assessments of the accuracy of their forecasts—something that few organizations transparently do to date. Furthermore, even if genocide *is* correctly predicted, researchers have yet to develop consensus regarding the best evidenced-based practices for preventing its onset. This is likely due, in part, to a lack of public knowledge about how governments take diplomatic steps to prevent violence. As such, researchers have not been able to study diplomatic steps in order to ascertain what works and what does not. Additional research should be devoted to this topic—as possible given available information—though prevention is ultimately a matter of political will that transcends early warning efforts. Put another way, even the most accurate early warning endeavours are useless if countries and organizations are not willing to respond.

Future of Atrocity Prediction and Prevention

While political will may always be hard to attract and sustain, atrocity prediction and prevention will undoubtedly continue to improve. Though there are many possible ways to advance prediction efforts, I conclude this chapter by looking towards the future of geocide prediction and suggesting that moving beyond the state is particularly important for further enhancing forecasts.

The vast majority of the aforementioned studies analyse state-level factors in line with theories suggesting that a certain degree of capacity—traditionally only held by states—is necessary to commit genocide. In turn, predictive bodies create lists of *countries* at risk.

These endeavours are not misguided, as the state is vital to understanding the onset of genocide. Government officials and their armies initiated most genocides that occurred during the twentieth and twenty-first centuries, and factors related to the state, such as the type of government, can certainly influence the likelihood of genocide as reviewed above.

Genocide scholarship and related prediction efforts nonetheless run the risk of placing undue emphasis on the state.[95] Limiting predictive models of genocide to violence committed by the state disregards the fact that non-state actors can and do commit genocide, as research on paramilitaries has made clear. Analysing the onset of genocide at the state level also eclipses other meaningful ways to examine genocide, such as at the conflict level, since there can be multiple conflicts within a state at any given time. Furthermore, genocide often occurs in only part of a state or unfolds at different times within countries. Thus, as a complement to state-centric approaches, genocide prevention efforts should 1) better address genocide committed by non-state actors, 2) take conflicts as the unit of analysis, and 3) examine the onset and triggers of genocide at subnational levels.

Although the vast majority of genocides have been committed with active or tacit involvement of the state, non-state actors can and do commit genocide. In August 2014, for instance, ISIL militants swept across the Sinjar region of northern Iraq, which is home to the majority of the world's Yazidi people. The entire male population of the village of Khocho was executed, while many women and children were kidnapped.[96] This targeted destruction on the basis of religion and group membership is indeed genocide, but most early warning efforts would not have predicted this violence because it was committed by non-state actors. To be clear, numerous studies have documented non-state actors' involvement in genocide, but these studies

---

[95] Alexander Laban Hinton, 'Critical Genocide Studies', *Genocide Studies and Prevention* 7:1 (2012), 10; Cyanne Loyle, 'Understanding Nonstate Actor Behavior: The Determinants of Mass Atrocities', *Simon-Skjodt Center for the Prevention of Genocide Series of Occasional Papers* 9 (2018), 2.

[96] Human Rights Council, 'They Came to Destroy: ISIS Crimes Against the Yazidis,' Advance Version, 2016 (A/HRC/32/CRP.2), 6–8; Yazda Documentation Project, *Mass Graves of Yazidis Killed by the Islamic State Organization or Local Affiliates On or After August 3, 2014* (Yazda: Global Yazidi Organization, 2016), 4. See also Chapter 6, 'The State and Genocide' by Anton Weiss-Wendt.

focus on involvement as influenced by states rather than non-state actors *initiating* the violence.

As terror organizations, militias, and insurgent groups gain power, they act like states. They levy taxes, take territory, and wield a military—often in pursuit of creating their own government.[97] It consequently stands to reason that such groups would have the capacity to initiate and commit genocides, and researchers and practitioners should analyse the factors associated with non-state actor genocides. As many researchers have examined why and when non-state actors target civilians more broadly, this scholarship might be particularly useful for specifically predicting the onset of genocide committed by non-state actors. For example, genocide initiated by non-state actors may be linked to characteristics of the non-state actor (e.g. size, ideology, longevity), the non-state actor's relationships with civilians and governments, or the broader structural context in which the non-state actor operates.[98] This research could be informed by numerous disciplines and could likewise bring new disciplinary foci into genocide prevention, such as research in organizational sociology.

Furthermore, although researchers generally consider civil war and related conflicts as the strongest predictor of genocide, more could be done to analyse the particular facets of conflicts that influence genocide. While state-centric theories and models of genocide typically include a measure of ongoing conflict, they often do not account for differences between multiple conflicts within the same state. For example, most datasets cite two different civil wars occurring in Ethiopia in 1976, though only one of these conflicts involved genocide. According to the PITF State Failure Problem Set,[99] a year after the civil war began in 1975, '[the] army, internal security units, and civilian defence squads massacre[d] political and military elites, workers, students, bureaucrats, and others thought to oppose the

---

[97] David C. Rapoport, 'The Four Waves of Rebel Terror and September', *Anthropoetics* 8:1 (2002), http://wrldrels.org/wp-content/uploads/2016/02/Rapoport-Four-Waves-of-Terror.pdf.

[98] The Holocaust Memorial Museum's Early Warning Project has begun to forecast violence committed by non-state actors.

[99] https://www.systemicpeace.org/inscrdata.html

revolutionary regime'. When this genocide began, the Eritrean-Ethiopian war of independence was also taking place in the country, though this specific war did not involve genocide.

Quantitatively measured state-level factors likely cannot account for why one of these civil wars involved genocide while the other did not, but in-depth comparative case studies of the two conflicts likely can. Additionally, quantitative or comparative qualitative analyses of the onset of genocide in certain conflicts will surely shed light on the characteristics of conflicts that may lead to genocide, either as the conflicts are ongoing or in their aftermath. These characteristics include but are not limited to the type of conflict, who is involved, aspects of the violence, and, for genocides that begin *after* a conflict ends, how the conflict ended. This analysis may be especially important because some of the factors associated with civil war onset—like the roughness of terrain or the size of a country—are not typically associated with genocide. Although it is important to examine violence holistically, there may thus be important differences between conflicts that involve genocide and those that do not.

Finally, although genocides typically have a country-level onset date, violence can start at various times within or across countries. In order to predict genocide with more precision, researchers must understand *why* violence begins in specific locations. While state-level factors such as a state-led exclusionary ideology or threat to a government may inform why genocide occurs, they cannot fully explain why violence begins at a particular place. In fact, attempting to extend these theories to subnational units would neglect the fact that those committing the violence are, like all social actors, subject to the influence of their immediate social surroundings—surroundings that vary widely, meaning that other theories tailored to subnational spaces are needed to predict onset within subnational spaces.

To predict genocide at subnational levels, researchers can turn towards studies of other forms of violent conflict and crime. Analyses of civil and ethnic violence have documented how subnational dynamics influence where and when violence occurs.[100] For instance,

---

[100] Elisabeth Jean Wood, *Insurgent Collective Action and Civil War in El Salvador* (New York: Cambridge University Press, 2003), 226–56; Stathis Kalyvas, *The Logic*

civil conflict may be more likely in subnational spaces marked by low economic growth and capacity[101] or climate variability,[102] as well as in sparsely populated regions near borders and comparatively far from capital cities.[103] Studies of crime have also pointed towards many other factors (such as employment levels, community cohesion, and signs of social and physical disorder) that could influence the onset of violence at various subnational levels.[104]

of Violence in Civil War (New York: Cambridge University Press, 2006), 388–92; Alok K. Bohara, Neil J. Mitchell, and Mani Nepal, 'Opportunity, Democracy, and the Exchange of Political Violence: A Subnational Analysis of Conflict in Nepal', *Journal of Conflict Resolution* 50:1 (2006), 108–28; Gudrun Østby, Henrik Urdal, Mohammad Zulfan Tadjoeddin, S. Mansoob Murshed, and Håvard Strand, 'Population Pressure, Horizontal Inequality and Political Violence: A Disaggregated Study of Indonesian Provinces, 1990–2003', *Journal of Development Studies* 47:3 (2011), 377–98; Aas Rustad, Siri Camilla, Halvard Buhaug, Åshild Falch, and Scott Gates, 'All Conflict is Local: Modeling Sub-National Variation in Civil Conflict Risk', *Conflict Management and Peace Science* 28:1 (2011), 15–40.

[101] Halvard Buhaug, Scott Gates, and Päivi Lujala, 'Geography, Rebel Capability, and the Duration of Civil Conflict', *Journal of Conflict Resolution* 53:4 (2009), 544–69.

[102] Hanne Fjelde and Nina von Uexkull, 'Climate Triggers: Rainfall Anomalies, Vulnerability and Communal Conflict in Sub-Saharan Africa', *Political Geography* 31:7 (2012), 444–53.

[103] Halvard Buhaug and Jan Ketil Rød, 'Local Determinants of African Civil Wars, 1970–2001', *Political Geography* 25:3 (2006), 315–35. Clionadh Raleigh and Håvard Hegre, 'Population Size, Concentration, and Civil War: A Geographically Disaggregated Analysis', *Political Geography* 28:4 (2009), 224–38. Combining insights from numerous studies, Rustad and colleagues further propose a subnational conflict risk indicator based on population, socioeconomic status, conflict history, ethno-political exclusion, geographic location within a country, and neighbouring conflicts in other subnational administrative units. Rustad et al., 'All Conflict is Local'. See also Matthew Kupilik and Frank Witmer, 'Spatio-Temporal Violent Event Prediction Using Gaussian Process Regression', *Journal of Computational Social Science* 1:2 (2018): 437–51.

[104] Such data may be particularly useful in predicting the onset of violence that is largely undertaken by civilians, as was the case in Rwanda (Nyseth Brehm, 'Subnational Determinants of Killing in Rwanda'). Notably, the newly released political violence early-warning system called ViEWS produces monthly forecasts at the country *and* subnational level. This system does not explicitly forecast genocide but does examine state-based conflict, non-state conflict, and one-sided violence across the continent of Africa. Håvard Hegre, Marie Allansson, Matthias

Researchers could also analyse triggers at subnational levels. Although researchers have thus far conceptualized triggers at the state level, these events and processes likely occur in localized spaces as well. The trigger of the 1994 genocide in Rwanda was the President's plane crash, for example, but there may have been more proximate, localized triggers that contributed to the timing and severity within different subnational communities. Models of the diffusion of genocide will also be important to prediction in subnational spaces.[105]

As researchers and practitioners move beyond the state by analysing non-state actors, conflicts, and subnational spaces, they should draw upon a multitude of disciplines. Indeed, much of the scholarship reviewed in this chapter has stemmed from political science due to the predominance of this field in research related to predicting genocide. Yet, multiple disciplines and their related disciplinary approaches are necessary to better understand and, in turn, predict genocide. Literatures from criminology and organizational sociology briefly suggested above—alongside rich, critical work in anthropology, history, and psychology, among others—will be paramount to the future efforts suggested here.

Conclusion

Inspired in part by the horrific genocides of the 1990s, researchers and policymakers have been attempting to predict genocide. This has involved multi-methods research on broader risk factors of genocide as well as more immediate triggers and escalatory factors. Many individuals and organizations have incorporated this research into forecasting models that have, to date, identified countries that may be at risk of genocide. Though researchers and practitioners must do

---

Basedau, Michael Colaresi, Mihai Croicu, Hanne Fjelde, Frederick Hoyles et al., 'ViEWS: A Political Violence Early-Warning System', *Journal of Peace Research*, [online] (2019), https://doi.org/10.1177/0022343319823860.

[105] See Charles H. Anderton and Jurgen Brauer, 'The Onset, Spread, and Prevention of Mass Atrocities: Perspectives from Formal Network Models', *Journal of Genocide Research*, 21:4 (2019), 481–503.

more to assess the accuracy of these forecasts, research and related prediction efforts should also transcend the state to analyse non-state actors who commit genocide, conflicts that are associated with genocide, and subnational risk. In doing so, we will continue to move towards even more refined prediction efforts.

Select Bibliography

Goldsmith, Benjamin E., Charles R. Butcher, Dimitri Semenovich, and Arcot Sowmya, 'Forecasting the Onset of Genocide and Politicide: Annual Out-of-Sample Forecasts on a Global Dataset, 1988–2003', *Journal of Peace Research* 50:4 (2013), 437–52.

Harff, Barbara, 'No Lessons Learned from the Holocaust? Assessing Risks of Genocide and Political Mass Murder since 1955', *American Political Science Review* 97:1 (2003), 57–73.

Mayersen, Deborah, 'On the Timing of Genocide', *Genocide Studies and Prevention* 5:1 (2010), 20–38.

Nyseth Brehm, Hollie, 'Re-examining Risk Factors of Genocide', *Journal of Genocide Research* 19:1 (2017), 61–87.

Straus, Scott, 'Triggers of Mass Atrocities', *Politics and Governance* 3:3 (2015), 5–15.

Uzonyi, Gary, 'Interstate Rivalry, Genocide, and Politicide', *Journal of Peace Research* 55:4 (2018), 476–90.

Verdeja, Ernesto, 'Predicting Genocide and Mass Atrocities', *Genocide Studies and Prevention: An International Journal* 9:3 (2016), 13–32.

Ward, Michael D., Brian D. Greenhill, and Kristin M. Bakke, 'The Perils of Policy by P-Value: Predicting Civil Conflicts', *Journal of Peace Research*, 47:4 (2010), 363–75.

3

The Absence of Genocide in the Presence of Risk

When Genocide Does Not Occur

Deborah Mayersen and Stephen McLoughlin

Introduction

On 2 October 1937, Dominican President Rafael Trujillo ordered a massacre. Over the next week, somewhere between fifteen and twenty thousand ethnic Haitians along the northern frontier of the Dominican Republic were slaughtered.[1] At first, those Haitians that could make it to the border were allowed to flee, but by 5 October, checkpoints were closed and the military killed all those trying to escape.[2] By 8 October, the massacre was complete, the region having been virtually emptied of Haitians.[3] This massacre reflected a deeply rooted history of anti-Haitian sentiment in the Dominican Republic; one that has endured to the present day. Ethnic Haitians continue to experience discrimination, hatred, and violence. Former Dominican President Joaquín Balguer (1966–78, 1986–96), for example, spoke of 'Haitian imperialism' and 'peaceful invasion' as threats to the country,

---

[1] Richard Turits, 'A World Destroyed, A Nation Imposed: The 1937 Haitian Massacre in the Dominican Republic', *Hispanic American Historical Review* 82:3 (2002), 589–91; Richard Turits, *Foundations of Despotism: Peasants, The Trujillo Regime, and Modernity in Dominican History* (Paulo Alto: Stanford University, 2003), 161.

[2] Turits, 'A World Destroyed', 614.

[3] Ibid., 621.

referring to contact with Haitians as leading to 'ethnic corruption' and
'ethnic decay'.[4] Since the 1990s there have been concerted attempts
to deny citizenship to ethnic Haitians born in the Dominican Republic, despite their constitutional rights.[5] This led to an estimated seventy
to eighty thousand ethnic Haitians being forcibly deported in
2015–18.[6] Such events highlight that, for many decades, the Dominican Republic has exhibited some risk factors for genocide. Ethnic
Haitians can clearly be defined as an 'outgroup'; intergroup relations
are deeply politicized; and there is widespread state-led discrimination. Yet despite this, genocide has never occurred there. And while
it may seem surprising, such a scenario is far from unusual. It is this
subject, the absence of genocide in the presence of risk, that forms the
focus of this chapter.

Case studies such as that of the Dominican Republic, in which
genocide has not occurred despite demonstrable risk, have been
relatively overlooked in Genocide Studies.[7] This chapter therefore
begins within an examination of the historiography of Genocide
Studies. It considers the benefits, and limitations, of the root cause
model that has dominated many approaches to understanding the
causes of genocide, and how this model contributes to a focus on risk
progression. The chapter then examines the relative stability of risk in
many nations exhibiting some preconditions for genocide, exploring
why this stability is under-recognized. The following section considers
'negative' case studies, that is, those in which genocide has not
occurred despite demonstrable risk. First, we examine the methodological challenges associated with these cases, followed by highlighting
the unique potential they offer. Several case studies illustrate how

---

[4] Pedro Miguel, *The Imagined Island: History, Identity and Utopia in Hispaniola*, trans.
Jane Ramírez (Chapel Hill: University of North Carolina Press, 2005), 57–8.

[5] Jonathan Katz, 'What Happened When a Nation Erased Birthright Citizenship', *The Atlantic*, 12 November 2018, https://www.theatlantic.com/ideas/arch
ive/2018/11/dominican-republic-erased-birthright-citizenship/575527/

[6] Ibid.

[7] Stephen McLoughlin and Deborah Mayersen, 'Reconsidering Root Causes:
A New Framework for the Structural Prevention of Genocide and Mass Atroci-
ties', in Bert Ingelaere, Stephan Parmentier, Jacques Haers SJ, and Barbara
Segaert (eds.), *Genocide, Risk and Resilience: An Interdisciplinary Approach* (Houndmills:
Palgrave, 2013), 49–67.

genocide is far from inevitable. Even in circumstances in which many risk factors are present, such as in Iran in the early 1980s, risk stabilization and reduction is a likely outcome. When risk is more moderate, such as in Botswana and Zambia, productive pathways to risk amelioration can be found. Finally, the chapter concludes by reflecting on the transformative potential of negative case studies for genocide prevention.

The Root Cause Approach to Understanding the Causes of Genocide

A strong focus of the first generation of genocide scholars was to build an understanding of the causes of genocide. Very quickly, substantial progress was made in this area. Research by scholars such as Kuper, Fein, Melson, Staub, and others led to broad agreement around key preconditions.[8] These include a plural and divided society, in which there are one or more disadvantaged 'outgroups'; discrimination and persecution of outgroups; internal strife such as war, economic difficulties, or political crises in the at-risk nation; propaganda and incitement to violence against the target group; and a capacity to organize the genocide.[9] Scholars, whether utilizing qualitative or quantitative methods to understanding the causes of genocide, adopted quite similar research designs.[10] Case studies of major incidents of past genocide were selected for comparison. Through examining antecedents of genocides such as the Armenian genocide, the Holocaust,

---

[8] Leo Kuper, *Genocide: Its Political Use in the Twentieth Century* (New Haven: Yale University Press, 1982); Helen Fein, *Accounting for Genocide: Victims and Survivors of the Holocaust* (New York: Free Press, 1979); Ervin Staub, *The Roots of Evil: The Origins of Genocide and Other Group Violence* (New York: Cambridge University Press, 1989); Florence Mazian, *Why Genocide? The Armenian and Jewish Experiences in Perspective* (Ames: Iowa State University Press, 1990); Robert Melson, *Revolution and Genocide: On the Origins of the Armenian Genocide and the Holocaust* (Chicago: University of Chicago Press, 1992).

[9] For more details, see Deborah Mayersen, *On the Path to Genocide: Armenia and Rwanda Reexamined* (New York and Oxford: Berghahn Books, 2014).

[10] Scott Straus, 'Political Science and Genocide', in Donald Bloxham and A. Dirk Moses (eds.), *The Oxford Handbook of Genocide Studies* (Oxford: Oxford University Press, 2010), 163–81.

and the Cambodian genocide, cross-situational risk factors were identified. It is these that have framed our understanding of the causes of genocide, and led the 'root cause approach' to dominate. Yet while this paradigm has provided crucial insight into the causes of genocide, it provides an incomplete picture. By focusing exclusively on cases which have culminated in genocide, case study selection has been effectively limited to those cases in which risk factors dominated, and protective or mitigating factors were ineffective or inoperative.[11]

Current research with respect to the prevention of genocide has also developed from the root cause paradigm. The responsibility to protect, for example, heavily reflects this approach. The International Commission on Intervention and State Sovereignty (ICISS) report developing the concept identified the need to address root causes such as 'political needs and deficiencies', 'economic deprivation and the lack of economic opportunities', and 'strengthening legal protections and institutions'.[12] The 2009 report of then UN Secretary-General Ban Ki-moon, *Implementing the Responsibility to Protect*, emphasized the need to address 'underlying fissures in the social and political fabric particularly in states and regions where ethnic tensions run high and deep inequalities among groups persist'.[13] The report opined, 'Even relatively stable, developed and progressive societies need to ask themselves whether they are vulnerable . . . whether the seeds of intolerance, bigotry and exclusion could take root and grow into something horrific and self-destructive'.[14] The 2014 'Framework of Analysis for Atrocity Crimes: A Tool for Prevention', developed by the United Nations Office on Genocide Prevention and the Responsibility to Protect, adopts a similar approach. Of the ten factors relevant to risk of genocide, nine are squarely focused on risk. Only

---

[11] McLoughlin and Mayersen, 'Reconsidering Root Causes', 54–5; Hollie Nyseth Brehm, 'Re-examining Risk Factors of Genocide', *Journal of Genocide Research* 19:1 (2017), 61–87.

[12] International Commission on Intervention and State Sovereignty (ICISS), *The Responsibility to Protect* (Ottawa: International Development Research Centre, 2001), xi.

[13] United Nations General Assembly (UNGA), *Implementing the Responsibility to Protect*, 12 January 2009, A/63/677, 19.

[14] Ibid., 13.

one, still termed a 'risk factor', focuses on the 'absence of mitigating factors'.[15]

Relatively few scholars have moved beyond the root cause paradigm to explore the aetiology of genocide from a broader perspective. Leo Kuper, a foundational scholar in the field, examined the negative case studies of South Africa under Apartheid and Northern Ireland.[16] In each case he found powerful, case-specific restraints that counterbalanced risk factors and contributed to limiting the scope of the violence. Manus Midlarsky also examined the protective factors at play in the negative case studies of Finland and Bulgaria (but not the Balkan territories occupied by Bulgaria, from which deportations took place) during the Holocaust.[17] He found an 'absence of loss', including territorial loss, in each case contributed to a more empathetic response to the Jews.[18] In other case studies, the presence of an affine population proved protective. The protective role of Greece, over the ethnic Greek population in the Ottoman Empire during the First World War, provides an illustrative example. More recently, as the field of Genocide Studies has grown and complexified, new approaches are increasingly diversifying our understanding of the processes that lead to genocide and—importantly—how that trajectory can be interrupted. In recent years, for example, microhistories and the work of practitioners in the field of genocide prevention have led to an increased focus on the role of local factors. Local agency, with appropriate support, for example, has been recognized as making a crucial difference in stabilizing or reducing risk of genocide.[19] As a result, organizations such as Peace Direct have directed their efforts towards preventing genocide and mass atrocities into supporting local

[15] United Nations, Framework of Analysis for Atrocity Crimes: A Tool for Prevention (United Nations, 2014), https://www.un.org/en/genocideprevention/documents/about-us/Doc.3_Framework%20of%20Analysis%20for%20Atrocity%20Crimes_EN.pdf.

[16] Kuper, *Genocide*.

[17] Manus Midlarsky, *The Killing Trap: Genocide in the Twentieth Century* (New York: Cambridge University Press, 2005).

[18] Ibid., 325.

[19] Bridget Moix, 'Turning Atrocity Prevention Inside-out: Community-based Approaches to Preventing, Protecting, and Recovering from Mass Violence', *Genocide Studies and Prevention* 9:3 (2016), 59–69; Deborah Mayersen, 'Building

agency.[20] This has included activities such as training community mediators in the Democratic Republic of Congo to resolve conflicts locally, prior to any broader escalation. Collectively, this wider range of approaches has contributed to a more complete understanding of the factors that contribute to genocide.

To address the disproportionate focus on the root cause paradigm, in 2012 we proposed a new framework for the prevention of genocide and mass atrocities.[21] The risk and resilience framework gives equal credence to the role of risk factors and that of factors that mitigate against genocide. The model recognizes that genocide results not just from the presence and accumulation of risk factors, but equally from the absence or inoperability of factors that promote resilience. It rejects conceptions of risk as static, linear, and progressive. Rather, it identifies that a state's risk profile for genocide reflects the relative dominance and interaction of risk and resilience factors as they fluctuate over time. For example, a state may legally discriminate against a vulnerable minority, increasing risk, but this may be counterbalanced by an independent legal system, offering some protection. By thereby focusing on resilience alongside risk, this model inherently recognizes that genocide is far from inevitable, even in the presence of multiple risk factors.[22] The accumulation of risk and the failure of mitigating factors is only one pathway among many that might be taken. This explains why negative cases, such as that of ethnic Haitians in the Dominican Republic, are a common outcome. Moreover, it provides a new dataset of cases beyond the previous focus on paradigmatic examples of genocide. Through analysis of negative case studies, factors that promote resilience—and potentially might contribute to genocide prevention—can be identified. After examining the relative stability of risk in many at-risk nations, it is these negative case studies that this chapter will explore.

Resilience to Genocide: Ten Practical Measures' (Auschwitz Institute for Peace and Reconciliation, Policy Brief in Prevention, 2018), http://www.auschwitzinstitute. org/wp-content/uploads/2016/01/AIPR-Brief-Building-Resilience-to-Genocide.pdf.

[20] Moix, 'Turning Atrocity Prevention Inside-out'.

[21] McLoughlin and Mayersen, 'Reconsidering Root Causes'.

[22] Ibid.

Risk as a Relatively Stable Factor

The relative stability of nations demonstrating some risk factors for genocide is often overlooked. Perhaps somewhat naturally, the focus of scholars, policymakers, and practitioners is frequently on nations experiencing crises and rapid acceleration of risk. Yet societies with some risk factors are typically characterized by relative stability rather than risk escalation.[23] As Andrea Bartoli et al. have observed, 'Most states do not commit genocide most of the time. State interest normally does not coincide with genocidal intent, and the predisposition of governments is generally not genocidal.'[24] In Rwanda, for example, risk factors for genocide were present from the time of decolonization in the early 1960s.[25] Yet for most of the period between independence in 1962 and the genocide in 1994 the country was relatively stable. In the 1970s and 1980s the country experienced economic growth and improvements on key developmental indicators such as education, maternal and infant mortality rates, and access to clean drinking water.[26] Certainly, there were episodes of violence, such as in 1963–64 and 1973, and these are common in countries at risk of mass violence. Fluctuations in risk levels, with processes of risk escalation followed by some retreat, can serve as warning signs and reminders that the risk is very real. Overall, however, Rwanda was relatively stable for decades, despite the ongoing presence of risk factors.[27] This highlights that—even in countries where hindsight provides us with certainty about the very real risk of genocide—stability can be the dominant characteristic. Many countries that appear on risk lists, moreover, may never go on to experience genocide, exhibiting stability for indefinite periods.

For the last decade or so, countries exhibiting some risk factors for genocide have been tracked on numerous risk lists, and the data from

---

[23] Ibid., 60.

[24] Andrea Bartoli, Tetsushi Ogata, and Gregory Stanton, 'Emerging Paradigms in Genocide Prevention', *Politorbis* 47:2 (2009), 15–24, 21.

[25] Mayersen, *On the Path to Genocide.*

[26] Ibid., 152.

[27] Deborah Mayersen and Stephen McLoughlin, 'Risk and Resilience to Mass Atrocities in Africa: A Comparison of Rwanda and Botswana', *Journal of Genocide Research* 13:3 (2011), 247–69.

these also demonstrate the relative stability of risk. Risk lists are published annually (or regularly) by a number of organizations, including Genocide Watch, Minority Rights Group International, the Early Warning Project (by the United States Holocaust Memorial Museum), the Genocide Prevention Advisory Network, and the Atrocity Forecasting Project. There is some difference in the focus of each on genocide or a wider array of mass atrocities, but overall there is substantial consensus in their risk assessments. With some now having more than a decade of data, the high degree of stability within risk rankings is becoming apparent. The 'Peoples Under Threat' risk list, published by Minority Rights International, provides an illustrative example.[28] There is a very high level of stability between the top five countries identified as at risk in 2008–11, and those identified in 2019. Four of the top five countries in 2009—Somalia, Sudan, Afghanistan, and Iraq—remained in the top five in 2019.[29] The only country to exit in this period was Myanmar, which reflects risk reduction as a consequence of the massive ethnic cleansing that took place in 2017—that is, the occurrence of mass atrocities. Syria, ranked at highest risk in 2020, is the only country to have exhibited a rapid risk escalation, leaping from a ranking of 30 in 2011 to 3 in 2014, as a result of the regime's violent response to the Arab Spring.[30] Across the top 10, there is a similar level of stability, with most countries that have moved in or out of the top 10 in the past decade doing so by only a couple of places in the rankings.[31] Only Côte D'Ivoire, ranked tenth in 2011 (although lower in 2008–10) has experienced a very substantial risk reduction, dropping to fiftieth in 2019.[32] This reflects intensive international involvement in preventing mass violence there, including the deployment of the UN peacekeeping mission UNOCI.

---

[28] Minority Rights Group International, Peoples Under Threat, 2019, https://peoplesunderthreat.org/.

[29] Ibid.; McLoughlin and Mayersen, 'Reconsidering Root Causes'. In 2019, South Sudan ranked third. This has been compared with Sudan's 2009 ranking, as South Sudan did not yet exist in 2009.

[30] Minority Rights Group International, Peoples Under Threat.

[31] Ibid.

[32] Ibid.

Stability in risk rankings is also a characteristic of the majority—but not all—nations with mid-level rankings of risk. In the four years between 2008 and 2011, for example, more than half the states appearing on Genocide Watch's risk list of countries at risk of genocide, politicide, or mass atrocities, experienced no movement to a higher or lower stage of risk within the (then) eight-stage model.[33] The overwhelming majority experienced either no change or a movement of only one stage. The People's Under Threat list provides an informative and nuanced picture with respect to the stability of risk.[34] In 2019, for example, the average movement of rankings in countries ranked 11–20 in risk was 2.6. Half of that figure, however, can be accounted for by one country—Cameroon—which experienced a rapid rise of fourteen places in the rankings since 2018. Removing that outlier gives an average movement of 1.3. In 2018, there was a similar average of 1.0. In 2017 the average was 2.4, but again half of that figure can be accounted for by one country, Eritrea. While of course we must be aware that such ranking systems are imperfect devices, overall this suggests that in the overwhelming majority of countries risk levels are relatively stable, while a small number of countries experience relatively rapid risk escalation. Thus the quantitative data also confirm the relative stability of risk.

It is also important to recognize that many countries that exhibit some risk factors for genocide will experience a reduction, rather than an accumulation, of risk over time. Indonesia, for example, has appeared on multiple risk lists. In the past the Indonesian government has perpetrated genocide, including the 1965–66 Indonesian killings and the violence in East Timor (1975–99). Currently, ethnic, indigenous, and religious minorities are recognized as at risk, including the Acehnese, Papuans, and Dayaks.[35] In the period between 2011 and 2019, however, Indonesia's ranking has dropped significantly in the Peoples Under Threat risk list, from 34 to 69.[36] Similar risk reductions

---

[33] McLoughlin and Mayersen, 'Reconsidering Root Causes', 62; Genocide Watch, http://www.genocidewatch.org/ (older material on this website) and http://www.genocidewatch.com/.
[34] Minority Rights Group International, Peoples Under Threat.
[35] Ibid.
[36] Ibid.

can be charted in countries that have not previously experienced genocide, such as Nepal. In 2011, Nepal was ranked twentieth in risk, but following steady reductions it was ranked sixty-second in 2019.[37] Countries that experience such reductions of risk do not typically attract attention for doing so, however. To a large extent it is both to be expected and appropriate that countries experiencing crises and/or rapid risk escalation will dominate rhetoric in the field of genocide prevention. Nonetheless, this can lead to skewed perceptions, whereby the far more numerous cases of relative stability, and cases of risk reduction, are under-recognized.

Methodological Challenges with Negative Case Study Selection

But how do we select cases where risk either remains stable, or de-escalates over time? In methodological terms, understanding why risk does not escalate into genocide requires the selection of negative cases—cases where the dependent variable (in this instance, genocide) does not occur, despite the presence of one or more independent variables (causal factors, or risk factors). In other words, the selection of a negative case is based on proving a causal relationship between risk factors and an outcome that did not unfold. To do this meaningfully, negative cases need to be selected by establishing that genocide was a likely, or *possible* outcome.

In the social sciences, there is very little scholarship to draw on when it comes to methodological considerations around negative cases.[38] The most useful guide for establishing a causal connection between causal factors and an outcome that did not occur is Mahoney and Goertz's 'The Possibility Principle'. Mahoney and Goertz argue that negative case selection can be done on the basis of 'possibility' rather than likelihood. It is not necessary to prove that an outcome is

---

[37] Ibid.
[38] Two exceptions include Rebecca Jean Emigh, 'The Power of Negative Thinking: The Use of Negative Case Methodology in the Development of Sociological Theory', *Theory and Society* 26 (1997), 649–84; and James Mahoney and Gary Goertz, 'The Possibility Principle: Choosing Negative Cases in Comparative Research', *American Political Science Review* 98:4 (2004), 653–69.

likely or imminent—rather, it is sufficient to demonstrate that its occurrence is possible. In order to determine whether an outcome is possible, they developed the 'possibility principle', whereby possibility is determined by two factors. The first factor is that the case must contain at least one independent variable that is associated with the outcome in question. The second is that a case should be ruled out 'if it possesses a value on a variable that is known from previous research to make the outcome of interest impossible'.[39] What does this mean for negative cases in relation to genocide? They use genocide scholar Barbara Harff's research to demonstrate this. First, Harff identifies a number of preconditions associated with genocide and politicide,[40] which pass the first test (the existence of one or more independent variables). Second, they refer to Harff's claim about upheaval as a fulfilment of the second test. Harff found that the key pivotal factor that drives countries towards genocide are those with certain preconditions, which have also experienced upheaval: 'an abrupt change in the political community caused by the formation of a state or regime through violent conflict, redrawing of state boundaries, or war'.[41] In the absence of upheaval, then, it is not clear that genocide is 'possible'. Thus, to select negative cases of genocide according to the 'possibility principle', a case would need to contain at least one risk factor, and have experienced upheaval.

However, there are limitations to this approach to negative case selection. While this methodological justification captures cases on the path to dangerous risk escalation, it overlooks numerous cases of moderate risk that have not yet endured upheaval. Indeed, it is often the case that the more moderate the risk is over a long period of time, the more insights there are for prevention. When tensions reach the point of violence, the type of preventive strategies that are needed are far more controversial and invasive, and more often than

[39] Mahoney and Geortz, 'The Possibility Principle', 658.

[40] Barbara Harff, 'No Lessons Learned from the Holocaust? Assessing the Risks of Genocide and Political Mass Murder Since 1955', *American Political Science Review* 97:1 (2003), 57–73, 61–2.

[41] Ibid., 62.

not require international involvement.[42] However, often the required
political will from international actors to diffuse such tensions does not
exist, as the experience of Rwanda in 1994, and the more recent cases
of Myanmar and Syria, demonstrate. When it comes to understanding
prevention, we can learn much from states that have managed moderate levels of risk over long periods of time. There are insights to be
gained from cases that qualify under Mahoney and Goertz's 'possibility principle' and there are insights to be gained from states that
have managed long-term risk and avoided upheaval. In terms of
prevention, it is far better if states are able to avoid a scenario where
crisis or upheaval unfolds, and dangerous risk escalation becomes
much harder to mitigate.

Thus, in terms of studying why genocides do not happen, a paradox
exists. The greatest insights for prevention come from countries that
have, with some success, mitigated long-term risk and avoided
upheaval. The problem for scholars is that the more distant a country
appears from the perpetration of genocide, the more difficult it is to
establish a causal connection with this outcome, deeming it harder to
justify such cases as objects of investigation. Yet in better understanding why it is that genocides do not occur, the preventive value of such
scholarship lies in insights not only from cases of heightened risk, but
also from cases of moderate and relatively stable risk.

Negative cases provide important insights for prevention. They
bring into focus the role that not only external actors, but also local
and national actors, play in mitigating risk associated with genocide.
When it comes to negative cases of high risk, the key preventive actors
are often a combination of domestic and international. With moderate risk, the key preventive stakeholders are largely internal, and the
ways that various local-level and national-level leaders and other
players have managed risk has the potential to be instructive for others
facing similar challenges. Local and national actors know best how to
tailor insights to their own specific contexts, and where international
political will is forthcoming, complementing domestically-based ini-
tiatives works far better than one-size-fits-all approaches that overlook

---

[42] Jennifer M. Welsh, 'Turning Words into Deeds? The Implementation of the
"Responsibility to Protect"', *Global Responsibility to Protect* 2:1–2 (2010), 149–54, 153.

the unique calculus of risk and risk mitigation across communities and countries. It makes sense then, to investigate negative cases across the risk spectrum, to better understand that ways that various actors have navigated societies through periods of stress. The remainder of this chapter provides an overview of negative cases that represent both high and moderate levels of risk.

Negative Case Studies

The Bahá'í minority in Iran

Genocide is far from an inevitable outcome, even in circumstances that suggest there is a high risk of genocide onset. The case study of the Bahá'í minority in Iran provides an illustrative example. The Bahá'í faith emerged in Persia (now Iran) in the 1840s, as an offshoot of Shi'i Islam. Its central tenets include the oneness of humanity, universal peace, the eradication of all forms of prejudice, equality between men and women, the harmony between science and religion, and the importance of universal compulsory education.[43] Around the world there are approximately five million Bahá'í, of whom about 350,000 are located in Iran (it is difficult to give a precise estimate of Bahá'í in Iran, as official censuses there do not identify ethnic or religious minorities).[44] Almost since its inception, followers of the Bahá'í faith have been targeted for persecution in Iran. They experienced riots, massacres, seizure of property, and so on, and have been repeated targets of inflammatory anti-Bahá'í propaganda. During the period of unrest leading up to the 1979 Iranian revolution, the Bahá'í minority experienced increased persecution. In late 1978, for example, an incident in Sarvestan, in south-western Iran, led to violent attacks

---

[43] Baha'i Faith, 'Principles of the Baha'i Faith', http://www.bahai.com/Bahaullah/principles.htm.

[44] Peter Smith, 'A Note on Babi and Baha'i numbers in Iran', *Iranian Studies* 17:2–3 (1984), 295–301; Baha'i Topics, 'A Global Community', http://info.bahai.org/article-1-6-0-1.html; Iran Human Rights Documentation Center (IHRDC), *A Faith Denied: The Persecution of the Baha'is of Iran*, 2006, 4; Kerim Yildiz, *Kurds in Iran: The Past, Present and Future* (London: Pluto Press, 2007), 55.

against Bahá'í, and looting and burning of hundreds of houses.[45] Ayatollah Khomeini, the leader of the revolution, expressed his negative perception of Bahá'ís in an interview he gave just prior to taking power in 1979. 'They are a political faction; they are harmful; they will not be accepted', he stated.[46]

Following the revolution, the new republic's constitution did not recognize the Bahá'í. Bahá'í school teachers were dismissed from their positions, and the holiest Bahá'í shrine in Iran was destroyed.[47] The government began to target the Bahá'í leadership. Executions, political imprisonment, and torture of Bahá'í leaders became widespread.[48] One of the most tragic cases was that of ten Bahá'í women hanged in June 1983, for teaching religious classes to Bahá'í children.[49] During this period, the Bahá'í community also experienced a range of other persecutions. Bahá'í property was confiscated, looted, and sometimes destroyed.[50] Bahá'í community centres were destroyed and cemeteries desecrated.[51] Bahá'í were banned from the civil service, and by 1987, more than 11,000 had lost their government positions.[52] Bahá'í students were prohibited from enrolling in schools, and many students that were already enrolled were expelled.[53] In 1981 Bahá'í students were also banned from the university system. There were also expressions of genocidal rhetoric amongst high-level government officials. Iran's Attorney General, Siyyid Moussavi-Tabrizi, for example, stated 'The Qur'an recognised

---

[45] IHRDC, *A Faith Denied*, 17–19.

[46] Quoted in Denis MacEoin, 'The Baha'is of Iran: The Roots of Controversy', *Bulletin (British Society for Middle Eastern Studies)* 14:1 (1987), 75.

[47] Reza Afshari, 'The Discourse and Practice of Human Rights Violations of Iranian Baha'is in the Islamic Republic of Iran', in Dominic Brookshaw and Seena Fazel (eds.), *The Baha'is of Iran* (London: Routledge, 2008), 235; Roger Cooper, *The Baha'is of Iran: A Minority Rights Group Report* (London: Minority Rights Group, 1985), 11.

[48] Cooper, *The Baha'is of Iran*, 13; Bahá'í International Community (BIC), *The Baha'i Question: Cultural Cleansing in Iran* (New York: Baha'i International Community, 2008), 60–3.

[49] BIC, *The Baha'i Question*, 46–7.

[50] MacEoin, 'The Baha'is of Iran', 75.

[51] IHRDC, *A Faith Denied*, 38.

[52] Ibid., 43–5.

[53] Ibid., 46.

only the People of the Book as religious communities. Others are pagans. Pagans must be eliminated.'[54]

As the plight of the Bahá'í in Iran came to light, the international community began to express alarm. Human rights groups, which had been observing repression in Iran well before the revolution, rapidly began documenting violations of human rights experienced by the Bahá'í and other minority groups. In 1982, the International Commission of Jurists reported ' "[T]he treatment of Bahá'ís is motivated by religious intolerance and a desire to eliminate the Bahá'í Faith from the land of its birth." This comes close to an allegation of genocide.'[55] A number of factors, however, contributed to the risk of genocide in Iran stabilizing rather than escalating into genocide onset. Most importantly, concerted efforts from the global Bahá'í community led to strong international awareness and condemnation of the Iranian government's actions.[56] The situation received sustained attention at the UN, with resolutions being passed almost every year since 1980.[57] Significantly, Iran's major trading partners also expressed their displeasure.[58] As Iran's economy declined in 1980s, maintaining trade relationships became increasingly important. These factors contributed to repression of the Bahá'í minority easing in the latter part of the 1980s. By 1990, genocide scholar Leo Kuper commented that 'I think the persecution of the Bahá'ís is correctly described as a threatened genocide, averted only by the skilled representations of the Bahá'í international community and resolute action in the United Nations and the European Parliamentary Assembly'.[59] Nonetheless, the Bahá'í minority have continued to experience social, economic, and cultural restrictions. The risk stabilized for a time, and

[54] Quoted in BIC, *The Baha'i Question*, 44.

[55] Quoted in Paul Allen, 'The Baha'is of Iran: A Proposal for Enforcement of International Human Rights Standards', *Cornell International Law Journal* 20 (1987), 338.

[56] Katharine Bigelow, 'A Campaign to Deter Genocide: The Baha'i Experience', in Helen Fein (ed.), *Genocide Watch* (New Haven: Yale University Press, 1992), 192.

[57] BIC, *The Baha'i Question*, appendix II.

[58] Moojan Momen, 'The Babi and Baha'i Community of Iran: A Case of "Suspended Genocide"?' *Journal of Genocide Research* 7:2 (2005), 238.

[59] Quoted in Momen, 'The Babi and Baha'i Community of Iran', 235.

continues to fluctuate. While the situation hasn't escalated into genocide, there continues to be a very real risk of it doing so. In 2020, Iran
was currently ranked fourteenth on the Peoples Under Threat risk list,
having oscillated between tenth and twentieth place over the last
several years.[60] Such ongoing risk is quite typical of negative case
studies of genocide.

Ethnic Minorities in Botswana

In cases of moderate risk, local and national actors often devise and
enact strategies that have a prohibitive effect, as the cases of Botswana
and Zambia demonstrate. While Botswana is not a country associated
with genocide, since independence in 1966, it has displayed evidence
of a number of long-term risk factors associated with such a crime,
including entrenched ethnic-based discrimination, political exclusion,
and horizontal inequalities. Botswana comprises thirty-seven different
minority groups, including the demographically dominant Tswana, as
well as many smaller groups including the Bakgaligadi, the Wayeyi,
and the Khoisan.[61] In the country's postcolonial history (and indeed
prior to independence), these smaller ethnic groups have been subject
to discrimination and political exclusion. There has been an exclusion
of minority languages, a situation that is particularly felt in the
education sector, especially in remote areas where minority groups
predominate. In such areas levels of literacy and school completion
are much lower.[62] In terms of political exclusion, Botswana's upper
house, the House of Chiefs, initially only recognized the eight Tswana
chieftaincies, at the expense of other tribal groups. While the House of
Chiefs has been expanded, the chamber continues to differentiate
between the Tswana chiefs—who hold permanent positions—and

[60] Minority Rights Group International, Peoples Under Threat.
[61] RETENG, *Alternative Report Submitted to the UN Committee on the Elimination of all forms of Racial Discrimination (CERD)* (Gaborone: RETENG: The Multicultural Coalition of Botswana, 2006); Clark J. Leith, *Why Botswana Prospered* (Montreal and Kingston: McGill-Queens University Press, 2005), 29; Kenneth Good, *Diamonds, Dispossession and Democracy in Botswana* (Woodbridge: James Curry and Jacana Media, 2008), 85.
[62] Good, *Diamonds, Dispossession and Democracy*, 94.

other members, who have non-permanent seats.[63] Horizontal inequality within the country reveals that the gap between rich and poor (one of the highest in the world) has an ethnic dimension, with these groups—particularly the Khoisan—experiencing greater poverty than the rest of the population. This entrenched discrimination found expression in more acute expressions of human rights violations, one example being the government-instigated forceful eviction of some Khoisan groups from their ancestral territory of the Central Kalahari Game Reserve between 1997 and 2002. In doing so, the government in Botswana—contrary to their own constitution—denied this group its basic citizenship rights.[64]

These risk factors do not in and of themselves directly lead to genocide. In the absence of upheaval, such risk can exist for years, decades, or even longer without leading to mass violence. However, genocide rarely, if ever occurs in the absence of such long-term risk. There is much to learn from the way that states actually manage such risk over time, as the ability to do so may well provide insights into why and how such societies not only manage structural risk in relation to genocide, but also how upheaval is avoided. In avoiding upheaval, the chances of genocide (or other forms of mass violence) decrease considerably. Thus, the management of long-term risk is enormously instructive in terms of the roles that local and national actors play in preventing genocide. The combination of social and political discrimination, and inequality of economic opportunity have been recognized by Genocide Watch as containing moderate risk.[65]

The fact that this risk has been managed (albeit not ameliorated) over more than five decades is the result of three things—the country's relatively robust democracy, a strong rule of law (especially its independent judiciary), and the equitable provision of services. While education was not provided in the mother tongue of all groups, education was indeed accessible to all, and has given even the most

---

[63] RETENG, *Alternative Report*, 7, 28.

[64] See e.g. Justice Unity Dow, *Judgement* (Lobatse, Botswana, 2006); Justice M. P. Phumaphi, *Judgement* (Lobatse, Botswana, 2006).

[65] Genocide Watch, 'Genocides, Politicides and other Mass Murder since 1945, with Stages in 2008' (2009), http://www.genocidewatch.org/images/GenocidesandPoliticidessince1945withstagesin2008.pdf.

marginalized groups in the country the capacity to confront discrimination and to campaign for better representation.[66] Indeed it was the very provision of state education that prompted many to raise questions about national identity, and the predominant role of Setswana as the language of instruction. Members of various minority groups have formed activist groups that have advocated for their rights—RETENG, Kamanakao, and First Peoples of the Kalahari being three examples.

Botswana's robust democratic system and strong rule of law have been at the heart of the country's more than five decades of post-independence stability. The country's independent judiciary has been particularly crucial in allowing such organizations a voice to formally challenge government policies and practices. This is largely a product of the vision of inaugural president, Seretse Khama, who established a two-tiered legal system based on a combination of traditional law and statutory law.[67] Indeed, Botswana's judiciary has on numerous occasions overturned policies and laws that had entrenched and formalized ethnic-based discrimination and marginalization. The High Court has provided a means for the country's most marginalized group—the Khoisan—to challenge the most powerful—the government—in two landmark cases.

These two cases concerned the forceful evictions of Khoisan groups from their ancestral lands within the Central Kalahari Game Reserve (CKGR). The Khoisan-formed First Peoples of the Kalahari took the government to court over the evictions, and in 2006, the High Court ruled that a 2002 government order authorizing this eviction was illegal.[68] In a measure of the Court's independence the government recognized the decision and declared that they would honour it. Yet the government tried other tactics to prevent the groups from returning. Authorities shut down the area's only borehole—depriving the group of the only access to a constant water supply in the area—and

---

[66] Jacqueline Solway, 'Navigating the "Neutral" State: "Minority" Rights in Botswana', *Journal of Southern African Studies* 28:4 (2002), 711–29, 717.

[67] McLoughlin, *The Structural Prevention of Mass Atrocities*, 92.

[68] BBC News, 'Botswana Bushmen Win Land Ruling' (2006), http://news.bbc.co.uk/1/hi/world/africa/6174709.stm; Dow, *Judgement*; Phumaphi, *Judgement*.

prohibited them from drilling new boreholes.[69] This prompted the First Peoples of the Kalahari to open another court case against the government. In January 2011 the Court of Appeal ruled that those who had been given the right to dwell in the CKGR also were legally justified in re-opening the closed borehole, as well as drilling others as they saw fit.[70]

The importance of these court cases is not that they changed government attitudes to marginalized groups like the Khoisan. Indeed the Khoisan remain among the poorest groups in the country, and continue to suffer from social discrimination.[71] Rather, the importance is twofold—first, the judiciary in Botswana provided a safety net in the midst of discrimination. Second, it gave those who were the subject of discrimination and human rights violations a trust in due process as a means of redressing these issues. Thus, there existed in Botswana's democratic system opportunities to fight for change and win back rights, which diminishes the need to resort to violent means to struggle for rights. Botswana's democratic system and strong rule of law has not eliminated discrimination, but has put a limit on it, and in doing so has had an inhibitory effect on the long-term risk of genocide. Far from being the 'African Success Story' that it is sometimes labelled,[72] Botswana is a country that has endured enormous challenges since independence. Social divisions and discrimination persist, but risk has not escalated. The country's equitable provision of services, as well as its good governance, has had the effect of mitigating risk associated with genocide.

---

[69] Survival International, 'The Bushmen', (2019), https://www.survivalinternational.org/tribes/bushmen8.

[70] John Simpson, 'The Kalahari Bushmen are Home Again', *The Guardian*, 13 December 2011, https://www.theguardian.com/commentisfree/2011/dec/13/kalahari-bushmen-home-again-botswana-diamonds.

[71] The World Bank, 'Overview', *The World Bank in Botswana* (2019), https://www.worldbank.org/en/country/botswana/overview; Kenneth Good, 'At the Ends of the Ladder: Radical Inequalities in Botswana', *The Journal of Modern African Studies* 31:2 (1993), 203–30.

[72] See e.g. Daron Acemoglu, Simon Johnson, and James A. Robinson, 'An African Success Story: Botswana', Massachusetts Institute of Technology Department of Economics, Working Paper Series 01–37 (2001), https://papers.ssrn.com/sol3/papers.cfm?abstract_id=290791.

Ethno-linguistic Minorities in Zambia

Like Botswana, neighbouring Zambia also provides insights into the avoidance of genocide and other mass atrocities. Despite ethno-linguistic tensions, a limited democracy, and economic inequality, Zambia has managed such risks without the advent of dangerous escalation or upheaval. These risks have been inhibited by two key factors—the inclusive ideas of the country's first president, Kenneth Kaunda, and civil society-based activism.[73] This risk was particularly acute in the first two decades of independence, when five of its neighbours were mired in civil wars, and its economic options were contingent on two white minority-ruled countries, Zimbabwe and South Africa, who were both hostile to Zambia for its support of anti-government resistance groups. These complex and charged international dynamics compounded Zambia's domestic challenges, and raised the question of how it was that Zambia did not go down the path of many of its neighbours.

In Zambia's formative years of independence, it was faced with calls for secession from the Western Province, and growing ethno-linguistic divisions that looked likely to become institutionally entrenched. The Western Province, formerly known as the Kingdom of Barotseland, had been administered as a separate protectorate during British colonial rule, which prompted leaders there to call for greater autonomy within independent Zambia. This led to inaugural president, Kenneth Kaunda, signing the Barotseland agreement with the province, which allowed them to have a greater say in terms of local governance.[74] Throughout the 1960s many of its terms were gradually rescinded, until the entire agreement was abandoned in 1969,

---

[73] Stephen McLoughlin, 'Reconceptualising Mass Atrocity Prevention: Understanding Risk and Resilience in Zambia', *International Journal of Politics, Culture and Society* 27:4 (2014), 427–41.

[74] Cherry Gertzel, 'Western Province: Tradition, Economic Deprivation and Political Alienation', in Cherry Gertzel, Carolyne Bayliss, and Morris Szeftel (eds.), *The Dynamics of One-Party State in Zambia* (Manchester: Manchester University Press, 1984), 206; Stefan Lindemann, *Inclusive Elite Bargains and Civil War Avoidance: The Case of Zambia* (London: Crisis States Research Centre, 2010), 12.

prompting some leaders in the province to call for secession.[75] Of the roughly seventy-three different tribal groups, four major language groups emerged in different parts of the country—Bemba, Nyanga, Tonga, and Lozi. Although there were no inherent historical tensions between these groups,[76] they became the basis of factional division within the party of government, the United National Independence Party (UNIP), as well as other parties. This factional division played out in three key ways. The first was that members of particular ethno-linguistic groups tended to consolidate their own positions by recruiting other members of the same group within government departments, risking the prospect of such divisions becoming institutionally entrenched. Second, such spoils of governance prompted tensions between political elites. Third, these tensions precipitated a number of new breakaway parties, all formed on the basis of ethnolinguistic identity, a pattern which further threatened to aggravate tensions along identity lines.[77] This had a destabilizing effect on political competition, particularly in the first decade of independence. By the early 1970s, Zambia looked to be on a path of growing and irreversible identity-based division.

Political leadership and the fostering of an inclusive national identity were instrumental in addressing these growing tensions, and in the process, mitigating the risk of mass atrocities. Kenneth Kaunda—himself not a member any of the four ethno-linguistic blocks—worked at fostering an inclusive national identity from the outset. Aware of the need for both elites and the general population to eclipse tribal and ethnic divisions, he declared, 'with any luck, this generation will think of itself not in tribal terms as Bemba, Lozi or Tonga, but as Zambians. This is the only guarantee of future stability.'[78]

Kaunda weakened the position of those calling for secession not through violence, but through astute political positioning. Recognizing that these calls were coming not from everyone, but principally

---

[75] Lindemann, *Inclusive Elite Bargains*, 12, 15.

[76] These four languages were elevated above scores of tribal languages and dialects due to missionary activity and colonial practices.

[77] Marcia M. Burdette, *Zambia: Between Two Worlds* (Boulder: Westview Press, 1988), 72–3.

[78] Kenneth Kaunda, *A Humanist in Africa* (London: Longmans, 1967), 91.

from traditional rulers, Kaunda rewarded young and educated Lozi leaders by giving them key positions within both the public centre and UNIP, empowering them, and enriching the Western Province.[79] This undermined the calls for secession, and ensured that there remained, within the province, a lot of support for a united Zambia. This is in stark contrast to responses to calls for secession in the immediate region. At the same time in neighbouring Congo, calls for secession in Katanga province triggered a protracted civil war, resulting in widespread civilian casualties.[80]

Kaunda used similar tactics to deal with rising inter-factional tensions within UNIP in the 1960s.[81] To offset the tendency of UNIP members of parliament securing the spoils of governance for their ethno-linguistic block, Kaunda initiated frequent ministerial reshuffles, to ensure that no one faction maintained dominance over government departments. Likewise, within the public sector, he ensured that there were frequent changes of personnel, particularly at the managerial level.[82] This helped manage division, and offset competing claims for a time, though tensions continued to rise towards the end of the 1960s, prompting some to break away from UNIP to form new parties, many drawing support from specific ethnic groups.[83] Kaunda's response was to prohibit opposition parties outright, heralding a period of one-party rule from the early 1970s to 1991.[84] This period of authoritarian rule created other problems, including growing popular unrest amidst increasing poverty.[85] Kaunda's response to the growing ethno-linguistic tensions in the 1960s was effective in managing those tensions, but his prohibition of opposition parties

---

[79] Lindemann, *Inclusive Elite Bargains*, 36.

[80] Rene Lemarchand, 'The Limits of Self-Determination: The Case of the Katanga', *American Political Science Review* 56:2 (1962), 404–16.

[81] See Robert Molteno, 'Cleavage and Conflict in Zambian Politics: A Study of Sectionalism', in William Tordoff (ed.), *Politics in Zambia* (Manchester: Manchester University Press, 1974).

[82] Burdette, *Zambia*, 69; Lindemann, *Inclusive Elite Bargains*, 13.

[83] Burdette, *Zambia*, 71–2.

[84] Bizeck Jube Phiri, *A Political History of Zambia: From the Colonial Period to the 3rd Republic* (Trenton: Africa World Press, 2006), 163–9.

[85] Michael Bratton, 'Zambia Starts Over', *Journal of Democracy*, 3:2 (1992), 81–94, 85–6.

eventually posed other risks in relation to political instability. However, the absence of an exclusionary ideology during Kaunda's tenure precipitated a popular movement against his authoritarianism, which was itself inclusive and absent of inter-ethnic tension. This is in stark contrast to transitions in Rwanda and Burundi, where the advent of multi-party politics in the 1990s aggravated ethnic tensions.[86]

This points to the fact that risk mitigation in Zambia has not been simple. Kaunda's tactics in response to factional division were effective in containing factional divisions, but precipitated a prolonged period of authoritarian rule, which led to growing unrest and rioting in the late 1980s. When it comes to long-term risk mitigation, there is no endpoint. Circumstances change and new challenges arise, prompting new responses. The processes of risk and its mitigation in Zambia—as in Botswana and Iran—are ongoing and worthy of examination alongside the monitoring of countries that raise the alarms due to dangerous risk escalation, or the onset of genocide or other mass atrocities.

Conclusion

Genocide is not an inescapable outcome in at-risk countries. Two key factors have contributed to widespread misperceptions that risk is highly likely to culminate in genocide. The first is the 'root cause paradigm' that dominated early scholarship into understanding the causes of genocide. By identifying causation through working backwards from major incidents of genocide, this approach led to a strong focus on risk factors, and a neglect of factors that promote resilience. The resulting models of the preconditions of genocide also implied a linear, progressive development of risk. In recent years, scholars have increasingly challenged this paradigm. We have contributed to this, through proposing a 'Risk and Resilience' model, that gives equal credence to escalatory and de-escalatory factors.[87] A nation's risk

[86] McLoughlin, *The Structural Prevention of Mass Atrocities*, 160–3; Peter Uvin, 'Ethnicity and Power in Burundi and Rwanda: Different Paths to Mass Violence', *Comparative Politics* 31:3 (1999), 253–71.

[87] McLoughlin and Mayersen, 'Reconsidering Root Causes'; Mayersen and McLoughlin, 'Risk and Resilience'.

profile at any given point in time is best understood as a combination of these factors, each contributing to the overall picture. Escalation to genocide is just one of many possible outcomes, and indeed not the most likely. Even in circumstances of high risk, such as the experiences of the Bahá'í minority in Iran, there may only be a moderate probability of risk escalation. When the risk profile is lower, such as in Botswana and Zambia, risk stabilization or amelioration is even more likely. The second key factor that has contributed to a strong focus on risk escalation is that it is countries in crisis, that are experiencing rapid growth in risk, that command the most attention. This is rightly so—such countries may require significant assistance to stall that process. Yet it has also contributed to misperceptions about the relative likelihood of such processes more broadly. Countries experiencing relative stability of risk, or declining risk, rarely receive attention for doing so. Nonetheless, these experiences are far more typical.

In recent years, a new subfield focused on genocide prevention has emerged from the growing field of Genocide Studies. For the first time, practitioners, advocates, and policymakers are actively working to prevent genocides in at-risk nations. This includes not only in countries in crisis, on the cusp of extreme violence, but also in countries with much lower risk profiles. This work makes deepening our understanding of risk and resilience more important, and more urgent, than ever. Scholarly analysis of negative case studies facilitates identification of processes and factors that have successfully stabilized or reduced the risk of genocide in the past. This can potentially provide evidence-based strategies for use by practitioners. Understanding resilience to genocide, therefore, is arguably the most important challenge in Genocide Studies today.

Select Bibliography

Bellamy, Alex J., 'Reducing Risk, Strengthening Resilience: Towards the Structural Prevention of Atrocity Crimes', *Stanley Foundation Policy Analysis Brief*, April 2016, https://stanleycenter.org/publications/pab/Risk-Resilience-BellamyPAB416.pdf.

Harff, Barbara, 'No Lessons Learned from the Holocaust? Assessing the Risks of Genocide and Political Mass Murder since 1955', *American Political Science Review* 97:1 (2003), 57–73.

Ingelaere, Bert, Stephan Parmentier, Jacques Haers SJ, and Barbara Segaert (eds.), *Genocide, Risk and Resilience: An Interdisciplinary Approach* (Houndmills: Palgrave, 2013).

Mahoney, James and Gary Goertz, 'The Possibility Principle: Choosing Negative Cases in Comparative Research', *American Political Science Review* 98: 4 (2004), 653–69.

Mayersen, Deborah, *On the Path to Genocide: Armenia and Rwanda Reexamined* (New York and Oxford: Berghahn Books, 2014).

Mayersen, Deborah and Stephen McLoughlin, 'Risk and Resilience to Mass Atrocities in Africa: A Comparison of Rwanda and Botswana', *Journal of Genocide Research* 13:3 (2011), 247–69.

McLoughlin, Stephen, *The Structural Prevention of Mass Atrocities: Understanding Risk and Resilience* (London: Routledge, 2014).

Midlarsky, Manus, *The Killing Trap: Genocide in the Twentieth Century* (New York: Cambridge University Press, 2005).

Moix, Bridget, 'Turning Atrocity Prevention Inside-out: Community-based Approaches to Preventing, Protecting, and Recovering from Mass Violence', *Genocide Studies and Prevention* 9:3 (2016), 59–69.

4

Gender and Genocide

Elisa von Joeden-Forgey

Introduction

The scholarship on gender and genocide has matured significantly since the last edition of this volume. Rather than being peripheral to the field as a whole, gender and genocide has become an established subfield. Two new edited volumes on women and genocide, a feminist history of the Holocaust, and new edited volumes on gender and genocide, on rape as a weapon of war and genocide, and on gender and the Holocaust have appeared since 2010.[1] Case studies have multiplied and have enriched our understanding of how gender works comparatively in the development, commission, and adjudication of the crime. The 'gender lens' is likewise more broadly accepted as an important contribution to understanding and responding to genocidal processes. Nevertheless, the insights offered by

[1] Elissa Bemporad and Joyce W. Warren, *Women and Genocide: Survivors, Victims, Perpetrators* (Bloomington: Indiana University Press, 2018); Zoë Waxman, *Women in the Holocaust: A Feminist History* (New York: Oxford University Press, 2017); JoAnn DiGeorgio-Lutz and Donna Gosbee (eds.), *Women and Genocide: Gendered Experiences of Violence, Survival, and Resistance* (Toronto: Women's Press, 2016); Carol Rittner and John K. Roth (eds.), *Teaching About Rape as a Weapon of War and Genocide* (London: Palgrave Macmillan, 2016); Amy Randall (ed.), *Genocide and Gender in the Twentieth Century: A Comparative Survey* (London: Bloomsbury, 2015); Myrna Goldenberg and Amy H. Shapiro (eds.), *Different Horrors, Same Hell: Gender and the Holocaust* (Seattle/London: University of Washington Press, 2013); Carol Rittner and John K. Roth (eds.), *Rape: Weapon of War and Genocide* (Minnesota: Paragon House, 2012).

gender-sensitive research are still often treated as subjects of interest solely to gender scholars and to studies specifically of women and girls, which therefore marginalizes this scholarship as well as the scholars— most of whom are women—who use a gendered lens to analyse the genocidal processes in its entirety. In large part, this marginalization must be understood as a consequence of enduring sexist practices within the field of Genocide Studies and within academia more generally. As a consequence, the mainstream synthetic and theoretical works on genocide continue to fail to integrate the work of gender scholarship. While there have been great moves forward in the past ten years, a great deal of work remains to be done.

In this chapter, I analyse how a consideration of gender is crucial to our understanding of the crime, because genocide is a process that is, at its core, about identity and therefore about group reproduction, both biologically and culturally understood. As Helen Fein pointed out in a seminal essay on the subject, '[r]eproduction serves to con- tinue the group; genocide to destroy it. Thus, perpetrators must either annul reproduction within the group or appropriate the progeny in order to destroy the group in the long run'.[2] In my analysis, genocide is a crime of reproductive violence that targets people according to their perceived and actual positions within the biological and cultural reproductive process; the perpetrators' ultimate aim is the destruction of the target group as a functioning historical entity. Genocides are characterized by 'life force atrocities', highly symbolic and ritualized dramatizations of the perpetrator's obsession with demonstrating his or her destructive power over the target group's very life force. One finds in most, if not all, genocides tortures involving generative sym- bols and generative institutions (reproductive organs, infants and small children, special markings of identity, the bonds that promote family and community coherence, and the physical spaces document- ing group existence in this world, including religious institutions, burial grounds, and symbols of cultural life). Such symbols can be destroyed in ways that do not require the wholesale physical killing of all members of a group. In fact, it appears that the 'total' genocides,

[2] Helen Fein, 'Genocide and Gender: The Uses of Women and Group Des- tiny', *Journal of Genocide Research* 1:1 (1999), 43.

such as the Holocaust and Rwanda, where men and women are killed in roughly equal numbers, are the exceptions; the norm is rather the sex-selective killing of specific members of a group combined with a host of strategies, including especially sexual violence, aimed at destroying the group's ability to survive into the future. In all cases, genocide involves widespread life force atrocity.

Gender is a set of cultural practices and beliefs that organize relations of power.[3] 'Gender', as a concept, is usually treated as distinct from 'sex', which is generally understood to be a physical or biological phenomenon. Recent studies of sexual development in utero, however, have called into question the neat separation between constructed 'gender' and immutable 'sex', as well as the capacity of existing language to capture the full spectrum sexual and gender identity.[4] Such research has challenged not only the 'gender binary', which is little more than an ideology, but also the assumption that there is something inherently 'female' or 'male' within the human body. The fluidity that exists between material and constructed aspects of sex and gender is well captured by the masculinities scholar R. W. Connell, who defines gender as 'the structure of social relations that centers on the reproductive arena, and the set of practices that bring reproductive distinctions between bodies into social processes'.[5] The engine of dominant forms of sex and gender differentiation, for Connell, are the heterosexual, cisgender social relations of reproduction against which 'gender' and 'sexuality' are measured. For the purposes of this chapter, what is important about these new insights is that they point to the extent to which categories of sexual differentiation are as much a construct as categories of gender differentiation. Therefore, when I speak of 'gender', gender roles, women, men, girls, and boys, I am not positing something natural but rather referring to the constructed and dominant operation of categories within the

---

[3] Joan Wallach Scott, *Gender and the Politics of History* (New York: Columbia University Press, 1988), 42.

[4] Anne Fausto-Sterling, 'Why Sex Is Not Binary', *New York Times*, 25 October 2018.

[5] R. W. Connell, *Gender: In World Perspective*, 3rd ed. (Cambridge and New York: Polity, 2014).

gender regimes of groups of people—whether they are victims, perpetrators, bystanders, rescuers, or exist somewhere else along the
spectrum of agency.

Research on genocidal ideology has shown that ideologies usually
emerge within gender binaries, weaponize gender binaries, and seek
to ossify gender binaries. As a consequence, genocidaires exhibit a
preoccupation with group reproduction and target groups based on
perpetrator theories of how they reproduce themselves. Genocidaires
further seek to impose a strict adherence to gendered norms—usually
including enforced heterosexuality—within perpetrating societies,
even in cases, like Cambodia, where perpetrators adhere to an official
ideology of gender nondifferentiation. A good illustration of a genocidal project in enforced heterosexuality is Nazi policy towards homosexual men during the Third Reich. Gay men were targeted for their
supposed resistance to and undermining of heterosexual race reproduction. They were targeted not simply in their bodies but also in the
spaces that Nazis blamed for their reproduction: bars and clubs, but
also research institutes and books. The first book burnings included
the library and archives of Magnus Hirschfeld's Institute for Sexual
Science.[6] The Nazi Party used many different means to achieve the
goal of eradicating male homosexuality from Germany, focusing on
what they considered to be the 'life force' behind the existence of the
social group.[7] Most modern genocides demonstrate a pronounced
homophobia and targeting of queer people. In fact, extreme homophobia can be seen as an early warning of genocide against other
groups as well.

Considering the experiences of men and women, male-identified
people and female-identified people, and queer and straight people
simultaneously can help us see genocide as a process that combines
many different means of (reproductive) destruction in order permanently to undermine the future of a group. Although direct killing can

---

[6] Joanne Meyerowitz, *How Sex Changed: The History of Transsexuality in the United
States* (Cambridge, MA, and London: Harvard University Press, 2002), 21.

[7] For a legal analysis of Nazi policies toward the LGBTQ community as a form
of genocide, see Matthew Waites, 'Genocide and Global Queer Politics', *Journal of
Genocide Research* 20:1 (2018), 44–67.

be a central part of the genocidal process, it is not the whole story. Studying gender in genocide can help identify frequently overlooked long-term causes of genocide as well as enduring genocidal patterns faced by societies as they seek to rebuild in the wake of genocide. In other words, gender is central to the crime of genocide and should be central to the study of it rather than treated as a specialized subfield.

Definitions of Genocide

Up until recently, there have been only two scholars who have incorporated what we might call a 'gender lens' in their definitions of genocide. In 1990 sociologist Helen Fein defined genocide as the 'sustained purposeful action by a perpetrator to physically destroy a collectivity directly or indirectly, through interdiction of the biological and social reproduction of group members, sustained regardless of the surrender or lack of threat offered by the victim'.[8] A decade later, Claudia Card offered a definition that echoes Fein's concern with biological and social reproduction, what Card calls 'social vitality':

> This essay develops the hypothesis that social death is utterly central to the evil of genocide, not just when a genocide is primarily cultural but even when it is homicidal on a massive scale. It is social death that enables us to distinguish the peculiar evil of genocide from the evils of other mass murders . . . . Putting social death at the center takes the focus off individual choice, individual goals, individual careers, and body counts, and puts it on relationships that create community and set the context that gives meaning to choices and goals.[9]

These two definitions refine Raphael Lemkin's quite gendered concern with 'spiritual' and 'biological' techniques of genocide, which included things like the malnourishment of parents who are then unable to properly care for children and bestow on them cultural forms—a definition that predates Fein and Card by almost half a

---

[8] Helen Fein, 'Genocide: A Sociological Perspective', *Current Sociology* 38 (1990), 1–126.

[9] Claudia Card, 'Genocide and Social Death', *Hypatia* 18:1 (Winter 2003), 63–79.

century.[10] During this time, little attention was paid to gender—and women—in the scholarship on the Holocaust and genocide.

The foundation for an investigation of gender and genocide was laid by women scholars of the Holocaust, who in the 1980s began to research the experiences of women survivors.[11] Until then Holocaust research had reflected the gendered assumptions of masculinist historical scholarship wherein the history of men stood in for the history of humankind. Women's experiences were considered to be derivative of and ancillary to men's, and consequently of little importance to history. It was the testimony of male survivors that come to comprise the literary and historical canon of the Holocaust, despite the fact that women were a majority in the Jewish population of Europe before the Second World War.[12] Indeed, women wrote the majority of memoirs and testimonials in the first years after 1945,[13] despite having a lower survival rate overall.[14]

It is clear from the existing research that gender directly influenced people's experience of Nazi persecution at various moments within the overall patterns of destruction. Gender norms shaped how Jews in Germany and elsewhere responded to the Nazi threat.[15] Gender also shaped the specific nature of people's vulnerabilities, which were, in significant respects, different for Jewish men and women. For example, sexualized violence against women was common at every step of the process of destruction—from Gestapo prisons and *Kristallnacht* in Germany, to the Nazi process of expansion across Europe, to

---

[10] 'Gendering Lemkin: Unearthing Sexual Violence (and Other Gendered Atrocities) in Raphael Lemkin's Writings', Paper Presented at the Twelfth Conference of the International Association of Genocide Scholars, Yerevan, Armenia, 8–12 July 2015.

[11] For a more complete discussion of this literature, please see the previous version of this chapter in Dirk Moses and Donald Bloxham (eds.), *The Oxford Handbook of Genocide Studies* (Oxford: Oxford University Press, 2010), 61–80.

[12] Raul Hilberg, *Perpetrators, Victims, Bystanders: The Jewish Catastrophe, 1933–1945* (New York: Harper Perennial, 1993), 127.

[13] Judith Taylor Baumel, *Double Jeopardy: Gender and the Holocaust* (London and Portland: Vallentine Mitchell, 1998), 41.

[14] Hilberg, *Perpetrators*, 127, 130.

[15] The classic study of this is Marion Kaplan, *Between Dignity and Despair: Jewish Life in Nazi Germany* (Oxford University Press, 1998).

round ups, shooting actions, deportations, the concentration and
death camps, death marches, in hiding, and from Allied soldiers
after the war.[16] The historian Nechama Tec found cases of Jewish
women partisans who were sexually exploited and also raped by their
comrades.[17] The very real threat of sexual exploitation that Jewish
women faced from a variety of men alters the dominant image of the
Holocaust as a 'closed' historical event by demonstrating the multiple
trajectories of violence that coalesce in genocide and later feed back
into post-genocide societies.[18]

Apart from defining key difference in the way that men and women
experienced persecution, feminist study of the Holocaust has shown
that in both ideology and practice National Socialism was an expression of misogyny as well as racism.[19] The Nazis sought to control
women's bodies both within and outside of the *Volksgemeinschaft*.[20] In
addition to demonstrating the importance of misogyny to genocidal
ideology, the study of gender and genocide also sheds light on the
ways that perpetrators instrumentalize gender in the killing process.
Even in what have been called 'gender neutral' genocides, such as the
Holocaust and Cambodia, perpetrators treat the sexes differently,

---

[16] Waxman, *Women in the Holocaust*; Myrna Goldenberg, 'Sex-Based Violence
and the Politics and Ethics of Survival', in Goldenberg and Shapiro, *Different
Horrors, Same Hell*, 99–127; Sonja Hedgepeth and Rochelle Saidel (eds.), *Sexual
Violence against Jewish Women during the Holocaust* (Hanover, NH and London: Brandeis University Press/University Press of New England, 2010); Joan Ringleheim,
'Genocide and Gender: A Split Memory', in Ronit Lentin (ed.), *Gender and Catastrophe* (London and New York: Zed Books, 1997), 26–8.

[17] Nechama Tec, 'The Fate of Women', in *Defiance: The Bielski Partisans* (New
York and London: Oxford University Press, 1994), 154–69.

[18] Zoë Waxman examines the re-inscription of traditional gender roles after the
Holocaust in Chapter 4, 'After the War', in *Women in the Holocaust*, 113–46.

[19] The classic studies of Nazi misogyny are Gisela Bock, *Zwangssterilisation im
Nationalsozialismus: Studien zur Rassenpolitik und Frauenpolitik* (Opladen: Westdeutscher
Verlag, 1986), and Claudia Koonz, *Mothers in the Fatherland: Women, the Family, and
Nazi Politics* (New York: St. Martin's, 1986).

[20] See e.g. the chapters in Bridenthal et al. (eds.), *When Biology Became Destiny*.
See also David Patterson, 'The Nazi Assault on the Jewish Soul through the
Murder of the Jewish Mother', in Goldenberg and Shapiro (eds.), *Different Horrors*,
163–76.

though not in ways that significantly affect overall survival rates.[21] In a careful study of gender and the Holocaust in Veszprém, Hungary, Tim Cole shows that while Jewish men aged eighteen to forty-eight were much more likely to die as forced labourers before deportations to the death camps began, by 1944 many of them were able to avoid deportations, and almost certain death, precisely because of their labour power.[22] According to Raul Hilberg, men in general died much more quickly than women in the early phases of the Nazi occupation of Eastern Europe.[23] Men died at much higher rates in the ghettos, in part because of the hard labour they were forced to do.[24] Men also tended to be killed first in the massacres committed by mobile killing squads in Poland, Russia, and Serbia because it was easier for soldiers and police reservists to rationalize and justify the killing of men, whom they identified as security threats.[25] Even Heinrich Himmler, who clearly had no qualms about killing Jewish men, needed an additional rationalization for killing Jewish women and children.[26]

Adding Men

As the case of the Holocaust demonstrates, men's fates are also determined by gender norms, gender assumptions, and gendered ideologies. Nevertheless, the explicit focus on men's gendered experience during genocide is still very new. Patriarchal assumptions about 'women and children' and women's more peaceful nature have

---

[21] Fein, 'Genocide and Gender', 43–63.

[22] Tim Cole, 'A Gendered Holocaust? The Experiences of "Jewish" Men and Women in Hungary, 1944', in Randolph L. Braham and Brewster S. Chamberlin (eds.), *The Holocaust in Hungary: Sixty Years Later* (New York: Columbia University Press, 2006), 54.

[23] Hilberg, *Perpetrators*, 128. He notes that there was a 'reversal of fortunes' after the development of the gas vans and the death camps, which made killing women and children psychologically less taxing on the killers.

[24] Ibid. Hilberg notes that many women were also forced to do hard labour, though perhaps in smaller numbers. See also Nechama Tec, *Resilience and Courage: Women, Men, and the Holocaust* (New Haven: Yale University Press, 2003), 11.

[25] Hilberg, *Perpetrators*, 129.

[26] Roth, 'Equality, Neutrality, Particularity', 11.

exercised a direct, though often subtle, influence on the ways that observers measure atrocities and can leave civilian men and disarmed male soldiers vulnerable to massacre.[27] Attacks on women and children frequently appear to generate greater outrage than attacks on men, largely because attacks on men can be so easily explained away with reference to their supposed 'battle age'. Although public outrage at atrocities against women and children is usually short-lived (it has rarely translated itself into gender-sensitive priorities in war crimes tribunals or gender-sensitive economic development efforts in post-genocidal societies), it is nevertheless significant inasmuch as it can serve to bring a particular conflict to the forefront of international media attention. The Yazidi leadership's response to ISIS genocide was to encourage women and girls to speak about the sexualized violence they experienced to help bring attention to the genocide being suffered by the entire Yazidi community. Though this resulted in global visibility, it unfortunately did not benefit Yazidis on the ground in northern Iraq, where international and regional humanitarian organizations have provided IDPs with few, if any, resources to help them heal from their traumatic experiences.[28]

Adam Jones's research on gender and genocide has brought male victimization to the forefront of analysis. He has shown that a policy of killing men first constitutes a 'tripwire or harbinger of fuller-scale root-and-branch genocides', an insight that is very useful to early warning systems.[29] We have already discussed this pattern in the Holocaust. This pattern is also evident to varying degrees in the Armenian genocide, the genocides in Bosnia and Rwanda, in Kosovo, in East Timor, in Sudan, and in the genocides committed by ISIS against the Yazidi and other minorities in northern Iraq. Jones's work demonstrates that patriarchal assumptions about men as perpetrators and

[27] Cynthia Enloe, 'Women and Children: Making Feminist Sense of the Persian Gulf Crisis', *Village Voice*, 25 September 1990; R. Charli Carpenter, *'Innocent Women and Children': Gender, Norms and the Protection of Civilians* (Burlington: Ashgate, 2006).

[28] See e.g. Johanna E. Foster and Sherizaan Minwallab, 'Voices of Yazidi Women: Perceptions of Journalistic Practices in the Reporting on ISIS Sexual Violence', *Women's Studies International Forum* 67 (March–April 2018), 53–64.

[29] Adam Jones, 'Gendercide and Genocide', in Adam Jones (ed.), *Gendercide and Genocide* (Nashville: Vanderbildt University Press, 2004), 23.

combatants can serve to occlude genocidal practices and even outright deny their existence by dismissing the sex-selective massacre of men. Equally, patriarchal assumptions about women's suffering (that it is less important) can serve denial strategies that point to the small numbers of people killed, ignoring rape and other forms of violence that are not immediately lethal. Genocidaires can also use both of these patriarchal traditions in international law semantically to hide their crimes behind putative 'counterinsurgency efforts', as the government of Sudan has done in Darfur and the government of Myanmar is doing with reference to the Rohingya people in Rakhine State.

Recognition that civilian men are often the initial targets of murder in genocide is therefore crucial to any attempt to fashion an early warning system and end the impunity with which genocidaires have committed mass murder up to the present day. For Jones, these sex-selective massacres, in addition to being harbingers of root-and-branch genocides, are also instances of 'gendercide', or 'gender-selective mass killing', and he argues that gendercide in and of itself is a form of genocide.[30] Two international court rulings on the Srebrenica massacre, where in July 1995 over 8,000 Bosnian Muslim men and boys were killed by Bosnian Serb forces under the command of the indicted General Radko Mladic, support the notion of gendercide as genocide, though only in the limited sense that the gendercidal massacre at Srebrenica was embedded in a wider ethnic conflict.[31]

Femicide and Feminicide

The growing literature on femicide, especially in Latin America, raises many of the same questions that the term 'gendercide' does. Femicide

---

[30] For an overview of the concept of 'gendercide', see Jones, *Gendercide and Genocide*, 1–38. See also his Gendercide Watch website: http://www.gendercide. org. The term gendercide was first used by Many Ann Warren, whose 1985 book of the same title examined instances in which women and girls were the targets. Mary Anne Warren, *Gendercide: The Implications of Sex Selection* (Totowa: Rowman and Allanheld, 1985). There has been a substantial debate about whether gendercide is itself a genocidal process. See e.g. the contributions of Stuart Stein and R. Charli Carpenter to *Gendercide and Genocide*.

[31] ICTY, *Prosecutor v. Krstić*, 19 April 2004, http://www.un.org/icty/krstic/ Appeal/judgment/index.htm; ICJ, Press Release, 26 February 2007.

is a concept first developed by feminist sociologist Diana Russell in the 1970s. She defines femicide as 'the killing of females by males *because* they are female' and includes in this definition such phenomena as intimate partner violence and sex-selective termination of pregnancy in India and China.[32] Although Russell never conceptualized femicide in and of itself as a form of genocide, when the term entered Spanish-language scholarship, largely through the works of Mexican feminist anthropologist Marcela Lagarde y de los Ríos, it was translated as *feminicidio* (feminicide), rather than *femicidio* (the direct translation), specifically to emphasize the genocidal aspects of the phenomenon, that is, that women are being targeted for destruction because of their membership in a gender-defined social group and that their targeting is part of a larger destructive process against this group. The term *feminicidio* widens the scope of the crime as well as the number of its perpetrators, calling attention to the structural and systemic dynamics that create a society in which the destruction of women—and 'the feminine' as such—is naturalized and accepted.[33] In this way, feminicide resembles arguments about structural and systemic genocide and 'genocidal societies'.[34]

Latin American scholars, especially those working in Guatemala, which experienced genocide in the 1980s during a period known as *La Violencia*, have in fact theorized genocide within more enduring historical processes of violence against women (*feminicidio*) to demonstrate that periods before and after mass killing events are rife with accepted forms of violence against women, including murder, that share important technologies of domination with the genocidal process.[35]

---

[32] Diana E. H. Russell and Nicole Van de Ven, *Crimes Against Women: Proceedings of the International Tribunal* (Berkeley: Russell Publications, 1990). Subsequent works have expanded the definition of femicide to include the killing of females by other females to serve the interests of men.

[33] In common parlance, the terms femicide and feminicide are often used interchangeably to mean simply the 'the killing of females'.

[34] See e.g. Tony Barta, 'Relations of Genocide: Land and Lives in the Colonization of Australia', in I. Wallimann and M. N. Dobkowski (eds.), *Genocide and the Modern Age: Etiology and Case Studies of Mass Death* (New York: Greenwood, 1987).

[35] Roselyn Costantino, 'Guatemaltecas Have Not Forgotten: From Victims of Sexual Violence to Architects of Empowerment in Guatemala', in Carol Rittner and John K. Roth (eds.), *Rape: Weapon of War and Genocide* (St. Paul: Paragon House, 2012).

For example, David Carey and M. Gabriela Torres argue that successive Guatemalan regimes since the colonial era have tolerated gender terror against women and have used it as a means of imposing patriarchal control over the population as a whole. Over time, nurtured by official approval, gender terror became more entrenched and extreme, facilitating the turn towards mass killing in the 1980s.[36] The impunity with which genocidal violence was committed, and the impunity that has reigned in Guatemala since, has made the country one of the most violent in the world, with the third highest femicide rate (behind only El Salvador and Jamaica).[37] Feminist research into the Kurdish conflict in Mesopotamia has begun to make connections between femicide and genocide.[38] Here too we see the use of historical forms of gender-based violence and control that have been traditionally directed at women to enact wider genocidal patterns against both women and men.

The overlap between processes of feminicide (directed at women, girls, and female-identifying persons) and genocide (directed at other groups) raises the possibility that examinations of 'peacetime' gender dynamics can offer important insights into the development of genocidal ideology, genocidal concepts, genocidal institutions, and, eventually, large-scale genocidal processes. In and of itself, the crime of rape, which feminist philosopher Ann Cahill defines as 'a sexually specific act that destroys . . . the intersubjective, embodied agency and therefore personhood of woman', shares with genocide the intentional destruction of identity.[39] In the book *Sex and World Peace*, Valerie Hudson and her co-editors demonstrate statistically that there is a direct relationship between levels of gender equity in nations and their

---

[36] David Carey Jr. and M. Gabriela Torres, 'Precursors to Femicide: Guatemalan Women in a Vortex of Violence', *Latin American Research Review* 45:3 (2010), 142–64.

[37] Small Arms Survey, 'Femicide: A Global Problem', *Research Note 14* (2012).

[38] Hilal Alkan, 'The Sexual Politics of War: Reading the Kurdish Through Images of Women', *Les Cahiers du CEDREF 22* (2018), 68–92; Elisa von Joeden-Forgey, 'Genocide Watch Releases Genocide Warning for Kurds in the Middle East', 2 April 2018, https://www.genocidewatch.com/single-post/2018/04/02/Genocide-Watch-Releases-Genocide-Warning-for-Kurds-in-the-Middle-East.

[39] Ann J. Cahill, *Rethinking Rape* (Ithaca: Cornell University Press, 2001), 13.

vulnerability to internal and inter-state conflict.[40] States that tolerate greater levels of gender inequity have a greater propensity to domestic conflict and international war. The authors argue that given the primacy of gender as a sign of difference in basic units of social organization, such as the family, inequalities between genders, and especially violence against women by men, can feed directly into the way that people approach difference later in life. Applying this insight to the precursors to genocide, high levels of annihilative violence against women clearly could set the stage for annihilative projects against other marginalized groups.

The feminist historian Andrea Smith recognizes the powerful model rape provides for genocidal projects. In the book *Conquest,* she demonstrates how North American settlers applied the idea of 'rapable and violable' bodies not just to indigenous women but to indigenous people as a whole.[41] As a consequence, levels of gender-based violence against women and their families were and continue to be very high in the US and Canada (as well as in Central and South America).[42] In this respect, today's discriminatory policies of child removal, the disappearance and murder of Native women, and ongoing efforts by federal authorities to undermine Native sovereignty—all policies that attack the integrity of the individual and the corporate body—can be seen as a continuation of systemic genocidal dynamics against violable bodies within US settler colonialism.

The emerging link between violence against women in 'peacetime' societies and genocidal processes as a whole offers us new possibilities for the early detection of genocidal policies and genocidal ways of thinking. A similar link potentially exists, as I noted earlier, between violence against queer people and the emergence of genocidal social forms. For the most part, scholars and policymakers have been concerned with the impact of long-term ethnic, religious, and national

[40] Valerie M. Hudson, Bonnie Ballif-Spanvill, Mary Caprioli, and Chad F. Emmett, *Sex and World Peace* (New York: Columbia University Press, 2012).

[41] Andrea Smith, *Conquest: Sexual Violence and American Indian Genocide* (Durham, NC: Duke University Press, 2015).

[42] Marion Buller et al. (eds.), *Reclaiming Power and Place: The Final Report of the National Inquiry into Missing and Murdered Indigenous Women and Girls* (June 2019).

cleavages on a society's vulnerability to conflict, as these social categories so often determine the targets of genocide. Gender-based violence, if seen at all, has been understood as a symptom of conflict, whether genocidal or not. But gender-based violence may also be an important precursor to genocide, a petri dish of genocidal ideology, and a driver of genocidal atrocity.[43]

Genocidal Rape

When Serbia started its war with Bosnia in 1992 one of the major news stories coming out of the region was the systematic use of rape by the Serb forces to enforce a policy of 'ethnic cleansing', as it was then routinely called.[44] This was the first time that women around the world were successful in organizing an international movement to have rape explicitly recognized and prosecuted as a war crime, a crime against humanity, and a crime of genocide.[45] The massive international effort to bring this about began with the groundbreaking article by Catherine MacKinnon, who argued early on in the war that rape was being used by Serb forces as a tool of genocide.[46] Her article was followed by books by Alexandra Stiglmayer (1994) and Beverly Allen (1996), both of which called attention to the particularly genocidal role that rape was playing in the violence.

[43] Elisa von Joeden-Forgey, 'Gender, Sexualized Violence and the Prevention of Genocide', in Sheri P. Rosenberg, Tibi Galis, and Alex Zucker (eds.), *Reconstructing Atrocity Prevention* (Cambridge: Cambridge University Press, 2016), 125–50.

[44] Roy Gutman, *A Witness to Genocide* (New York: Macmillan, 1993).

[45] Louise Chappell, 'Gender Mainstreaming in International Institutions: Developments at the UN Ad Hoc Tribunals and the International Criminal Court', *Paper Presented at the International Meeting of the International Studies Association, Hilton Hawaiian Village, Honolulu, Hawaii*, 5 March 2005; Marsha Freeman, 'International Institutions and Gendered Justice', *Journal of International Affairs* 52:2 (1999), 513; Kelly Dawn Askin, 'Prosecuting Wartime Rape and Other Gender-Related Crimes under International Law: Extraordinary Advances, Enduring Obstacles', *Berkeley Journal of International Law* 21:2 (2003), 317.

[46] Catherine A. MacKinnon, 'Turning Rape into Pornography: Postmodern Genocide', *MS* 5 (July/August 1993), 24–30. MacKinnon's article was later published in Alexandra Siglmayer (ed.), *Mass Rape: The War against Women in Bosnia-Herzegovina* (Lincoln/London: University of Nebraska Press, 1994), 74–81.

MacKinnon developed her ideas about the relationship between rape and genocide in several articles where she calls attention to the fact that genocides are sexualized (and often pornographic) for a reason. In her analysis, perpetrators use sexualized violence as a tool of domination of groups of men and women because it has worked so well for so long in enforcing domination of men *over* women. 'Sexual abuse', she writes, 'is a perfect genocidal tool. It does to ethnic, racial, religious, and national groups as such what has been done to women as such from time immemorial in one of the most effective systems of domination-to-destruction in history'.[47] Her argument has been borne out by many of the studies of hypermasculinity and genocidal masculinity mentioned later in this chapter.

It is estimated that between 20,000 and 50,000 women and girls were raped during the wars in the former Yugoslavia between 1991 and 1995. An estimated 3,000 men and boys were raped and otherwise sexually violated.[48] 'While all sides in the Bosnian conflict have committed rapes', notes Joana Daniel-Wrabetz, 'Serbian forces appear to have used rape on the largest scale, principally against Muslim women.'[49] Usually rape was accompanied by various tortures, including branding with the Serbian cross, burning, slashing, beating, and threats of death against the women and their family members, especially their children. Men and boys faced castration, circumcision, enforced rape of one another or of family members, rape by guards, and enforced rape of corpses. Rape frequently was used as a means of murder, but Serb forces also used a policy of forced maternity against Bosniak women to create more 'Serbian' children. Women's bodies were used to humiliate families and communities as the perpetrators raped girls in front of their parents or forced family members to rape each other.

---

[47] Catherine A. MacKinnon, 'Genocide's Sexuality', in *Are Women Human?* (Cambridge, MA: Belknap Press, 2006), 233.

[48] Survivors Project, *Legacies and Lessons: Sexual Violence Against Men and Boys in Sri Lanka and Bosnia & Herzegovina* (Los Angeles: UCLA School of Law, 2017).

[49] Siobhan K. Fisher, 'Occupation of the Womb: Forced Impregnation and Genocide', *Duke Law Journal* 46:1 (1996), 109; Joana Daniel-Wrabitz, 'Children Born of War Rape in Bosnia-Herzegovina and the Convention on the Rights of the Child', in Carpenter (ed.), *Born of War*, 23.

Rape in Rwanda shared with rape in Bosnia these genocidal qualities, though here it was much more widespread and usually used as a
means of murder. The estimates of the number of women raped reach
to 500,000, few of whom were allowed to survive.[50] While perpetrators used rape in this case primarily as a part of a terrifying and
drawn-out ritual of killing, some Tutsi women were also subjected to
forced maternity under the logic that they would bear Hutu children,
demonstrating the multiple and self-contradictory levels on which
perpetrators pursue the destruction of the target group's reproductive
powers.[51] Thousands of women survivors were rendered permanently
disabled from the brutality of the rapes, many having been left
incapable of bearing children. Furthermore, many assailants seem to
have knowingly infected raped women with HIV, thereby ensuring
their eventual and untimely deaths even if they were to survive the
genocide.[52]

In the face of heavy media attention on the use of rape in both the
Bosnian and the Rwandan genocides, questions were raised about the
best way to characterize these rapes. The controversy has revolved
around the question of whether to conceptualize 'genocidal rape' as a
special category of rape. Catherine MacKinnon sparked this debate
when she argued that 'rapes in the Serbian war of aggression against
Bosnia-Herzegovina and Croatia are to everyday rape what the
Holocaust was to everyday anti-Semitism: both like it and not like it
at all, both continuous with it and a whole new departure, a unique
atrocity yet also a pinnacle moment in something that goes on all the
time'.[53] Initially, the case for rape as a crime of genocide was most
forcefully made in the case of forced pregnancy and forced maternity.

[50] SURF-Survivor's Fund, 'Statistics of the Genocide', https://survivors-fund.org.uk/learn/statistics/.

[51] Human Rights Watch, *Shattered Lives: Sexual Violence during the Rwandan Genocide and its Aftermath* (New York: HRW, 1996); Jones, 'Gender and Genocide in Rwanda', in Jones (ed.), *Gendercide and Genocide*, 98–137; Marie Consolee Mukan-gendo, 'Caring for Children Born of Rape in Rwanda', in Carpenter (ed.), *Born of War*, 40–52.

[52] Mukangendo, 'Caring for Children Born of Rape in Rwanda', 45.

[53] MacKinnon, 'Turning Rape into Pornography', 74. Several feminists have voiced concern about the high-profile public attention that has been focused on 'genocidal rape'. See e.g. Rhonda Copelon, 'Surfacing Gender:

The international law scholar Siobhan Fisher characterized the Serbian policy of forced maternity as a genocidal 'occupation of the
womb'.[54] Writing on the Armenian genocide, Donald Bloxham has
similarly identified forced marriage and sexual slavery as a 'colonization of the female body' that was an important part of the genocidal
process.[55] Such policies are genocidal because the purpose is to force
women to give birth to children defined as issuing from the perpetrator group, thereby preventing them from carrying children from their
own group.[56] The philosopher Claudia Card goes one step further to
argue that forced impregnation can be a crime of genocide even when
the intent was not specifically to create new children of the perpetrator's group. In her view, rape brings social death to a person and
forced impregnation 'uses sperm as a biological weapon intended to
destroy social vitality in a people'.[57]

Decisions by the international tribunals set up for Bosnia and
Rwanda, established in 1993 and 1994, respectively, have upheld
much of the scholarly work on genocidal rape. Fisher's interpretation
of forced maternity was confirmed by both the International Criminal
Tribunal for Rwanda (ICTR) in *Prosecutor v. Akayesu* and the International Criminal Tribunal for the former Yugoslavia (ICTY) in the
Karadžić and *Mladić* decisions.[58] In *Prosecutor v. Akayesu*, the ICTR
further found that rape and sexual violence 'constitute genocide in
the same way as any other act as long as they were committed with the
specific intent to destroy, in whole or in part, a particular group,

---

Reconceptualizing Crimes against Women in Time of War', in Stiglmayer (ed.),
Mass Rape, 197; Susan Brownmiller, 'Making Female Bodies the Battlefield', in
Stiglmayer (ed.), *Mass Rape*, 180.

[54] Fisher, 'Occupation of the Womb', 124.

[55] Donald Bloxham, 'Internal Colonization, Inter-Imperial Conflict and the
Armenian Genocide', in A. Dirk Moses (ed.), *Empire, Colony, Genocide: Conquest,
Occupation, and Subaltern Resistance in World History* (New York: Berghahn Books,
2008), 338.

[56] Fisher, 'Occupation of the Womb', 93.

[57] Claudia Card, *Confronting Evils: Terrorism, Torture, Genocide* (Cambridge: Cambridge University Press, 2010), 293.

[58] Mark Ellis, 'Breaking the Silence: Rape as an International Crime', *Case
Western Reserve Journal of International Law* 38 (2006/2007), 232–5.

targeted as such'.[59] While the Statute of the International Criminal Court (ICC) does not list sexual violence or rape as specific elements of the crime of genocide, the ICTY and ICTR decisions have set important precedents for trying gender-based violence as genocide.[60]

Relational Violence, Life Force Atrocities, and Prevention

The debate about the status of rape in genocide and whether it itself is genocidal neglects to consider the wider 'relational' context of much gender-based violence.[61] Rape in genocide is frequently part of an elaborate and sustained ritual on the part of perpetrators in which they focus not only on killing, raping, and expelling living members of a group, but also on the intensive targeting of symbols of the group's life force, rituals that I have called 'life force atrocities'.[62] Recognizing the wide-ranging targets of genocidal violence, Dirk Moses has called genocide 'a "total social practice" that [affects] all aspects of group life'.[63] In such a context, rape can indeed be a crime of genocide. During genocide, people are usually targeted in terms of their familial roles, that is, the roles the perpetrators perceive them to play in the reproductive process of the group. Common practices across genocides include killing infants in front of their parents, forcing family members to rape one another, destroying women's reproductive capacity through rape and mutilation, castrating men, eviscerating pregnant women, and otherwise engaging in ritual cruelties aimed directly at the spiritually sacred, biologically generative, and emotionally nurturing structures of family and community life.[64] A common life force atrocity across genocides is the targeting of pregnant women for particularly symbolic tortures. In the Nazi camps, for example,

[59] ICTR, *Prosecutor v. Akayesu*, Case No. IT-96-4-T, 731.

[60] Rape is specifically recognized as a crime of war and a crime against humanity. Ellis, 'Breaking the Silence', 240.

[61] Jones, 'Gender and Genocide', 25.

[62] Elisa von Joeden-Forgey, 'Devil in the Details: "Life Force Atrocity" and the Assault on the Family in Times of Conflict', *Genocide Studies and Prevention* 5:1 (Spring 2010), 1–19.

[63] A. Dirk Moses, 'Empire, Colony, Genocide: Keywords and the Philosophy of History', in Moses (ed.), *Empire, Colony, Genocide*, 13.

[64] Joeden-Forgey, 'Devil in the Details'; see also Card, *Confronting Evils*, 276–83.

pregnancy was treated with particular cruelty in accord with its potent symbolism.[65]

The Armenian genocide is a classic example of gender-based geno-cidal patterns. Men were overwhelmingly killed first, especially Arme-nian elites, intellectuals, and soldiers in the Ottoman army.[66] After these initial sex-selective massacres, the Committee of Union and Progress perpetrators followed a family-based pattern of destruction. When villages were attacked, men were murdered first and their surviving family members were raped, expelled, and killed. Perpet-rators frequently engaged in inversion rituals and ritual desecrations in the process.[67] As in other cases, rape during the Armenian genocide served many purposes: it was part of the process of eliticide, the destruction of a group's leadership, in that it emphasized the 'unpro-tected' nature of women and children in a patriarchal society; it publicly demonstrated the perpetrators' mastery over the Armenian life force; it inflicted 'total suffering' on both the men and the women (and the boys and girls) who were tortured in two ways—through violent attacks on their own bodies and by having to witness the immense suffering of their loved ones; and it compromised the future integrity of the group by sowing the seeds of psychic and familial dissolution. Some women and girls were kidnapped by Turkish, Kurdish, and Arab men and absorbed into their families as domestic servants, 'wives', and sex slaves. Although there was a coordinated international effort after the genocide to free these women from their captors, surviving captive Armenian women faced many 'choiceless choices' as a consequence of their treatment during the genocide: According to Ottoman law, for example, women who had children

[65] Gisela Perl, *I Was a Doctor in Auschwitz* (Salem: Ayer, 1984), 80. Quoted from Goldenberg, 'Lessons Learned from Gentle Heroism: Women's Holocaust Nar-ratives', *The Annals of the American Academy of Political and Social Science*, 548 (1996), 86; Raul Hilberg, *The Destruction of the European Jews* (New York: Holmes and Meier, 1985), 146.

[66] Matthias Bjørnlund, ' "A Fate Worse than Dying": Sexual Violence during the Armenian Genocide', in Dagmar Herzog (ed.), *Brutality and Desire: War and Sexuality in Europe's Twentieth Century* (New York: Palgrave Macmillan, 2009), 17.

[67] Katherine Derderian, 'Common Fate, Different Experience: Gender-Specific Aspects of the Armenian Genocide, 1915–1917', *Holocaust and Genocide Studies* 19:1 (Spring 2005), 5.

born in forced marriages would usually have to leave these children behind with the fathers and set out for an uncertain future alone, often as the only surviving member of their Armenian families.[68]

Since 2010 we have seen this type of violence manifested in northern Syria, in Iraq, in Myanmar, and in Xinjiang, China against the Uighur Muslim population.[69] Despite this, few scholars and policymakers have recognized the central importance of relational violence to genocide, or its terrifying efficacy, even though it is a consistent characteristic of survivor testimony. The absence of a 'relational framework' in genocide scholarship, to use Adam Jones's phrase, has ensured that some of the crimes common to genocide have languished in scholarly and legal obscurity.[70] Most often these genocidal life force atrocities are categorized simply as 'rape' in the literature, even though they encompass so many other crimes and victims.[71]

Focusing on relational violence and life force atrocities draws in many other instances of gross violations of human rights that do not easily conform to the common understanding of genocide. During the 1971 war in Bangladesh, for example, many of the estimated 200,000 rapes were accompanied by relational violence similar to that found in Armenia, Bosnia, and Rwanda, including the evisceration of pregnant women and the mutilation of foetuses.[72] Other instances include the Japanese Army's attack on Nanking in the Second World War, its

[68] Anna Aleksanyan, 'Between Love, Pain and Identity: Armenian Women After World War I', in Ulrike Ziemer (ed.), *Women's Everyday Lives in War and Peace in the South Caucuses* (New York: Palgrave Macmillan, 2020).

[69] Austin Ramzy and Chris Buckley, '"Absolutely No Mercy": Leaked Files Expose How China Organized Mass Detentions of Muslims', *New York Times*, 16 November 2019; Fortify Rights, '"They Gave Them Long Swords": Preparations for Genocide and Crimes Against Humanity Against Rohingya Muslims in Rakhine State, Myanmar' (July 2018), http://www.fortifyrights.org/downloads/Fortify_Rights_Long_Swords_July_2018.pdf.

[70] Jones, 'Gender and Genocide', 25.

[71] For an example, see Kelly Dawn Askin, 'Prosecuting Gender Crimes Committed in Darfur', in Samuel Totten and Eric Markusen (eds.), *Genocide in Darfur: Investigating the Atrocities in the Sudan* (New York: Routledge, 2006), 146–8.

[72] Yasmin Saikia, 'Beyond the Archive of Silence: Narratives of Violence of the 1971 Liberation War of Bangladesh', *History Workshop Journal* 58 (2004), 275–87.

'comfort women' system, and the recent war in Sierra Leone.[73] Some of the election-related violence in the Rift Valley region in Kenya in 2008 also showed a genocidal logic, especially as regards the treatment of children.[74] Non-lethal patterns of genocide, such as child removal in Australia, Canada, and the US, are also easier to see if we appreciate the importance and depth of relational violence.[75]

Despite the continuing neglect of the insights of gender scholarship into the overall crime of genocide, the importance of relational violence, life force atrocities, and gender-based violence during genocide is slowly beginning to gain recognition within official as well as scholarly circles.[76] Just as the Bosnian and Rwandan cases of genocide brought to international attention the important role played by

[73] Masahiro Yamamoto, *Nanking: Anatomy of an Atrocity* (Westport: Praeger, 2000); James Yin and Shi Young, *The Rape of Nanking: An Undeniable History in Photographs* (Chicago: Innovative Publishing Group, 1996); Iris Chang, *The Rape of Nanking: The Forgotten Holocaust of WWII* (New York: Basic Books, 1997); Yuki Tanaka, *Japan's Comfort Women: Sexual Slavery and Prostitution during World War II and the US Occupation* (New York: Routledge, 2002); Kelly Dawn Askin, 'Comfort Women: Shifting Shame and Stigma from Victims to Victimizers', *International Criminal Law Review* I (2001), 5–32; *The Women's International War Crimes Tribunal 2000 for the Trial of Japanese Military Sexual Slavery, Summary of Findings*, 12 December 2000; Amnesty International, *Sierra Leone: Rape and other Sexual Crimes against Girls and Women* (New York: Amnesty International, 2000); Amnesty International, *Democratic Republic of Congo, Mass Rape: Time for Remedies* (New York: Amnesty International, 2004); Jan Goodwin, 'Silence=Rape', *The Nation*, 8 March 2008.

[74] Xan Rice, 'Murder of the Children who Sought Sanctuary in Church', *The Guardian*, 3 January 2008.

[75] For more on relational violence and the 'genocidal economy', see Elisa von Joeden-Forgey, 'Gender and the Genocidal Economy', in Charles H. Anderton and Jürgen Brauer (eds.), *Economic Aspects of Genocides, Other Mass Atrocities, and Their Prevention* (Oxford: Oxford University Press, 2016), 378–95. For child removal, see e.g. A. Dirk Moses (ed), *Genocide and Settler Society: Frontier Violence and Stolen Indigenous Children in Australian History* (New York/Oxford: Berghahn Books, 2005); The Truth and Reconciliation Commission of Canada, *They Came for the Children* (Winnipeg, Manitoba, 2012), http://www.trc.ca/websites/trcinstitution/index.php?p=580.

[76] See e.g. John Kerry, 'Remarks on Daesh and Genocide', 17 March 2016, https://2009-2017.state.gov/secretary/remarks/2016/03/254782.htm, as well as the United Nation's *Framework of Analysis for Atrocity Crimes* (New York: United Nations, 2014), https://www.un.org/en/genocideprevention/documents/about-us/Doc.3_Framework%20of%20Analysis%20for%20Atrocity%20Crimes_EN.pdf.

sexualized violence in the 'big three' atrocity crimes (war crimes, crimes against humanity, and genocide), ISIS genocide against the Yazidis and other minorities in Iraq and Syria, Myanmar's genocide against the Rohingya and Karen peoples, and the ongoing state genocides against many different peoples in western and southern Sudan have brought public attention to gendered patterns of genocide that do not conform to the sometimes simplistic conceptualizations of 'total genocide' that emerge from the classic, massive, root-and-branch genocides of the twentieth century (the Armenian Genocide, the Holocaust, and the 1994 Genocide against the Tutsi in Rwanda).[77] A recent special issue of *Genocide Studies International* has introduced the idea that we begin to focus on a 'Mesopotamian' model of genocide that, in contrast with the Holocaust model, surfaces the important role of sexual violence, expulsion, kidnapping and enslavement (absorption), and denial of identity in genocidal processes.[78]

Genocidal Masculinities and Genocidal Femininities

The widespread nature of sexual violence against women and men during genocide indicates that genocide is a crime intimately connected to particular types of masculinity.[79] Masculinity is a construct, a meaning system, and a performance; it is therefore subject to multiple interpretations by different male-identified people at any given time. Specific sorts of masculinity can be harnessed to the patriarchal power structure and reproduced, as well as radicalized, to pursue violent ends. Some Holocaust scholars, for example, have begun to use the term 'hypermasculinity' to refer to the particular Nazi masculine ideal represented by the German military and

[77] Elisa von Joeden-Forgey, 'Patterns of Genocide: A Critical Tool for Genocide Prevention', *OnGenocide Blog*, 6 December 2019.

[78] Thomas McGee and Elisa von Joeden-Forgey (eds.), *Genocide Studies International* 13:1, Special Issue on 'Genocide and the Kurds' (Spring 2019).

[79] Ronit Lentin, 'Introduction: (En)gendering Genocides', in Ronit Lentin (ed.), *Gender and Catastrophe* (London and New York: Zed Books, 1997), 7.

particularly the SS.[80] My work has identified a specific 'genocidal masculinity' across various cases that pits itself both against status quo institutions—including existing patriarchal systems—and against the target groups, each of which are seen to set limits upon, and constitute existential threats to, the full expression of the perpetrators' historical and existential power, which they associate with the generative power of 'their' group.[81]

The study of masculinity in genocide has evolved significantly in the past decade. Holocaust scholars have examined hypermasculinity, rituals of violence, and how these combined to create the conditions for genocide in Nazi-occupied Europe. Since genocide often is crime intimately linked with war,[82] the ways that men make sense of war and seek to cope with it can shed light on political, social, moral, and cultural processes that can hasten the development and spread of particularly violent forms of masculine identity. Promising work has been done on this front regarding veterans of the First World War in interwar Germany, especially the veteran and writer Ernst Jünger, who called war the 'male form of procreation'.[83] Andreas Huyssen has linked interwar fascist gender constructs like Jünger's to soldiers' 'traumatic experience of emasculation' during the war.[84] In his view, interwar fascism was a means of 'remasculinizing' the self by rejecting the feminized civilian peacetime world and insisting on the liberatory and elevating power of violence, a construct that took on

---

[80] See e.g. Edward B. Westerman, 'Drinking Rituals, Masculinity, and Mass Murder in Nazi Germany', *Central European History* 51 (2018), 367–89; Thomas Kühne, *The Rise and Fall of Comradeship: Hitler's Soldiers, Male Bonding and Mass Violence in the Twentieth Century* (Cambridge: Cambridge University Press, 2017); Christina Wieland, *The Fascist State of Mind and the Manufacturing of Masculinity: A Psychoanalytic Approach* (London: Routledge, 2015); Jane Caplan, 'Gender and the Concentration Camps', in Jane Caplan and Nikolaus Wachsmann (eds.), *Concentration Camps in Nazi Germany: The New Histories* (New York: Routledge, 2012).

[81] Elisa von Joeden-Forgey, 'Genocidal Masculinity', in Adam Jones (ed.), *New Directions in Genocide Research* (London: Routledge, 2012), 89.

[82] Martin Shaw, *War and Genocide: Organized Killing in Modern Society* (Cambridge: Polity Press, 2003).

[83] Ernst Jünger, *Der Kampf als inneres Erlebnis, Sämtliche Werke* 2.1, vol. 7 (Stuttgart: Klett-Cotta, 1980), 50.

[84] Andreas Huyssen, 'Fortifying the Heart-Totally Ernst Jünger's Armored Texts', *New German Critique* 59 (Spring/Summer 1993), 9.

genocidal dimensions within the Nazi party. Thomas Kühne and Edward Westerman have looked at how masculinity served to create strong bonds of loyalty between Wehrmacht soldiers and members of the SS, who engaged in ritualized cruelties as part of this bonding. Kühne writes that 'excessive drinking, tales of sexual adventures, misogynistic rhetoric, rowdyism, even collective rape—all this gained its social momentum from being celebrated—practiced, reported, or applauded—together'.[85]

Kühne's research shares commonalities with research on male comradeship in other genocidal contexts. For example, Euan Hague has shown how the all-male rituals of genocidal rape in Bosnia-Herzegovina were a means of performing the potency of their Serbian national identity.[86] The link between masculinist potency and national power can also help explain why the rape of men during genocide is rarely discussed even within the societies that share national identity with the male rape victims.[87] In Hague's interpretation, when Serb soldiers raped Muslim and Croat women and men, girls and boys, they were exercising their masculinist domination over civilians that they identified specifically as *feminized* ethnic enemies, and this drama was a core feature of 'hetero-masculinist' constructions of Serbian national identity under Milošević.[88] Such an approach frames genocide as an expressive act that, in large part because of its gendered nature, requires constant recapitulation. Such an understanding helps explain why genocides tend to radicalize even further at the peripheries and expand to new victim groups.[89]

Another promising line of enquiry is the relationship between institutions of male domination and genocidal ideology. Christopher

[85] Kühne, *The Rise and Fall of Comradeship*, 293.

[86] Euan Hague, 'Rape, Power and Masculinity: The Construction of Gender and National Identities in the War in Bosnia-Herzegovina', in Lentin (ed.), *Gender and Catastrophe*, 50–63.

[87] Janine Natalya Clark, 'Masculinity and Male Survivors of Wartime Sexual Violence: A Bosnian Case Study', *Conflict, Security and Development* 17:4 (2017), 287–311.

[88] Hague, 'Rape, Power and Masculinity', 55.

[89] Robert Gellately, 'The Third Reich, the Holocaust, and Visions of Serial Genocide', in Robert Gellately and Ben Kiernan (eds.), *The Specter of Genocide: Mass Murder in Historical Perspective* (Cambridge: Cambridge University Press, 2003),

Taylor highlighted the gendered nature of genocidal utopia when, writing on the Rwanda genocide, he described Hutu Power ideology as one that sought 'an imagined past condition of patriarchy as well as the perpetuation of Hutu dominance'.[90] The link between male domination within the perpetrator group and genocide against 'outside' groups is a common one, and usually expresses itself in terms of an ersatz patriarch (the leader, the party) who is both god and father in that he exercises final power over reproductive choices and determines who shall live and who shall die. This explains why political leaders who oversee genocides also often promote authoritarian and coercive reproductive policies within their own groups, as was especially the case during the Cambodian genocide.[91] Their efforts to erode institutions of autonomous generation among insiders (by reducing women to breeders, co-opting children, and forcibly separating preexisting family members) are intimately intertwined with their plans to destroy outside groups, in whole or in part.

Finally, the ways that women find agency in these explicitly masculinist projects needs to be better explained.[92] There can be no doubt that women have participated in genocides as perpetrators in very high numbers. Their support for genocidal projects has also been very strong. Laura Sjoberg and Caron Gentry contend that 'as women's

---

241–63; Helen Fein, 'Genocide, Terror, Life Integrity, and War Crimes: The Case for Discrimination', in George J. Andreoloulos (ed.), *Genocide: Conceptual and Historical Dimensions* (Philadelphia: University of Pennsylvania Press, 1994).

[90] Jones, 'Gender and Genocide in Rwanda', 101–2; Christopher C. Taylor, *Sacrifice as Terror: The Rwandan Genocide of 1994* (Oxford/New York: Berg, 1999), 151–79.

[91] M. O'Brien, 'Jurisprudential Evolution: Genocide and Forced Marriage in ECCC Case 002/02', Paper presented at Fourteenth Conference of the International Association of Genocide Scholars, Phnom Penh, Cambodia, 2019; Judith Strasser, Thida Kim, Silke Studzinsky, and Sopheap Taing, *A Study about Victims' Participation at the Extraordinary Chambers in the Courts of Cambodia and Gender-Based Violence under the Khmer Rouge Regime* (Phnom Penh, Cambodia: Transcultural Psychosocial Organization, 2015).

[92] For a detailed discussion of the scholarly work on male and female perpetration, see Adam Jones, 'Gender and Genocide', in *Genocide: A Comprehensive Introduction* (New York: Routledge, 2017), 625–60.

freedoms increase, so will their violence', which appears to assume that as human beings gain more control over their fates they naturally turn towards violence.[93] Recent works on women perpetrators of genocide, particularly historian Wendy Lower's *Hitler's Furies*, appear to support this view of 'freedom', though only within an overall masculinist, misogynist, fascist dictatorship. German women found liberation from gender and class limitations by signing up for service on the eastern front, where they participated in the tens of thousands in making sure the genocidal machine was working smoothly.[94] Within the context of patriarchy and enforced conformity to the gender binary, genocide scholar Sara Brown may have come up with the best conceptualization of women's perpetration during genocide: 'constrained agency'. She located Rwandan women's perpetration within 'the process of identity formation and the policing of intra and inter-group boundaries' that took place as part of a society-wide transformation towards genocide.[95]

Normalizing the reception and analysis of women's perpetration is a necessary response to patriarchal fictions about inherent female passivity.[96] Lower's book shows that any large-scale genocidal project will require its 'domesticization' within the spheres of activity traditionally controlled (at least at a local level) by women, not merely the family, but also public activities in which women are usually a majority, such as (in the case of Nazi Germany) secretarial work, the nursing and teaching professions, social hosting, and volunteer activities.[97]

[93] Laura Sjoberg and Caron E. Gentry, *Mothers, Monsters, Whores: Women's Violence in Global Politics* (London: Zed Books, 2007), 4.
[94] Wendy Lower, *Hitler's Furies: German Women in the Nazi Killing Fields* (Boston: Houghton Mifflin, 2013). Lower makes it clear that women cannot be held responsible for the formation of extreme right-wing parties in Weimar Germany or for the fact that the National Socialist German Workers' Party came to power in January 1933. She recognizes that the Nazis were stridently anti-feminist, persecuted many non-Jewish German women, and did not allow women into the party leadership or to rise up the ranks of the state bureaucracy.
[95] Sara Brown, *Gender and the Genocide in Rwanda* (New York: Routledge, 2018), 10.
[96] See e.g. James Waller, *Becoming Evil* (Oxford: Oxford University Press, 2007), 269.
[97] Joeden-Forgey, 'Domesticating Genocide', *East Central Europe* 44:1 (2017), 160–3.

Nevertheless, we should be careful not to naturalize violence—for women or for men—in a way that moves our focus away from interrogations of power systems. In patriarchal gender regimes, the expression of heterosexual, cisgender masculinity and femininity can be an expression of a particularly aggressive form of power that exists at quite a distance from whatever inner qualities individual men and women may possess. It is worth considering the contributions that anti-patriarchal liberatory projects based in ideologies of gender equality, such as the Rojava experiment in northern Syria and the Zapatista movement in Chiapas, Mexico, might make to genocide prevention, and asking whether, and under what circumstances, they would turn to genocide as a form of domination and control.[98] We do know that these gender liberatory projects, when incorporated into armed struggle, often seem to contribute to impressive troop discipline in avoiding sexual violence.[99]

It is further worth analysing whether not only unequal gender relations of patriarchy, but also the gender binary itself—its imposition and the forms of social meaning that revolve around it—is an important incubator of genocidal potential. Recent ground-breaking research on violence against transgender women and its genocidal components raises precisely the question of the role of sexual identities, the gender binary, and hegemonic cis- and hetero-normative agendas in creating the conditions for genocide. Haley Marie Brown has convincingly argued that the high rates of murder of transgender women around the world is an expression of genocidal intent on the part of the perpetrators, who appear to be targeting and seeking to completely annihilate the transgender woman's body as the location of her identity and the source of trans generative power.[100] The life

---

[98] Arianne Shahvisi, 'Beyond Orientalism: Exploring the Distinctive Feminism of Democratic Confederalism in Rojava', *Geopolitics* 2018.

[99] Elisabeth Jean Wood, 'Rape in Not Inevitable During War', in Kathleen Kuehnast, Chantal de Jonge Oudraat, and Helga Hernes (eds.), *Women and War: Power and Protection in the 21st Century* (Washington: US institute of Peace, 2011), 37–64.

[100] Haley Marie Brown, 'The Forgotten Murders: Gendercide in the 21st Century and the Destruction of the Transgender Body', in John Cox, Amal Khoury, and Sarah Minslow (eds.), *Denial: The Final Stage of Genocide?* (New York: Routledge, forthcoming 2020). See also: Jeremy D. Kidd and Taryn Witten,

force atrocities committed against transgender women are suggestive: transgender women have been beheaded, burned, and mutilated.[101] The destruction of transgender identity is also pursued through what Brown calls 'conversion rituals', the goal of which is to 'to "convert" transgender women back into cisgender people through gendered bodily destruction'.[102] Brown's research, though currently focusing on the murder of transgender women, has broad applicability. For example, much of the social violence against transgender men and women and gender variant people in the US is happening against a backdrop of official identity denial, which itself points to the genocidal nature of transphobia.[103]

When we look at the victims of genocide in terms of their gendered destruction, we are able to identify genocidal intent very early on in a conflict. As we well know, genocide looks very different at different stages of its development. Atrocities against the life force, which are so often focused on small groups like extended families, can be used as evidence of genocidal intent for the purpose of early warning and intervention. In the case of the murders of trans women, we have seen that violence focused on single individuals may be evidence of genocidal intent. Certain policies, such as separating families, kidnapping children, casting 'outside' group men as sexually violent or 'outside' group women as conniving and disloyal (such as is the case surrounding the 'anchor baby' and 'welfare queen' debates in the US), can be red flags of emerging genocidal ideation.[104] The microcosms of much genocidal violence have the potential to offer us deeper insight into the longer-term causes of genocides, particularly in terms of genocidal

---

'Transgender and Transsexual Identities: The Next Strange Fruit—Hate Crimes, Violence and Genocide Against the Global Trans Communities', *Journal of Hate Studies* 6 (2010).

[101] Brown, 'The Forgotten Murders'.

[102] Ibid.

[103] Erica L. Green, Katie Benner, and Robert Pear, ' "Transgender" Could Be Defined Out of Existence Under Trump Administration', *New York Times*, 21 October 2018.

[104] Joeden-Forgey, 'Gender, Sexualized Violence, and the Prevention of Genocide', 145.

ideologies and the creations of conditions under which people are tempted to embrace and participate in genocidal killing.

Aftermaths

If the study of gender in genocide is important to an early warning system, it is equally important to the rebuilding efforts in post-genocidal societies. Gender analysis brings attention to the intentional ways in which families and communities are disrupted and destroyed; therefore, special emphasis will need to be placed on rebuilding families and fostering community cohesion. This will require intensive public policy efforts to recognize and de-stigmatize male and female survivors of rape by giving due attention to the concentric circles of suffering caused by the relational nature of genocidal violence. Particular attention will need to be paid to women survivors who experience enormous structural vulnerability in post-genocidal societies in the form of social ostracism, impoverishment, and homelessness due to discriminatory customs of inheritance and limited occupational options. Many are forced to raise children alone, including children born of wartime rape and war orphans. Many are suffering from disabilities and illnesses related to genocidal violence. Many are unable to conceive or carry children, which can interfere with their ability to marry and thereby condemn them to a lifetime of economic hardship.[105] Male survivors of sexualized violence appear to suffer similar fates.[106]

Many genocidal systems and processes continue well past the end of armed conflict and can become exacerbated by international responses. International peacekeepers, for example, have committed rape and have exploited the economic vulnerability of targeted communities to exchange resources for sex with impunity.[107] Well-intentioned, and even successful, humanitarian programmes

[105] Ibid., 128.
[106] Will Storr, 'The Rape of Men: The Darkest Secret of War', *The Observer*, Saturday 16 July 2011, http://www.theguardian.com/society/2011/jul/17/the-rape-of-men.
[107] Melanie O'Brien, *Criminalising Peacekeepers: Modernising National Approaches to Sexual Exploitation and Abuse* (New York: Palgrave Macmillan, 2017).

can reinforce family dislocation and even undermine the agency of survivors.[108] Refugee and internally displaced person (IDP) camp policies can inadvertently continue the destructive consequences of genocidal rape by, for example, encouraging women with children born of war to register their children according to local laws. In Yazidi IDP camps in northern Iraq, this has had the consequence of alienating such children from the wider Yazidi community, since, according to Iraqi family law, children born to unknown fathers are immediately registered as 'Muslim'.[109]

Genocides can create massive human trafficking networks and many young women, and some young men, find their way into sex trafficking either as a direct result of the kidnapping during genocide or as an economic necessity afterwards.[110] These destructive patterns can continue for decades after genocides, as we see in the case of Cambodia especially. Studies indicate that early marriage, forced marriage, violence against women, and violence against children increases in postwar contexts.[111] In places like Bosnia, Rwanda, and Sierra Leone, where so many rapists have gone unpunished, women continue to live in fear of reprisals.[112] Finally, many post-genocidal societies end up reasserting patriarchal gender norms in the effort to rebuild social orders that have been ripped apart.[113] This can inadvertently reinforce some of the structures that make societies vulnerable to the commission of genocide in the first place.

[108] Thomas McGee, 'Saving the Survivors: Yezidi Women, Islamic State and the German Admissions Programme', *Kurdish Studies* 6:1 (2018), 85–109.

[109] Thomas McGee, 'Born in War: Risk of Statelessness and Stigmatized Nationality Acquisition for Children of Yezidi Survivors in Kurdistan', Paper presented at the Third Lalish Conference, Dohuk, Iraq, April 2017.

[110] Alys McAlpine, Mazeda Hossain, and Cathy Zimmerman, 'Sex Trafficking and Sexual Exploitation in Settings Affected by Armed Conflicts in Africa, Asia and the Middle East: Systematic Review', *BMC International Health and Human Rights* 16:34 (2016), 1–16.

[111] Ann Jones, *War Is Not Over When It's Over* (New York: Metropolitan Books, Henry Holt and Company, 2010), 8.

[112] Carpenter (ed.), *Born of War*.

[113] Waxman, *Women in the Holocaust*; Lerna Ekmekcioglu, *Recovering Armenia: The Limits of Belonging in Post-Genocide Turkey* (Stanford: Stanford University Press, 2016); Georgina Holmes, *Women and War in Rwanda: Gender, Media and the Representation of Genocide* (London and Oxford: Bloomsbury, 2013).

Alternately, and more hopefully, the skills women gain through socialization can contribute in important ways to peacebuilding, as Jennie Burnet argues in *Genocide Lives in Us: Women, Memory and Silence in Rwanda*: '[T]raditional Rwandan roles of women as social mediators between households in the community and between the patrilineages joined by their marriages gave women strategic access to remake, or at least to challenge, divisions within communities created or reinforced by violent conflict'.[114] Projects of gender equality also hold out the potential to reduce vulnerability to armed conflict and genocide.

If we are going to be serious about genocide prevention, gendered understandings of the crime will be critical. They offer us not only insights into the harm done to half of the human population, but also insights into the development of genocidal processes. These insights have the potential to identify red flags decades before armed conflict and offer more effective means of addressing genocide in its wake. Humanity is facing unparalleled challenges in the twenty-first century that will most certainly make our societies more vulnerable to genocide.[115] Gender research can contribute to more peaceful and sustainable societies, as well as a more peaceful and sustainable international order, which is our only hope of forging both the strength and the resilience we will need if we are to avoid the worst.

Select Bibliography

Bemporad, Elissa and Joyce W. Warren (eds.), *Women and Genocide: Survivors, Victims, Perpetrators* (Bloomington: Indiana University Press, 2018).

Brown, Sara, *Gender and the Genocide in Rwanda* (New York: Routledge, 2018).

Burnet, Jennie, *Genocide Lives in Us: Women, Memory and Silence in Rwanda* (Madison: University of Wisconsin Press, 2012).

Carpenter, R. Charli (ed.), *Born of War: Protecting Children of Sexual Violence Survivors in Conflict Zones* (Sterline: Kumarian Press, 2007).

DiGeorgio-Lutz, JoAnn and Donna Gosbee (eds.), *Women and Genocide: Gendered Experiences of Violence, Survival, and Resistance* (Toronto: Women's Press, 2016).

---

[114] Jennie Burnet, *Genocide Lives in Us: Women, Memory and Silence in Rwanda* (Madison: University of Wisconsin Press, 2012).

[115] Alex Alvarez, *Unstable Ground: Climate Change, Conflict and Genocide* (Lanham: Rowman & Littlefield, 2017).

Ekmekcioglu, Lerna, *Recovering Armenia: The Limits of Belonging in Post-Genocide Turkey* (Stanford: Stanford University Press, 2016).

Goldenberg, Myrna and Amy H. Shapiro (eds.), *Different Horrors, Same Hell: Gender and the Holocaust* (Seattle/London: University of Washington Press, 2013).

Hedgepeth, Sonja, and Rochelle Saidel (eds.), *Sexual Violence against Jewish Women during the Holocaust* (Hanover, NH and London: Brandeis University Press/University Press of New England, 2010).

Holmes, Georgina, *Women and War in Rwanda: Gender, Media and the Representation of Genocide* (London/Oxford: Bloomsbury, 2013).

Jones, Adam (ed.), *Gendercide and Genocide* (Nashville: Vanderbildt University Press, 2004).

Jones, Ann, *War Is Not Over When It's Over* (New York: Metropolitan Books, Henry Holt and Company, 2010).

Kühne, Thomas, *The Rise and Fall of Comradeship: Hitler's Soldiers, Male Bonding and Mass Violence in the Twentieth Century* (Cambridge: Cambridge University Press, 2017).

Lower, Wendy, *Hitler's Furies: German Women in the Nazi Killing Fields* (Boston: Houghton Mifflin, 2013).

O'Brien, Melanie, *Criminalising Peacekeepers: Modernising National Approaches to Sexual Exploitation and Abuse* (New York: Palgrave Macmillan, 2017).

Randall, Amy (ed.), *Genocide and Gender in the Twentieth Century: A Comparative Survey* (London: Bloomsbury, 2015).

Rittner, Carol, and John K. Roth. *Rape: Weapon of War and Genocide* (Minnesota: Paragon House, 2012).

Rittner, Carol, and John K. Roth (eds.), *Teaching About Rape as a Weapon of War and Genocide* (London: Palgrave Macmillan, 2016).

Taylor, Christopher C., *Sacrifice as Terror: The Rwandan Genocide of 1994* (Oxford/New York: Berg, 1999).

Waxman, Zoë, *Women in the Holocaust: A Feminist History* (New York: Oxford University Press, 2017).

5

Ideology and Genocide

Jonathan Leader Maynard

Introduction

The suggestion that genocidal violence is rooted in certain ideological foundations has been one of the most consistent arguments of Genocide Studies scholars throughout the history of the discipline. In *The Origins of Totalitarianism*, first published in 1951, Hannah Arendt emphasized the distinct character of totalitarian ideologies in generating the political demand for group elimination.[1] In his 1981 classic *Genocide: Its Political Use in the Twentieth Century*, Leo Kuper asserted that 'ideological is a necessary pre-condition for genocide',[2] since ideologies like Nazism or Stalinism dehumanize victims in ways critical for exterminatory violence. In 2003, Barbara Harff's influential quantitative analysis identified 'exclusionary ideology' as one of the six primary risk factors for genocides and politicides,[3] while Scott Straus, in one of the most prominent recent studies of genocide, concludes that: 'to explain variation—to explain why countries with similar crises experience different outcomes—the role of ideology is essential'.[4]

---

[1] Hannah Arendt, *The Origins of Totalitarianism* (Orlando: Harcourt Books, 1951/1976).

[2] Leo Kuper, *Genocide: Its Political Use in the Twentieth Century* (New Haven: Yale University Press, 1981), 84.

[3] Barbara Harff, 'No Lessons Learned from the Holocaust? Assessing Risks of Genocide and Political Mass Murder since 1955', *American Political Science Review* 97:1 (2003), 57–73.

[4] Scott Straus, *Making and Unmaking Nations: War, Leadership and Genocide in Modern Africa* (Ithaca: Cornell University Press, 2015), x.

Yet beneath this widespread awareness of ideology's relevance in genocide lies substantial disagreement and uncertainty over *how* it matters, and *how much* it matters compared to other factors. Is there a crucial ideological dimension to all genocides, or is it only central in a special 'ideological' subset of cases? What are the most crucial features of certain ideologies which imbues them with genocidal potential? Do ideologies provide driving motives for genocide or do they merely offer post-hoc rationalizations for the violence? For whom do genocidal ideologies typically resonate: are they only central for state leaders or does their influence penetrate deeper into the mass population and rank-and-file killers? While Genocide Studies has yielded outstanding research on the ideological backgrounds and dynamics of many specific cases, it has proven difficult to translate such work into any consensus answers to these comparative theoretical questions.

Scholarly disagreement is not, of course, intrinsically unwelcome. But the extent of uncertainty over ideology's role reflects, I suggest, some deeper problems with the way debates over ideology have evolved in Genocide Studies. For a start, many discussions have taken as their centre of gravity the controversy over Daniel Goldhagen's contention that widespread German enthusiasm for 'eliminationist antisemitism' provided the necessary and sufficient motivational cause for the Holocaust.[5] In 1998, Dirk Moses expressed the concern that 'the polarizing effect of Goldhagen's exaggerated emphasis on the power of anti-Semitism might make ideologically centered arguments implausible', and this is visible in several relatively sceptical analyses of ideology's role in genocide and mass killing.[6] Discussions of ideology's role in genocide have also been heavily structured by the 'intentionalist-functionalist debate' in Holocaust

---

[5] Daniel Goldhagen, *Hitler's Willing Executioners: Ordinary Germans and the Holocaust* (London: Abacus, 1996). See also Christopher R. Browning, *Ordinary Men: Reserve Police Battalion 101 and the Final Solution in Poland* (London: Penguin Books, 1992/ 2001), 191–224; Gavriel Rosenfeld, 'The Controversy That Isn't: The Debate Over Daniel J. Goldhagen's Hitler's Willing Executioners in Comparative Perspective', *Contemporary European History* 8:2 (1999), 249–73.

[6] A. Dirk Moses, 'Structure and Agency in the Holocaust: Daniel J. Goldhagen and His Critics', *History and Theory* 37:2 (1998), 194–219, here 218.

historiography between those who stress the centrality of elite ambitions
for genocidal policies (often seen as the natural home for ideological
explanations) and those who stress the 'cumulative radicalization'
towards genocide as a product of bureaucratic thinking and organizational imperatives (frequently characterized as implying a more constrained role for ideology).[7] Finally, scholars have often assumed that
ideologies must be fixed macro-level phenomena which therefore cannot
explain spatial or temporal variation within specific genocides (as though
ideologies must be unchanging and uniformly adhered to across society)
and cannot explain contrasting behaviour towards different victim
groups (as though ideologies make identical claims about every potential
category of victims).[8]

In mapping and consolidating contemporary research on ideology
and genocide in this chapter, I encourage Genocide Studies to move
beyond these assumptions and associations. Ideology should not be
narrowly identified with Goldhagen, intentionalism, or static macro-
level explanations. More recent research on genocide has increasingly
emphasized the complex links between ideologies and violence, has
highlighted intra-case variation in ideology, and has used such variation to explain regional, temporal, and target-group contrasts in
how genocide unfolds.[9] This chapter seeks to entrench this trend,

[7] See Moses, 'Structure and Agency', 199–209; Donald Bloxham, 'Organized
Mass Murder: Structure, Participation, and Motivation in Comparative Perspective', *Holocaust and Genocide Studies* 22:2 (2008), 203–45.

[8] Charles King, 'Can There Be a Political Science of the Holocaust?', *Perspectives
on Politics* 10:2 (2012), 323–41, here 331–2; Kjell Anderson, *Perpetrating Genocide:
A Criminological Account* (Abingdon: Routledge, 2017), 7; Maureen S. Hiebert,
Constructing Genocide and Mass Violence: Society, Crisis, Identity (Abingdon: Routledge,
2017), 138.

[9] See e.g. Aristotle A. Kallis, 'Race, "Value" and the Hierarchy of Human Life:
Ideological and Structural Determinants of National Socialist Policy-making',
Journal of Genocide Research 7:1 (2005), 5–30; Alexander Laban Hinton, *Why Did
They Kill? Cambodia in the Shadow of Genocide* (Berkeley: University of California Press,
2005), esp. 22–31; Aristotle A. Kallis, *Genocide and Fascism: The Eliminationist Drive in
Fascist Europe* (New York: Routledge, 2009); Diana Dumitru and Carter Johnson,
'Constructing Interethnic Conflict and Cooperation: Why Some People Harmed
Jews and Others Helped Them during the Holocaust in Romania', *World Politics*
63:1 (2011), 1–42; Geoffrey Robinson, '"Down to the Very Roots": The Indones-
ian Army's Role in the Mass Killings of 1965–66', *Journal of Genocide Research* 19:4

endorsing an approach to studying ideology in genocide which 'weaves macrolevel and microlevel analysis to comprehend local motivations and the cultural patterning of mass violence'.[10] I do so by examining three questions which are central to debates over ideology's role in genocide: first, what imbues certain ideologies with genocidal potential, and how 'extraordinary' a break from conventional politics do such ideologies represent; second, how do ideologies relate to more self-interested or 'pragmatic' motives for violence; and third, how do ideologies causally influence perpetrators' actions in genocide?

Since it is an infamously slippery concept, I should clarify that I conceptualize 'ideology' broadly, as the *distinctive political worldviews of individuals, groups, and organizations, that provide sets of interpretive and evaluative ideas for guiding political thought and action.*[11] Ideologies are, thus, sets of ideas both about how the political world *is* and how it *should be*—involving distinctive narratives and purportedly factual beliefs as much as values and ideals.[12] This broad conceptualization is consistent with how most modern research understands ideology, and treats ideologies as normal and ubiquitous features of politics rather than some sort of 'special', highly systematic, dogmatic, or idealistic belief-system.[13] This does not make ideology matter by conceptual fiat—ideologies could be commonplace but matter little for

(2017), 465–86; Adam Scharpf, 'Ideology and State Terror: How Officer Beliefs Shaped Repression During Argentina's "Dirty War"', *Journal of Peace Research* 55:2 (2018), 206–21.

[10] Hinton, *Why Did They Kill?*, 31.

[11] See also Malcolm B. Hamilton, 'The Elements of the Concept of Ideology', *Political Studies* 35 (1987), 18–38; Michael Freeden, *Ideologies and Political Theory: A Conceptual Approach* (Oxford: Oxford University Press, 1996), 3; John T. Jost, Christopher M. Federico, and Jaime Napier, 'Political Ideology: Its Structure, Functions and Elective Affinities', *Annual Review of Psychology* 60 (2009), 307–37, here 309.

[12] Pamela E. Oliver and Hank Johnston, 'What a Good Idea! Ideologies and Frames in Social Movement Research', *Mobilization: An International Quarterly Review* 4:1 (2000), 37–54, here 44.

[13] See e.g. Aletta Norval, 'The Things We Do With Words—Contemporary Approaches to the Analysis of Ideology', *British Journal of Political Science* 30:2 (2000), 313–46, here 316; Alex Alvarez, 'Destructive Beliefs: Genocide and the Role of

behaviour. But it does allow for a broad range of different theoretical perspectives on how ideologies might matter and what kinds of ideologies may be most pernicious in encouraging genocide.

Characterizing Genocidal Ideologies

What gives certain ideologies genocidal potential? Up to a point, genocide scholars appear to agree on a basic answer to this question: genocidal ideologies are vitally characterized by ideas that make certain categories of persons appear outside, and irreconcilably threatening to, the perpetrators' political community. They are, in Harff's terminology, *exclusionary* ideologies, or for Goldhagen, *eliminationist* ideologies.[14] This, indeed, is why genocidal ideologies are often seen as crucial. While all sorts of prejudices, political crises, and material circumstances may promote general hostility and violence against a certain group, genocide goes beyond this—it involves *eliminationist categorical violence* aimed at destroying, in some sense, a group as such. The basic argument for ideology's importance in genocide is that more 'objective' material or political circumstances can rarely, if ever, explain why a state would resort to such a policy, especially given the heavy costs, risks, and moral violations associated with genocide. It takes a special ideological construction of the victims as constituting an *intense and intrinsic collective threat*, scholars argue, to explain why genocide, rather than some more limited coercive or repressive measure, is deployed.[15] Ideological dehumanization of victims is also widely emphasized, as this helps to frame victims as intrinsic threats, and

---

Ideology', in A. Smeulers and R. Haveman (eds.), *Supranational Criminology: Towards a Criminology of International Crimes* (Antwerpen: Intersentia, 2008), 213–32, here 217; Francisco Gutiérrez Sanín and Elisabeth Jean Wood, 'Ideology in Civil War: Instrumental Adoption and Beyond', *Journal of Peace Research* 51:2 (2014), 213–26, here 214.

[14] Harff, 'No Lessons Learned', 62–3; Daniel Goldhagen, *Worse Than War: Genocide, Eliminationism and the Ongoing Assault on Humanity* (London: Abacus, 2010).

[15] Straus, *Making and Unmaking Nations*, ch.1; Hiebert, *Constructing Genocide*; Anderson, *Perpetrating Genocide*, 73–4.

also facilitates violence by allowing many perpetrators to 'morally disengage' from the human consequences of their actions.[16]

Beyond this, however, scholars diverge in their characterization of the essential ideological foundations of such exclusionary or eliminationist sentiments. What might be identified as the prevailing 'traditional' view portrays genocide as driven by relatively *extraordinary ideological goals* centred around totalitarian, revolutionary, utopian, and/or supremacist aims and values.[17] Eric Weitz, for example, presents genocides as generally the product of 'ideologies of race and nation, revolutionary regimes with vast utopian ambitions [and] moments of crisis generated by war and domestic upheaval'.[18] Similarly, Robert Melson stresses the interaction of revolution and ideology in genocides where '[t]o respond to the revolutionary situation and to implement their ideological desires [revolutionaries] may destroy not only the old regime's institutions but also their political opponents and the communal groups and classes that they identify with their enemies'.[19] Manus Midlarsky likewise presents the roots of mass violence and genocide as lying in 'totalist' forms of extremism which 'share a vision of society which is radically at variance with that existing at the time of their formulation'.[20] Many of the most studied cases—the Armenian genocide, the Holocaust, genocidal campaigns in Stalin's USSR, mass atrocities and genocides under the Khmer Rouge, and the Rwandan genocide—have been invoked in support of this view.[21]

---

[16] Albert Bandura, 'Moral Disengagement in the Perpetration of Inhumanities', *Personality and Social Psychology Review* 3:3 (1999), 193–209.

[17] Kuper, *Genocide*, ch. 5; Goldhagen, *Hitler's Willing Executioners*, chs. 1 and 16; Elihu D. Richter, Dror Kris Markus, and Casey Tait, 'Incitement, Genocide, Genocidal Terror, and the Upstream Role of Indoctrination: Can Epidemiologic Models Predict and Prevent?', *Public Health Reviews* 39:30 (2018), 1–22.

[18] Eric D. Weitz, *A Century of Genocide: Utopias of Race and Nation* (Princeton: Princeton University Press, 2003), 15. See also Alex Alvarez, *Genocidal Crimes* (Abingdon: Routledge, 2010), 62–73.

[19] Robert Melson, *Revolution and Genocide: On the Origins of the Armenian Genocide and the Holocaust* (Chicago: University of Chicago Press, 1992), 260.

[20] Manus Midlarsky, *Origins of Political Extremism: Mass Violence in the Twentieth Century and Beyond* (Cambridge: Cambridge University Press, 2011), 12.

[21] Karl D. Jackson, 'The Ideology of Total Revolution', in Karl D. Jackson (ed.), *Cambodia 1975–1978: Rendezvous with Death* (Princeton: Princeton University Press, 1989), 37–78; Melson, *Revolution and Genocide*, chs. 5–7 and 9; Robert Melson,

At the same time, several scholars express concerns about this characterization. With Goldhagen primarily in his sights, James Waller contends that: 'It is too easy [to focus on] *only* an extraordinary culture, like Germany, and *only* an allegedly extraordinary ideology, like eliminationist anti-Semitism'.[22] Mark Levene challenges the emphasis on extraordinarily racist or totalitarian ideologies for portraying genocide as 'both a radically criminal and abhorrent act, outside of, and distinct from, the dominant and accepted norms of liberal state and society'.[23] Donald Bloxham and Dirk Moses likewise suggest that we should be suspicious of 'a classically liberal understanding of genocide, where the crime results above all from aberrant political ideologies and oppressive political systems, and where the problem of genocide can be solved by the reassertion of the healthy norms of international democratic society'.[24] Such scholars often emphasize that, as Weitz himself notes: 'Historically all sorts of regimes have perpetrated genocides.'[25] While less well studied, both relatively liberal states and non-revolutionary autocracies have been charged with employing genocidal violence in, for example, California, German South West Africa, British Tasmania, Guatemala, and Indonesia.[26] While it may be tempting to conclude that these are simply not 'ideological genocides', this relies on a circular limitation of

---

'Modern Genocide in Rwanda: Ideology, Revolution, War and Mass Murder in an African State', in Robert Gellately and Ben Kiernan (eds.), *The Specter of Genocide: Mass Murder in Historical Perspective* (Cambridge: Cambridge University Press, 2003), 325–38; Weitz, *Century of Genocide*, chs. 2–4; Norman Naimark, *Stalin's Genocides* (Princeton: Princeton University Press, 2010).

[22] James Waller, *Becoming Evil: How Ordinary People Commit Genocide and Mass Killing* (Oxford: Oxford University Press, 2007), 53.

[23] Mark Levene, *Genocide in the Age of the Nation State I: The Meaning of Genocide* (London: I.B. Tauris & Co. Ltd., 2008), 9.

[24] Donald Bloxham and A. Dirk Moses, 'Editors' Introduction: Changing Themes in the Study of Genocide', in Donald Bloxham and A. Dirk Moses (eds.), *The Oxford Handbook of Genocide Studies* (Oxford: Oxford University Press, 2010), 1–16, here 9.

[25] Weitz, *Century of Genocide*, 12. See also Weitz, *Century of Genocide*, 236–7.

[26] Benjamin Madley, 'Patterns of Frontier Genocide 1803–1910: The Aboriginal Tasmanians, the Yuki of California and the Herero of Namibia', *Journal of Genocide Research* 6:2 (2004), 167–92; Ashley Riley Sousa, ' "They will be hunted

'ideology' to extraordinary revolutionary or utopian worldviews. Scholars of these genocides generally agree that colonial and ultra-conservative ideologies were crucial in motivating and legitimating the violence.

In contrast to the traditional emphasis on *extraordinary ideological goals and values*, then, an alternative view suggests that the crucial ideological foundations of genocide are generally rooted in *radicalized or distorted versions of what are nevertheless familiar and conventional political claims and concerns*. Jürgen Zimmerer suggests, for example, that genocide can be sustained by an 'ideology [which] can be as basic as the belief in the existence of inferior and superior human beings, i.e. of a racial hierarchy. It does not necessarily need the "elaborate" and long standing specificity of anti-Semitism, for example.'[27] In particular, scholars who emphasize the link between genocide and modern nation-building projects stress that *nationalism* is a ubiquitous component of modern politics, and is intrinsically dependent on the definition of certain segments of the population as legitimate parts of the political community, with other segments necessarily excluded or subordinated.[28] It is in this sense that Daniel Moshman suggests that 'genocide is an extreme result of normal identity processes'.[29] If those groups seen as 'outside' the national community are also perceived as severe threats, elites may contemplate genocide under conditions of social crisis. By contrast, when ideological narratives of the nation

---

down like wild beasts and destroyed!'": A Comparative Study of Genocide in California and Tasmania', *Journal of Genocide Research* 6:2 (2004), 193–209; Benjamin Madley, *An American Genocide: The United States and the California Indian Catastrophe* (New Haven: Yale University Press, 2016); Roddy Brett, *The Origins and Dynamics of Genocide: Political Violence in Guatemala* (Houndmills: Palgrave Macmillan, 2016).

[27] Jurgen Zimmerer, 'From the Editors: Environmental Genocide? Climate Change, Mass Violence and the Question of Ideology', *Journal of Genocide Research* 9:3 (2007), 349–51, here 350.

[28] Michael Mann, *The Dark Side of Democracy: Explaining Ethnic Cleansing* (Cambridge: Cambridge University Press, 2005); Levene, *Meaning of Genocide*; Christopher Powell, *Barbaric Civilization: A Critical Sociology of Genocide* (Montreal: McGill-Queen's University Press, 2011).

[29] Daniel Moshman, 'Us and Them: Identity and Genocide', *Identity* 7:2 (2007), 115–35, here 115.

involve an inclusive vision of the political community, with minority groups still understood as members, such threat perceptions are much less likely, and restraints on genocide much stronger.[30]

A distinct though compatible argument focuses more on the ideological roots of genocide in *war and national security* than on nationalism and nation-building per se—though these clearly overlap. Several scholars emphasize that ideological justifications of genocide are built on conventional claims about threat, self-defence, national security, and state authority. In this sense, Martin Shaw suggests, genocide is a form of 'degenerate war' guided by a 'construction of civilian groups as enemies, not only in a social or political but also in a military sense, to be destroyed'.[31] While such an ideological construction *can* be encouraged by revolutionary ambitions and vast supremacist projects of racial purification, such extraordinary aims are not necessary. Especially in conditions of social crisis and conflict, conventional security politics can be used to promote genocide once connections between serious threats and civilian groups are ideologically promoted. Thus Hutu military elites in Rwanda issued warnings, prior to the genocide in 1994, of 'Tutsi inside or outside the country, extremist and nostalgic for power . . . and who wish to reconquer power by all means necessary including arms'.[32] The Memorandum of the Serbian Academy of Sciences, often cited as laying the ideological foundations for Serbian violence in the 1990s, similarly affirmed that: 'Except for the period of the existence of the NDH,

---

[30] Straus, *Making and Unmaking Nations*, ch. 3.

[31] Martin Shaw, *What is Genocide?* (Cambridge: Polity Press, 2007), 111. See also Omar Shahabudin McDoom, 'The Psychology of Threat in Intergroup Conflict: Emotions, Rationality, and Opportunity in the Rwandan Genocide', *International Security* 37:2 (2012), 119–55.

[32] Benjamin A. Valentino, *Final Solutions: Mass Killing and Genocide in the 20th Century* (Ithaca: Cornell University Press, 2004), 182; Scott Straus, 'Retreating from the Brink: Theorizing Mass Violence and the Dynamics of Restraint', *Perspectives on Politics* 10 (2012), 342–62, here 353. See also Philip Zimbardo, *The Lucifer Effect: How Good People Turn Evil* (London: Rider Books, 2007), 13; Donald G. Dutton, *The Psychology of Genocide, Massacres and Extreme Violence: Why 'Normal' People Come to Commit Atrocities* (Westport: Praeger Security International, 2007), 106.

Serbs were never so endangered as they are today.'[33] As genocidal ideologies incorporate and employ such constructions of threat, observes Jacques Sémelin, 'massacre takes on the appearance of an act of war'.[34]

This ideological radicalization of relatively conventional security politics has been most strongly emphasized in anti-communist campaigns in Latin America guided by the 'National Security Doctrine'—a set of US-promoted ideas which encouraged the association of almost all left-wing groups with a purported international communist conspiracy and identified massive collective violence as a necessary 'defensive' response. Latin American autocracies were principally ultraconservative rather than revolutionary or utopian regimes, yet their embrace of the National Security Doctrine encouraged the identification of broad civilian groups, including indigenous populations, as dangerous threats to society that needed to be crushed. Thus, at the height of the Argentinian 'Dirty War', the military regime targeted mass violence against the extremely general category of 'subversion'—defined as 'anyone who opposes the Argentine way of life'.[35] Daniel Feierstein has influentially argued that this campaign ultimately took on a genocidal form.[36] In the fight against a left-wing insurgency in Guatemala, genocidal killings against the Maya population in the early 1980s were likewise justified by the claim that, as the press secretary to *de facto* President Efraín Ríos Montt summarized:

> The guerrillas won over many Indian collaborators . . . Therefore the Indians were subversives, right? And how do you fight subversion? Clearly, you had to kill Indians because they were collaborating with subversion. And [human rights advocates] would say, 'you're

---

[33] Weitz, *Century of Genocide*, 195–6. The NDH was the fascist Ustaše state of Croatia established by Nazi Germany and Fascist Italy during the Second World War.

[34] Jacques Semelin, *Purify and Destroy: The Political Uses of Massacre and Genocide* (London: Hurst & Company, 2007), 145.

[35] David Pion-Berlin, 'The National Security Doctrine, Military Threat Perception, and the "Dirty War" in Argentina', *Comparative Political Studies* 21:3 (1988), 382–407, here 401.

[36] Daniel Feierstein, 'Political Violence in Argentina and Its Genocidal Characteristics', *Journal of Genocide Research* 8:2 (2006), 149–68.

massacring innocent people'. But they weren't innocent. They had sold
out to subversion.[37]

This conception of the indigenous 'Indian' population was likewise
used to justify genocidal violence to soldiers at the rank-and-file level
in Guatemala. Roddy Brett reports how, at a three-day massacre in
Cuarto Pueblo:

> According to those interviewed, a lieutenant encouraged the soldiers to
> finish things off *properly*, explaining that all the inhabitants were allies of
> the guerrilla and that the only way to end the conflict was by exter-
> minating them all. The lieutenant carried a list of other villages whose
> residents allegedly supported the guerrilla, and he congratulated the
> troops on their success, boasting that the guerrilla had one less village to
> turn to.[38]

The resulting violence did not reflect a rationally necessary response
to counterinsurgency—indeed, it frequently proved counterproductive.[39]
But nor did it reflect especially 'extraordinary' ideological ambitions.
Racism was—as Weitz would suggest—important, but it was not
exceptional by the standards of many countries, and cannot explain
the significant number of non-indigenous victims of state violence in
Guatemala.[40] What linked racism to genocide was an ultraconservative militaristic ideology that melded intense anticommunism, US-
influenced counterinsurgency doctrine, and a harsh developmentalist
project of nation-building. All three represented highly brutal versions
of what are nevertheless familiar right-wing, security-centric, and
nationalist ideological themes. Similar arguments could be made
regarding campaigns of genocide/politicide in, for example, Indonesia 1965–66, Iraq 1988–91, or the Former Yugoslavia 1992–95.

Growing attention to such cases suggests, then, a re-evaluation of
the truly *essential* character of genocidal ideologies. It remains the case
that the most violent regimes of the twentieth century—including

[37] Valentino, *Final Solutions*, 212.

[38] Brett, *Origins and Dynamics of Genocide*, 168–9.

[39] Virginia Garrard-Burnett, *Terror in the Land of the Holy Spirit: Guatemala Under
General Efraín Ríos Montt, 1982–1983* (Oxford: Oxford University Press, 2009),
25–6; Brett, *Origins and Dynamics of Genocide*, 115 and 31–2.

[40] Garrard-Burnett, *Terror in the Land of the Holy Spirit*, 17.

Nazi Germany, the Soviet Union, Mao's China, the Khmer Rouge, and the Ottoman Empire under the Young Turks—have typically adhered to revolutionary, utopian, and supremacist ideologies of some form, and such ideologies are a demonstrable risk factor for genocides and mass violence.[41] Moreover, even in non-revolutionary states, nationalist and militarist justifications of violence frequently involve transformative, racist, and supremacist ideas in a broad sense.[42] But truly *extraordinary* ideological projects may be better seen as intensifiers of violence—which expand its likely scale and scope— rather than necessary ideological preconditions of genocide. Geno- cidal ideologies can be built, instead, on commonplace notions of a primary moral and political community, self-defence, and military necessity, which are linked to highly distorted representations of civilian groups as deeply and collectively threatening.

Ideology, Pragmatism, and Self-Interest

Closely related to these debates over the degree to which genocidal ideologies represent an extraordinary break from conventional polit- ics are questions concerning the relationship between ideology and what are variously described as more 'strategic', 'material', 'eco- nomic', 'self-interested', or 'pragmatic' drivers of genocidal violence. Typically, genocide scholars have assumed a fundamental contrast between ideology and such pragmatic concerns. This is most visible in the many efforts to typologize genocides. Helen Fein influentially distinguishes, for example, between ideological, retributive, despotic, and developmental genocides, while Frank Chalk and Kurt Jonassohn distinguish between genocides which 'implement . . . an ideology' from those which 'eliminate a real or potential threat . . . spread terror among real or potential enemies . . . [or] acquire economic wealth'.[43]

---

[41] Nam Kyu Kim, 'Revolutionary Leaders and Mass Killing', *Journal of Conflict Resolution* 62:2 (2018), 289–317.

[42] See e.g. Feierstein, 'Political violence in Argentina', 159.

[43] Helen Fein, *Genocide: A Sociological Perspective* (London: Sage Publications, 1990); Frank Chalk and Kurt Jonassohn, *The History and Sociology of Genocide: Analyses and Case Studies* (New Haven: Yale University Press, 1990), 29; Harff, 'No Lessons Learned', 61.

Indeed, some scholars suggest that ideology *requires* a kind of 'killing for killing's sake' genocidal campaign disconnected from broader political goals.[44] In parallel, some scholars dispute the helpfulness of 'genocide' as a theoretical construct, on the grounds that it overstates singular ideologically-grounded motives and thereby misrepresents the messy overlap of fear, local rivalries, and self-interest that actually drives mass violence on the ground.[45]

Though this firm distinction between ideology and pragmatic self-interest may strike some as intuitive, it is increasingly rejected in both genocide scholarship and specialist work on ideology. Few ideologies are actually silent on pragmatic concerns with power, security, economics, or self-interest. Indeed, retribution, elimination of threats and enemies, the upholding of a despotic regime, or the pursuit of economic wealth and development *can all be deeply ideological activities*. The US's massacres of Native Americans, Belgium's murderous exploitation of the Congo, and Germany's annihilation of the Herero people of South West Africa were, for example, variously motivated by economic interests and the perceived need to repress or punish dangerous 'rebels'. But they were also, as Alex Bellamy points out, inextricably bound up with European colonialist ideology, and its denigration of indigenous populations as inferior beings deprived of moral rights.[46]

Moreover, many genocidal ideologies rely in large part on appeals to material and practical grievances in justifying extreme violence against civilian groups. Mere intergroup differences are not pervasively linked to conflict—indeed, there is no statistical relationship between the degree of group diversity within societies and their propensity towards violence.[47] What matters, as Randall Collins

[44] John E. Roemer, 'Rationalizing Revolutionary Ideology', *Econometrica* 53:1 (1985), 85–108; Neil J. Mitchell, *Agents of Atrocity: Leaders, Followers, and the Violation of Human Rights in Civil War* (New York: Palgrave Macmillan, 2004), 38 and 41.

[45] See e.g. Christian Gerlach, *Extremely Violent Societies: Mass Violence in the Twentieth-Century World* (Cambridge: Cambridge University Press, 2010), ch. 1.

[46] Alex J. Bellamy, *Massacres and Morality: Mass Atrocities in an Age of Civilian Immunity* (Oxford: Oxford University Press, 2012), 81–95.

[47] Matthew Krain, 'State-Sponsored Mass Murder: The Onset and Severity of Genocides and Politicides', *Journal of Conflict Resolution* 41:3 (1997), 331–60; James D. Fearon and David D. Laitin, 'Ethnicity, Insurgency, and Civil War', *The*

puts it, is how 'allegedly long-standing ethnic hostilities nevertheless are ideologically mobilized at particular points in time'.[48] It is frequently via the assertion of material grievances that such ideological mobilization occurs, and the combination of intergroup divisions with significant material or political inequalities is associated with violent conflict.[49] In the Cambodian 'autogenocide' and Stalinist 'dekulakization', for example, material inequalities were weaponized via ideological narratives of criminally exploitative segments of society who had to be purged. Often the grievances may be largely or wholly an invention of the genocidal ideology, but nevertheless successful in generating a belief of deeply unjust exploitation subjected on society by a minority group. In both the Holocaust and Armenian genocide, a pervasive narrative of the parasitic prosperity of Jewish and Armenian communities was utilized to generate the perception of such groups as threats. In all such cases, material and pragmatic concerns cannot be divorced from the ideological claims and narratives within which they are understood.

In consequence, limiting ideology to only denote highly idealistic motives for genocide disconnected from economics, security, and self-interest significantly distorts our thinking about genocidal violence. Consider, for example, Peter du Preez's effort to elucidate such a distinction:

> An ideological form of genocide [includes] the concept of ideological
> xenophobia as in the Nazi and the Armenian cases, where the purpose

American Political Science Review 97:1 (2003), 75–90; Erik Gartzke and Kristian Skrede Gleditsch, 'Identity and Conflict: Ties that Bind and Differences that Divide', *European Journal of International Relations* 12:1 (2006), 53–87; Alexander B. Downes, *Targeting Civilians in War* (Ithaca: Cornell University Press, 2008), 48–56.

[48] Randall Collins, 'Micro and Macro Causes of Violence', *International Journal of Conflict and Violence* 3:1 (2009), 9–22, here 20.

[49] See Joan Esteban and Gerald Schneider, 'Polarization and Conflict: Theoretical and Empirical Issues', *Journal of Peace Research* 45, 2 (2008), 131–41; Lars Erik Cederman, Nils B. Weidmann, and Kristian Skrede Gleditsch, 'Horizontal Inequalities and Ethnonationalist Civil War: A Global Comparison', *American Political Science Review* 105, 3 (2011), 478–95. See also Ervin Staub, *The Roots of Evil* (Cambridge: Cambridge University Press, 1989).

was to purify the nation by eliminating all alien elements . . . What of pragmatic genocides, driven by fear, hatred, material needs and the desire to dominate? Theory is rudimentary, though some mimicry may occur. Noticeably absent though is the influence of intellectuals . . . Where the ideologues write massive romances about the destiny of the people, the nature of the enemy and the course of history . . . the pragmatists reduce things to the self-evident. There are enemies. They are dangerous . . .[50]

This passage highlights the problems of dichotomizing ideology and pragmatic self-interest. The cases du Preez classifies as ideological (including the Nazi Holocaust, Stalinist dekulakization, or Armenian genocide) are hardly lacking in the dynamics of 'fear, hatred, material needs and the desire to dominate' found in those cases he describes as pragmatic (such as the Herero genocide and Cold War-era violence in Rwanda). It is also false to suggest that the influence of 'intellectuals' and 'theory' is absent in the latter campaigns. What of the racial pseudoscience invoked to justify colonial domination, or the invented foundation myths of modern Rwanda, fostered and encouraged by Belgian colonial masters in order to facilitate their hegemony?[51] These are not just 'self-evident' features of how the world is, but ideological constructs central to the justification of violence. Indeed, as du Preez acknowledges at other points, 'pragmatic' genocides are *not* usually wars on 'real' enemies who present a genuine threat, but imagined enemies constructed through the distinctive worldviews of the perpetrators. In what sense, then, do 'pragmatists reduce things to the self-evident'?[52]

By contrast, questioning this dichotomy between ideology and pragmatism has allowed recent Genocide Studies scholarship to explore the important interactions between ideologies and various categories of motives in genocidal perpetration. As Alvarez emphasizes: '[G]enocides take place for a variety of reasons and can include economic, political, nationalistic, ethnic, and religious motivations. In

[50] Peter du Preez, *Genocide: The Psychology of Mass Murder* (London: Bowerdean and Boyars, 1994), 69–70.

[51] Melson, 'Modern Genocide in Rwanda', 326–9.

[52] Notably, du Preez ultimately waters down the tightness of this categorization considerably, observing that 'pragmatic genocides are really just debased forms of ideological genocide'—see du Preez, *Genocide*, 80.

every case, however, these motivations are intertwined with and buttressed by genocidal ideologies that provide the intellectual scaffolding upon which the genocide is constructed.'[53] This observation reflects, after all, the essential claim for the importance of ideology in genocide observed earlier—relatively 'objective' material and political self-interest may be able to predict a general willingness to employ violence, but they cannot explain why decisionmakers pursue *genocidal* violence in response. As Straus observes: '[T]he ideological vision of the leadership will shape how a state defines strategic enemies and strategic objectives, thus indicating which states are likely to respond to perceived threat with mass violence and which are not.'[54] Moreover, even the most prosaic forms of self-interest—such as desires for economic enrichment or career advancement—can be importantly interwoven with ideology within those organizations and bureaucracies engaged in the perpetration of genocide. In his leading study of the employment of slave labour in the concentration camps, for example, Michael Thad Allen stresses how many SS functionaries 'identified their individual interest so strongly with those of "the German people" or other grand entities beyond themselves [that] they readily developed genuine attachments to the ideals of those organisations which promoted their careers'.[55]

Consequently, while 'pragmatic' considerations do bear on genocidal violence, and sometimes push regimes and groups to make compromises over their ultimate ideological ideals, how they do so *itself depends on perpetrators' ideological frameworks.* For example, Aristotle Kallis observes how the Second World War created strong pragmatic pressures on the Nazi leadership to relax a range of persecutory policies—such as restrictions on female participation in the labour force, incarceration of homosexuals, and, most obviously, annihilation of Jews, Roma/Sinti, Slavs, and the medically disabled—which

---

[53] Alvarez, 'Destructive Beliefs', 220.

[54] Scott Straus, '"Destroy Them to Save Us": Theories of Genocide and the Logics of Political Violence', *Terrorism and Political Violence* 24:4 (2012), 544–60, here 549.

[55] Michael Thad Allen, *The Business of Genocide: The S.S., Slave Labour, and the Concentration Camps* (Chapel Hill: University of North Carolina Press, 2002), 114–15.

reflected ultimate Nazi ideals but fundamentally undermined Nazi war-waging.[56] In some cases, the Nazis proved somewhat responsive to such pressures: increasingly employing female labour from 1942 onwards and redesignating certain (Aryan) homosexual groups as admissible for military service. Regarding 'inferior' races, however, the Nazis made few such concessions to pragmatism. On the contrary, policy radicalization accelerated dramatically during the war. As Kallis explains, this contrasting Nazi sensitivity to practical trade-offs was itself rooted in the Nazis' varying ideological understandings of these issues. The shift in policies towards Aryan homosexuals, for example, 'was possible on the basis of both their otherwise "racial" value and the pliability that the notion of [certain forms of homosexuality as a] "curable condition" allowed—two elements that were conspicuously lacking in the case of other groups, such as the Jews and the mentally ill'.[57]

This interpenetration of ideology and pragmatic/material/strategic concerns is inevitable, because while it is common in political discourse to appeal for a 'pragmatic' rather than 'ideological' course of action, what *seems* pragmatically sensible depends on ideological assumptions about the relative importance of different goals and the likely efficacy of different policies. As Slavoj Žižek observes: '[T]he very gesture of stepping out of ideology pulls us back into it.'[58] The tendency to conceive of 'ideologies' as only very abstract, idealistic worldviews, whereas pragmatism or realpolitik are assumed to denote just 'seeing the world as it is', is both wrong and dangerous. 'There are', Neta Crawford reminds us, 'few "real" material interests that cannot be viewed in more than one way.'[59] Consequently, while pragmatic considerations assuredly matter in genocide, the conceptions of interests and strategy they appeal to are fundamentally embedded in perpetrators' ideologies.

---

[56] Kallis, 'Race, "Value" and the Hierarchy', 14–18.

[57] Ibid., 14–15.

[58] Slavoj Žižek, 'The Spectre of Ideology', in Slavoj Žižek (ed.), *Mapping Ideology* (London: Verso, 1994), 1–33, here 10.

[59] Neta C. Crawford, *Argument and Change in World Politics: Ethics, Decolonization and Humanitarian Intervention* (Cambridge: Cambridge University Press, 2002), 79.

Ideology and Action

In 1992, Robert Melson observed that while ideology appeared to be crucial in genocide, emphasizing it raised the question: 'What if anything does ideology have to do with action and behavior?'[60] Almost three decades later, there is still much uncertainty over how to answer this question. How exactly do ideologies influence the behaviour of genocide perpetrators or, for that matter, those who resist or avoid genocide? Do ideologies actually provide motives for genocidal violence, or do they play a more facilitative or enabling role? Do perpetrators follow an ideology's prescriptions because they deeply believe in the truth of the ideology, or simply rhetorically espouse the ideology out of peer pressure or cynical self-interest? No consensus answers exist to these questions.

The most conventional causal story contends that genocidal ideologies matter because perpetrators deeply believe in them, and are motivated by their ideological convictions to initiate and implement policies of mass murder. This story is advanced in its strongest form by Goldhagen, who stresses the Holocaust's roots in 'the autonomous motivating force of Nazi ideology, particularly its central component of antisemitism . . .'[61] and sees violence by the ordinary 'rank-and-file' killers as explained by the fact that 'the perpetrators, "ordinary Germans," were animated by antisemitism, by a particular *type* of antisemitism that led them to conclude that the Jews *ought to die*'.[62] Adherents to this causal story vary significantly, however, in how pervasive they present such 'true believers' in genocidal ideology as being. Goldhagen portrays almost all Germans as enthusiastic supporters of 'eliminationist antisemitism'; similarly, Elihu Richter et al. suggest that the danger and capacity for mass violence derives from the way 'ideologies are deeply embedded in the mindsets of affected populations'.[63] Other scholars, however, are more constrained. Early Holocaust scholarship typically saw true believers as dominant only amongst the Nazi leadership and its core constituencies, while much

---

[60] Melson, *Revolution and Genocide*, 7.

[61] Goldhagen, *Hitler's Willing Executioners*, 13.

[62] Ibid., 14 (emphasis in original).

[63] Richter, Markus, and Tait, 'Incitement, Genocide, Genocidal Terror', 15.

recent genocide scholarship suggests that ideological belief merely
needs to be *sufficiently* widespread—especially amongst key supporters
and rank-and-file perpetrators of the genocide—to reach a relative
tipping point that allows leaders to proceed with violence.[64]

Such scholars rarely if ever claim that ideologies are the *only*
relevant causal precondition for genocide. Manus Midlarsky, for
example, argues that 'extremists of virtually all persuasions believe
in a societal "natural order"' . . . If these convictions are held strongly,
and the political and social conditions to be detailed . . . hold, then extremist
behavior follows.'[65] Even Goldhagen, widely criticized for the 'mono-
causal' nature of his account, emphasizes that anti-Semitism provided
the necessary and sufficient *motivational* cause of the Holocaust, leaving
room for other enabling conditions. But in such accounts of ideology,
animosity towards victims rooted in strong ideological convictions
typically becomes *the central motor* of genocide. Other causal factors—
such as crisis, war, authoritarianism, or economic interests—serve as
facilitators, or even mere excuses, for violence. Concerning the Rwandan genocide, for example, Philip Verwimp contends that: 'The annihilation resulted from the revolutionary Hutu ideology which pictured
the Hutu peasantry as a subordinated and exploited class . . . There is
no doubt of the importance of the civil war [but] the civil war was not
the cause of the genocidal plan. The civil war offered merely the
pretext, the occasion to execute the final solution.'[66] What unites all
these accounts is what I call a 'true believer' account of ideology: they
all emphasize *strong ideological belief and conviction* as the key causal
mechanism linking ideology to the perpetration of genocide. Such
beliefs allow genocidal ideologies to make even horrific mass violence
look morally justified and praiseworthy to its perpetrators. As Claudia

[64] See e.g. John Weiss, *Ideology of Death: Why the Holocaust Happened in Germany*
(Chicago: Elephant Paperbacks, 1997); John Weiss, 'Daniel Goldhagen, *Hitler's
Willing Executioners*: An Historian's View', *Journal of Genocide Research* 1:2 (1999),
257–72.

[65] Midlarsky, *Origins of Political Extremism*, 20.

[66] Philip Verwimp, 'Development Ideology, the Peasantry and Genocide:
Rwanda Represented in Habyarimana's Speeches', *Journal of Genocide Research* 2:3
(2000), 325–61, here 327.

Koonz's study of *The Nazi Conscience* observes at its outset: 'The road to Auschwitz was paved with righteousness.'[67]

Many scholars are, however, rather sceptical of the claim that genocides are mainly driven by ideological true believers. They point to decades of cross-case research which suggests that relatively few perpetrators appear to match stereotypes of the 'raving ideologue'[68] motivated by 'deep, historic passions and hatreds'[69] and 'fanaticism'.[70] Reversing Verwimp's argument above, such sceptics often contend that genocide's most important roots lie elsewhere—it is ideologies which merely provide a 'pretext',[71] 'rationalization',[72] or 'afterthought'[73] for violence. Many such sceptics are influenced by research on social psychology on the way peer pressure, organizational roles, or orders from authority can induce individuals to harm others even when they lack any true belief in the rightness of such actions.[74] Others point to conditions of social and political breakdown which create incentives for violence that have little to do with ideological objectives or hatreds.[75]

In much existing genocide scholarship, then, '[i]deology is generally either viewed as a constant, inflexible political and cultural platform [or] is dismissed as the deluded justifications expressed by elite

---

[67] Claudia Koonz, *The Nazi Conscience* (Cambridge, MA: The Belknap Press of Harvard University Press, 2003), 3.

[68] Waller, *Becoming Evil*, 102.

[69] John Mueller, 'The Banality of "Ethnic War"', *International Security* 25:1 (2000), 42–70, here 43.

[70] Stathis N. Kalyvas, *The Logic of Violence in Civil War* (Cambridge: Cambridge University Press, 2006), 64–6.

[71] Lee Ann Fujii, 'The Power of Local Ties: Popular Participation in the Rwandan Genocide', *Security Studies* 17:3 (2008), 568–97, here 570.

[72] Waller, *Becoming Evil*, 49.

[73] Zimbardo, *Lucifer Effect*, 11.

[74] Paul A. Roth, 'Social Psychology and Genocide', in Donald Bloxham and A. Dirk Moses (eds.), *The Oxford Handbook of Genocide Studies* (Oxford: Oxford University Press, 2005), 198–216, here 199; Paul A. Roth, 'Hearts of Darkness: "Perpetrator History" and Why There Is No Why', *History of the Human Sciences* 17:2/3 (2004), 211–51, here 237.

[75] Gerlach, *Extremely Violent Societies*, 1–7; Susanne Karstedt, 'Contextualizing Mass Atrocity Crimes: The Dynamics of "Extremely Violent Societies"', *European Journal of Criminology* 9:5 (2012), 499–513; Charles H. Anderton and Jurgen Brauer (eds.), *Economic Aspects of Genocides, Other Mass Atrocities, and Their Prevention* (Oxford: Oxford University Press, 2016).

individuals when it suits their desires'.[76] Both these perspectives ultimately rest, however, on what I have called a 'true believer' account of ideology—the assumption that *if ideology matters*, it does so through strong ideological convictions and motives. It is the purported presence of such convictions and motives which makes ideology so important for the first camp, and their rarity which makes it relatively peripheral for the second camp. But this 'true believer' account of ideology is flawed. It is now widely appreciated across the humanities and social sciences that ideas can often influence actions even in the absence of deep belief. As such, a growing range of genocide scholars simultaneously suggest that true believers may be a minority of genocide perpetrators while also refusing to simply dismiss ideology as irrelevant for the remaining majority. Instead, such scholars focus on a broader range of psychological and social mechanisms through which ideology might shape genocidal behaviour.[77]

For a start, ideologies may be sincerely accepted and *internalized* by perpetrators in ways that are much weaker than the deep convictions of archetypal 'true believers'. Indeed, modern psychological research suggests that deep, well-formulated, and consciously convicted beliefs are relatively unusual—most ideological worldviews are rooted in a mixture of relatively intuitive values, unquestioned narratives, vague beliefs, and temporary frames of situations, policies, and actions.[78] But this does not render ideology's influence weak, since these more inchoate ideological elements can still profoundly shape how individuals interpret and evaluate different political situations and courses of action. In his analysis of ethnic violence in the Yugoslav Wars, for

[76] Elisabeth Hope Murray, *Disrupting Pathways to Genocide: The Process of Ideological Radicalization* (Houndmills: Palgrave Macmillan, 2015), 3.

[77] See also George C. Browder, 'Perpetrator Character and Motivation: An Emerging Consensus?', *Holocaust and Genocide Studies* 17:3 (2003), 480–97, here 494–5; Hinton, *Why Did They Kill?*, 25–8.

[78] Jost, Federico, and Napier, 'Political Ideology', 315–26; Jonathan Haidt, *The Righteous Mind: Why Good People are Divided by Religion and Politics* (London: Allen Lane, 2012); Paul Thagard, 'The Cognitive-Affective Structure of Political Ideologies', in Bilyana Martinovski (ed.), *Emotion in Group Decision and Negotiation* (Berlin: Springer, 2014), 51–72; Peter Hays Gries, *The Politics of American Foreign Policy: How Ideology Divides Liberals and Conservatives over Foreign Affairs* (Stanford: Stanford University Press, 2014), 43–8.

example, Anthony Oberschall emphasizes that deep, longstanding commitments to aggressive ethnic nationalism appear to have been rare. But he proposes that an ethnonationalist 'crisis frame', resonant in light of historical legacies of conflict, could be activated by elites to transform interethnic relations and justify violence.[79] Even tentative or partial acceptance of such a frame could serve to motivate individuals to engage in violence to 'defend' their community or to legitimate violence that was guided by baser motives. In his theoretical reformation of genocidal dehumanization, Rowan Savage similarly emphasizes that 'the only necessity is a narrative that legitimizes the action in question. In order to fulfil a psychological need such a "script" does not actually require wholehearted or long-term belief.'[80]

As this view suggests, even in the absence of ideological *motives* for violence, tentative or limited acceptance of ideological justifications of genocide can often serve to *legitimate* violence. This is generally an essential precondition for genocidal action since, as the political psychologists John Jost and Brenda Major observe: 'the carrying out of extreme acts of exploitation, violence and evil is socially and psychologically feasible only to the extent that perpetrators are able to make their actions seem legitimate'.[81] Alex Alvarez likewise argues that:

> To marginalize, disenfranchise, and persecute a group of people requires many citizens to accept the necessity and morality of policies of destruction and this is largely done through the manipulation of belief systems by politicians . . . genocidal killers are not generally motivated by sociopathic needs and desires but rather because they have accepted ideologies that portray the killing as necessary, just, and moral.[82]

---

[79] Anthony Oberschall, 'The Manipulation of Ethnicity: From Ethnic Cooperation to Violence and War in Yugoslavia', *Ethnic and Racial Studies* 23:6 (2000), 982–1001.

[80] Rowan Savage, 'Modern Genocidal Dehumanization: A New Model', *Patterns of Prejudice* 47:2 (2013), 139–61, here 149.

[81] John T. Jost and Brenda Major (eds.), *The Psychology of Legitimacy: Emerging Perspectives on Ideology, Justice and Intergroup Relations* (Cambridge: Cambridge University Press, 2001), 5.

[82] Alvarez, 'Destructive Beliefs', 217–18.

Consequently, even in the absence of strong ideological convictions, or central ideological motives for violence, ideologies may be essential in explaining how genocide becomes possible, and why many perpetrators willingly participate.

Sceptics might doubt that ideological legitimation is really so crucial. Individuals, it may be thought, can always come up with some suitable justifications for mass killing when other motives or incentives to engage in it are strong. Ideological justifications are thus reduced, again, to 'post-hoc rationalizations'. But the immense body of research on legitimacy, norms, and decision-making does not generally support this argument.[83] People certainly do rationalize: stretching, twisting, and reinterpreting existing moral norms to suit their material or psychological self-interest. But the capacity to engage in such reinterpretation is not universally guaranteed. Some people rationalize willingly, in ways that open the doors to enthusiastic participation in ever-escalating horrors. Others rationalize just enough to facilitate involvement but retain underlying sentiments that problematize the legitimacy of the violence and may explain their simultaneous engagement in small acts of rescue, resistance, or reluctant implementation. Still others veer away from rationalization at some point: consider Oskar Schindler's determination to save Jews in the Holocaust after witnessing the brutal liquidation of the Warsaw ghetto, despite his previous collaboration in the Nazi occupation of Poland and opportunistic membership of the Nazi party.[84] Some individuals, moreover, never rationalize—underlying convictions in the illegitimacy of action render them unwilling or unable to do so. Even when individuals are not 'true believers' guided by strong ideological motives, their private ideological attitudes and broader ideological environment may still significantly affect their capacity to become involved in genocidal violence.[85]

[83] See, in general Jost and Major, *Psychology of Legitimacy*; Crawford, *Argument and Change*.

[84] Luitgard N. Wundheiler, 'Oskar Schindler's Moral Development During the Holocaust', *Humboldt Journal of Social Relations* 13:1/2 (1986), 333–56.

[85] See Kristen Renwick Monroe, *Ethics in an Age of Terror and Genocide: Identity and Moral Choice* (Princeton: Princeton University Press, 2011).

The above arguments all still focus, however, on genuine acceptance of ideological justifications of genocide, with perpetrators cast as
individuals who 'believe in the rightness and necessity of their actions'
to at least some degree.[86] This is a crucial form of ideological influence, but it is a mistake to see it as the only link between ideologies and
action, since ideologies can also influence perpetrators who scarcely
believe in the ideology *at all*. When an ideology becomes embedded in
the institutions, norms, and policy platforms of groups, organizations,
and societies, the apparent dominance of that ideology creates pressures, incentives, opportunities, and constraints for an individual
irrespective of their personal ideological views. If most people *expect* that
most people will continue to comply with certain ideological norms,
pursue certain ideological goals, or follow certain ideological routines
and rituals, this creates strong social pressures and incentives to do
likewise, creating a self-reinforcing dynamic that reproduces such
expectations and sustains the ideological structure. Members of a
ruling party, a state security agency, or an ad hoc killing unit, for
example, may all feel pressured to further those organizations' stated
ideological missions even if none of them privately supports it. They
may be incentivized to 'wear'[87] the ideology of the party, agency, or
unit, and espouse and enact its prescriptions for action, without deep
attachment to or even understanding of the political claims and
aims which underlie those prescriptions. The fact that such espousal
and enactment of ideology is driven by social influence rather than
private belief does not mean that 'unideological factors' are 'the real
cause'. The *direction of action*—the specific behaviour that is actually
encouraged—depends on the content of the ideologies in question.
Ideologies are more than sincerely-held belief-systems in the minds
of individuals. They also provide focal points of social expectations,
foundations for group norms, and coordinating scripts for collective
action.

Understanding ideology as linked to action in *both* these broad
ways—through varying degrees of internalization and various social
pressures and incentives—highlights the interconnection of ideologies

---

[86] Alvarez, *Genocidal Crimes*, 59.
[87] Browder, 'Perpetrator Character', 494–5.

with peer pressure, social conformity, norms, organizational structure, and, again, self-interest.[88] Indeed, early groundwork for this dualistic account of ideology and action can be found in the work of those 'structuralist' historians of the Holocaust who highlighted, not the irrelevance of ideology, but the way organizational configurations allowed leadership ideologies to mold individual and collective action even when underlying ideological belief was limited. Ian Kershaw, for example, explicated how in Nazi Germany:

> [i]ndividuals seeking material gain through career advancement in party or state bureaucracy, the small businessman aiming to destroy a competitor through a slur on his 'aryan' credentials, or ordinary citizens settling scores with neighbours by denouncing them to the Gestapo, were all, in a way, 'working towards the Führer' . . . The result was the unstoppable radicalization of the system and the gradual emergence of policy objectives closely related to the ideological imperatives represented by Hitler . . . the 'vision' embodied in Hitler's leadership claim served *to funnel a variety of social motivations, at times contradictory and conflicting, into furthering—intentionally or unwittingly—Nazi aims closely associated with Hitler's own ideological obsessions.*[89]

In this manner, ideology can act as a critical 'organizing principle'[90] or 'script or dramaturgical blueprint'[91] for violence, powerfully shaping when genocides occur and the way killings unfold, even for perpetrators who are not guided by deep ideological convictions.

None of this should downplay sincere internalization or obscure the important roles genuine true believers often play. Ultimately, genocide perpetrators are guided by multiple motives and most will act out of varying degrees of sincere ideological internalization and the social

---

[88] See also Stanley Milgram, *Obedience to Authority: An Experimental View* (London: Pinter & Martin Ltd., 1974/2010), 143–4; Ravi Bhavnani, 'Ethnic Norms and Interethnic Violence: Accounting for Mass Participation in the Rwandan Genocide', *Journal of Peace Research* 43:6 (2006), 651–69; Lee Ann Fujii, *Killing Neighbors: Webs of Violence in Rwanda* (Ithaca: Cornell University Press, 2009), chs. 5–6.

[89] Ian Kershaw, ' "Working Towards the Führer." Reflections on the Nature of the Hitler Dictatorship', *Contemporary European History* 2:2 (1993), 103–18, here 117–18 (emphasis added).

[90] Anderson, *Perpetrating Genocide*, 28.

[91] Fujii, *Killing Neighbours*, 104.

influence of the broader ideological environment.[92] But this emphasis on the *multiple mechanisms by which ideology can shape action* fits better with contemporary understandings of genocide perpetrators as highly heterogenous, and encourages 'a more distributive view' of ideology in which varying levels of sincere belief and social influence can be mapped across different perpetrating groups.[93] It also highlights that processes of ideological radicalization towards genocide are not simply about mass persuasion of potential perpetrators—they are just as vitally a matter of cornering social expectations, shifting prevailing discourses, and dominating institutions and organizational structures.[94]

The respective balance of sincere internalization of ideology on the one hand and compliance with ideology due to social pressures and incentives on the other is hard to assess both for a given perpetrator and for genocidal campaigns as a whole, and this remains an important area for future research. But since the two are compatible, and either path can induce compliance with ideological rationales for violence, complete knowledge of the precise balance is not necessary to convincingly link ideology to genocide. As Bloxham observes: 'In this complex of ideological imperative, organizational flux, competition, and collaboration, delineating the roles played by ideological commitment, material interest, and "just doing one's job" is difficult—but there is no sign that any one contradicted the others during the genocide.'[95] Sincere belief in ideology and the social institutionalization of ideology both matter, and it is by understanding the mutually reinforcing processes through which they allow key elements of genocidal ideologies to encourage and mold mass violence that scholars can continue to shed light on the key preconditions and dynamics of genocide.

---

[92] See also Hinton, *Why Did They Kill?*, 25–7.

[93] Ibid., 27. See also Jonathan Leader Maynard, *Ideology and Mass Killing: The Radicalized Security Politics of Genocides and Deadly Atrocities* (Oxford: Oxford University Press, 2022).

[94] See Murray, *Disrupting Pathways*, 4–5 and 185; Anderson, *Perpetrating Genocide*, 69.

[95] Bloxham, 'Organized Mass Murder', 207.

Conclusion

Ideologies are never the only important driver of genocide, but the current state of Genocide Studies research suggests that they do provide vital preconditions for exterminatory violence and shape the internal dynamics of such violence through a range of causal processes. In this chapter, I have sought to map the increasingly sophisticated ways in which genocide scholars have theorized those preconditions and processes. Such theoretical progress has, in my view, neutralized most simplistic forms of scepticism about ideology's importance. Genocides are not 'unideological' because they are perpetrated by regimes that do not match the stereotype of revolutionary utopianism, because they are partly driven by self-interest, or because most perpetrators are not fanatical true believers. The reduction of ideology to a static, universally internalized, utterly fantastical, and behaviourally deterministic worldview is a caricature, and not representative of leading contemporary work on ideology and genocide.

This still leaves room for important debates and disagreements over ideology's role in genocide. The relative causal priority of ideology remains somewhat uncertain—some scholars will continue to present ideologies as the vital independent motor of genocidal campaigns, while others will suspect that the emergence of genocidal ideologies is itself explained by deeper causes such as conflict, cultural cleavages, periods of radical state modernization, and so forth. But since ideologies evolve over time *in interaction* with broader social, political, and cultural changes, there is likely to be no straightforward or universalizable answer to this issue. Everything is caused by something—what theorists who stress ideology might most productively claim is that while the causes of ideological radicalization towards genocide are extremely diverse and unpredictable, once ideological foundations for genocide emerge, and other permissive social and political conditions are in place, the link to genocidal perpetration is extremely strong. But the dynamics of ideological radicalization towards genocide—especially outside the Holocaust—remain under-studied and are an important area for future research.[96] So too is the degree of similarity and difference between genocidal ideologies. As genocide scholars

[96] Murray, *Disrupting Pathways*, 35.

continue to expand the range of genocides subjected to detailed research, we need an ongoing conversation over the most powerful and recurring forms of ideological justification for genocide, as well as an appreciation of how case-specific ideological content shapes the particular way in which violence unfolds. The relative centrality of 'top-down' processes of ideological dissemination by elites versus more bottom-up, spontaneous ideological meaning-making by ordinary citizens or 'on the ground' perpetrators is also uncertain. Much research assumes, plausibly, that intellectual elites are best placed to promote ideological innovations, but there are significant limits to elite influence, and non-elite actors are clearly also ideological inter-preters and innovators.[97]

Broad-brush ideological categories cannot provide neatly predict-ive 'grand theories' of genocide. But the analytical strategy of studying ideological content in depth and unpacking the processes by which such content influences national elites, bureaucratic functionaries, local leaders, and rank-and-file killers can make essential contributions to our efforts to explain when genocides occur and how they unfold. By moving beyond older stereotypes of genocidal ideology and the-orizing the complex links between ideologies and violent action in more detail, such research offers one of the most exciting avenues of progress in our efforts to better understand, forecast, and prevent genocide.

Select Bibliography

Alvarez, Alex, 'Destructive Beliefs: Genocide and the Role of Ideology', in A. Smeulers and R. Haveman (eds.), *Supranational Criminology: Towards a Criminology of International Crimes* (Antwerpen: Intersentia, 2008).

Bellamy, Alex J., *Massacres and Morality: Mass Atrocities in an Age of Civilian Immunity.* (Oxford: Oxford University Press, 2012).

Bloxham, Donald, 'Organized Mass Murder: Structure, Participation, and Motivation in Comparative Perspective', *Holocaust and Genocide Studies* 22:2 (2008), 203–45.

Browder, George C., 'Perpetrator Character and Motivation: An Emerging Consensus?', *Holocaust and Genocide Studies* 17:3 (2003), 480–97.

---

[97] See also Hinton, *Why Did They Kill?*, 28–31.

Freeden, Michael, *Ideologies and Political Theory: A Conceptual Approach* (Oxford: Oxford University Press, 1996).

Jost, John T. and Brenda Major (eds.), *The Psychology of Legitimacy: Emerging Perspectives on Ideology, Justice and Intergroup Relations* (Cambridge: Cambridge University Press, 2001).

Kallis, Aristotle A., *Genocide and Fascism: The Eliminationist Drive in Fascist Europe* (New York: Routledge, 2009).

Oberschall, Anthony, 'The Manipulation of Ethnicity: From Ethnic Cooperation to Violence and War in Yugoslavia', *Ethnic and Racial Studies* 23:6 (2000), 982–1001.

Straus, Scott, *Making and Unmaking Nations: War, Leadership and Genocide in Modern Africa* (Ithaca: Cornell University Press, 2015).

Weitz, Eric D., *A Century of Genocide: Utopias of Race and Nation* (Princeton: Princeton University Press, 2003).

6

Genocide and the State

Anton Weiss-Wendt

Introduction

This chapter explores the connection between genocide and the state.
My contention is that no form of mass violence, and least of all
genocide, erupts spontaneously. It requires premeditation, usually
by a government with a record of gross human rights violations.
Indeed, I argue, genocide is intricately linked to the idea of the
modern state, despite a body of scholarship that questions that link.
Non-state agents such as radical political parties or armed militias are
usually incorporated into the governing structure and therefore rarely
perform on their own. The state may deliberately use them as proxies
to obfuscate the decision-making process and thus to shift responsibility for the crimes committed. Even though the ruling body may not
always emphasize the state interests in genocide, the painstaking
reconstruction of the chain of command, where possible, inevitably
points to the upper echelons of power as the original source of mass
violence. In some cases the subjects may not even be able to identify
the leading individuals who constitute the state. This, however, does
not make the state less present at the crime scene.

I use the conventional definition of state, as an organized political
community under one government. In cases where the forces in
control of the government penetrate through the entire state apparatus, including the civil service and military, this political system
becomes a 'regime'. The discussion of an 'ideal type of state' in my
opinion is as fruitless as the construction of an 'ideal type of genocide'.
Neither the state nor any of its constituencies possess certain innate

characteristics that would make it prone to violence. Like any other outcome of human activity, the crime of genocide is developmental and can always be traced back to a particular set of circumstances unique to a specific time and place.[1]

Until the early 1990s, the state had been considered the prime, if not the only, agent of genocide. The Yugoslav wars of secession and Rwanda genocide, however, have bred dissent among scholars, some of whom began arguing that non-state actors can at times perpetrate violence on a genocidal scale without the highest authorities' sanction and organizational capacity. The attack on the Yazidi minority in Iraq by the Islamic State jihadists in 2014, unprecedented in its brutality, made state authority appear even less a factor in genocide. This chapter asserts the original view, by deconstructing the arguments that emphasize the role of military units and the ambiguity of dictatorship. The analysis of the centre–periphery interaction further affirms the primacy of the state.

While acknowledging the role of the state in drafting and implementing the policies of mass murder, some scholars also consider auxiliary agents of genocide. This is particularly true with scholars examining earlier cases of premeditated mass death. When dealing with the phenomenon of genocide beyond Nazi Germany, Lemkin barely spent any time discussing the perpetrators. In his pioneering book, *Axis Rule in Occupied Europe*, he used general terms such as 'occupant', 'oppressor', or 'conqueror'. However, Lemkin's ambition to write a global history of genocide demonstrates his intention to consider, among others, church authorities, local warlords, and civil rulers as agents of genocide.[2] Thus his unpublished manuscript includes a chapter on Spanish colonies in America abundant with references to non-state agents of genocide. Lemkin held responsible for the crimes the local administration, but also the colonists of New Spain, and sometimes their indigenous collaborators. Simultaneously, he emphasized that the Spanish government never authorized

---

[1] Frank Chalk and Kurt Jonassohn (eds.), *The History and Sociology of Genocide: Analyses and Case Studies* (New Haven: Yale University Press, 1990), 23.

[2] Raphael Lemkin, *Axis Rule in Occupied Europe: Laws of Occupation, Analysis of Government, Proposals for Redress* (Washington: Carnegie Endowment for International Law, 1944), 79–93.

slavery as such and actually tried to ameliorate the conditions of the indigenous people.[3]

It is true that the UN Genocide Convention does not consider genocide a crime planned and executed necessarily by the state. Although Article IX does refer to the 'responsibility of a State for genocide', Article IV defines potential offenders as 'constitutionally responsible rulers, public officials, or private individuals'. Respective positions on state responsibility in genocide, which had been aired during the debates on the draft treaty in 1947 and 1948, were mainly informed by realpolitik, and sometimes the dark past. The US, for example, was only willing to consider individual state officials within the context of genocide, so as not to implicate its own government in crimes such as lynching. The British, for their part, wanted to ensure that the monarch could not stand accused on charges of genocide. An earlier amendment, which proclaimed a state or government the most likely offender, had thus been defeated. The British, who had preferred this particular wording, eventually conceded that states could bear only civil, not criminal responsibility following a violation of the convention.[4] Regardless, the UK had assumed a pessimistic view that, if a state had been keen on committing genocide, it could do so in spite of the convention. Meanwhile the Soviets and the French, who had originally been opposed to declaring state responsibility for genocide, came to eventually embrace this idea. All of this comes as no surprise, taking into consideration that the UN Genocide Convention came about as a result of a political compromise whose major goal was to safeguard the interests of the signing parties rather than accurately reflect on patterns of history.[5]

When applying the concept of genocide to the colonial Americas and Australia, historians tend to interpret the Genocide Convention in the light of Lemkin's early writings. Thus, Ben Kiernan writes that

[3] Michael McDonnell and Dirk Moses, 'Raphael Lemkin as Historian of Genocide in the Americas', *Journal of Genocide Research* 7:4 (2005), 510, 512.

[4] Docs nos. 13, 41, 43, 56, 73, 97–8, 113, reproduced in Anton Weiss-Wendt, *Documents on the Genocide Convention from the American, British, and Soviet Archives* (London: Bloomsbury, 2018), 37–8, 76–7, 84, 149–50, 171, 191, 195–7, 216.

[5] Cf. Anton Weiss-Wendt, *The Soviet Union and the Gutting of the UN Genocide Convention* (Madison: University of Wisconsin Press, 2017).

some English settlers committed genocide in some parts of North America and later in Australia. He then adds that Virginia Indians on occasion repaid the white settlers in kind. He attempts to differentiate by using the term 'genocidal massacres' instead of genocide. This enables him to argue that the so-called 'genocidal moments' can in equal measure be referred back to communal violence. Like Lemkin did fifty years earlier, Kiernan names particular governors, trade companies, and splinter groups that carried out, wittingly or unwittingly, partial genocide. At the same time, Kiernan does not let British colonial authorities and American federal officials off the hook, suggesting the crime of omission, and, indeed, legitimation by their general support of the colonization project.[6] Dirk Moses and Benjamin Madley pursue a similar line of argumentation, discerning criminal intent from the enormous cost of colonization of Australia and California, respectively. The dramatic decline of Australia's indigenous population from 750,000 in 1788 to 31,000 in 1911 makes Moses implicate both central and local authorities in pursuing policies calculated to bring about their physical destruction, pursuant to Article II of the Genocide Convention. The more negotiating power the local settlers community had vis-à-vis the Colonial Office, the more radical the outcome, according to Moses.[7] Madley, following many other scholars, reaches the exact same conclusion in the case of California in 1846–73, wherein systematic policies by multiple actors reduced the native population by some 80 per cent. More consistently than any other student of Native American history before him, Madley has painstakingly related a massive body of evidence to specific crimes of the sort enumerated in Article II.[8]

[6] Ben Kiernan, *Blood and Soil: A World History of Genocide and Extermination from Sparta to Darfur* (New Haven: Yale University Press, 2007), 7, 14, 16, 35, 221–5, 232, 244–7.

[7] Dirk Moses, 'Genocide and Settler Society in Australian History', in Dirk Moses (ed.), *Genocide and Settler Society: Frontier Violence and Stolen Indigenous Children in Australian History* (New York and Oxford: Berghahn Books, 2004), 24–36.

[8] Benjamin Madley, *An American Genocide: The United States and the California Indian Catastrophe* (New Haven: Yale University Press, 2016), 3–14, 346–59.

Despite the complex classification elaborated by social scientists—who distinguish between retributive, institutional, utilitarian, monopolistic, developmental, despotic, optimal, etc. genocide—this particular crime is ultimately driven by ideology.[9] In view of the intent to destroy, in whole or in part, tactical and integral functions of genocide become indistinguishable. Alternately, the act of physical or biological destruction of an entire group, no matter to what ends, is inanely ideological in its intent. The traditional understanding of ideology as a rigid system of ideas and beliefs regarded as justifying action is usually augmented in the context of genocide by a pseudo-scientific dogma. Obviously, violent ideology is not confined to the state and may exist on different levels down to radical splinter group, repressive communities, or individual fanatics. In fact, an ideology is usually a product of intellectuals. It does not mean though, contrary to what John Heidenrich has argued, that the 'bloodiest genocides of human history, especially in the twentieth century, were orchestrated by intellectuals'.[10] If it had not been for shrewd and fanatical politicians, Charles Darwin's postulate of survival of the fittest—to cite just one, classical example—would have remained nothing more than what it was, namely a theory. Nonetheless, accession to political power is a prerequisite for implementing that ideology, however important other forms of less formal power may be in shaping or stimulating genocide. In most cases, however, violent rhetoric and/or terror are a means of attaining power rather than a goal. From the vantage point of the rulers to be, resorting to genocide to hold sway is counterproductive. Even the most brutal among the actors concede the necessity of sustaining popular support. Therefore, genocide is rarely, if at all, used to build or take over the state. The policies of exclusion, segregation, and mass murder usually emerge from within

[9] Roger Smith, 'Human Destructiveness and Politics: The Twentieth Century as an Age of Genocide', in Isidor Wallimann and Michael Dobkowski (eds.), *Genocide and the Modern Age: Etiology and Case Studies of Mass Death* (Syracuse: Syracuse University Press, 2000 [1987]), 21–39; Kurt Jonassohn and Frank Chalk, 'A Typology of Genocide and Some Implications for the Human Rights Agenda', in ibid.; Helen Fein, *Genocide: A Sociological Perspective* (London: Sage Publications, 1993), 32–50.

[10] John Heidenrich, *How to Prevent Genocide: A Guide for Policymakers, Scholars, and Concerned Citizens* (Westport: Praeger, 2001), 34.

the state that has already attained or striving to attain legitimacy by whatever means.

Theoretical Approaches

Social and political scientists were among the first scholars of genocide. Unsurprisingly, then, the scholars working in those fields have also developed a theoretical discourse on state and genocide. Helen Fein postulated that in order to uncover the origins of modern premeditated genocide we must first recognize it as organized state murder. Centrally planned and purposeful, genocide is instrumental to the perpetrators' ends, Fein argued. From the viewpoint of a ruling elite, genocide has a function that helps to legitimize the existence of the state. An ideology may justify eradicating peoples that do not fit into the new nation, by assimilating, expelling, or annihilating them. Fein put much emphasis on the rationality of the perpetrators, who allegedly weigh opportunities, costs, and sanctions before setting on a course of destruction. She established a straight connection between war and genocide, contending that the former reduces the deterrence against the latter. This awards the perpetrators both freedom or action and *post facto* justification. Finally, she projected a higher risk of genocide in a situation of a crisis of national identity caused by the defeat in war.[11] Later on Fein broadened her theoretical framework, restating that genocide may be both a premeditated and improvised response to a problem or opportunity. Simultaneously, she began differentiating between the functions of group destruction, one of which is to eliminate a collectivity allegedly disloyal to the present regime and another to reinforce cohesion by restructuring the population.[12]

Frank Chalk and Kurt Jonassohn agree with Fein that genocide has always required a high degree of centralized authority and

[11] Helen Fein, *Accounting for Genocide: Victims and Survivors of the Holocaust* (New York: The Free Press, 1979), 7–9; Fein, *Genocide*, 36.

[12] Helen Fein, 'Scenarios of Genocide: Models of Genocide and Critical Responses', in Israel Charny (ed.), *Toward the Understanding and Prevention of Genocide: Proceedings of the International Conference on the Holocaust and Genocide* (Boulder: Westview Press, 1989), 5.

bureaucratic organization. However, they provide a different explanation, by assuming that most people are reluctant to slaughter innocent civilians en masse. Irving Horowitz, too, places the state at the
centre of his analysis of genocide. He views genocide as the ultimate
means of social control by a totalitarian state. Norman Cohn, against
Fein and Horowitz, views genocide not as a result of calculated action
but as an attempt to realize fantasies of redemption, messianic and
apocalyptic at the same time.[13] Jonassohn tends to side with Cohn, by
arguing that ideological genocides have been committed in the name
of a fundamentalist religion, a millenarian political theory, or racial
purity.[14] Barbara Harff, who has coined the term *politicide*, considers
revolutionary upheaval a likely cause of genocide, much like defeat in
war. For her, genocide is an instance of state terrorism.[15] Following
Fein and Harff, Jack Nusan Porter emphasizes war or a defeat in war
as one of the preconditions for genocide. The perpetrator can stigmatize victims as traitors and conceal mass murder as an extension of
military warfare.[16]

During the last decade scholars have introduced several variables in
the initial debate on the role of the state in genocide. Among the most
important qualifications is the fact that the regimes rarely exercise
absolute authority and that the ranks of genocide perpetrators include
non-state actors claiming state authority. Harff has provided probably
the most nuanced account of state-generated violence. A scenario
leading to an ideological genocide involves a new elite coming to
power, usually through a coup or revolution, with a radical vision of
a new society purified of unwanted or threatening elements. Besides
exclusionary ideology, another factor contributing to escalation of
conflict to genocidal levels is the narrow ethnic base of a regime.
A situation in which the elite disproportionately represent one

[13] Fein, *Genocide*, 37, 42, 49.

[14] Kurt Jonassohn, *Genocide and Gross Human Rights Violations in Comparative
Perspective* (New Brunswick: Transaction Publishers, 1993), 23; Kurt Jonassohn,
'What is Genocide?', in Helen Fein (ed.), *Genocide Watch* (New Haven: Yale
University Press, 1992), 24.

[15] Fein, *Genocide*, 38–9, 50.

[16] Jack Nusan Porter, *Genocide and Human Rights: A Global Anthology* (Lanham:
University Press of America, 1982), 15.

segment in a heterogeneous society may potentially lead to mass violence or even genocide. The elites are likely to safeguard their interests by designing policies of exclusion, prompting the underrepresented groups to challenge them, and thus perpetuating the authorities' insecurity.

Harff notes that the Genocide Convention fails to take into account the possibility that non-state actors can and do attempt to destroy rival ethnic and political groups. However, mass murder is never accidental nor is it an act of individuals. According to her, genocide and politicide are carried out with the explicit or tacit approval of powers that be or those who claim state authority. Harff sums up her arguments as follows: 'any persistent, coherent pattern of action by the state and its agents that brings about the destruction of a collectivity, in whole or part, is prima facie evidence of authorities' responsibility'.[17]

Scott Straus tends to agree with Harff. He argues that state involvement exposes the causes and shapes the character of annihilation. It is essentially impossible to find a case of modern genocide occurring without state participation. The state can provide massive resources and coordinated planning required in a campaign of systematic destruction. A state project involves ideology and institutions. The questions that scholars should be asking are how state officials decide on a policy of extermination, how do they convince a subject population to commit or condone genocide, and which institutional configurations induce the commission of the crime?[18] Straus allows that non-state actors and/or coalitions of local actors, through what he calls 'decentralized coordination', could execute genocide. Yet the involvement on state level remains paramount, for only the nation-state has the capacity to exercise control over larger territory, integrate local actors, and supervise multiagency operations. At the least, it presupposes the tacit approval and, more likely, 'vertical

[17] Barbara Harff, 'No Lessons Learned from the Holocaust? Assessing Risks of Genocide and Political Mass Murder Since 1955', *American Political Science Review* 97:1 (February 2003), 57–70, quotation at 59.

[18] Scott Straus, 'Contested Meanings and Conflicting Imperatives: A Conceptual Analysis of Genocide', *Journal of Genocide Research* 3:3 (2001), 365.

coordination' by state authorities.[19] Among the first generation of genocide scholars, Leo Kuper is one who has accounted for all historical eventualities when he wrote, that 'genocide is generally, though not exclusively, a state crime, committed by governments or with their knowledge and complicity'.[20] The scholars mentioned above disagree on the degree of involvement of the state in genocide, without negating the relationship between the two. One particular historian, Christian Gerlach, however, has embarked on a mission to erase that link completely. Gerlach, who is best known for his works on the Holocaust, shifted the attention from the state to what he calls 'extremely violent societies'. Gerlach appears as the most radical critic of the theory of state, as it has developed in the field of comparative Genocide Studies. He downplays the state policies by emphasizing the importance of multi-causality and context on the one hand and by referring to methodological problems with the term genocide on the other. The focus on the state and its attributes such as ideology, bureaucracy, and elites—according to him—is a residue of the totalitarian, Eurocentric model. In his quest for a new terminology, Gerlach unwittingly substitutes a top-down approach to the study of genocide for a one-dimensional model of explanation from below. For example, in his interpretation, a state and its functionaries act more as representatives of the larger population strata, making 'intent' irrelevant in establishing whether genocide was perpetrated. By discarding intent to commit mass murder and denying regimes the decision-making power, Gerlach shrugs off all the complexities of the term genocide, including implications of state involvement, through his criticism of the function of prevention.[21] In the final analysis, the phenomenon of participatory violence in no way excludes the intrinsic, structural links between the authorities, various levels of

[19] Scott Straus, *Making and Unmaking Nations: War, Leadership, and Genocide in Modern Africa* (Ithaca and London: Cornell University Press, 2015), 17–18, 23–4, 53, 54.

[20] Leo Kuper, 'The Genocidal State: An Overview', in Pierre van den Berghe (ed.), *State Violence and Ethnicity* (Niwot: University Press of Colorado, 1990), 19.

[21] Christian Gerlach, 'Extremely Violent Societies: An Alternative to the Concept of Genocide', *Journal of Genocide Research* 8:4 (December 2006), 458–65; Christian Gerlach, *Extremely Violent Societies: Mass Violence in the Twentieth-Century World* (Cambridge: Cambridge University Press, 2010).

state administration, and broader masses. Indeed, a more sophisticated conception of intent and of the way it is shaped at different levels
could accommodate Gerlach's case studies within more conventional
conceptions of genocide.

Studies by Michael Mann and Mark Levene make a significant
contribution to our understanding of mass violence, including the role
of the state. Written by a sociologist and a historian respectively, *The
Dark Side of Democracy* and *The Meaning of Genocide* are remarkable books
with novel theses worth comparing. Mann and Levene take a different
perspective discussing one and the same phenomenon, which they call
by different names. Conspicuously, the subtitle of Mann's book is
'Explaining Ethnic Cleansing', while Levene put as an overall title
for the first instalment of his four-volume study *Genocide in the Age of the
Nation State*. The massive investigation into the roots of human destructiveness rendered interesting results.

Levene argues that we should examine the broader context in
which genocide has arisen in the modern world rather than the
particularities of each instance of genocide. As he argues also in his
chapter in this volume, the phenomenon of genocide is linked to the
emergence of Western powers and their expansion outside Europe.
Although the rise of the West was not identical with a comprehensive
program of annihilation, it did create a cultural discourse that had
made such policy possible. Otherwise, the project of modern state is
bound to create a better society. In pursuit of that goal, the state set
out to organize its human resources accordingly. We are talking not
about a totalizing state—Levene reminds the readers—but a homogenous nation-state.[22] Genocide is integral to the trajectory of
nation-states—argues, somewhat provocatively, Levene.[23]

---

[22] Mark Levene, *Genocide in the Age of the Nation State*, vol. i: *The Meaning of Genocide*
(London: I. B. Tauris, 2005), 155–6; Mark Levene, *Genocide in the Age of the Nation
State*, vol. ii: *The Rise of the West and the Coming of Genocide* (London: I. B. Tauris, 2005),
103–19.

[23] Mark Levene, *The Crisis of Genocide*, vol. i: *Devastation: The European Rimlands,
1912–1938* (Oxford: Oxford University Press, 2013), xiii; Mark Levene, *The Crisis
of Genocide*, vol. ii: *Annihilation: The European Rimlands, 1939–1953* (Oxford: Oxford
University Press, 2013), 5.

The term 'pathological homogenization' introduced by political scientist Heather Rae may serve as a corrective to Levene's *longue durée* analysis. Echoing Levene, Rae contends that one of the methods of state-building throughout the modern period had been cultivating identification through exclusion of minority groups, often by violent means. Unlike the former, however, Rae states that pathological means of homogenization used in the past by state-builders had led to forced assimilation and expulsion, rather than outright genocide. The propensity for mass murder and genocide increased in the twentieth century along with the bureaucratic and technological capacity of the state.[24]

Mann isolates causation in specific types of violence by differentiating between different forms of mass violence and focusing more narrowly on the twentieth century. In the absence of a precise definition of ethnic cleansing, Mann uses the term inclusively, much like Norman Naimark before him. Whereas Levene explores the causal link between modernity, nation-state, and genocide, Mann draws a connection between modernity, democracy, and ethnic cleansing. His first argument is that 'murderous cleansing is modern, because it is the dark side of democracy'. The extreme forms of ethnic cleansing require state coherence and capacity and therefore are usually directed by states. When it comes to a situation when a state slides towards ethnic cleansing, according to Mann, radicalization and factional split is more dangerous than disintegration. The novelty of his approach is that he considers different *levels* of perpetrator rather than merely identifying perpetrators. The top three levels include, respectively, radical elites operating party-states, paramilitaries, and the popular power base. The elites, militants, and core constituencies are interlinked and exercise power in three distinctive ways—top-down, bottom-up, and sideways, respectively. Mann contends that ethnic refugees fleeing from threatened borderlands constitute one of the main core constituencies, as they are more dependent on the state for their subsistence and values. Unlike Levene, Mann differentiates between mass murder as a crime common throughout human history

[24] Heather Rae, *State Identities and the Homogenization of Peoples* (Cambridge: Cambridge University Press, 2002), 1–6, 14, 19, 212.

and murderous ethnic cleansing which is distinctively modern.[25] What Mann and Harff have to say about the relationship between the modern state and genocide constitutes the core argument advanced in this chapter.

Bureaucracy

In their conceptualization of genocide, several social and political scientists refer to the state as the source of mass violence. Irving Horowitz went the farthest, proposing the following definition of genocide: a 'structural and systematic destruction of innocent people by a state bureaucratic apparatus'.[26] The idea of bureaucracy as a soulless machine that may acquire a life of its own modifies the notion of the destruction process. We do not any longer deal with the predictable situation in which the authorities see their order passed down the chain of command to be executed. Difficult to comprehend, the bureaucratic mode of operation makes the path to destruction more convoluted and thus less apparent. Set in motion by humans, it runs on autopilot. Although the outcome of this process rarely departs from the original vision of the leadership, the genocidal intent gets reinterpreted in terms of productivity and expediency. Internal tensions and power struggles inform the decisions of the officials on all levels of state bureaucracy much the same they affect the clique. However independent in its decisions it may appear, bureaucracy is an extension of the state and therefore has only limited freedom of action. Regimes typically control the administrative bureaucracy through patronage and enforced ideology.

Most extensively, the role of state bureaucracy in genocide has been elaborated on the example of the Holocaust. Raul Hilberg, who had come up with the concept of 'desk murderer', presented the linear model of operation of the German state and party bureaucracy involved with the 'Final Solution of the Jewish Question'. According to Hilberg, a new agency was engaged every time its predecessor had

[25] Michael Mann, *The Dark Side of Democracy: Explaining Ethnic Cleansing* (Cambridge: Cambridge University Press, 2005), 1–34, 70.

[26] Irving Horowitz, *Genocide: State, Power and Mass Murder* (New Brunswick: Transaction Books, 1976), 18.

failed the task. Karl Schleunes described the bureaucratic endeavour as a stopgap process in which several agencies worked on the 'problem' simultaneously. Neither Hilberg nor Schleunes doubted the role of Hitler as a prime behind-the-scenes mover. Zygmunt Bauman moved the discussion into the realm of abstraction, talking about compartmentalization of tasks that stifle moral judgement. Building upon the research mentioned above, Götz Aly and Susanne Heim reached the farthest-reaching conclusion regarding the capacity of a bureaucratic apparatus to further the mass murder agenda. In their interpretation, Nazi racial planners—or 'architects of genocide' as they called them—enjoyed almost unlimited freedom of action while mapping the future of the occupied East.[27] One step further and the intricate link between state as ultimate authority and bureaucracy as conduit of ascendancy would be severed. This is unlikely to happen, though, because state bureaucracy is and remains an essential part of the power structure, also when it comes to genocide.

Donald Bloxham has arrived at a similar conclusion in his analysis of the role of bureaucracy in mass murder. Like many other scholars, though, he began with a question: 'To what extent can bureaucracies themselves show the genocidal way as a result of their professional problem-solving abilities, leading rather than simply enacting policies decided on from above?' Bloxham observes that genocide, as predominantly a crime of state, is usually executed by the administration in the service of the state. He demonstrates in the example of Nazi Germany how an extremist political group managed to penetrate and subvert existing state organs, taking over the functions of the 'normative state'. A new bureaucracy thus created incorporates ideologically motivated young officials striving for rapid career advancement and older authoritarian conservatives acquiescing to radical policies. Both groups perform in anticipation of rewards and at times personal security, which they can only receive from the state that employs them. By encompassing ideological engagement and systematic

---

[27] Raul Hilberg, *The Destruction of the European Jews* (Chicago: Quadrangle Books, 1961); Karl Schleunes, *The Twisted Road to Auschwitz: Nazi Policy toward German Jews, 1933–39* (London: Andre Deutsch, 1970); Zygmunt Bauman, *Modernity and the Holocaust* (Ithaca: Cornell University Press, 1989); Götz Aly and Susanne Heim, *Architects of Annihilation: Auschwitz and the Logic of Destruction* (London: Phoenix, 2003).

174 *Anton Weiss-Wendt*

problem-solving, state bureaucracies ultimately reflect regime values. The state is important in regulating popular versus organizational participation in mass violence, Bloxham concludes.[28] The escalation of political mass violence in the Soviet Union in the 1930s can be attributed in part to the bureaucratic mode of operation characteristic of the first socialist society.

When it comes to bureaucracy, the most peculiar feature of Stalinist terror was the quota system. The Soviet Security Police (NKVD) headquarters in Moscow provided local party and security police branches with the figures of how many thousands or tens of thousands 'enemies of the people' or members of the 'enemy nationalities' should be deported from any given locality. In the process, local officials often appealed to their superior to increase the quotas, which had a snow-ball effect, particularly during the Great Terror of 1937–8. This phenomenon can be explained through the nature of the Soviet system on the one hand and a survival instinct on the other. Many a historian sees the planned economy (as opposed to market economy) as the grounding principle of the socialist system. Mass collectivization and industrialization was the kernel of the First Five-Year Plan intro-duced in the Soviet Union in 1928. Mass deportations of peasants and the famine could be viewed respectively as an intentional and unin-tentional consequence of social engineering. The expression 'fulfill and over-fulfill the Five-Year Plan' had persisted throughout the Soviet period. However, it was more than just material rewards and career advancement that made the officials in charge perpetuate the class and ethnic cleansing. The erratic nature of Soviet terror—which puts it into the category of revolutionary terror but sets it apart from Nazi terror, for example—meant that no one was safe, including the individuals who administered it. An official who did not show enough zeal in exercising an assigned task, in this case population manage-ment, could potentially join the ranks of the unfortunate individuals he or she had sent on paper to faraway destinations. Just consider the rotation within the NKVD organization whose former heads, Gen-rikh Yagoda and Nikolai Ezhov, were executed as 'the enemies of the

[28] Donald Bloxham, 'Bureaucracy and Organized Mass Murder: A Comparative Historical Analysis', *Holocaust and Genocide Studies* 22:1 (2008), 203–45.

people' in 1938 and 1940 respectively. Despite the arguments advanced by revisionist historians, the element of fear was indeed omnipresent in the Soviet society in the late 1930s and early 1940s.[29]

Military

Some scholars have de-emphasized the role of the state in genocide by drawing attention to the military as a self-governing body capable of generating violent impulses. The discourse usually centres on military leaders in the field or the military establishment at large. Particular instances of mass murder that have prompted the military-centred analysis range from colonial genocides such as German South West Africa to political genocides such as Indonesia. Those who consider the Roma ('Gypsies'), alongside the Jews, as victims of Nazi genocide, point to the indiscriminate shooting of the Ukrainian and Russian Roma by the Wehrmacht units in 1941.[30]

Isobel Hull argued in the case of German South West Africa that the extermination of the native populations in 1904–6 developed out of imperial military practices and was not ordered in Berlin. To ensure the unconditional implementation of his 'destruction order' from October 1904, Lieutenant General Lothar von Trotha first had to establish total military control over the colony. By unseating the governor, who did not subscribe to his brutal policies, von Trotha felt free to circumvent the normal chain of command in the colonies. In his order to hunt down and starve the defeated Herero, von Trotha followed the nineteenth-century German military doctrine that pre-scribed the destruction of the enemy as a final goal of warfare. However, as Hull has explained, it was Kaiser Wilhelm who issued the order 'to crush the uprising by all means'—a standard formulation used with regard to colonial revolts. The extent of the violence has as

[29] The strongest exponent of the 'push from below' theory is Robert Thurston, *Life and Terror in Stalin's Russia, 1934–1941* (New Haven: Yale University Press, 1996).

[30] Cf. Martin Holler, *Der nationalsozialistische Völkermord an den Roma in der besetzten Sowjetunion (1941–1944)* (Heidelberg: Neumann, 2009); Anton Weiss-Wendt (ed.), *The Nazi Genocide of the Roma: Reassessment and Commemoration* (New York and Oxford: Berghahn Books, 2013), 7–12, 16–18, 120–80.

much to do with the personality of von Trotha, who had been known for a ruthless suppression of native uprisings prior to his appointment in German South West Africa.[31] In other words, he had arrived in Windhoek 'to do the job', as he understood it. Moreover, governor Leutwein, who had opposed von Trotha's extermination policy, was himself a soldier experienced in putting down revolts. The General Staff that had installed von Trotha in his position convinced the Kaiser to reverse the 'destruction order'. As Hull writes, Bismarck's ultimate intention in masterminding a policy that had granted the military a free hand was to safeguard the monarchy. Therefore, it would be incorrect to present the German military, the General Staff, and specifically General von Trotha as acting *in opposition* to the central authorities. Rather, they discharged duties in accordance with con-temporaneous norms and preconceptions and in anticipation of sanc-tion from above. By the same token, the parliamentary debates and the public outcry caused by the inhuman treatment of colonial sub-jects in places like Tasmania and German South West Africa testifies to the emergence of pluralistic society in Europe rather than to a presumed goodwill of the European governments.

The emphasis on the military runs counter to a tendency of dissoci-ating genocide from warfare. Activists hailed as groundbreaking the clause in the Genocide Convention specifying that genocide can be committed not only in time of war but also in time of peace. This may be regarded as a personal victory for Raphael Lemkin, who had failed to introduce the charges of genocide in the decision of the Inter-national Military Tribunal (IMT) in Nuremberg in 1946. The mar-ginal treatment of the Holocaust in the IMT proceedings was partially due to the Allied decision to tie Nazi war crimes with so-called crimes against peace. Having taken the outbreak of the Second World War as a starting point for the legal investigation, the prosecution effectively excluded the 1930s' policies of exclusion and discrimination—which

---

[31] Isabel Hull, 'Military Culture and the Production of "Final Solutions" in the Colonies: The Example of Wilhelminian Germany', in Robert Gellately and Ben Kiernan (eds.), *The Specter of Genocide: Mass Murder in Historical Perspective* (New York: Cambridge University Press, 2003), 144–62.

had paved the way to genocide—from consideration.[32] The legal innovation that erased the distinction between the maltreatment of civilians in time of war and peace has led some social scientists to reject the link between war and genocide. According to Paul Bartrop, for example, five out of fifteen major genocides in the twentieth century took place outside of a military conflict. He mentions specifically the 1932–3 famine in the Soviet Union, the Indonesian massacres of 1965–6, the Burundi killings in 1972, and routine executions in the Khmer Rouge Cambodia between 1975 and 1979.[33] This and similar analyses ingrained in the quantitative method tend to disregard context. To the same extent to which the violent regimes invent enemies, they conjure up wars. This is particularly true in the case of communist dictatorships, which perpetuate the siege mentality.

The fear of losing control over the subject population, or even worse of being forced from power, is a potent factor when it comes to unleashing ethnic violent. Common sense and history teach us that democracies are less prone to committing mass crimes than dictatorships. Much like in human relationships, the shrewd ways of gaining influence or misuse of office at the state level breed suspicion of those in power. Although the outside threat to the ruling clique may be real, more often than not it is imaginary. The statesmen in the 1930s Soviet Union and 1970s Cambodia acted out of fear of war. Both countries were overtaken by violence. Russia experienced a world war, a revolution, a civil war, a foreign intervention, and famine before Stalin began implementing mass collectivization and industrialization, which in its turn brought about the horrendous famine of 1932–3. Confiscation of grain was part and parcel of a defence programme that was meant to ensure the Soviet Union's survival. Stalin was one of many old Bolsheviks who had been obsessed with hostile encirclement, border infiltration, and eventually full-scale war against the

[32] Donald Bloxham, *Genocide on Trial: War Crimes Trials and the Formation of Holocaust History and Memory* (Oxford: Oxford University Press, 2001), 57–89. For a qualifying perspective see Kim C. Priemel, 'Beyond the Saturation Point of Horror: The Holocaust at Nuremberg Revisited', *Journal of Modern European History* 14:4 (2016), 522–47.

[33] Paul Bartrop, 'The Relationship Between War and Genocide in the Twentieth Century: A Consideration', *Journal of Genocide Research* 4:4 (2002), 519–32.

nascent socialist state. In Stalin's mind, whatever he did—including starving its own people—made the country stronger in the face of an inevitable military confrontation with the capitalist world. In the case of Stalin, magnified suspicion crossed the line to political paranoia.

It was not substantially different in the case of the Khmer Rouge whose war rhetoric had become a self-fulfilled prophecy. Cambodia went through a foreign occupation during the Second World War, a struggle for independence, a civil war, and the American bombing prior to the communist takeover in 1975. The alienation from the Vietnamese patron soon escalated into the persecution of the Vietnamese minority, the incursion into the neighbouring country's territory, and eventually defeat of Pol Pot's Cambodia at the hands of the Vietnamese. The impending war with 'Western imperialism' and Vietnam served as the ultimate rationale for spreading terror within Cambodia. Thus there exists a direct connection between war scare and cumulative radicalization. Simultaneously, it discredits the notion of total war as a conduit for genocide. It may be true in some cases— for example Ottoman Turkey, as Jay Winter has demonstrated, and Nazi Germany—but not in others.[34]

Paramilitaries

Mann considers the military as one of four power networks—along with ideological, political, and economic factors—that may produce the rationale for genocide (Mann continually uses the term 'ethnic cleansing'). Armies, police forces, and irregulars are the main agencies of military power.[35] Whereas the armed forces are expected to protect the interests of the state, the paramilitaries often serve as an extension of the military, as was the case in Indonesia, for example. At other times, the initiative to build irregular troops comes directly from the state authorities, without any mediation. Ottoman Turkey would be a good example of that. The shock units formed by political parties in their quest for power (units whose deployment is typically explained away as a means of self-defence) represent the third type of auxiliaries.

---

[34] Jay Winter, 'Under Cover of War: The Armenian Genocide in the Context of Total War', in Gellately and Kiernan (eds.), *The Specter of Genocide*, 189–213.

[35] Mann, *The Dark Side of Democracy*, 32.

This kind of militia emerged in Rwanda in the wake of the Arusha Accord and the Ndadaye assassination. Bands of armed men can also form spontaneously—or so it may appear—in secessionist territories, as occurred in the Serb-settled areas of Bosnia-Herzegovina. The most extensive use of irregular forces is possible under condition of prolonged military occupation, particularly in territories that have experienced enemy rule before. Depending upon the background of the irregular forces, this phenomenon is usually described as collaboration, however imperfect the term may be. Nazi Germany was fairly successful at raising local units amongst the Estonians, Latvians, Lithuanians, Ukrainians, and some Muslim peoples in the occupied Soviet territories.

The state is eager to use militias, which it has clandestinely trained and armed, to simulate the condition of civil war. That disposition can afford two types of action, both beneficial to the state: denial or intervention. The officials may denounce the 'rumours' of state involvement, letting the bloodshed run its course. The role of militias in spearheading and/or meticulously carrying out mass murder is difficult to gauge due to the multiple chains of command, which can only be established with certainty *ex post facto*. The ruling of the International Court of Justice (ICJ) in the case of Bosnia-Herzegovina against Serbia indirectly touched upon this problem. Some observers commented that the judgment from February 2007, which pronounced Serbia not guilty of the crime of genocide, could have been different if the government in Belgrade had not insisted on withdrawing some important documents that had allegedly exposed the subordinate position of the Bosnian Serb administration vis-à-vis Milošević's regime.[36]

In the modern period, the use of proxies has been associated with the colonial conquest of, and the subsequent wars of liberation in, Africa and Asia. During the Cold War the superpowers fought each other in the name of a superior ideology, ostensibly by deploying indigenous troops that they had armed and trained. What might have looked like a conventional civil war to the outside world was

---

[36] See *New York Times*, 9 April 2007. See also Kate Ferguson, *Architectures of Violence: The Command Structures of Modern Mass Atrocities* (London: Hurst, 2020).

planned and accounted for thousands of kilometres away. At times violence got out of hand: the armed units that were supposed to fight ideological warfare split and regrouped along alternate lines, massacring each other instead of a designated enemy and their patrons. In certain cases, magnified many times over, this scenario played out also in the context of genocide. While the US sponsored the southerners in their fight against the 'Viet Cong', the Vietnamese communists supported the Khmer Rouge guerrillas in neighbouring Cambodia. Once the Khmer Rouge seized power in the country, they turned against their political backers and the Vietnamese people at large. No matter what the political setup, the type of irregulars, or the extent of atrocities they commit, the traces inevitably go back to the state or the shadowy forces acting in its name. No scholar has succeeded so far in proving otherwise.[37]

In Sudan and the former Yugoslavia the relationship between paramilitaries and the state was rather unambiguous. Thanks to compulsory military service, by 1990 the Yugoslav People's Army (JNA) numbered 185,000 men on active duty and half a million reservists. Up to three million men were subject to conscription by the Territorial Defence. Those who remained in the country when war broke out in 1991 had few choices. They could either join the armed forces or one of the militias that operated in Croatia and Bosnia-Herzegovina. While the federal state was falling apart, the nationalist authorities in Belgrade bet on paramilitaries, who could control territory and thus strengthen the Serbian state. Out of 10,000 Serb volunteers who fought in Bosnia, half had previously served in the Yugoslav People's Army. Unsurprisingly, then, the military controlled most of the militias, with the rest run by the State Security Service. The latter group of paramilitary units, including the notorious 'Tigers' under the command of Željko Ražnatović (Arkan), stressed their links to the security service. In some cases, though, the rank-and-file of the paramilitary units were unaware of that arrangement.[38]

[37] Ugur Ümit Üngör, *Paramilitarism: Mass Violence in the Shadow of the State* (Oxford: Oxford University Press, 2019) may prove a seminal work on the subject.

[38] Aleksandra Milićević, 'Joining the War: Masculinity, Nationalism and War Participation in the Balkans War of Secession, 1991–1995', *Nationalities Papers* 34:3

Bosnian Serb forces and Serb paramilitaries account for most deaths in 1991–5 (c. 97,000). Evidence of central planning is in abundance. The JNA provided arms to the local Serbs in Bosnia-Herzegovina, and on several occasions participated in the atrocities. Paramilitary units were particularly efficient at carrying out the policy of ethnic cleansing when attached directly to regular army units. Even though direct guidance for individual operations was normally exercised at the commander's level, the leadership set certain policy goals, allowing their subordinates the latitude to achieve them. If it were otherwise, Serbian political and military authorities in Bosnia and Belgrade would have made an effort to suppress local gunmen, as did the legitimate Bosnian government. The Belgrade leadership bears ultimate responsibility for the crimes committed, as Norman Cigar insists. Milošević evidently provided financial and logistic support for some of the most brutal Serb militias operating in Bosnia, channelling it through Serbia's Ministry of Defence. According to a militia leader Vojislav Šešelj, Milošević was in charge, even though he had given verbal rather than written orders. It is true that at a later point Milošević reined in some militias, including that of Šešelj. However he acted only after he started viewing these groups as a political threat. Along with other state agencies and nationalist organizations, the Serbian Orthodox Church also lent its hand to organizing, financing, and arming the infamous Serbian Volunteer Guard, as its leader Arkan had subsequently acknowledged. Arkan once stated that 'every member of paramilitary units must in the first place be responsible to the Serbian people and must respect the parliament and the president of the Republic'.[39]

(July 2006), 266; Milićević, 'Paramilitaries and the State: The Case of Serbia', paper delivered at the 7th Convention of the International Association of Genocide Scholars, Sarajevo, 12 July 2007.

[39] Norman Cigar, *Genocide in Bosnia: The Policy of 'Ethnic Cleansing'* (College Station: Texas A&M University, 1995), 36, 48–55, 64–5, 104; Benjamin Lieberman, *Terrible Fate: Ethnic Cleansing in the Making of Modern Europe* (Chicago: Ivan R. Dee, 2006), 307; Norman Naimark, *Fires of Hatred: Ethnic Cleansing in Twentieth-Century Europe* (Cambridge, MA: Harvard University Press, 2001), 161.

The Sudanese authorities have been using militias as a counter-insurgency strategy since 1985. The government in Khartoum began mobilizing the Arab tribes against the Sudanese People's Liberation Army during the civil war in the south of the country. Baggara Arab militias received arms and military training to strike against the Dinka and Nuba peoples suspected of supporting the rebels. The use of Arab militias enabled Khartoum not only to conserve its own, overstretched resources, but also to disguise its intervention as 'age-old tribal conflict'. Between 1985 and 2003, militias supported by military intelligence and aerial bombardment carried out a brutal policy of scorched earth, massacring, pillaging, and raping civilians. In 2003, General Omar al-Bashir, who had seized power in the country fourteen years earlier, began using the same strategy in the Darfur region. The Sudanese army, untrained in desert warfare, was ineffective against the rebels, who used hit-and-run tactics. Experiencing a humiliating defeat, the government of Sudan set out to crush rebellion in Darfur by arming militias from among local Arab tribes, collectively known as *Janjaweed*. The *Janjaweed* struck against the civilian populations of those non-Arab tribes from which the rebels had largely drew their recruits, that is, the Fur, Zaghawa, Massalit, and others. Arab militias resorted to a brutal practice of ethnic cleansing aimed at replacing the local population with Arab settlers, just as they had done in oil-producing areas of the south and the Nuba Mountains.[40]

A loosely organized Arab militia force, on horseback and camel, was comprised of some 20,000 men. Many criminals were released on the promise of joining the militia. This force was better trained, armed, and supplied than similar units in the past. The recruits were paid a decent salary considering the economic situation of the region. Many militiamen received regular army uniforms and insignias of ranks. More importantly, Khartoum coordinated the activities of its regular forces with those of *Janjaweeds*. Thus the government directed militia activities rather than merely condoned them. The most powerful militia leader, Musa Hilal, did not even try to deny his links to the government in Khartoum, from which he had received marching orders. In fact, except for their sandals, turbans, and the emblem—an armed man on camelback—the *Janjaweed* were indistinguishable from regular troops. Hilal stated that he had raised a tribal militia at the request of the government to fight the rebellion in Darfur. From the beginning of the aggression in Darfur, the *Janjaweed* became increasingly integrated into the Sudanese military structure. Many militia members were incorporated into the police, security service, and various paramilitary organizations.[41]

Dictator, One-Party Rule, State

An intelligent doubt about the preponderant role of the state in the genocide is rooted in the continuous debate in the social sciences between those who emphasize the role of individual and collective actors and those who accentuate institutional structures.[42] For Holocaust historians it may sound like the old Intentionalist–Functionalist debate.

When it comes to initiating and sanctioning destruction, the visibility of the leader makes him or her a natural subject of inquiry. Unable to comprehend the complex relationship between various levels of civil and military administration, survivors instinctively search for answers in the personality of a dictator, who is believed, and rightly so, to carry the burden of responsibility for committed atrocities. As with the previous discussions of bureaucratic, military, and paramilitary structures, the question is whether it is possible to dissociate the elites from the state. The evidence suggests a negative answer.

Despite the significant body of literature that examines the world's dictators from a comparative perspective, personality characteristics

[41] Ibid. 36–41, 86, 101–14; Gerard Prunier, *Darfur: The Ambiguous Genocide* (Ithaca: Cornell University Press, 2005), 97–109, 117, 134, 152–5; Joyce Apsel (ed.), *Darfur: Genocide before Our Eyes* (New York: Institute for the Study of Genocide, 2005), 23, 26, 33, 40, 54–5, 62–3, 67.

[42] George Andreopoulos, 'Introduction: The Calculus of Genocide', in Andreopoulos (ed.), *Genocide: Conceptual and Historical Dimensions* (Philadelphia: University of Pennsylvania Press, 1994), 8. On a theoretical level, Michael P. Jasinski has succeeded in bridging all those perspectives in his recent book, *Examining Genocides: Means, Motive, and Opportunity* (London: Rowman & Littlefield, 2017).

of the leaders associated with genocidal violence rarely match.[43] What they all do have in common is the quest for power. By explicating the synergy between the ruler and the ruled one can better understand the motives behind the crime. Leaders and the ruling elites are often motivated by self-interest. To achieve their goals, they may claim that the purpose of destruction is to bolster the power of an entire people. The ultimate skill of an authoritarian leader is to mobilize the population, by cultivating and channelling violent impulses. They strive to move a culture down a path of mass violence; they promote destructive ideologies, which can win them fanatical supporters; and they create critical infrastructure in the form of a bureaucracy and/or a military.[44]

The perception of a leader who single-handedly decides on genocide runs the danger of overlooking both structural factors and collective prejudices that may fuel the machine of destruction. The one scholar who rejects this thesis is Benjamin Valentino. Valentino argues that the violence is typically performed by a relatively small group of people, usually members of military or paramilitary organizations. A regime's leaders do not need to seek the broader public support, as they are capable of recruiting the few individuals to carry our genocide (Valentino uses a substitute term, 'mass killing'). Societies at large come to play a role in genocide mainly as comprising passive onlookers, compliant with authority and indifferent to the fate of victims. A relatively small group of political or military leaders, according to Valentino, can ensure the acquiescence to their radical policies even in societies that are actively opposed to them. He admits the factor of situational pressure only as far as it relates to leaders' strategic goals and beliefs. As an argument, he invites his critics to

---

[43] See e.g. Ben Kiernan, 'Pol Pot and Enver Pasha: A Comparison of the Cambodian and Armenian Genocides', in Levon Chorbajian and George Shirinian (eds.), *Studies in Comparative Genocide* (New York: St. Martin's Press, 1999), 165–78.

[44] Israel Charny, *How Can We Commit the Unthinkable? Genocide: The Human Cancer* (Boulder: Westview Press, 1982), 193–9; Linda Woolf and Michael Hulsizer, 'Psychological Roots of Genocide: Risk, Prevention, and Intervention', *Journal of Genocide Research* 7:1 (2005), 106–8.

imagine the Great Terror without Stalin or the Holocaust without Hitler.[45]

The worn out Hitler–Stalin comparison does not suggest a one-man dictatorship in each and every instance of genocide. The towering figure of a tyrant is clearly missing in the case of Rwanda, and should be multiplied by three in the case of Ottoman Turkey. The Khmer Rouge genocide by all accounts lacked a charismatic leader. For quite some time, foreign observers were unable to tell who was actually running the Democratic Republic of Kampuchea. Officially, Cambodia continued to be ruled by the government in exile headed by Norodom Sihanouk, until his forced removal in March 1976. Important decisions, however, were made by the mysterious body called Revolutionary Organization (*angkar padevat*). The Khmer cadre pledged absolute loyalty to the Organization, without necessarily knowing its leading personalities. The Khmer Rouge denied the authoritarian nature of their regime by stressing the collective nature of the leadership. For the same reason the names of the leaders of the 'Organization' were kept secret. Pol Pot went by the name Brother no. 1, Nuon Chea Brother no. 2, and so on.[46] The assassination of the Rwandan President, whose plane was shot down on 6 April 1994, in circumstances which remain murky to this day, propelled into power a group of relatives and close associates of Juvénal Habyarimana who had reasons to seek his death. The interim government that was subsequently sworn in consisted of extremist Hutu politicians. However, it appears that those individuals were mere puppets in the hands of the actual genocidaires. The Committee of Union and Progress in Turkey was led by three men—Talat Pasha, Enver Pasha, and Djemal Pasha—who had collectively devised a policy leading to the demise of the Armenian minority.

The complex processes leading up to genocide should not be reduced to a regime's leaders and their 'insanity'. Whether economic gain or territorial acquisition, revenge, or security motivate a

---

[45] Benjamin Valentino, *Final Solutions: Mass Killing and Genocide in the Twentieth Century* (Ithaca: Cornell University Press, 2004), 2–7.

[46] David Chandler, *The Tragedy of Cambodian History: Politics, War, and Revolution since 1945* (New Haven: Yale University Press, 1991), 246, 258.

genocidal campaign against a certain group, the leaders of the regime believe in the justice of their cause and therefore are incapable of conceding that their policy was criminal. In that respect Talat Pasha, Hitler, Pol Pot, and even al-Bashir, all resemble each other. The closest that Stalin came to regret after he had ended the Great Terror in 1938 was his concession that some 'mistakes' were made.[47] Pol Pot fought to the last against the government in Phnom Penh, however undemocratic it had been. Hitler preferred to go up in smoke rather than surrender to his mortal enemies, and Talat Pasha died unrepentant, cut down by the bullet of an Armenian assassin. Although genocide is almost always directed by state elites, this is the end process of state disintegration, reconstitution, and radicalization.[48]

Jihadists

The meteoric rise of, and appalling crimes committed by, the so-called Islamic State (IS) pose a challenge to the discourse on state and genocide. The IS shot to prominence after sweeping over large parts of Iraq in the summer of 2014 and claiming authority over Muslims worldwide. The most horrific act of violence occurred in Northern Iraq in August of 2014, when the IS systematically targeted the Yazidis—a Kurdish religious minority—for destruction. *Dabiq*, the official publication of the Islamic State, declared the Yazidi community an 'apostate sect'. In reference to the Quran, it spoke of a Muslim duty to make the Yazidis extinct, including by means of killing.[49] Consequently, an estimated 3,100 Yazidis were murdered and a further 6,800 kidnapped/enslaved.[50] Thousands more were forcefully converted and/or expelled from their ancestral lands, all with the stated goal of eradicating Yazidis as a group. The United Nations and

[47] Hiroaki Kuromiya, *Stalin: Profiles in Power* (Harlow: Pearson-Longman, 2005), 126.

[48] Mann, *The Dark Side of Democracy*, 23.

[49] *Dabiq*, 'The Revival of Slavery: Before the Hour' 1:4 (2014), 14–17, https://clarionproject.org/docs/islamic-state-isis-magazine-Issue-4-the-failed-crusade.pdf.

[50] Figures from Sefik Tagay et al., 'The 2014 Yazidi Genocide and Its Effect on Yazidi Diaspora' *The Lancet* 10106:390 (2017), 1946.

the US government subsequently defined as genocide the concerted attack on the Yazidi minority by the Islamic State.

The problem in hand may be postulated as a two-pronged question: is a terrorist organization generally capable of committing genocide, and is a superstructure established for the purpose of governing a captured territory a prerequisite for carrying out genocide? The first question prompts a simple statement of fact: no jihadist organization before the IS—including the most expansive and ferocious of them all, al-Qaida, from which it had branched out—had ever attempted genocide. Answering the second question requires a closer look at the Islamic State as both a propaganda brand and a functioning apparatus.

Notably, as William McCants has pointed out, the group chose to call itself a *state* rather than an *emirate*, the word commonly used by jihadists. The ambiguity of seeking either a modern nation-state or a version of medieval caliphate was thus deliberate.[51] The promise of a dystopian proto-state helped the IS first to attract fighters away from rival terrorist groups and subsequently overshadow those groups, and later to secure a steady flow of fresh recruits from around the world. Counterintuitively, the IS and its adherents banked on a positivist agenda of a state-like structure to wage a holy war—and in the case of the Yazidis, genocide—against infidels and apostates. Simultaneously, it amplified the impact of coalition strikes on the civilian population as a strategic legitimizer for the IS.[52] To begin with, the Islamic *State* had emerged in the vacuum created by the failed attempts at nation-building in the Middle East. Whether it was effective or not, the IS did have a government on the ground. The illusory sense of stability and order had been reinforced through a comprehensive system of repression. The crime of apostasy was automatically extended to the 'enemies of the state'. The ones who had installed a bureaucratic discipline in IS were former members of Saddam Hussein's Ba'ath

[51] William McCants, *The ISIS Apocalypse: The History, Strategy, and Doomsday Vision of the Islamic State* (New York: St. Martin's Press, 2015), 15–16, 21–2, 121–7.

[52] Cf. Charlie Winter, 'Apocalypse, Later: A Longitudinal Study of the Islamic State Brand', *Critical Studies in Media Communication* 1:35 (2017), 103–21.

Party.[53] The IS capital city, Raqqa, by all means and purposes, served as a 'formidable Islamist micro community'.[54]

It is exactly the clout of a state that enabled IS to kill with impunity. As an Islamic scholar and senior member of IS (who was eventually killed in a coalition airstrike) explained back in 2014, the Islamic State would not submit itself to independent arbitration in cases involving murdering members of rival rebel groups. One cannot make a state accountable for crimes, he cynically declared. The millenarian vision thus provided a licence to subjugate, and kill, those Sunnis and non-Muslim minorities who did not want to pledge allegiance to the Islamic State. Conversely, IS used mass violence as a state-building exercise. At the same time, the shift from warfare to governing had also, in part, precipitated the eventual demise of the Islamic State. Inadvertently, it made itself beholden to a population without being capable of and/or willing to ever comprehensively deliver on its state-building propaganda.[55] Hence, in the case of IS, the perverted idea of state serves as an enabling condition for genocide.

Conclusions

Scholars have been reluctant to use qualifying adjectives such as 'terrible', 'horrendous', 'inconceivable' when talking about genocide. These words lack precise meaning and thus may impede the detached analysis. When all is said and done, however, we are left with no other choice but to acknowledge that genocide occurs when deadly calculus meets desperate and paranoid minds. Pogroms, massacres, ethnic cleansing, or even mass killings—all these violent acts may have their origin in popular culture, perpetuated and perpetrated by the masses. But not genocide! The plan to wipe out an entire group— 'leaving none to tell the story', in the words of Alison des Forges—can only be born in the upper corridors of power, or alternatively to crystallize on its way up through the existing hierarchies. In either

[53] Jonathan Gatehouse, 'What the West Really Knows about the State of ISIS', *Maclean's*, 22 April 2016.

[54] Anthony Celso, *The Islamic State: A Comparative History of Jihadist Warfare* (Lanham: Lexington Books, 2018), xvi, 44–5, 56.

[55] *The ISIS Apocalypse*, 33–4, 38–9, 43–4, 89, 135–8, 148–55.

case, it requires the machinery of state to implement the utopian vision of society. Ideology, bureaucratic apparatus, political parties, the military, militias—these are the constituents of a state. These structures are complementary, not mutually exclusive.

From the vantage point of the perpetrators, genocide is *contradictio in adjecto*. They believe that their nation is on the verge of collapse yet must regain its past glory. They belittle and dread the victim group at the same time. They delegate the delicate act of destruction to various agencies, while reserving the last word for themselves. They want to implicate in murder as many people as possible, without lessening their grip on power. They may be few, styled as many. The only element that remains constant through all phases of genocide is the presence of the state. Elites, political parties, bureaucracies, armed forces, and paramilitaries—all these entities can enter agential state, in isolation or in aggregate. However weak the state may appear, it serves as an invariable reference point in the case of genocide. With all the variables, detours, ambiguities, and exceptions accounted for, genocide is still primarily a crime of state, as Frank Chalk has unequivocally stated.[56] Even those scholars who consider the emphasis on state agency to be a remnant of the Holocaust discourse eventually admit that 'genocide rarely takes place without government complicity'.[57] The authoritarian system of governance implies that subordinate agencies and individuals can only carry out acts of genocide with the active or tacit consent of the senior leadership. Whenever genocide appears to have been committed by individual actors in pursuit of their own goals, the latter inevitably act in concert with the government seeking to expand state control. Under all circumstances, the central authorities remain clear stakeholders in the outcome of the genocide.[58]

[56] Frank Chalk, 'Redefining Genocide', in Andreopoulos (ed.), *Genocide*, 60.

[57] Madley, *An American Genocide*, 356.

[58] Catherine Barnes, 'The Functional Utility of Genocide: Towards a Framework for Understanding the Connection Between Genocide and Regime Consolidation, Expansion, and Maintenance', *Journal of Genocide Research* 7:3 (2005), 311, 313.

Select Bibliography

Bloxham, Donald, *Genocide on Trial: War Crimes Trials and the Formation of Holocaust History and Memory* (Oxford: Oxford University Press, 2001).

Bloxham, Donald, 'Bureaucracy and Organized Mass Murder: A Comparative Historical Analysis', *Holocaust and Genocide Studies* 22:1 (2008), 203–45.

Flint, Julie, and Alex de Waal, *Darfur: A Short History of a Long War* (London/ New York: Zed Books, 2005).

Gerlach, Christian, *Extremely Violent Societies: Mass Violence in the Twentieth-Century World* (Cambridge: Cambridge University Press, 2010).

Horowitz, Irving, *Genocide: State, Power and Mass Murder* (New Brunswick: Transaction Books, 1976).

Kiernan, Ben, *Blood and Soil: A World History of Genocide and Extermination from Sparta to Darfur* (New Haven: Yale University Press, 2007).

Levene, Mark, *Genocide in the Age of the Nation State*, vols. i–ii (London: I. B. Tauris, 2005).

Levene, Mark, *The Crisis of Genocide*, vols. i–ii (Oxford: Oxford University Press, 2013).

Mann, Michael, *The Dark Side of Democracy: Explaining Ethnic Cleansing* (New York: Cambridge University Press, 2005).

Rae, Heather, *State Identities and the Homogenization of Peoples* (Cambridge: Cambridge University Press, 2002).

Straus, Scott, *Making and Unmaking Nations: War, Leadership, and Genocide in Modern Africa* (Ithaca and London: Cornell University Press, 2015).

Valentino, Benjamin, *Final Solutions: Mass Killing and Genocide in the Twentieth Century* (Ithaca: Cornell University Press, 2004).

Weiss-Wendt, Anton (ed.), *Documents on the Genocide Convention from the American, British, and Russian Archives*, vols. i–ii (London: Bloomsbury, 2018).

7

Genocide and Empire

Matthias Häussler, Andreas Stucki[1], and Lorenzo Veracini

Introduction

Many scholars agree with Jeffrey Rossman and others that '[e]mpire and genocide are intricately linked'.[2] Polish legal scholar Raphaël Lemkin, who coined the concept of genocide in 1944 in observing the Nazi empire, noted that '[g]enocide as a technique of empire has occurred throughout human history'. It comes as no surprise, therefore, that historians and publicists from the Global South connected their recent or continuing experience of colonial violence with the terror 'imposed upon the occupied countries of Europe by the Axis Powers' during the Second World War.[3] In the early 1940s, Cuban historians, for example, linked massive civilian deaths during the Cuban War of Independence (1895–8) to the violent 'totalitarian methods' targeting civilian populations in war-torn Europe. Cubans had 'suffered the terrible results of being the precursors' of

---

[1] Andreas Stucki would like to thank Christian Gerlach for commenting on an earlier draft of this essay.

[2] Jeffrey J. Rossman, 'Genocide and Empire', in John M. MacKenzie (ed.), *The Encyclopedia of Empire* (Chichester: John Wiley [online], 2016), 1. See also Leo Kuper, *Genocide: Its Political Use in the Twentieth Century* (New Haven and London: Yale University Press, 1981), 14–16, 44–5, and ch. 4, as well as the essays in A. Dirk Moses (ed.), *Empire, Colony, Genocide: Conquest, Occupation, and Subaltern Resistance in World History* (New York and Oxford: Berghahn Books, 2008).

[3] Raphaël Lemkin, *Axis Rule in Occupied Europe: Laws of Occupation, Analysis of Government, Proposals for Redress* (Washington: Carnegie Endowment for International Peace, 1944), ix.

indiscriminate violence, Luis Martínez y Gereda concluded in 1942; this violence aimed at 'the annihilation of the peaceful population of the adversary', he explained.[4] Similar points about the colonial origin of genocidal practices had been made by many intellectuals during the Second World War, and shortly after by Aimé Césaire and Frantz Fanon.[5]

These and related contentions about the continuity and transfer of repressive policies and exterminatory practices from the colonial arena to Europe during the Second World War have shaped philosophical and historiographical debates to this day. In particular, German colonialism in South West Africa, today's Namibia, during the war against the Herero and Nama peoples (1904–8) has come under scrutiny when trying to elaborate on the eliminatory dynamics which determined both the colonial war and later the Nazi period, although in different ways. Horst Drechsler, a scholar from the German Democratic Republic (GDR), focused on the genocidal aspects of German colonial rule in Namibia at an early stage of scholarly debate. According to Drechsler, the German commander in the African colony, Lieutenant General Lothar von Trotha, 'had but one aim: to destroy the Herero nation', thus embarking on a criminal campaign that 'can only be described as genocide'. It was the *first* war 'in which German imperialism', allegedly only to be overcome by the GDR, 'resorted to methods of genocide', Drechsler wrote in 1966.[6] The controversy about the alleged paths 'from Windhoek to Auschwitz'

[4] Luis Martínez y Gereda, 'La reconcentración', in *Primer Congreso Nacional de Historia* [1942], vol. 2, *Trabajos presentados* (La Habana: Imp. El Siglo XX, 1943), 316. See also Emilio Roig de Leuchsenring, *Weyler en Cuba: Un precursor de la barbarie fascista* (La Habana: Editorial Páginas, 1947), 211.

[5] German political theorist Karl Korsch remarked in 1942 that 'the Nazis have extended to "civilized" European peoples the methods hitherto reserved for the "natives" and "savages" living outside so-called civilization'. See Carroll P. Kakel, III, 'Patterns and Crimes of Empire: Comparative Perspectives on Fascist and Non-Fascist Extermination', *Journal of Holocaust Research* 33:1 (2019), 4–21; Aimé Césaire, *Discourse on Colonialism* (New York: Monthly Review, 1972 [1950]), 36; Frantz Fanon, *The Wretched of the Earth*, preface Jean-Paul Sartre, trans. Constance Farrington (New York: Grove, 1963), 101; Hannah Arendt, *The Origins of Totalitarianism* (New York: Harcourt, 1994 [1955]), 155.

[6] Horst Drechsler, *'Let Us Die Fighting': The Struggle of the Herero and Nama against German Imperialism (1884–1915)* (Berlin: Akademie-Verlag, 1980), 7, 155.

continues, attaining temporary peaks around the 100-year anniversary of the war in the early 2000s.[7]

Recent research on the entanglements of empire and genocide in world history has also focused on *settler colonialism* as a specific mode of domination, contending that 'the primary logic of settler colonialism can be characterized as one of elimination'.[8] Settler colonialism as a distinctive colonial formation differs from other forms of imperial control. In this chapter, we refer to both modes of domination in order to explore extreme violence in all its imperial manifestations. The settler 'neo-Europes' that had formed during the global 'settler revolution' of the nineteenth century were also sites of genocidal practices.[9]

A genocidal potential is indeed deeply woven into the social, cultural, and political fabric of empire, but the link between empire and genocide is contingent on a variety of factors.[10] We analyse the distinct forms of violence inhering in imperial spaces and emanating from the logics of imperial and settler-colonial rule. We refer to 'extreme violence' and not just 'genocide' because an approach from a broad variety of perspectives—beyond the state as the main perpetrator and beyond a focus on modernity—is paramount to understanding colonial and imperial violence in the *longue durée*.[11]

---

[7] See Matthias Häussler, *The Herero Genocide: War, Emotion and Extreme Violence in Colonial Namibia* (Oxford & New York: Berghahn Books, 2021, 5–9; Jürgen Zimmerer, *Von Windhuk nach Auschwitz? Beiträge zum Verhältnis von Kolonialismus und Holocaust* (Münster: Lit Verlag, 2011); Robert Gerwarth and Stephan Malinowski, 'Hannah Arendt's Ghosts: Reflections on the Disputable Path from Windhoek to Auschwitz', *Central European History* 42:2 (2009), 279–300.

[8] Patrick Wolfe, 'Land, Labor, and Difference: Elementary Structures of Race', *American Historical Review* 106:3 (2001), 868.

[9] Alfred Crosby, *Ecological Imperialism: The Biological Expansion of Europe, 900–1900* (Cambridge: Cambridge University Press, 2004); James Belich, *Replenishing the Earth: The Settler Revolution and the Rise of the Anglo–World, 1783–1939* (Oxford: Oxford University Press, 2009); A. Dirk Moses (ed.), *Genocide and Settler Society: Frontier Violence and Stolen Indigenous Children in Australian History* (New York and Oxford: Berghahn Books, 2004); Michael Mann, *The Dark Side of Democracy* (Cambridge: Cambridge University Press, 2004).

[10] Rossman, 'Genocide and Empire', 1; Kuper, *Genocide*, 44.

[11] According to Heinrich Popitz, '[v]iolence means a power action, leading to the intended bodily damaging of others, no matter whether for the actor it finds its

Structural features inherent in imperial rule contributed to a ubiquitous prevalence of violence in imperial spaces. Everyday violence—even only threatened violence—was pervasive in imperial formations. Conversely, empire's structural 'weakness' could in moments of perceived crisis lead to 'massive exterminatory overkill'.[12] This chapter emphasizes the imperial potential for both unleashing and containing violence.

Excluding the last section dedicated to settler colonialism as a specific mode of domination and the first section dedicated to a definition of empire, each section of this chapter deals with a specific imperial moment in relation to the 'imperial threshold', the moment when an imperial relation is instituted: the first one deals with extreme violence in pre-imperial formations, the second addresses a tendency to refrain from genocidal violence when hovering above the imperial threshold, while the third is about extreme violence when empire recrosses the imperial threshold. Extreme violence is especially relevant when imperial rule loses coherence, for example, when the Ottoman state is facing collapse, when France realizes that claims to dominion in Algeria are empty without subjugating the local populations, when what is left of imperial Spain perceives that the project of reshaping colonial relations has faded, when General von Trotha feels that the native insurgency threatens the very foundations of the colonial order, and, in earlier decades, when the imperial or national

---

meaning in its being carried out (as mere power of action) or, translated into threats, is supposed to establish the durable subjection of the other party (as binding power of action)'. Popitz emphasizes the 'removal of limits to the human relation of violence', pointing to a twofold anthropological basis of such a transgression, viz. the 'relative release, in men, from instinct, which goes along with a broad liberation from constrictions to act and impediments to acting', and the 'capacity of the human imagination, with its own lack of boundaries'. These observations point to a specifically human potential for violence, and, as a consequence, for extreme violence consisting of acts which are commonly condemned as 'barbaric', 'monstrous', or 'mad'. See Heinrich Popitz, *Phenomena of Power: Authority, Domination, and Violence* (New York: Columbia University Press, 2017), 29–31, and Monique Castillo, 'Can Extreme Violence Be Justified?', *Inflexions* 1:31 (2016), 193.

[12] Mark Levene, *Genocide in the Age of the Nation-State*, vol. 2: *The Rise of the West and the Coming of Genocide* (London: I.B. Tauris, 2005), 66.

states fail to reach distant settler-colonial frontiers, leaving the local settler community in charge of managing native affairs.[13]

For their heuristic potential, this chapter relies on two metaphors: the 'threshold' and the 'storage container'. Violence is to be found both below and above the imperial threshold, but it acquires a genocidal character primarily below it—either before the threshold is crossed, in tribal societies, for example, or when the prospect of recrossing it during the eclipse of empire becomes a real possibility. Likewise, widespread violence characterizes imperial, colonial, and settler-colonial settings, whether it is stored for the purpose of colonial exploitation, or spent in processes of indigenous elimination. In the latter case, however, when settlers operate at a distance from empire on remote frontiers, the imperial threshold is crossed in the opposite direction: empire is exhausted by distance in these locales and the settlers are in charge.

While we outline below how violence fundamentally characterizes imperial formations in general, in doing so we also revisit received narratives of empire. Empire has been linked to genocide, but we argue that it is not necessarily genocidal. This is not to reheat the fiction and self-understanding of empires as affording peace and stability—as in *Pax Romana, Pax Mongolica, Pax Ottomana,* or *Pax Britannica*—but to point to the empire's possibilities in containing violence after conquest. By contrast, settler colonialism has traditionally been seen as a process of 'peaceful' expansion but often it is defined by genocidal violence.

Empires in World History

Broadly understood, an empire can be defined as 'a political unit that is large and expansionist (or with memories of an expansionist past), reproducing differentiation and inequality among people it incorporates'; furthermore, empire might be perceived as 'a composite

---

[13] On the perception of imperial failure, see Maurus Reinkowski and Gregor Thum (eds.), *Helpless Imperialists: Imperial Failure, Fear and Radicalization* (Göttingen: Vandenhoeck & Ruprecht, 2012).

political unit with, generally, a ruling center and a dominated periphery'.[14] Overall, empires were (and are) flexible tools of governance and exploitation endowed with an astonishing ability for adaption to historical circumstances over long periods of time. Jane Burbank and Frederick Cooper have noted how '[p]olitical flexibility could give empires long lives'.[15] Throughout large periods of human history, imperial power structures were the norm of socio-political organization. The nation-state still constitutes an exception, especially if one considers that in Western Europe, in the UK and France, the 'imperial condition' persisted at least until the 1960s, while it lasted until the mid-1970s under the Portuguese and Spanish dictatorships.[16] Historian Romain Bertrand refers to the 'banality' of the imperial structure in historical perspective.[17] The 'echoes of empire' shape our world to this day.[18]

Obviously, empires and their repertoires of domination as well as exploitation differed from place to place and changed over time. The ancient Roman Empire with its regional particularities, for example,

[14]   Craig Calhoun, Frederick Cooper, and Kevin W. Moore, 'Introduction', in Calhoun, Cooper, and Moore (eds.), *Lessons of Empire: Imperial Histories and American Power* (New York: The New Press, 2006), 3; John M. MacKenzie, 'Empires in World History: Characteristics, Concepts, and Consequences', in MacKenzie (ed.), *Encyclopedia of Empire*, 1.

[15]   Jane Burbank and Frederick Cooper, *Empires in World History: Power and the Politics of Difference* (Princeton: Princeton University Press, 2010), 16. On flexibility, and on the endurance of the Portuguese and Spanish Empires, see Alfred W. McCoy, Josep M. Fradera, and Stephen Jacobson (eds.), *Endless Empire: Spain's Retreat, Europe's Eclipse, America's Decline* (Madison: University of Wisconsin Press, 2012).

[16]   'The nation plus the empire ruled by special laws is the "imperial nation"'. See Josep M. Fradera, *The Imperial Nation: Citizens and Subjects in the British, French, Spanish, and American* Empires (Princeton: Princeton University Press, 2018), 237.

[17]   Romain Bertrand refers to 'la banalité de la forme impériale'. See his 'Histoires d'empires: La question des "continuités du colonial" au prisme de l'histoire impériale comparée', in Pierre Robert Baduel (ed.), *Chantiers et défis de la recherche sur le Maghreb contemporain* (Paris: L'Harmattan, 2009), 538, 545 and 547.

[18]   The term is borrowed from Kalypso Nicolaïdis, Berny Sèbe, and Gabrielle Maas (eds.), *Echoes of Empire: Memory, Identity and Colonial Legacies* (London, I. B. Tauris, 2015). For a comparative analysis, see Elizabeth Buettner, *Europe after Empire: Decolonization, Society, and Culture* (Cambridge: Cambridge University Press, 2016).

cannot be simply equated to the British Empire, which, spanning the globe in the late nineteenth century, included distinct forms of control for different parts of the territories it ruled. Accordingly, despite the generic 'model' of the Roman Empire which was constructed as a form of rule to be adopted by early modern and modern empires such as the Spanish and the British, specific historical periods yielded their peculiar forms of imperial rule.

Pre- and early modern empires, including the Chinese, the Ottoman, Russian, and Habsburg ones that persisted into the twentieth century, were generally land-based and contiguous, featuring more or less fluid transitions between perceived 'centre' and 'periphery'. While premodern empires were mainly seeking tribute from functioning regional economies, non-contiguous early modern and modern empires—among them Portugal, Spain, the Netherlands, France, and Britain—more and more interfered in the demographic and economic structures of the invaded territories. In the Americas, Asia, and Africa, regional subsistence economies were often destroyed to give way to modes of production more in line with the alleged needs of the 'Western' centres. Increasingly globalized mercantilist and then capitalist markets bridged early modern and modern times: monocultures such as sugar cane, coffee, or tobacco plantations were a striking feature. Modern empires like France, Italy, Germany, the US, and Japan frequently emphasized the distinction between 'centre' and 'periphery' and between 'them' and the colonized 'other'.[19] In the light of modern colonialism, indigenous alterities were connoted negatively, being perceived as an impediment to domination and modernization. Although exploitation remained the main goal of colonial expansion, empires generated interferences that could be tantamount to destroying an ethnic group's culture.[20]

[19] One should bear in mind that non-contiguous imperial expansion went hand in hand with the formation of the modern nation-state, providing the 'metropole' with a strong and exclusive 'self-description, ... supported by ideological and institutional controls', giving rise also to modern racism. Racism came to be the ideology underlying modern expansion, having a considerable impact on imperial sociation. Greg Woolf, *Becoming Roman: The Origins of Provincial Civilization in Gaul* (Cambridge: Cambridge University Press 1998), 16; Häussler, *The Herero*, 10–12.

[20] See, for an overview, the essays in Robert Aldrich and Kirsten McKenzie (eds.), *The Routledge History of Western Empires* (London: Routledge, 2014).

Incidents of extreme violence occurred during the campaigns in Algeria led by French army officer Thomas Bugeaud in the 1830s and 1840s.[21] Indeed, military culture pushing for (total) subjugation of the enemy met with socio-economic changes and employed new ways of communication. The material tools of empire also underwent rapid change: steam and steel opened further spaces for imperial penetration. Whereas railway systems, steam-powered gunboats, and automatic guns (e.g. the Gatling gun employed by the British forces in South Africa in the Anglo-Zulu War in 1879) were the staples of empire in the nineteenth century, air-power added a whole new dimension to European colonial warfare in the twentieth century.[22] The new 'tools' of empire impacted military culture and allowed for prolonged campaigns, aiming at ever more radical goals. Sophisticated technologies, among other factors, did, however, not succeed in containing the global decolonization revolution, which was gaining traction after the First World War and accelerated its pace after 1945.[23]

After the Second World War, the African colonies, in particular, became an arena of renewed imperial efforts, triggering tenacious resistance. Both Britain and France sent legions of 'experts' and administrators to the colonies and elaborated sophisticated 'development' plans, allegedly in order to provide basic services (healthcare, education, infrastructure). The Belgians and others followed this general path, sometimes with a certain time-lag, as was also the case with the Portuguese and the Spanish. Scholars have described these developments as a second phase of colonization.[24] Despite the 'wind of change' and the general promotion of basic human rights, both

---

[21] Olivier Le Cour Grandmaison, *Coloniser, exterminer: Sur la guerre et l'État colonial* (Paris: Fayard, 2005), 137–73.

[22] See the essays in Dierk Walter and Birthe Kundrus (eds.), *Waffen Wissen Wandel: Anpassung und Lernen in transkulturellen Erstkonflikten* (Hamburg: Hamburger Edition, 2012).

[23] See Erez Manela, *The Wilsonian Moment: Self-Determination and the International Origins of Anticolonial Nationalism* (Oxford: Oxford University Press, 2017).

[24] Miguel Bandeira Jerónimo, 'Repressive Developmentalism: Idioms, Repertoires, and Trajectories in Late Colonialism', in Martin Thomas and Andrew Thompson (eds.), *The Oxford Handbook of the Ends of Empire* (Oxford: Oxford University Press, 2018), 537–54.

Western democracies and dictatorships fought their retreat from empire in extremely violent ways. This is true for the Dutch in Indonesia (1945–9), the British in Kenya (1952–60), the French in Vietnam (1946–54) and Algeria (1954–62), and the Portuguese in Angola, Guinea-Bissau, and Mozambique (1961–75). In these late-colonial wars, to name but a few, forced modernization (health care, infrastructure, 'education') met with large-scale resettlement schemes, and mass internment with torture and arbitrary mass killings. Extreme violence characterized both the beginnings and the ends of empires.[25]

Having said that, generations of historians have been captivated by the powerful metaphor of the 'rise and fall' of empires. Following this narrative, the course of history is neatly compartmentalized: The heydays of empire are followed by decline. In a supposedly 'natural' succession, one great power or civilization follows on the heels of the other. The global early modern Portuguese and Spanish empires in Asia and the Americas are superseded and replaced by formal and informal control by the British, the French, and the Dutch in southeast Asia as well as the Americas and Africa since the late eighteenth century. Emerging powers such as Japan and the US are added to the equation in the nineteenth century. While imperial overstretch, alleged decadence, and lack of innovation are the usual suspects when analysing decline, cultural, scientific, economic, and political modernization along with nationalism seem to explain the drive towards domination. Following this narrative, 'micro-militarism' and fragmentation of power around the world are seen as signs for US decline as a current global hegemon, which will probably be followed by China, the next rising star.[26]

This understanding of the history of empires and human evolution misses out on several levels. First, the alleged 'fall' of empires might be

[25] For the 'dirty wars' of the French and the British in Africa, see Fabian Klose, *Human Rights in the Shadow of Colonial Violence: The Wars of Independence in Kenya and Algeria* (Philadelphia: University of Pennsylvania Press, 2013); for the Portuguese and the Spanish in Africa, see Andreas Stucki, *Violence and Gender in Africa's Iberian Colonies: Feminizing the Portuguese and the Spanish Empire, 1950s–1970s* (Cham: Palgrave Macmillan: 2019), ch. 3.

[26] Alfrew W. McCoy, 'Fatal Florescence: Europe's Decolonization and America's Decline', in McCoy, Fradera, and Jacobson (eds.), *Endless Empire*, 3–39.

better described as 'transformation', as in the case of the Ottoman
Empire, or as 'eclipse', dragging on and phasing out sometimes for
centuries, as was the case with the Spanish and the Portuguese. The
history of the Ottoman Empire is indeed one of radical change and
transformations over time, keeping up with challenges both from
within and from the outside.[27] The remains of the once global Spanish
Empire—the empire on which the sun never set in the time of Philip
II—endured until well into the 1970s. After being forced to accept the
independence of Latin America in the 1820s, after the loss of Cuba,
Puerto Rico, and the Philippines to the US in 1898, after independence of the Moroccan protectorate in 1956 and Equatorial Guinea in
1968, the last soldiers of imperial Spain left what was 'Spanish Sahara'
in February 1976. One of Europe's oldest empires, that is, Spain, was
among the last to decolonize its colonies overseas. Adaptation over
time to local circumstances (withdrawal after costly and often bloody
wars of independence), adjustments to geopolitical realities (shrinking
and/or transformation), shifting continents in search of a new El
Dorado: all adds to the notion of the flexibility of imperial
formations.[28]

Furthermore, the narrative of the 'rise' of empires has often been
constructed in hindsight. There was in fact no blueprint for empire
and, as John M. MacKenzie reminds us, 'Empires are invariably
adept at propaganda since they control the acquisition and interpretation of data'.[29] Only in retrospect were the British or the French able
to invent a coherent space of domination, lumping together the

[27] In the early days a small warlord polity, the Ottoman Empire underwent
processes of centralization, turning the Sultan into one of the most powerful rulers
of the early sixteenth century. See Halil Inalcik, *An Economic and Social History of the
Ottoman Empire. Vol. One, 1300–1600* (Cambridge: Cambridge University Press,
1998), 12–13. According to Baki Tezcan, the transformations eventually resulted
in the emergence of 'The Second Ottoman Empire' lasting from 1580 to 1826. See
Baki Tezcan, *The Second Ottoman Empire: Political and Social Transformation in the Early
Modern World* (Cambridge: Cambridge University Press, 2010).

[28] See Josep M. Delgado Ribas, 'Eclipse and Collapse of the Spanish Empire,
1650–1898', and Josep M. Fradera, 'Empires in Retreat: Spain and Portugal after
the Napoleonic Wars', both in McCoy, Fradera, and Jacobson, (eds.), *Endless
Empire*, 43–54, resp. 55–73.

[29] MacKenzie, 'Empires in World History', 20–1.

conquered bits and pieces. For the empire's centre, the violent wars at the frontiers only acquired a meaning when neatly displayed—in hindsight—on the imperial red-, blue- and rose-coloured maps. In the early twentieth century, the map of the British Empire depicted Britain's rule over more than one-fifth of the globe and its populations. When domination 'on the spot' was in fact continuously challenged both by local populations and Britain's own settlers (the US declared its independence in 1776, the dominions of Canada, South Africa, and Australia subsequently enjoyed self-government from 1867), the map epitomized greatness and—most importantly—the cohesion of the empire.

Analytically, empire was often broken down into different forms of control and violent domination throughout long-lasting historical processes sketched above. In the early modern period, colonial expansion oscillated between trading and conquering, between informal domination and formal occupation. Throughout the centuries, imperialism and colonialism had many faces. At times colonization was disguised as scientific explorations or religious missions, sometimes exploitation was embodied by private companies or driven by state-led enterprises, such as (white) settlements. The latter, settler colonies, can be differentiated from plantation colonies or from imperial bases and trading hubs, such as Hong Kong or Macau.[30] However, despite the distinctiveness of each historical period and despite plausible differentiation of distinctive forms of empires and colonies, it is fair to say that the fundamental framework of empire as a form of socio-political organization proved able to adapt to ever changing social, cultural, political, and technical circumstances throughout time. Empire's flexibility allowed for continuity.

What is more, theories of modern imperialism aiming to explain the violent integration of new territories and economies in an expanding (capitalist) 'world system' dominated by Western powers, capture a feature that allows for the inclusion of ancient, early modern, and modern empires as well as land and blue-water empires in a single

---

[30] See for a thorough overview Trutz von Trotha, 'Was war Kolonialismus? Einige zusammenfassende Befunde zur Soziologie und Geschichte des Kolonialismus und der Kolonialherrschaft' *Saeculum* 55:1 (2004): 49–95.

analytical framework.[31] Aspects of imperial rule such as cooperation and collaboration of local people in imperial settings characterize empires from ancient times to decolonization after 1945. The same is true for settlers and their descendants. They have been—and still are—an unpredictable element in imperial settings.[32]

Having said that, this chapter responds to Sebastian Conrad's call to focus 'less on where and what empires are', and 'more on what they do'.[33] This means that instead of providing a phenomenology of empires and their particular characteristics, we include both ancient and modern empires within a single analytical framework. Our aim is to contribute to a better understanding of the significant triggers unleashing extreme violence on the one hand, and to elaborate on the key factors constraining the use of violence on the other. Both features characterize empires throughout human history, and an ambivalent 'imperial logic' carries both the potential of unleashing extreme violence as well as the drive for avoiding annihilation; devastated lands offer little opportunity for appropriating resources and expanding and securing one's own power base.

The Imperial Threshold

In order to identify the logic of imperial rule and its relation to violence, it is useful to refer to pre-imperial circumstances. Following Raymond C. Kelly, we assume that hunter-gatherer societies represent 'warless societies', and that war as an institution only evolved in more complex socio-political structures.[34] Unlike hunter-gatherer bands, more populous *tribal* groups depended on locally concentrated resources that they could not leave behind. In addition, tribal societies

---

[31] Flavio Eichmann, 'Expansion und imperiale Herrschaft: Zum epochenübergreifenden Charakter des Imperialismus', *Mittelweg 36* 4:21 (2012): 89–111.

[32] On Cuba, see John L. Tone, *War and Geocide in Cuba, 1895–1898* (Chapel Hill: The University of North Carolina Press, 2006); and on German settlers Häussler, *The Herero*, ch. 2. Further references are provided in the section on Settler Colonialism and Genocide in this chapter.

[33] Sebastian Conrad, 'Rethinking German Colonialism in a Global Age', *Journal of Imperial and Commonwealth History* 41:4 (2013), 554.

[34] Raymond C. Kelly, *Warless Societies and the Origin of War* (Ann Arbor: University of Michigan Press, 2000).

form anarchic, acephalous systems of politically autonomous local groups, which account for the pronounced bellicosity that has been observed in recent research.[35] Jürg Helbling explains the prevalence of war with reference to game theory: a confrontational strategy promises the greatest possible benefits regardless of the approach for which rival groups opt, whereas groups that focus unilaterally on a nonconfrontational strategy face the danger of defeat, annihilation, or expulsion. The late Roman military theorist Vegetius expressed this insight in only a seemingly paradoxical way: '*Si vis pacem, para bellum*' (if you want peace, prepare for war).[36]

The transition from tribal to complex societies marks a significant turning point in the history of conflict and warfare, as the aims and conduct of war changed fundamentally. In stark contrast to their tribal precursors, complex societies and their leading aristocracies waged wars to extend their power, which was attained by conquering new territories, subjugating enemies, and extracting tributes. Such novel aims and corresponding conducts are distinctive features of warfare in 'complex chieftaincies'.[37] By contrast, tribal groups not only wage 'constant' wars, as Steve LeBlanc has pointed out, they also wage *total* wars, targeting the entire enemy group, without distinguishing between combatants and the rest of the population.[38] If we perceive local groups as fundamental political units, offering a sense of collective adherence and identification to the individuals they comprise, we can assume that these wars were genocidal.

As Lawrence Keeley has elucidated, tribal wars regularly led to the complete extinction of defeated groups.[39] Men were most likely killed, women and children taken by the victors. To guarantee the security of their own group, dangerous rivals were eliminated by destroying the enemy collective as such. Tribal societies simply lacked the resources

[35] Lawrence H. Keeley, *War Before Civilization: The Myth of the Peaceful Savage* (New York and Oxford: Oxford University Press, 1996), 91.

[36] Jürg Helbling, *Tribale Kriege: Konflikte in Gesellschaften ohne Zentralgewalt* (Frankfurt and New York: Campus, 2006), 461–3.

[37] Helbling, *Tribale Kriege*, 119.

[38] Steven LeBlanc (with Katherine E. Register), *Constant Battles: The Myth of the Peaceful, Noble Savage* (New York: St. Martin's Press, 2003).

[39] Keeley, *War Before Civilization*, 92–3.

and organizational capacity to adopt a different approach to war, and subsistence economies could not generate surpluses to support professional warrior classes and a political administration. Even so, an eliminatory ideology did not accompany or drive tribal warfare, indicated by the fact that women and children could be absorbed by victors.

Complex chieftaincies aimed to transcend the anarchic order of acephalous societies, arising from the political autonomy of local groups by imposing an administrative hierarchy, which reduced the latter's independent organization to the status of dependent political sub-units.[40] This process can be seen as the imperial threshold. In contrast to the relatively egalitarian segmentary societies, new distinctions in rank emerged. The chieftain, who was now designated by rules of succession, possessed the power to claim goods and labour from dependent local groups. The chief's influence affected local production and sometimes stimulated the accumulation of a surplus that could be taxed.[41] Tribute formed the elites' economic basis in complex societies; the chiefs and the elites were interested in preserving the lives of the defeated, since they contributed to an increasing surplus as tax-paying subjects, servants, and slaves. As people became the preferred spoils of war, the occurrence of massacres decreased significantly. These political formations constituted incipient 'aristocratic empires', later complex imperial formations retained an interest in accumulating tribute generating subjects and lands.[42]

The imperial logic is characterized by an interest in refraining from total annihilation. Imperial authority is thus endowed with a broad

---

[40] Complex chieftaincies gathered at least several thousand members under the more or less prominent central power of a chief. See Steven LeBlanc, *Constant Battles*, 160. Non-complex chieftaincies, which were characterized by the absence of central power, usually disintegrated into politically autonomous groups of 75–300 members (Helbling, *Tribale Kriege*, 116). The difference between the two forms of social organization is not merely a quantitative one: complex chieftaincies integrated the different local groups politically, culturally, and economically into a unit that enabled diversification and specialization of production. See Marshall D. Sahlins, *Tribesmen* (Englewood Cliffs, NJ: Prentice Hill, 1968), 26.

[41] Sahlins, *Tribesmen*, 23, 25.

[42] John H. Kautsky, *The Politics of Aristocratic Empires* (New Brunswick: Transaction Publishers, 1997).

spectrum of possible forms of war and domination from which to choose. Whereas tribal groups regularly resort to annihilation to deal with the imponderables resulting from an anarchic political order, complex polities characterized by an imperial logic can still and often do resort either to annihilation whenever they deem it necessary or subjugate rivals and appropriate further revenue and manpower.[43] Complex polities neutralize their rivals by sparing their lives after vanquishing their military threat. Building on the terminology Sigmund Freud develops in *Beyond the Pleasure Principle* (1920), when it comes to conflict and war, imperial rule can be characterized by a drive to the augmentation and preservation of life (*'eros'*), while tribal societies are defined by the opposite, antagonistic drive (*'thanatos'*). The empire builders seek to create ever-larger units, even though a drive to restrict violence—to refrain from annihilation and instead strive for domination—is only *one* side of the imperial logic. The imperial logic displays also incentives for violence: domination was always based on violence or the threat of the use of force.

For the people *in situ*, the glorified peace under imperial authority entailed often extremely violent realities. Over the centuries, communities in large parts of vast imperial territories had hardly any contact with the representatives of the ruling centre. Some imperial officers described the few garrisons in the colonies 'as "lost isles" in a "boundless indigenous ocean"'.[44] Control and dominance were many times a fiction. Frequently, the sole interaction with the agents of empire was through the so-called pacification columns crossing remote regions, usually imposing new taxes and sometimes plundering and leaving a trail of destruction. Often 'pacification' triggered resistance while resistance called for further 'pacification': the violent 'dynamics of occupation-resistance-pacification-occupation' was a common feature of empire.[45]

[43] Ulrich Menzel, *Die Ordnung der Welt: Imperium oder Hegemonie in der Hierarchie der Staatenwelt* (Frankfurt: Suhrkamp, 2015), 39–41.

[44] Governor-General of Angola Caetano Almeida e Albuquerque (1877) is cited in Miguel Bandeira Jerónimo, 'The States of Empire', in Luís Trindade (ed.), *The Making of Modern Portugal* (Newcastle upon Tyne: Cambridge Scholars Publishing, 2013), 65.

[45] Bandeira Jerónimo, 'The States of Empire', 78.

A notable dose of paranoia was deeply rooted within imperial power structures. Scarce resources and the need to rely on the self-government of the subordinated units further fuelled the fear. The 'pacification' of imperial spaces repeatedly slipped into war and extreme violence. Given their autonomy, or potential autonomy, the political sub-units forming the imperial landscape always have the possibility of rebelling against imperial power. In these cases, the intervention of the empire shifts from 'policing' to outright war.[46] Broadly speaking, challenged imperial powers, facing the possibility of recrossing the imperial threshold, can seek the annihilation of their actual and perceived enemies. Extreme violence always remains one of the options available to them. Exemplary violence and the subsequent extermination of entire collectives follows this logic; 'pacifying' acquires a more sinister meaning and Tacitus' dictum a particular relevance: '[t]o ravage, to slaughter, to usurp under false titles, they call empire; and where they make a desert, they call it peace'.[47]

Violence alone, however, could not sustain imperial rule in the long run. Empires were bound to also seek indigenous collaboration and cooperation, not only during their genesis, but when conquest turned into occupation. They thus had to provide some opportunities for local populations to participate in imperial power structures, and were compelled to come to an arrangement with local societies, and even to foster a sense of solidarity and loyalty. The unequal 'terms of trade' in these 'unequal but incorporative polit[ies]' were renegotiated time and again with local leaders through violent means;[48] '[e]xploitation, brute force and forms of cooperation often occurred simultaneously'.[49]

---

[46] For an analysis of the blurred boundaries separating war and peace in imperial spaces, see Dierk Walter, *Colonial Violence: European Empires and the Use of Force* (London: Hurst, 2017); and Martin Thomas, 'Policing and Colonial Control', in MacKenzie (ed.), *Encyclopedia of Empire*.

[47] Publius Cornelius Tacitus, *De vita et moribus Iulii Agricolae*, https://la.wiki-source.org/wiki/De_vita_et_moribus_Iulii_Agricolae#XXX.

[48] See Alexander J. Motyl, *Imperial Ends: The Decay, Collapse, and Revival of Empires* (New York: Columbia University Press, 2001), 16, 4; Burbank and Cooper, *Empires in World History*, 10, 5 (quotations).

[49] Tanja Bührer et al., 'Introduction: Cooperation and Empire. Local Realities of Global Processes', in Tanja Bührer et al. (eds.), *Cooperation and Empire: Local Realities of Global Processes* (New York and Oxford: Berghahn Books, 2017), 6.

To illustrate the logic of imperial authority, oscillating between extreme violence and promises of integration and participation, the concepts of 'conquest' and 'pacification' are illuminating examples. In terms of conquest, the steps being taken to overcome an anarchic order are overwhelmingly violent.[50] And yet, a search for plunder could also become an end in itself.[51] This is particularly true when imperial expansion produced 'turbulent frontiers', spaces engendering a political economy that encouraged continuous expansion in its own right. In this particular constellation, imperial conquest called for 'pacification' and war was superseded by cooperative yet violently unequal interaction.[52] Imperial rule is thus routinely constructed as bringing long phases of peace.

Reordering the Imperial Space

The ordering of the imperial space—that is, actions and policies aimed at permanently securing conquest and the consolidation of rule—is closely linked to 'pacification'. Violence is now carried 'inward' in a process striving to create, at least in theory, a homogeneous political body.[53] Truly securing territory after conquest was always a crucial aspect of securing power in the long run if indirect rule—that is, empire on the cheap—would not do the job. Throughout the history of empire, reordering imperial spaces and constructing genuine 'imperial landscapes' included both the establishment of new

[50] See Trutz Von Trotha, *Koloniale Herrschaft: Zur soziologischen Theorie der Staatsentstehung am Beispiel des Schutzgebietes Togo* (Tübingen: Mohr, 1994), 33.

[51] The quest for booty at times became the empire's *raison d'être*. It is estimated that the neo-Assyrian expansion (911–609 BC) has claimed seven million lives, including a large number of deaths within Assyrian ranks. See Mario Liverani, *Assiria: La preistoria dell'imperialismo* (Bari and Rome: Laterza Editori, 2017), 265.

[52] John S. Galbraith, 'The "Turbulent Frontier" as a Factor in British Expansion', *Comparative Studies in Society and History* 2:2 (1960), 150–68. See also Charles Tilly, 'War Making and State Making as Organized Crime', in Peter B. Evans, Dietrich Rueschemeyer, and Theda Skocpol (eds.), *Bringing the State Back in* (Cambridge: Cambridge University Press, 1985), 169, 171.

[53] On the extreme reordering of space implied by the Nazi concept of *Lebensraum*, see Ulrike Jureit, 'Ordering Space: Intersections of Space, Racism, and Extermination', *Journal of Holocaust Research* 33:1 (2019), 64–82.

settlements and the employment of highly repressive tools such as forced resettlements.[54] While systematically applied by modern empires, both practices have a long imperial history dating back to antiquity.

The ancient Roman colonial practice is illuminating. While the Romans frequently deported entire populations, the Roman 'colonies' were about strategically turning formerly hostile locales into reliable hinterlands by providing reliable garrisons for emergencies and controlling strategic points. The Roman colonies, which enjoyed the highest status among cities since republican times, were originally military outposts established to permanently secure conquered territory but became trade hubs and exemplars of a Roman imperial lifestyle.[55] Military imperatives were thus entangled with envisioned efforts towards assimilation.

Examples of these entanglements are countless. In late nineteenth-century Cuba, Spanish colonial planners hoped for socio-economic stabilization of the island when promoting settlement schemes for Europeans. In the early 1870s one such project envisioned the settling of about forty to fifty thousand European families (mostly Germans) in the Cuban countryside. The German settlers' 'love of order and their sense of duty' would have a positive political and economic impact, it was argued. The settlement did not eventuate, probably due to Cuba's first war of independence (1868–78).[56] Almost 100 years later, the Portuguese colonial administration still pursued large-scale settlements of Europeans in its African colonies, particularly in Angola and Mozambique. The Portuguese Empire was promoting settlement throughout the 1950s and 1960s as other imperial powers in Africa

[54] See Mark Altaweel, *The Imperial Landscape of Ashur: Settlement and Land Use in the Assyrian Heartland* (Heidelberg: Heidelberger Orientverlag, 2008).

[55] See e.g. Jeremia Pelgrom and Tesse D. Stek, 'Roman Colonization Under the Republic: Historiographical Contextualisation of a Paradigm', in Tesse D. Stek and Jeremia Pelgrom (eds.), *Roman Republican Colonization: New Perspectives from Archaeology and Ancient History* (Rome, Palombi editori, 2014), 10–45.

[56] Luis Álvarez Gutiérrez, 'Un proyecto de colonización alemana para la Isla de Cuba en 1871', in Consuelo Naranjo Orovio and Tomás Mallo Gutiérrez (eds.), *Cuba, la perla de las Antillas: Actas de las I Jornadas sobre 'Cuba y su Historia'* (Aranjuez: Doce Calles, 1994), 111.

were rather concerned with exit strategies and the end of white rule.[57] But the aspiration to reorder the imperial space and the determination to display extreme violence when challenged remained. White settlements were a cornerstone of Portuguese development plans in Africa until the 1970s. They were envisioned as poles of 'civilization' that would uplift the African territories, even though they triggered conflicts over land and other resources, leading to the forced removal of local populations and sometimes contributing to extreme violence.

Establishing settlements and colonies was often paralleled by large-scale deportations. They were already a 'typical feature of the policy of the neo-Assyrian empire', and 'the policy of mass deportation had already been put into operation by Assyrian kings who reigned before Tiglath-Pileser III', while the 'large-scale deportation of a civilian population was practiced in Egypt, the Hittite Empire, and Mesopotamia'.[58] It was in the Assyrian Empire that extensive forced removals became a 'regular feature of Assyrian imperial policy and the most important means of its domination of other peoples, with far-reaching political, demographic and cultural consequences'.[59] It is likely that Assyrian mass resettlements have claimed the life of one-third of the deportees, as Mario Liverani's estimate suggests.[60] The vast dimensions of cross-imperial population transfers illustrate the intended scope of the Assyrian policy aimed at reordering the imperial landscape, the lives lost in the process are a reminder of the administrators and the defenders of empires' hubris, leading time and again to a humanitarian disaster. Notwithstanding the devastating outcomes, the deportation of entire populations within the borders and between parts of the empire remained a regularly employed device for ensuring domination.[61]

---

[57] Jeanne Marie Penvenne, 'Settling Against the Tide: The Layered Contradictions of Twentieth-Century Portuguese Settlement in Mozambique', in Caroline Elkins and Susan Pedersen (eds.), *Settler Colonialism in the Twentieth Century: Projects, Practices, Legacies* (New York: Routledge, 2005), 79–94.

[58] Bustenay Oded, *Mass Deportations and Deportees in the Neo-Assyrian Empire* (Wiesbaden: Dr. Ludwig Reichert Verlag, 1979), 1.

[59] Oded, *Mass Deportations and Deportees*, 2.

[60] Liverani, *Assiria*, 265.

[61] Andreas Stucki, '"Frequent Deaths": The Colonial Development of Concentration Camps Reconsidered, 1868–1974', *Journal of Genocide Research* 20:3 (2018), 305–26.

Population transfers and resettlements—sometimes in the context of anti-guerrilla warfare, sometimes in order to 'modernize' allegedly backward societies—are ubiquitous in the history of empire. In the early Ottoman Empire, for example, even though reason of state still called for tolerance, the rulers of empire pursued a policy called '*sürgün*', forced population transfers aiming at consolidating the acquisition of newly acquired territories such as the city of Istanbul in 1453 or the island of Cyprus in 1570.[62] The Ottomans also 'deported various unwanted groups', such as the Shia Kizilbashi, and the Yuruk pastoralists in their quest for undisputed rule.[63] The aim of these policies may not have been the homogenization of territory and the peoples inhabiting it, but they still envisaged a profound transformation of the imperial landscape, which had to be rendered legible and controllable. Whether intended or not, reordering the imperial landscape could readily result in the destruction of entire groups. Although Lemkin's understanding of empire was confined to national patterns, it is nevertheless revealing that he made both colonization and settlement intrinsic to his definition of genocide:

> Genocide has two phases: one, destruction of the national pattern of the oppressed group: the other, the imposition of the national pattern of the oppressor. This imposition, in turn, may be made upon the oppressed population which is allowed to remain, or upon the territory alone, after removal of the population and the colonization of the area by the oppressor's own nationals.[64]

Misguided projections of the 'nation' to the imperial past aside, the violent demographic reordering of imperial space could follow

[62] See Heath W. Lowry, *The Nature of the Early Ottoman State* (Albany: State University of New York Press, 2003), 92–3; Bernard Lewis, *Islam* (Paris: Editions Gallimard, 2005), 563–6.

[63] Alexander Lopasic, 'Islamization of the Balkans with Special Reference to Bosnia', *Journal of Islamic Studies* 5:2 (1994), 163–86, 173.

[64] Lemkin, *Axis Rule in Occupied Europe*, 79. On the intellectual history of genocide as a concept, see A. Dirk Moses, 'Empire, Colony, Genocide: Keywords and the Philosophy of History', in Moses (ed.), *Empire, Colony, Genocide*, 3–54 and Andrew Fitzmaurice 'Anti-Colonialism in Western Political Thought: The Colonial Origins of the Concept of Genocide', in Moses (ed.), *Empire, Colony, Genocide*, 55–81.

primarily military exigencies or more political ones. The siege of the island Melos during the Peloponnesian War between Athens and Sparta is a case in point. The Melians became the subject of genocidal destruction in 416 BC: the men were killed, the women and children were enslaved, and the island was repopulated with loyal Athenian citizens.[65] The polis no longer existed. One might argue that Athens only figured as a hegemon in the Attic League and not as an imperial power. This might have been true at the beginning of the war, yet in the course of events the respective leading forces, Athens and Sparta, increasingly behaved as imperial powers: Athens demanded much more than mere benevolent neutrality of the Melians. Melos' refusal led to total annihilation. This example was meant to discourage resistance from other units within the Athenian imperial formation. Imperial prestige was also a factor. Disobedience had to be punished with utmost severity.

In the context of the routine reordering of imperial spaces, the boundaries between what Jacques Sémelin describes as subjugating and annihilating extermination practices were often blurred.[66] A strategy of extermination could derive from a desire to permanently secure territory and from the perception of an existential challenge to imperial rule. Extermination in these cases superseded the imperial logic aiming to accumulate and preserve tribute-paying subjects.

Settler Colonialism and Genocidal Violence

Settler colonialism in world history

At times, dramatic demographic reorderings of space were conducted not by imperial administrators promoting settlements and/or deporting restive populations but by settler groups acting in their own capacity. These were colonists who were less interested in extracting tribute or exploiting subjugated populations than in acquiring

---

[65] Frank Chalk and Kurt Jonassohn, '"On Cases from Antiquity" and "Melos"', in Adam Jones (ed.) *Genocide*, vol. 2: *Genocide in History* (Los Angeles: Sage, 2008), 7.
[66] Jacques Sémelin, *Purify and Destroy: The Political Uses of Massacre and Genocide* (New York: Columbia University Press, 2007), 37–42, 332–42.

unfettered title and access to land. Where settlers could operate autonomously or semi-autonomously, the imperial threshold was also recrossed. Genocidal violence was perpetrated by the settlers who challenged imperial claims and suppressed indigenous challenges.

In instances of settler-colonial violence, the traditional relationship between perceived imperial centre and periphery is upended. Granted, imperialism and settler colonialism are both violent modes of domination, but settler autonomy results in a peculiar political geometry of empire: remote settler frontiers are dominated by civilian settlers, and the few representatives of the imperial state are often subordinate to the settlers.[67] Out there, on remote frontiers, the settlers often exercise the monopoly on the use of force that elsewhere is held by and fundamentally defines the state, as the sociologist Max Weber influentially intuited.[68] Out there, they form a militarized settler-colonial citizenry and claim special constitutive capabilities that exceed imperial orderings.

Settler communities had been established already in the seventeenth century, but they were for a long time marginal, located in unpromising areas, supported by colonial upstarts (England and France were late bloomers in the rush for colonies), populated by generally 'disreputable' individuals, seen as numbed by isolation, and far from the origins of 'civilization'. It is only with what James Belich has called the global 'settler revolution' of the nineteenth century that settlers typically became respectable, even though not always: the transport and the industrial revolutions had made the temperate prairies of North America and Australia, parts of South Africa, and the southernmost parts of South America and the easternmost parts of

[67] For genocidal developments in such locales, see Mohamed Adhikari (ed.), *Genocide on Settler Frontiers: When Hunter-Gatherers and Commercial Stock Farmers Clash* (New York and Oxford: Berghahn Books: 2014); Michael Grewcock, 'Settler-Colonial Violence, Primitive Accumulation and Australia's Genocide', *State Crime Journal* 7:2 (2018), 222–50.

[68] Max Weber, 'Politics as Vocation', in Tony Waters and Dagmar Waters (eds.), *Weber's Rationalism and Modern Society: New Translations on Politics, Bureaucracy, and Social Stratification* (Houndmills: Palgrave Macmillan, 2015), 129–98.

Asia, accessible, productive, and profitable.[69] The global settler
revolution aggressively reorganized space and resulted in several
'neo-Europes' firmly located where there previously were none: they
were unavoidable geopolitical facts on the ground.[70] These were all
areas subjected to processes that Belich defines as 'explosive colonisa-
tion'.[71] The settlers were able to demographically reorder these
imperial spaces and shape the forming settler societies without or
beside imperial intervention because they reproduced at a fierce
rate, welcomed sustained immigration (it is calculated that about
55 million Europeans departed the Old World for new ones in the
century after 1820), and because they controlled the local institutions
of the state, including the ability to shape native policies.[72]

Later, the settlers often became the state, either by acquiring self-
governing capacities through territorial or colonial devolution, or by
declaring their independence outright. Their state is typically aggressively expansionist but remains different from an imperial state, even if
the practice of frontier massacres is eventually discontinued. Rather
than managing subjected heterogeneity like imperial states do, the
settler state aims to constitute demographic homogeneity by the
violent application of a variety of administrative and assimilatory
means against surviving indigenous peoples. Cultural genocide, a
most violent practice, characterizes the operation of settler states.
Boarding schools and other bureaucratic apparatuses designed to
separate indigenous children from their parents and communities
mark the operation of settler colonialism after a violent phase of
dispossession and removal. The boarding schools of Canada and the
US were spaces of death and deculturation—inmate mortality rates

[69] Belich, *Replenishing the Earth*.

[70] 'Neo-Europe' is Alfred Crosby's definition of settler society. See Crosby,
Ecological Imperialism..

[71] Belich, *Replenishing the Earth*, 281, 288; see also Edward Cavanagh, and
Lorenzo Veracini (eds.), *The Routledge Handbook of the History of Settler Colonialism*
(London: Routledge, 2016).

[72] See e.g. Marjory Harper, 'British Migration and the Peopling of the Empire',
in Andrew Porter (ed.), *The Oxford History of the British Empire, Vol. III: The Nineteenth
Century* (Oxford: Oxford University Press, 1999), 75–87.

were staggering. Of course, these were also spaces of resistance and survival, but only recently were there serious attempts to address the legacies of this traumatic and genocidal past.[73]

During the twentieth century, settler-colonial projects persisted in a remarkable number of settings, even though during this phase the settlers had typically lost the political initiative they had on expanding frontiers and were usually relying on state support for their endeavours rather than exceeding the boundaries of the state to pursue their own.[74] When and if they lost the support of the imperial state, the very viability of the settler community became compromised, as in the case of French Algeria during the very early 1960s. Nearly a million settlers faced an uncertain future and decided to leave the independent postcolony and return to a metropole most of them had never visited.[75] Elsewhere, in Kenya and Rhodesia/Zimbabwe, for example, and in South Africa, the presence of an entrenched community of settlers and a violent history of dispossession ensured that protracted and bitter struggles for independence would ensue.[76]

---

[73] See Truth and Reconciliation of Canada, Honouring the Truth, Reconciling for the Future: Summary of the final report of the Truth and Reconciliation of Canada, 2015, http://nctr.ca/assets/reports/Final%20Reports/Executive_Summary_English_Web.pdf. The Report cites Patrick Wolfe and explicitly refers to settler colonialism as a mode of domination. See ibid., 388, 391, 399. See also, for Australia, see Australian Human Rights Commission, Bringing Them Home Report, 1997, https://www.humanrights.gov.au/sites/default/files/content/pdf/social_justice/bringing_them_home_report.pdf.

[74] Elkins and Pedersen (eds.), *Settler Colonialism in the Twentieth Century*. On settler autonomy away from the state, see e.g. Thomas Richard, '"Farewell to America": The Expatriation Politics of Overland Migration, 1841–1846', *Pacific Historical Review*, 86:1 (2017), 114–52; and Sarah K. M. Rodriguez, '"The Greatest Nation on Earth": The Politics and Patriotism of the First Anglo American Immigrants to Mexican Texas, 1820–1824', *Pacific Historical Review*, 86:1, (2017), 50–83.

[75] See e.g. Todd Shepard, *The Invention of Decolonization: The Algerian War and the Remaking of France* (Ithaca, NY: Cornell University Press, 2006).

[76] See e.g. Dane Kennedy, *Islands of White: Settler Society and Culture in Kenya and Southern Rhodesia, 1890–1939* (Durham, NC: Duke University Press, 1987).

Logic of elimination?

The relationship between settler colonialism as a distinct mode of domination and genocide has now been analysed in an important debate.[77] Patrick Wolfe argued that settler colonialism is not always genocidal but is instead governed by a 'logic of elimination', meaning that settler polities eliminate in a variety of ways and not necessarily by physically exterminating indigenous collectives. He had the forcible assimilation of indigenous communities and autonomies in mind.[78] In another seminal intervention, Michael Mann also emphasized how settler democracies more than imperial powers display an eliminationist drive when facing indigenous unsurrendered autonomy.[79]

At the same time, many have noted that the state was not necessarily involved in genocidal efforts in the settler frontiers, even though at times it definitely was. Often the soldiers that colonial governments sent out to the frontier would be settlers and the settlers were former soldiers, which makes distinguishing between civilian and state agencies quite difficult. Referring to genocide in Tasmania, Nicholas Dean Brodie has recently emphasized a 'combined apparatus of civil and military governance and personnel'.[80] Various historians, for example, argue that in the nineteenth century the US did not enact a policy of 'intentional genocide', while civilian militias did (and while Nazi Germany in the twentieth century did). One of them recently concluded that this was because *at the centre*, in Washington, DC, there

[77] Moses (ed.), *Genocide and Settler Society*; A. Dirk Moses and Dan Stone (eds.), *Colonialism and Genocide* (Abingdon: Routledge, 2008). For specific cases, see e.g. William Gallois, 'Genocide in Nineteenth-Century Algeria', *Journal of Genocide Research* 15:1 (2013), 69–88; Susan I. Blackbeard, 'Acts of Severity: Colonial Settler Massacre of amaXhosa and abaThembu on the Eastern Frontier of the Cape Colony, c.1826–47', *Journal of Genocide Research* 17:2 (2015), 107–32; and Thomas James Rogers and Stephen Bain, 'Genocide and Frontier Violence in Australia', *Journal of Genocide Research* 18:1 (2016), 83–100.

[78] Patrick Wolfe, 'Settler Colonialism and the Elimination of the Native', *Journal of Genocide Research* 8:4 (2016), 387–409.

[79] Mann, *The Dark Side of Democracy*.

[80] Nicholas Dean Brodie, 'The Vandemonian War as Genocidal Moment: Historiographical Refrains and Archival Secrets', *Journal of Genocide Research*, 20:3 (2018) 472–81, 479.

was 'no consensus'.[81] They do acknowledge, though, that there were frequent calls for extermination *at the margins*, but consider that the Indian reservations enabled survival, whereas this would not be the case in Eastern Europe for targeted populations.

But searching for the state in frontier genocides can be a moot undertaking; either because the state is largely absent or because, paradoxically, in a political vacuum even a minimal state presence can become immediately and murderously significant. Recent debates surrounding the question of genocide in California and Australia, for example, have faced the question of state or civilian agency in driving colonial genocides.[82] Debates on genocide on other settler frontiers in North America, including its eastern half, and in parts of Southern Africa and in Patagonia have followed a similar pattern.[83] In any case,

[81] Edward B. Westermann, *Hitler's Ostkrieg and the Indian Wars: Comparing Genocide and Conquest* (Norman: University of Oklahoma Press, 2016); Alex Alvarez, *Native America and the Question of Genocide* (Lanham: Rowman and Littlefield, 2014), Gary Clayton Anderson, *Ethnic Cleansing and the Indian: The Crime that Should Haunt America* (Norman: University of Oklahoma Press 2014). For the same argument that includes the Australian context, see Paul Bartrop, 'Punitive Expeditions and Massacres: Gippsland, Colorado, and the Question of Genocide', in Moses (ed.), *Genocide and Settler Society*, 194–216.

[82] See, on California, Brendan C. Lindsay, *Murder State: California's Native American Genocide, 1846–1873* (Lincoln: University of Nebraska Press, 2012); Benjamin Madley, *An American Genocide: The United States and the California Indian Catastrophe, 1846–1873* (New Haven: Yale University Press, 2016). On Australia, see Lyndall Ryan, 'Settler Massacres on the Australian Colonial Frontier 1836–1851', in Paul Dwyer and Lyndall Ryan (eds.), *Theatres of Violence: Massacre, Mass Killing and Atrocity Throughout History* (New York and Oxford: Berghahn Books, 2012) 94–109; Stephen Gapps, *The Sydney Wars: Conflict in the Early Colony 1788–1817* (Sydney: NewSouth Publishing, 2018); Tony Roberts, *Frontier Justice: A History of the Gulf Country to 1900* (St. Lucia: University of Queensland Press, 2005); Jonathan Richards, *The Secret War: A True History of Queensland's Native Police* (St. Lucia: University of Queensland Press, 2008).

[83] On the US, see Russell Thornton, *American Indian Holocaust and Survival: A Population History Since 1492* (Norman: University of Oklahoma Press 1987); David E. Stannard, *American Holocaust: The Conquest of the New World* (New York: Oxford University Press, 1994); Ward Churchill, *A Little Matter Of Genocide: Holocaust and Denial In the Americas, 1492 to The Present* (San Francisco: City Lights Books, 1998); Andrew Woolford, Jeff Benvenuto, and Alexander Hinton (eds.), *Colonial Genocide in Indigenous North America* (Durham, NC: Duke University Press, 2014); Jeffrey Ostler, '"Just and Lawful War" as Genocidal War in the (United States) Northwest

the indigenous economies were especially vulnerable to settler invasions—settler herbivores and a settler commons established and enforced on indigenous resources and lands effectively disabled indigenous subsistence.[84] Pastoral and agricultural settler colonialisms impacted differently on the indigenous hunting-gathering economies; the pastoral invasions were especially disruptive. As Mohamed Adhikari has noted, the invasions of commercial stock farmers were 'rapid' and 'intent on thoroughgoing and permanent confiscation of land and resources, and far less compromising in dealing with indigenous resistance' than 'colonising crop growers'. While 'crop farming was locally more destructive of indigenous societies because it supported denser populations and occupied land more comprehensively and permanently', he concluded, 'the impact of stock farming extended much more swiftly over larger areas, and was nonetheless devastating to hunter-gatherer communities'.[85]

A decentred political geometry has important consequences for the distinct ways in which violence, including genocidal violence, operates in settler-colonial frontiers. As argued above, all empires unleash violence as they are constituted in institutional forms. That's why Marx, for example, who was developing an understanding of 'primitive accumulation' (or originary: *Ursprüngliche*) looked at the colonies as well as England.[86] He understood capital as stored-up labour.

Ordinance and Northwest Territory, 1787–1832', *Journal of Genocide Research*, 18:1 (2016), 1–20; Laurelyn Whitt and Alan W. Clarke, *North American Genocides: Indigenous Nations, Settler Colonialism, and International Law* (Cambridge: Cambridge University Press, 2019); and Jeffrey Ostler, *Surviving Genocide: Native Nations and the United States from the American Revolution to Bleeding Kansas* (New Haven: Yale University Press, 2019). For a global perspective, see Mohamed Adhikari (ed.), *Civilian-Driven Genocides and the Genocide of Indigenous Peoples in Settler Societies* (Cape Town: University of Cape Town Press, 2020).

[84] Allan Greer, 'Commons and Enclosure in the Colonization of North America', *American Historical Review* 117:2 (2012), 365–86; Allan Greer, 'Settler Colonialism and Empire in Early America', *William and Mary Quarterly* 76:3 (2019), 383–90.

[85] Mohamed Adhikari, '"We are Determined to Exterminate Them": The Genocidal Impetus Behind Commercial Stock Farmer Invasions of Hunter-Gatherer Territories', in Adhikari (ed.), *Genocide on Settler Frontiers*, 4.

[86] Karl Marx, *Capital*, Vol. I, Chapter 28 (1867), https://www.marxists.org/archive/marx/works/1867-c1/ch28.htm.

Similarly, instituted colonialism, the imperial condition that follows primitive accumulation, can be understood as stored-up violence. And like capital can be reproduced or expended, colonial violence can be reproduced or superseded. Colonialism—empire—and settler colonialism can thus be conceptualized as distinct modes of domination because the former relies on violence in moving beyond the imperial threshold and then exacts tribute, while the other overcomes it through the elimination of indigenous alterities. Primitive accumulation is violent appropriation and dispossession—in the case of imperialism it is originary and results in an ongoing violent and unequal relationship, but in the case of settler colonialism, as a mode of domination premised on a logic of elimination, it is at once originary and final. Wolfe's conclusion that 'settler colonialism is a structure' in this context is another way of saying that settler colonialism perpetually appropriates in an originary way.[87] Marx focused mainly on England because the industrial revolution began there, but Wolfe and others have drawn attention to the settler colonial conditions of capitalist development, which entailed a massive land theft.[88]

Violence that is originary and final is a good definition of genocide: at the end of settler colonialism (and yet indigenous people resist the settler-colonial onslaught and survive and reclaim their unsurrendered sovereignty), like at the end of genocide, there is no relationship between victim and perpetrator. Tacitus' 'desert' comes to mind: violence on settler frontiers erases the conditions for its reproduction. Zygmunt Bauman believes that genocides are most likely when the sovereign has consolidated, when it has developed powerful destructive capabilities, but it is at the other extreme of this spectrum of possibility that genocide is also most likely: where the state has not yet

[87] Patrick Wolfe, *Settler Colonialism and the Transformation of Anthropology: The Politics and Poetics of an Ethnographic Event* (London: Cassell, 1999), 163.

[88] See Patrick Wolfe, *Traces of History: Elementary Structures of Race* (London, Verso, 2016); Gabriel Piterberg and Lorenzo Veracini, 'Wakefield, Marx and the World Turned Inside Out', *Journal of Global History*, 10:3 (2015), 457–78; Andrew Zimmerman, 'From the Second American Revolution to the First International and Back Again: Marxism, the Popular Front, and the American Civil War', in Gregory Downs, Kate Masur (eds.), *The World the Civil War Made* (Chapel Hill: University of North Carolina Press, 2015) 304–26.

entered the scene, and where bureaucratic apparatuses are unable or unwilling to exercise their restraining potential.[89]

Conclusion: Violence, Empire, Genocide

Imperial rule is thus ambivalent. On the one hand, surpassing the 'imperial threshold' (i.e. the transition from tribal to complex societies) was a step towards the preservation of the conquered instead of their total annihilation. This was also a move towards shielding a polity from the imponderables of an anarchic structure. That is where—somewhat counterintuitively—imperial rule could display its potential to limit violence. On the other hand, the emergence of large entities, focusing on the extraction of a surplus, did not bring the end of extreme violence. As we have shown, violence was inherent to imperial formation; at times it could be unleashed as extreme and genocidal violence.

Throughout the history of empires, the dynamics of violence and war led to escalation and sometimes degenerated into genocide. In general, these dynamics are related to two characteristics of imperial control. First, as we have argued, empires were 'weak states', composite entities that could break apart. As the agents of empires—administrators and military commanders—tried to conceal their weakness, emotions were often paramount in shaping policy responses: when the grandiose self-perception of the builders of empire was shattered, substantial destructive energies could be unleashed. The genocidal potential inherent in imperial power was thus responding to more and less rational drivers.[90]

---

[89] See Zygmunt Bauman, *Modernity and the Holocaust* (Cambridge: Polity Press, 1989). For a critique of Bauman's contention, see A. Dirk Moses, 'Genocide and Modernity', in Dan Stone (ed.), *The Historiography of Genocide* (Houndmills: Palgrave Macmillan, 2008), 156–93.

[90] One episode epitomizes this dynamic. An assassination attempt against the local colonial governor in Addis Ababa in 1937 was followed by an orgy of indiscriminate violence, and about 20,000 Ethiopians were massacred in the capital, while about 10,000 more were slaughtered elsewhere in the country. From his hospital bed, General Rodolfo Graziani coordinated the massacres; he knew about persistent rumours insinuating that he had been emasculated in the explosions that had injured him and was especially interested in exacting

Given the often ephemeral presence of the empire's institutions beyond the scattered 'islands' of imperial power in the major cities and trading posts, the intensity of rule in the colonies and imperial provinces was way less developed than in modern nation-states. The larger the imperial space, the more dispersed its forces. This was usually true for both the colonial administration (if it did not remain largely in the hands of the 'conquered' through forms of indirect rule), the imperial troops, and the dispersed settlers. The imperial powers often confronted anti-imperial insurgencies relatively late, and depending on the dynamics of these counterinsurgency efforts—affected by settler paranoia, the soldiers' and the officials' emotions, and the administrators' willingness to set an example (and the local populations' resistance when fighting ferociously for their livelihood)—war could lead to the extinction of whole groups, thus to genocidal outcomes.

And yet, despite its sometimes total character, imperial rule was precarious by definition. Empires were composites of (formally dependent) political units. This means that each of the semi-independent components had a potential for rebellion, and if successful, autonomous existence, a potential autonomy that relatively weak empires had to take into consideration when responding to challenges to imperial rule. And yet, as the imperial powers aimed to avoid any appearance of weakness and to ensure that rebellion did not set a precedent that could shake the empire to its foundations, responses to resistance were often extreme. Once challenged, the empire and the settlers on the ground tended to respond with extreme cruelty, resorting repeatedly to exemplary, excessive, and corrupting wrathful violence.

Select Bibliography

Barkey, Karen, *Empire of Difference: The Ottomans in Comparative Perspective* (Cambridge: Cambridge University Press, 2008).

---

exemplary revenge. See Ian Campbell, *The Addis Ababa Massacre: Italy's National Shame* (Oxford: Oxford University Press, 2017), and Giuseppe Finaldi, 'Fascism, Violence, and Italian Colonialism', *Journal of Holocaust Research* 33:1 (2019), 22–42.

Belich, James, *Replenishing the Earth: The Settler Revolution and the Rise of the Anglo–World, 1783–1939* (Oxford: Oxford University Press, 2009).

Burbank, Jane and Frederick Cooper, *Empires in World History: Power and the Politics of Difference* (Princeton: Princeton University Press, 2010).

Cavanagh, Edward and Lorenzo Veracini (eds.), *The Routledge Handbook of the History of Settler Colonialism* (London: Routledge, 2016).

Fradera, Josep, *The Imperial Nation: Citizens and Subjects in the British, French, Spanish, and American Empires* (Princeton: Princeton University Press, 2018).

Häussler, Matthias, *The Herero Genocide: War, Emotion, and Extreme Violence in Colonial Namibia* (New York: Berghahn, 2021).

Kautsky, John H., *The Politics of Aristocratic Empires* (New Brunswick: Transaction Publishers, 1997).

Keeley, Lawrence H., *War Before Civilization: The Myth of the Peaceful Savage* (New York and Oxford: Oxford University Press, 1996).

Levene, Mark, *Genocide in the Age of the Nation-State*, 2 vols. (London: I.B. Tauris, 2005).

Moses, A. Dirk (ed.), *Empire, Colony, Genocide: Conquest, Occupation, and Subaltern Resistance in World History* (New York and Oxford: Berghahn Books, 2008).

Levine, Philippa, *The Rise and Fall of Modern Empires*, 3 vols. (Farnham: Ashgate, 2013).

Veracini, Lorenzo, *Settler Colonialism: A Theoretical Overview* (Basingstoke: Palgrave Macmillan, 2010).

Walter, Dierk, *Colonial Violence: European Empires and the Use of Force* (London: Hurst, 2017).

Wolfe, Patrick, *Traces of History: Elementary Structures of Race* (London: Verso, 2016).

8

Genocide and War

Michelle Moyd

Introduction

In 1951, Black members of the Civil Rights Congress, an affiliate of the US Communist Party, submitted to the United Nations (UN) a petition entitled *We Charge Genocide*. The document enumerated acts of state-sanctioned violence against Black people, with a particular focus on lynchings carried out between 1945 and 1951. The introduction, authored by the group's National Executive Secretary William L. Patterson, named the grounds on which the charge of genocide rested: 'Out of the inhuman black ghettos of American cities, out of the cotton plantations of the South, comes this record of mass slayings on the basis of race, of lives deliberately warped and distorted by the willful creation of conditions making for premature death, poverty, and disease'.[1] *We Charge Genocide* explained in forceful terms why the treatment of Black people in the US should be considered genocide. It used the 1948 Genocide Convention to anchor its argumentation. Situated in the midst of the Cold War, the women and men of the Civil Rights Congress presented clear evidence of the US's longstanding war against Black people, arguing that 'there is ample historical precedent for genocidal crime increasing against the Negro people in

---

[1] *We Charge Genocide: The Historic Petition to the United Nations for Relief from a Crime of the United States Government Against the Negro People* (New York: Civil Rights Congress, 1951), xi.

time of war or threat of war as it is now increasing and has been since 1945'.[2]

The Civil Rights Congress's petition to the UN, the evidence the organization brought to bear, and its argumentation, gesture to the possibilities that new lenses might bring to the analysis of genocide. People living through entrenched, repetitive state-sanctioned violence perceive that the state is at war with them. This chapter argues that war and genocide connect to each other visibly and invisibly in ways that are, in the end, best discerned by identifying and listening to the perspectives of those who are most likely to experience eliminationist violence. Their perspectives merit at least as much attention as the monitoring and interventionist practices of international agencies, concerned states, and humanitarian organizations. Rather than attempting to distinguish between 'war' and 'genocide', I assume that they are entangled and contingent, and explore three ways of analysing their interrelationships.[3] As an historian of East Africa and colonial warfare, I find few meaningful ways to distinguish between the two concepts that do not ultimately diminish the harrowing, deadly ordeals experienced by peoples victimized by states, corporations, militaries, and settlers over a much longer time span, and

---

[2] Ibid., 26.

[3] Hirad Abahi and Philippa Webb, *The Genocide Convention: The Travaux Préparatoires*, Vol. 1 (Leiden and Boston: Martinus Nijhoff Publishers, 2008), 230–2. The relevant section appears in Secretariat Draft E/447. A subsection entitled 'International War and Civil War' explains the legal distinction between war and genocide. It appears within a section (II. Article I—Section II) that explains the definition of genocide as a deliberate act, which means 'that its object must be the destruction of a group of human beings' (230). It then notes that 'certain acts which may result in the total or partial destruction of a group of human beings are in principle excluded from the notion of genocide, namely international or civil war, isolated acts of violence not aimed at the destruction of a group of human beings, the policy of compulsory assimilation of a national element, mass displacement of population' (231). After outlining acts of war that are *not* genocide, the draft acknowledges, 'War may, however, be accompanied by the crime of genocide. This happens when one of the belligerents aims at exterminating the population of enemy territory and systematically destroys what are not genuine objectives. Examples of this are the execution of prisoners of war, the massacre of the populations of occupied territory and their gradual extermination. These are clearly cases of genocide.'

across much wider geographies, than is typically acknowledged. The 1948 Genocide Convention barely acknowledged the possibility that genocidal colonial violence had occurred in the past, and ignored the possibility of its existing in the postwar present or future.[4] As Mark Mazower has argued regarding South African Prime Minister Jan Smuts's role in creating both the League of Nations and the United Nations, these organizations, and the 1948 Genocide Convention itself, emerged out of fundamentally racist and civilizationist colonial paradigms. Indeed, Mazower asks, 'Could it be, in short, that the United Nations started out life not as the instrument to end colonialism, but rather—at least in the minds of men like Smuts—as the means to preserve it?'.[5] W. E. B. DuBois, among others, immediately recognized that this question demanded an affirmative response.[6]

I therefore approach this topic in a decolonizing spirit, centring the notion that those who are most likely to experience annihilationist violence have a keen sense of how war and genocide intertwine, intersect, and reinforce each other. They wield, per Dylan Rodriquez, a potentially 'disruptive political audacity and transformative power'. This power resides 'in the fact that their conditions of urgency . . . override the question of whether their use of the term *genocide* is fully abiding by proper legal standards or academic definitions'.[7] In other words, the legalism of much discourse around genocide is of little consequence for

[4] I base this assessment on a text search of the names of former colonies in Africa, as well as terms such as 'Africa', 'colonies', 'colonial', 'Aboriginal', 'Native', and 'Indigenous' in Abahi and Webb, *The Genocide Convention: The Travaux Préparatoires*, cited above. While 'South Africa' appears with some regularity, other mentions of colonies are notably sparse in the volume's more than 2,000 pages of text.

[5] Mark Mazower, *No Enchanted Palace: The End of Empire and the Ideological Origins of the United Nations* (Princeton: Princeton University Press, 2009), 30–1.

[6] W. E. B. Du Bois, 'None Who Saw Paris Will Ever Forget', *National Guardian*, 16 May 1949 in David Levering Lewis (ed.), *W.E.B. DuBois: A Reader* (New York: Henry Holt and Company, 1995), 755–6. See also Mazower, *No Enchanted Palace*, 62–3; and Adom Getachew, *Worldmaking after Empire: The Rise and Fall of Self-Determination* (Princeton and Oxford: Princeton University Press, 2019), 81–7.

[7] Dylan Rodriguez, 'Inhabiting the Impasse: Racial/Racial-Colonial Power, Genocide Poetics, and the Logic of Evisceration', *Social Text* 33:3 (2015), 26. See also Alfred Frankowski and Lisa Skitolsky, 'Lang's Defence and the Morbid Sensibility of Genocide Studies', *Journal of Genocide Research* 20:3 (2018), 423–8.

the lived experiences of those whose day-to-day existence is shaped by ongoing forms of eliminationist violence. I also foreground colonial warfare as a provocative means of illuminating how scholarship might more fully represent the varieties of ways that war and genocide interconnect.

This chapter proceeds through five sections. First, I explain why studying genocide from the perspective of colonial warfare enhances analytical possibilities for understanding their entanglement. Second, I provide an overview of existing scholarship on war and genocide in order to show why such analysis matters for scholars and students who want better tools for understanding this complex subject. The third, fourth, and fifth sections offer three different lenses, or heuristics, for seeing how war and genocide relate to each other.[8] My intent in presenting these lenses is not to discipline different examples into fixed typologies. Rather, each of these sections suggest different ways of interpreting historical and current examples that might aid in recognizing how war and genocide interconnect in different times and places. I conclude with brief reflections on what these heuristics might contribute to the ongoing work of analysing war and genocide as part of a decolonizing project.

War and Genocide: Decolonizing Perspectives

War, or the threat of war, creates conditions that political or military regimes use as justification for planning and carrying out mass violence against their enemies. These enemies may be real, perceived, or conjured to suit particular political agendas. Rhetorics of security, purity, and belonging undergird administrative and violent practices in which soldiers, police, auxiliaries, militias, and ordinary people commit genocidal violence. These connections between war and genocide have been deeply analysed for certain contexts, such as the First and Second World Wars, Armenia in 1915, and Darfur, for example. Far less attention has been dedicated to understanding this nexus in other global history contexts, such as colonial warfare, where analytical imprecision leads to confusing categorizations. For instance,

---

[8] Thanks to Donald Bloxham for suggesting this approach.

historians largely agree that German violence against Herero and Nama peoples in German Southwest Africa between 1904 and 1907 constituted genocide.[9] Yet on the other side of the continent during roughly the same years, the colonial army in German East Africa killed hundreds of thousands of people in the Maji Maji war. The dead included the East African combatants who had engaged in armed anti-colonial struggle against German colonial agents. But the majority of deaths during Maji Maji resulted from the *Schutztruppe*'s ruthless scorched earth campaign that caused widespread famine and displacement in much of the southern half of German East Africa. This sustained, multifaceted lethal violence is rarely described as genocide, though it killed as many as 300,000 Tanzanians.

This begs the question, why is this instance of colonial violence not classed as genocidal?[10] One answer is that the analytical focus in examining these simultaneous examples of mass violence has been split up in unproductive ways. The Herero-Nama War is characterized as a genocide, and Maji Maji is characterized as a colonial war. But a more fruitful description is that they were both genocidal colonial wars, and this premise is a necessary starting point for rethinking how war and genocide interrelate. In both cases, German colonial armies used purposeful combinations of lethal tactics to defeat and subjugate African peoples. In both instances, mass death was the outcome. Turn-of-the-century genocidal colonial wars against indigenous peoples in Africa, North America, Australia, and other colonized spaces presaged genocides that occurred later in the twentieth century. They were not a separate species of warfare. They therefore warrant closer study in assessing relationships between war and genocide.

---

[9] Jürgen Zimmerer and Joachim Zeller (eds.), *Genocide in German South-West Africa: the Colonial War (1904–1908) in Namibia and its Aftermath* (Monmouth: Merlin Press, 2008).

[10] One exception to this tendency is Dominik J. Schaller, 'From Conquest to Genocide: Colonial Rule in German Southwest Africa and German East Africa', in A. Dirk Moses (ed.), *Empire, Colony Genocide: Conquest, Occupation, and Subaltern Resistance in World History* (New York and Oxford: Berghahn Books, 2008), 296–324.

A second answer to the question of why some wars are considered genocide while others are not is that a focus on prevention, as articulated by international agencies, non-governmental organizations (NGOs), or states, can obscure the perspectives of those most likely to experience genocidal violence as part of war. Shifting perspective to foreground the victims' vantage points offers different possibilities for recognizing, interrupting, and perhaps even preventing new genocides, exposing processes that, if not interrupted, can culminate in eliminationist violence.

States, settlers, and others who have consolidated authority over people, land, and resources mobilize the tools at their disposal for implementing their visions of homogenous futures. In literal terms, these powerful entities go to war against enemies overseas, across borders or, as in the case of counterinsurgency, within territorial boundaries of nation-states and colonial territories. Indeed, one scholar posits that genocides 'actually more often occur in the context of *intrastate* warfare' than other contexts.[11] Recent examples that demonstrate such a progression include military attacks on Rohingya Muslims in Myanmar, pogroms against Indian Muslims in Delhi by Hindu nationalists, and the US's detention and neglect of Central American and other immigrants held in its carceral archipelago.

In metaphorical terms though, these kinds of powerful entities can also go to war against populations constructed as anathema to their fantasies of homogeneity, notions of purity, or security logics. The passage of the UN Convention on the Punishment and Prevention of Genocide in 1948 focused international legal attention on the question of intent to annihilate groups. But this focus has not been terribly successful in preventing the occurrence of new genocides. As Dirk Moses writes with reference to the International Criminal Tribunal for the former Yugoslavia (ICTY), 'The tribunal's use of the law of conspiracy, complicity, and incitement means that international jurisprudence is catching up with social scientists who realized long ago that narrow, black-letter interpretations of the convention's stipulations regarding genocidal intention cannot do justice to the messy

---

[11] Cheng Xu, 'Draining the Sea: Counterinsurgency as an Instrument of Genocide', *Genocide Studies International* 12:1 (2018), 7.

reality in which such intentions evolve'.[12] Seeing these 'messy realities' after the fact may enable bringing some perpetrators to justice for violating international law. But they do not save lives, because they do not disrupt or prevent genocidal processes before they reach annihilationist dimensions.

Deliberative efforts to discern between 'war' and 'genocide' as defined by international law seem incapable of expediting interventions to arrest these processes. Wartime violence is in fact very difficult, if not impossible, to contain, meaning that harm to civilians is not exceptional. Rather, it is to be expected. And in attempting to narrowly define genocide as mass violence that conforms to specific definitions, most notably the intentional targeting of groups for elimination, those with the power and resources to prevent genocide are not listening to those most likely to experience such violence. In a better world, international bodies and governments would take seriously those who predict and are witnesses to their own potential destruction. Prioritizing these perspectives highlights how colonial ways of war, including massacres, expulsions, and atrocities that pre-existed the 1948 Genocide Convention—have produced, and continue to produce—genocidal outcomes.[13]

A more finely honed sensibility about entanglements between war and genocide opens possibilities for discerning vulnerable populations and the risks for genocidal violence that shape their day-to-day existence. Colonial examples illustrate these entanglements with great clarity, since peoples living under colonialism often existed in states of precarity, the threat of quotidian and extraordinary violence looming over their everyday lives. Those who are most likely to become targets of eliminationist violence are also most familiar with the behaviours of those who commit such violence. They are thus best positioned to sound the alarm against its manifestations, whether

---

[12] A. Dirk Moses, 'Empire, Colony, Genocide: Keywords and the Philosophy of History', in Moses, *Empire, Colony, Genocide*, 20.

[13] Elisa von Joeden-Forgey, 'The Devil in the Details: "Life Force Atrocities" and the Assault on the Family in Times of Conflict', *Genocide Studies and Prevention* 5:1 (2010), 1–19.

slow-moving or (seemingly) sudden.[14] Too often, violence against vulnerable groups escapes analysis because it is legitimated by state, corporate, or settler priorities, or because it occurs in less visible forms than the more familiar and widely known variants of genocidal violence that shape public understanding. If the goal is to end such violence, we need different ways of seeing it. My purpose is not to redefine genocide or to contest existing definitions.[15] Rather, I want to call attention to how a narrow focus on 'genocide' as defined by the 1948 Convention limits consideration of a wide range of genocidal violence that often affects people who inhabit the margins of their societies. These people are deeply familiar with the processes that place them on the margins and keep them there, creating conditions that can tighten the knots connecting war and genocide.

War and Genocide in Existing Scholarship

Existing interdisciplinary scholarship on the connections between war and genocide is robust, offering important context for navigating the moral, legal, and political considerations that have informed thinking on the topic since 1948. In 2000, Helen Fein laid out these connections:

> The links between genocide and war are manifold. War releases aggression, allows the perpetrator to mask the crime and blame the victim for the war; indeed, the victim group may be the enemy. Wars lead to crises that destabilize society and may lead to the rise of revolutionary elites with genocidal ideologies which seek to reconstruct the society to fit the new order imposed by the state.[16]

Fein challenged what she perceived as an unhelpful demarcation drawn between genocide and civil war. She argued that the term 'civil wars' often allowed for 'modes of genocide denial'.[17] In other

---

[14] Elizabeth Hoover, *The River Is in Us: Fighting Toxics in a Mohawk Community* (Minneapolis and London: University of Minnesota Press, 2017), 9–12.

[15] Krista K. Thomason, 'If Everything Is Genocide, Nothing Is: Scepticism and the Concept of Genocide', *Journal of Genocide Research* 20:3 (2018), 412–16.

[16] Helen Fein, 'Civil Wars and Genocide: Paths and Circles', *Human Rights Review* 1:3 (2000), 49–61.

[17] Ibid., 50.

230 *Michelle Moyd*

work, Fein asserted the importance of definitions for '[honing] our critical faculties' in order to avoid mislabelling victims of different scales of 'violations . . . with a superblanket of generalized compassion as certified victims of "genocide"'.[18] Fein's work thus instructs readers in a precise, disciplined reading of war and genocide that forecloses wide applicability of the term. Still, she also calls for guarding against using euphemistic language that 'mask[s] genocide in a number of ways'.[19]

Other scholars have approached this problem differently, fore-grounding processes, political outcomes, and actors' behaviours rather than strict boundary-keeping around the concept of 'genocide'. Eric Markusen called for more 'expanded thinking', acknowledging that 'genocide, whether perpetrated during a war or not, clearly overlaps with crimes against civilian populations that are committed during warfare'.[20] In a controversial 1995 co-authored book, Markusen and Kopf argued that the logics and processes that had enabled the Holocaust were akin to those that underpinned Allied strategic bombing campaigns during the Second World War. The 'mass killing' caused by Allied strategic bomber crews in a context of 'total war', according to Markusen and Kopf, warranted comparison to the Holocaust.[21]

Scholars have also sought to explain the small-scale and contingent processes that often link war and genocide. Nancy Scheper-Hughes describes the 'everyday violence—"peacetime crimes"—[that make] structural violence and genocide possible', using multi-sited research as well as intimate family histories to support her argument.[22]

[18] Helen Fein, 'Genocide, Terror, Life Integrity, and War Crimes: The Case for Discrimination', in George Andreopoulos (ed.), *Genocide: Conceptual and Historical Dimensions* (Philadelphia: University of Pennsylvania Press, 1997), 105.

[19] Fein, 'Civil Wars and Genocide', 58.

[20] Eric Markusen, 'Genocide and Warfare', in Charles B. Strozier and Michael Flynn (eds.), *Genocide, War, and Human Survival* (London: Rowman and Littlefield, 1996), 83.

[21] Eric Markusen and David Kopf, *The Holocaust and Strategic Bombing: Genocide and Total War in the Twentieth Century* (Boulder, CO: Westview Press, 1995), 1–5.

[22] Nancy Scheper-Hughes, 'The Genocidal Continuum: Peace-Time Crimes', in Jeannette Mageo (ed.), *Power and the Self* (Cambridge: Cambridge University Press, 2002), 30.

Catherine Barnes emphasizes the political outcomes of genocide, noting the importance of understanding how 'genocide is functionally useful for its organizers and, in particular, ... how it helps a regime to consolidate, expand or maintain its control over a domain'. In this way, war and genocide produce similar outcomes.[23] Janine Natalya Clark shows how perpetrators' behaviours can shift depending on the local social contexts of violence within which they operate, arguing that perpetrators exhibit a 'sliding scale' of conduct that can 'rapidly fluctuate between acts of cruelty and kindness'.[24] These contextual, local shifts hinge on the smallest changes in conditions that then convince soldiers and auxiliaries to do things they otherwise might not have. Martin Shaw contends that 'genocide may constitute a widespread potential of contemporary armed conflict', and that scholars must be attentive both to the distinctions between war and genocide as well as their enmeshment.[25]

Like other scholars, Mark Levene has argued that war creates conditions for genocide. However, the vast geographic and temporal scope of his body of work is distinct. His two-volume study *The Crisis of Genocide* identifies three 'types' of war that, he argues, can help to analytically 'isolate genocide's incidence'.[26] In contrast to Martin Shaw's concept of 'degenerate war', Levene uses 'degenerative' to emphasize dynamic processes and shifting conditions over fixity.[27] He notes that 'unfolding, worsening, and by degree more "totalist" pursuit of war by belligerents over time might bring in its wake a greater

---

[23] Catherine Barnes, 'The Functional Utility of Genocide: Towards a Framework for Understanding the Connection between Genocide and Regime Consolidation, Expansion and Maintenance', *Journal of Genocide Research* 7:3 (2005), 309.

[24] Janine Natalya Clark, 'Genocide, War Crimes and the Conflict in Bosnia: Understanding the Perpetrators', *Journal of Genocide Research* 11:4 (2009), 421–45. See also Lee Ann Fujii, *Killing Neighbors: Webs of Violence in Rwanda* (Ithaca: Cornell University Press, 2009), 170–9.

[25] Martin Shaw, 'The General Hybridity of War and Genocide,' *Journal of Genocide Research* 9:3 (2007), 461–73.

[26] Mark Levene, *The Crisis of Genocide*, Vol. 2, *Annihilation: The European Rimlands 1939–1953* (Oxford: Oxford University Press, 2014), 236. Levene developed this typology in *Genocide in the Age of the Nation-State: The Meaning of Genocide* (London: I. B. Tauris, 2005), 56.

[27] As Shaw explains in *War and Genocide*: 'while genocide is a distinctive form of war, it is, nevertheless, an extension of ... *degenerate* war', in which unarmed civilian

readiness to dispense with normative rules distinguishing surrendered POWs, or non-combatants, from active enemy participants, a consequence could well be genocidal outcomes'.[28] Although rare in the war in Western Europe, he argued, this pattern was frequent in European 'rimlands arenas'—areas like the Balkans and other zones where antisemitism, imperial aspirations, and nation-states intersected to produce genocidal probabilities.[29] Attentive to layered geopolitical and spatial conditions, Levene's analysis offers fluidity and registers, and unlike Shaw's, does not attempt to distinguish a theoretical generic *war* from *degenerate* war.[30]

Genocide survey texts tend to explain the relationships between war and genocide by noting, like others mentioned above, that war produces conditions that enable genocide. John Cox's *To Kill a People: Genocide in the Twentieth Century* (2017) studies four examples—Armenia, the Holocaust, Cambodia, and Rwanda.[31] He differentiates between 'nongenocidal atrocities' and genocide, though he cautions against 'rigidly delineat[ing]' between them. '[T]o the family, witness or survivor of a brutal massacre in a village in Sierra Leone or Afghanistan or El Salvador', he writes, 'it would not be the least bit comforting to learn that someone far away determined that the killing was "merely" a human rights abuse or war crime rather than "genocide"'.[32] He concludes that war is 'the principal source of genocide'. War creates opportunities to objectify enemies, allows 'perpetrator regimes' to cast target groups as security threats, produces a permissive environment for exterminatory violence, and gives violence

populations are deliberately targeted, resulting in mass death. Martin Shaw, *War and Genocide* (Cambridge: Polity Press, 2003), 5. See also Levene, *The Crisis of Genocide*, Vol. 2, 234.

[28] Levene, *The Crisis of Genocide*, Vol. 2, 35.

[29] Mark Levene, *The Crisis of Genocide*, Vol. 1, *Devastation: The European Rimlands 1912–1938* (Oxford: Oxford University Press, 2014), 5–6.

[30] Shaw, *War and Genocide*, 5. Shaw's idea of degenerate war contrasts with what he calls 'legitimate war', by which he means war that is 'restricted to combatants' and 'qualified by rules of war'.

[31] John Cox, *To Kill a People: Genocide in the Twentieth Century* (Oxford: Oxford University Press, 2017), 4.

[32] Ibid., 12.

workers unfettered access to vulnerable civilian populations.[33] War also 'obscures or hides terrible atrocities', and 'provides a cover for the radical goals and actions of violent regimes'.[34] Michael Mann's *The Dark Side of Democracy* echoes this point regarding the history of ethnic cleansing, noting that higher numbers of deaths result from its occurrence during war.[35] Adam Jones's *Genocide: A Comprehensive Introduction* describes war and genocide as 'conjoined twins', noting that 'many rank war as genocide's greatest single enabling factor',[36] and identifying seven 'points of connection between war and genocide'.[37] Thus the idea that war creates the conditions for genocide is reinforced in all of these texts.

Unstated assumptions embedded in conceptual discussions of genocide convey a sense that only certain kinds of mass violence in war warrant categorization as genocide. Paul Bartrop, for example, ties the origin of the acceptance of 'mass death' to the Great War, 'which provided humans with the belief that they could, with impunity, slaughter massive numbers of their own kind'.[38] The Great War, according to Bartrop, showed 'ordinary people' that mass death was not difficult to accomplish, and 'played an enormous role as midwife to the modern concept of genocide', the gendered metaphor left unexamined.[39]

This argument mostly ignores the main sites where warfare frequently caused mass death well before the First World War: colonized spaces in Africa, North America, Australia, and elsewhere. The unacknowledged, probably unrecognized, criterion for what qualifies as genocide is a white European analytical perspective that renders

[33] Cox, *To Kill a People*, 204–6. See also Scott Straus, *The Order of Genocide: Race, Power, and War in Rwanda* (Ithaca: Cornell University Press, 2006). On violence workers, see Micol Seigel, *Violence Workers: State Power and the Limits of Police* (Durham, NC: Duke University Press, 2018).

[34] Cox, *To Kill a People*, 208.

[35] Michael Mann, *The Dark Side of Democracy* (Cambridge: Cambridge University Press, 2005), 32.

[36] Adam Jones, *Genocide: A Comprehensive Introduction*, 118.

[37] ibid., 118–22.

[38] Paul Bartrop, 'The Relationship Between War and Genocide in the Twentieth Century: A Consideration,' *Journal of Genocide Research* 4:4 (2002), 522.

[39] Ibid., 524.

invisible the genocidal potential of colonial wars. Bartrop's brief mention of the Herero-Nama genocide in German Southwest Africa only brings into sharper relief the many other examples of devastating colonial wars his analysis elides. Inclusion of these would immediately undermine the notion that the Great War was the first time people came to understand mass killing. In ignoring the many colonial wars that occurred in different parts of the world before 1914, Bartrop renders most colonial warfare outside of consideration as genocidal.[40]

The fact is that colonial contexts offer ample and clear reasons to question the utility of narrowly defining whether or not genocide took place. They illustrate the intertwining of war and genocide in their tendencies towards uncontainable violence. The parallels between imperial histories rooted in settler colonial violence against indigenous peoples, and the patterns that resemble later genocides, are impossible to ignore. US military and settler wars against indigenous peoples, for example, used forms of violence that resulted in genocide. Yet most scholars have seemed resistant to making such arguments.[41] This is beginning to change. Historian Benjamin Madley proposes a method for analysing whether or not violence against indigenous peoples constituted genocide. His comprehensive research on US Army violence against indigenous peoples of California uses a 'case study' method that 'reframe[s] the debate [on colonial genocide] by focusing on the question of genocide for particular tribes rather than all Native Americans'.[42] Using the UN Genocide Convention as a rubric, he closely analyses wartime violence against the Pequot and Yuki, identifying four 'markers' that denote 'ways of locating, and ultimately defining, *prima facie* cases of genocide'.[43] His markers for classifying violence against the Pequot and Yuki as genocide are the presence of

[40] See Dylan Rodriquez, 'Inhabiting the Impasse: Racial/Racial-Colonial Power, Genocide Poetics, and the Logic of Evisceration', *Social Text* 33:3 (2015), 19–44.

[41] Marouf Hasian, Jr., *Debates on Colonial Genocide in the 21st Century* (Basingstoke: Palgrave Macmillan, 2020), 16–17, 139–41.

[42] Benjamin Madley, 'Reexamining the American Genocide Debate: Meaning, Historiography, and New Methods', *American Historical Review* 120:1 (2015), 99. See also Benjamin Madley, *An American Genocide: The United States and the California Indian Catastrophe* (New Haven: Yale University Press, 2016).

[43] Madley, 'Reexamining the American Genocide Debate', 109.

'annihilationist statements, massacres, state-sponsored body-part bounties, and mass death in government custody'.[44] This 'mosaic' method, he argues, can be applied to analyses in other US and global historical contexts as well.[45]

Because Madley's primary goal is to prove that the US Army perpetrated genocide against Native peoples in California in the nineteenth century, his main focus is on the violent actors responsible for genocide. Markers for classifying genocidal violence that might be consequential for certain cases might not apply in others. Madley's powerful analysis, for instance, might have done more to explore gendered forms of violence as determinants of the longer-term structural cruelties perpetrated against Native peoples during US expansionist and settler colonial wars.[46] For indigenous peoples who survived genocide, peace brought an end to the overt forms of violence recognized by the UN Convention. But peace also often simply meant the continuation of warfare by other means—removal, expropriation, confinement, neglect, death. These factors do not register as genocide in the UN Convention. But they were part of genocidal colonial violence against Native peoples nonetheless.[47]

Considering war's similarities to genocide under certain circumstances clarifies the perspectives of indigenous and colonized peoples who suffered sustained violence during expansionist wars, as well as their aftermaths, including removal to reservations and other systematic abuses that caused lasting harm to their communities. William Bauer, Jr., in a favourable review of Madley's book, nonetheless pointed out that 'the lack of Native voices and perspectives created a flattened picture of how California Indians responded to and attempted to shape the genocidal policies aimed at them', adopting

[44] Ibid.

[45] Ibid., 133.

[46] Margaret Jacobs, 'Bearing Witness to California Genocide', *Journal of Genocide Research* 19:1 (2017), 143–9; and Jeffrey Ostler, 'California and the American Genocide Debate,' *Journal of Genocide Studies* 19:1 (2017), 149–54.

[47] Nick Estes, *Our History is the Future: Standing Rock versus the Dakota Access Pipeline, and the Long Tradition of Indigenous Resistance* (London and New York: Verso, 2019), 74–8. Jeffrey Ostler, *Surviving Genocide Native Nations and the United States from the American Revolution to Bleeding Kansas* (New Haven: Yale University Press, 2019).

religious and other meaningful strategies.[48] From this vantage point, it is much harder to justify classifying certain kinds of organized violence as genocide and others not. For indigenous peoples who experienced the ravages of colonial warfare, distinguishing between war and genocide would have been largely meaningless. For many Native peoples in the US in the nineteenth century, as well as those who experienced colonialism in other parts of the world, war was genocide.

In considering how war and genocide relate to each other then, centring indigenous peoples in the histories of settler-colonial wars highlights their inherent genocidal violence, and becomes 'a method for understanding these understudied worlds'.[49] Foregrounding indigenous frameworks for understanding the violence of settler colonialism immediately makes clear that 'not only are genocides always colonial, but colonial rule and colonialism as such are constantly genocidal'.[50] By extension then, colonial wars are a productive lens for sharpening our understandings of the intertwined relationships between war and genocide.

War Creates Conditions for Genocide

The most straightforward way of understanding the relationship between war and genocide is to recognize that war facilitates genocidal violence. Armies, other armed entities such as settler militia, and government agents, have all participated in recurrent patterns of mass

[48] William Bauer, Jr. 'Ghost Dances, Bears and the Legacies of Genocide in California', *Journal of Genocide Research* 19:1 (2017), 139–40. Madley consulted with many people from various American Indian nations, who helped him shape his perspectives. However, he 'could not obtain permission from the tribes involved to quote them' in his book. Benjamin Madley, 'Genocide in the Golden State: A Response to Reviews by William Bauer, Margaret Jacobs, Karl Jacoby and Jeffrey Ostler', *Journal of Genocide Research* 19:1 (2017), 161.

[49] Ned Blackhawk, *Violence Over the Land* (Cambridge, MA: Harvard University Press, 2008), 5–6. See also Michael A. McDonnell and A. Dirk Moses, 'Raphael Lemkin as Historian of Genocide in the Americas', *Journal of Genocide Research* 7:4 (2005), 521–2; and Roxanne Dunbar-Ortiz, *An Indigenous Peoples' History of the United States* (Boston: Beacon Press, 2014), 8–10; and Jeffrey Ostler, ' "Just and Lawful War" as Genocidal War in the (United States) Northwest Ordinance and Northwest Territory, 1787–1832', *Journal of Genocide Research* 18:1 (2016), 1–20.

[50] Schaller, 'From Conquest to Genocide', 317.

violence that qualify as genocides.[51] Soldiers, auxiliaries, and ordinary
people equipped with weapons can kill with brutal efficiency when
encouraged, expected, or ordered to do so by their leaders. Hitler's
war in the East provided the context within which German soldiers,
police, and auxiliaries killed thousands of Jews, Poles, Soviets, and
others as they occupied vast swathes of territory in Eastern Europe.
These combatants carried out genocide, fulfilling Nazi visions of
Lebensraum and racial purification of the East. In many ways, this
example best illustrates how wars create the conditions and mechanisms for genocide. An extensive body of scholarship documents the
processes that led to the genocide of millions of Jews, Roma, and Sinti,
queer people, disabled people, and political enemies who did not fit
the National Socialist vision of a homogenous Aryan population and
future.

The contours of this brutal history are well-known. Well before
Operation Barbarossa began in June 1941, military and security
officials knew Hitler's intentions in the East: 'to effect a racist war of
annihilation'.[52] Numerous 'commands and criminal orders' were
issued to provide guidance to the Wehrmacht. Parallel to these orders,
Reichsführer SS Heinrich Himmler undertook planning for 'the
physical liquidation of "Jewish-Bolshevik" elements in the population'
with the help of SS *Einsatzgruppen*. These operations were to take place
'directly behind the front in the rear of the army areas'.[53] Officials
formulated these 'directives and procedures' with complete disregard
for international law or the rules of war, and their ideological roots
were indisputably to be found in Hitler's racist and murderous program of *Lebensraum*.[54]

[51] See also Mark Levene, 'Empires, Native Peoples, and Genocide', in Moses,
Empire, Colony, Genocide, 184–5.

[52] Gerd R. Überschär, 'The Ideologically Motivated War of Annihilation in the
East', in Rolf-Dieter Müller and Gerd R. Überschär (eds.), *Hitler's War in the East:
A Critical Assessment*, 2nd rev. ed., trans. Bruce D. Little (New York: Berghahn
Books, 2002), 209. See also Ian Kershaw, 'Hitler's Prophecy and the "Final
Solution"' in A. Dirk Moses (ed.), *Genocide: Critical Concepts in Historical Studies*,
Vol. 4 (London: Routledge, 2010), 218–33.

[53] Ueberschär, 'The Ideologically Motivated War of Annihilation', 210.

[54] Ibid., 211–12. For more on *Lebensraum*, see Shelley Baranowski, 'Against
"Human Diversity as Such": *Lebensraum* and Genocide in the Third Reich', in

In keeping with this ideological objective, the *Wehrmacht*, police units, the SS, and other auxiliaries carried out atrocities, mass killings, and deportations. The war created a space where soldiers committed mass violence against vulnerable populations with efficiency. As Browning puts it, 'nothing helped the Nazis to wage a race war so much as the war itself'.[55] During Operation Barbarossa, Order Police units carried out mass executions as part of the wider 'liquidation' programme that aimed to remove all Jews from occupied territory through deportation or death.[56]

As Hitler's war in the East demonstrates, war 'creates a polarized world in which "the enemy" is easily objectified and removed from the community of human obligation'.[57] Soldiers, police, and others deputized or empowered by the state to carry out such violence may act under explicit orders, or they may act on less explicit but no less powerful understandings that enemies must be expelled or eliminated.[58] State narratives about security and the necessity of protecting homelands, occupied lands, and other state-defined interests from the enemy, bolster officers' and soldiers' internalized narratives about the rightness of their wartime conduct.[59] These narratives are also supported by soldiers' desire and opportunity to do things that otherwise might not be permitted, to gain or defend respectability, or to impress peers through performance of expected gender roles, such as

Volker Langbehn and Mohammad Salama (eds.), *German Colonialism: Race, the Holocaust, and Postwar Germany* (New York: Columbia University Press, 2011), 51–71.

[55] Christopher Browning, *Ordinary Men: Reserve Police Battalion 101 and the Final Solution in Poland* (New York: Harper Perennial, 1998), 186.

[56] Ibid., 9–25.

[57] Ibid., 162.

[58] Ibid., 73, 161–2, 184, 186.

[59] Sönke Neitzel and Harald Welzer, *Soldaten: On Fighting, Killing and Dying: The Secret Second World War Tapes of German POWs*, trans. Jefferson Chase (London: Simon and Schuster, 2011), 120–63. For an example drawn from a much earlier French colonial context, see William Gallois, 'Dahra and the History of Violence in Early Colonial Algeria', in Martin Thomas (ed.), *The French Colonial Mind*, Vol. 2, *Violence, Military Encounters, and Colonialism* (Lincoln: University of Nebraska Press, 2011), 3–25.

military or police masculinities that value the enactment of violence on defenceless others.[60] After the fact, the cover of war also obfuscates individual complicity and involvement in genocidal violence, allowing perpetrators to claim that they were just following orders.

The twentieth and twenty-first centuries provided many other examples of wars that enabled genocide beyond the well-known examples of Hitler's war in the East. Rwanda, Bosnia, and Syria all come to mind as sites where war created conditions for genocide and ethnic cleansing.[61] It makes more sense to expect this outcome than not. Lack of information is not the main problem. Rather, the continuing uncritical practice of viewing wars through the frame of state, settler, or corporate legitimacy invariably means failing to hear what those targeted for genocide have to say about their own experiences and conditions, until it is too late.

War and Genocide Are Similar Forms of Violence

War and genocide often have significant similarities, making it hard to differentiate between them. Colonial wars in German Southwest Africa and German East Africa, fought in different spaces, but roughly at the same time, caused comparable levels of death and devastation. As noted above, historians typically only label the war in German Southwest Africa a genocide. On closer examination of Maji Maji, as the war in German East Africa became known, substantial questions emerge about why German colonial violence against the peoples of southern Tanzania has evaded scrutiny as an example of genocidal warfare, given the similarities between them.

With few exceptions, officers and soldiers in colonial armies did not have to concern themselves with defending their actions when they waged war against peoples whom they did not consider fully human. They acted with impunity, backed by racist and civilizationist ideologies that justified indiscriminate violence and by extension, wars of annihilation.[62] Military priorities superseded those of the civilian

---

[60] Neitzel and Welzer, *Soldaten*, 137, 149; Browning, *Ordinary Men*, 185–6.

[61] Lee Ann Fujii, 'Transforming the Moral Landscape: The Diffusion of a Genocidal Norm in Rwanda', *Journal of Genocide Research* 6:1 (2004), 99–114.

[62] Schaller, 'From Conquest to Genocide', 310–11.

governor, Theodor Leutwein, and other German actors such as missionaries who sought other approaches to the escalating conflict between the Herero and Germans. In January 1904, Herero initiated attacks against German military strongholds and farms with the goal of ousting the settlers from the land following intensified colonial administrative, material, and land encroachments that had eroded Herero sovereignty. They killed 123 German settlers, but 'failed to gain a final victory', which allowed Germany time to send reinforcements.[63] Following a series of smaller engagements between *Schutztruppe* and Herero in which the latter suffered significant losses, the Herero retreated to the Waterberg, where there was ample water for them and their livestock. There, some 60,000 Herero waited, expecting to negotiate an end to hostilities with the Germans.

But negotiation was not part of the *Schutztruppe*'s plans. In August 1904, under the leadership of Lieutenant General Lothar von Trotha, the *Schutztruppe* pursued a final Herero defeat by attempting to encircle them at the Waterberg. According to Isabel Hull, 'it was supposed to be the decisive battle that would end the war'.[64] The *Schutztruppe* amassed a significant force, including 'some 4000 men, 1500 rifles, thirty artillery pieces, and twelve machine guns', against some 6000 armed Herero fighters. The *Schutztruppe* defeated the Herero, forcing the survivors from the Waterberg.[65] These survivors escaped through a weak spot in German lines into the Omaheke Desert. German soldiers pursued the Herero survivors into this unforgiving terrain, where shootings, exposure, and deprivation may have killed half of the surviving Herero population between August 1904 and early 1905.[66] Lothar von Trotha's infamous *Vernichtungsbefehl* (extermination order),

[63] Jürgen Zimmerer, 'Colonial Genocide: The Herero and Nama War (1904–8) in German South West Africa and Its Significance', in Dan Stone (ed.), *The Historiography of Genocide* (Basingstoke: Palgrave Macmillan, 2010), 326.

[64] Isabel V. Hull, *Absolute Destruction: Military Culture and the Practices of War in Imperial Germany* (Ithaca: Cornell University Press, 2005), 33.

[65] Susanne Kuss, *German Colonial Wars and the Context of Military Violence* (Cambridge, MA: Harvard University Press, 2017), 46. Kuss notes however that 'the poor performance of the artillery and machine gun sections in the Battle of Waterberg meant that they exerted no influence on the outcome of the engagement'. See 117.

[66] Hull, *Absolute Destruction*, 89.

issued on 2 October 1904, simultaneously encapsulated a set of
genocidal practices that were already underway, and outlined expectations for troops from that moment forward. Soldiers continued to
pursue, kill, and round up Herero until January 1905, when a new
phase in the destruction of the Herero began—the captivity phase.
Having 'embraced the notion that every Herero—man, woman, or
child—was a prisoner of war',[67] the Germans imprisoned thousands
of Herero and Nama in 'collection camps', before they were then
'shipped by train or wagon' to labour camps, prison camps, or private
companies 'which often ran camps of their own'.[68] In these unsani-
tary, barren camps, thousands of Herero succumbed to hunger,
disease, and exposure brought on by the Germans' politics of neglect.
As Hull puts it, 'Administering prisoners at all, much less in a way that
might guarantee their survival, was so alien to the proper task of a
"real" soldier that prisoner management was the stepchild of military
administration'.[69] The *Schutztruppe*'s inability or unwillingness to care
for prisoners (who they viewed as sub-human and therefore without
human rights) worked alongside the many other decisions made by
military officials during the Herero-Nama War to cause mass death
that was part and parcel of the overall genocidal colonial war. The
Schutztruppe's racism infused the construction of the Herero as security
threats. One need not draw a straight line from German Southwest
Africa to the Holocaust to argue that the *Schutztruppe* was responsible
for genocide there.

The Nama, who had also been at war with the Germans since
October 1904, met similar fates as the Herero. Their guerrilla style of
warfare allowed small bands of Nama to continue fighting the Germans into 1907. Trotha issued a threatening proclamation against the
Nama in April 1905, modelled after the one he had issued to the
Herero in October 1904. The October 1905 death of the key Nama
leader, Hendrik Witbooi, marked the beginning of Nama destruction
as well, though small bands continued fighting against the Germans
until 1907. In the second half of 1906, the Germans began sending all

[67] 'embraced the notion': Andrea Pitzer, *One Long Night: A Global History of
Concentration Camps* (New York: Little, Brown, and Company, 2018), 81.

[68] Hull, *Absolute Destruction*, 74, 75.

[69] Ibid., 71–2.

surviving Nama to Shark Island, where the appalling conditions caused an 'average annualized death rate' of 121 per cent, meaning that 'the original camp population plus twenty percent more new-comers would all have died in the course of a year'.[70] Hull calls this 'the greatest scandal of military occupation administration'.[71] 'Impris-onment', she writes, 'was a continuation of annihilation by other means'.[72] For both the Herero and the Nama, war and genocide were more similar than different. From their perspectives, and those of many historians, the German way of war in Southwest Africa was genocidal.[73]

Given the 300,000 Africans killed in German East Africa in the brutal German counterinsurgency that ended Maji Maji, the failure to name the outcome of this war a genocide is striking.[74] In July 1905, in the southern highlands of today's mainland Tanzania, a local anti-colonial protest against the cultivation of cotton grew exponentially within a month. Resistance to German colonial demands for cotton cultivation received spiritual heft from the prophet Kinjikitile Ngwale, whose millenarian message of resistance to the Germans and their African intermediaries resonated with large crowds who had been gathering in his presence since 1904.[75] His message was spread through the distribution of *maji* (water), a medicine that Kinjikitile claimed would protect believers from German bullets.[76] German colonial officials executed Kinjikitile in early August 1905, but the medicine and message had already been carried far and wide, north-wards and southwards, its 'changing character' driven by several

[70] Ibid., 90.

[71] Ibid., 85.

[72] Ibid., 90.

[73] Schaller, 'From Conquest to Genocide', 316–17. See also Jeremy Silvester and Jan-Bart Gewald (eds.), *Words Cannot Be Found: German Colonial Rule in Namibia: An Annotated Reprint of the 1918 Blue Book* (Leiden: Brill, 2003).

[74] Douglas Porch, *Counterinsurgency: Exposing the Myths of the New Way of War* (Cambridge: Cambridge University Press, 2013), 72.

[75] John Iliffe, *A Modern History of Tanganyika* (Cambridge: Cambridge University Press, 1979), 168–70.

[76] Ibid. See also Jamie Monson, 'War of Words: The Narrative Efficacy of Medicine in the Maji Maji War', in James Giblin and Jamie Monson (eds.), *Maji Maji: Lifting the Fog of War* (Leiden: Brill, 2010), 42–9.

'impulses spreading inland' from its origins. Between August 1905 and July 1906, as messengers (*hongo*) carried the medicine and the message to different parts of German East Africa, a number of distinct polities were enjoined to Kinjikitile's vision of a world without colonizers.[77]

The *Schutztruppe*'s logic in confronting Maji Maji fighters in German East Africa was more similar to what occurred in Southwest Africa than different. During the initial phase of the war, Maji Maji combatants scored some military successes against the *Schutztruppe*. But after reinforcements arrived from Germany in October 1905, the army began pursuing a systematic advance inland against the rebels along three routes. Maji Maji combatants turned to guerrilla-style tactics as the *Schutztruppe* turned to 'patrol warfare in which military engagements were secondary to seizure of food and destruction of crops'.[78] This scorched earth strategy, which incorporated a deliberate goal of starving the population, killed hundreds of thousands in southern Tanzania before the last insurgent leaders were killed in May and July 1908, ending the rebellion. The *Schutztruppe* summarily executed men of military age as 'ringleaders', with or without evidence of insurgent activity.

In German East Africa during Maji Maji, war and genocide were similar because the *Schutztruppe* indiscriminately, but with purpose, destroyed entire societies and economies based on suspected connections to combatants described as threats to colonial authority. With these actions, German officers intended to quash any remaining oppositional sentiment in areas they planned to reshape—or develop—once they defeated the military threat.

As in German Southwest Africa, military defeat of Maji Maji fighters did not end the violence, and the end of open fighting did not mean peace. Rather, the effects of colonial military occupation, exacerbated by the German *Hungerstrategie,* produced a sustained politics of neglect in southern Tanzania. The peoples of southern Tanzania suffered from lost productive and reproductive possibilities, their crops destroyed, livestock stolen, and many of their young men and women killed, imprisoned, or forced to work. Scorched earth

---

[77] Iliffe, *A Modern History of Tanganyika*, 190–91.
[78] Ibid., 193.

tactics undermined military opposition, simultaneously destroying communities' food supplies, subsistence, and abilities to plan for future survival. Those who survived experienced utter exhaustion, and were forced to turn their complete focus to surviving famine and multidimensional poverty.[79] Such work typically fell to women and children since men had been subject to summary executions and forced labour in the end stages of the war and its aftermath. The long-term difficulties of their recovery, which were profoundly gendered in their effects, extended well beyond the end of active fighting.[80] Understanding how the war continued to undercut southern Tanzanian peoples' futures takes on added significance in light of its simultaneity with the Herero-Nama war, which is widely acknowledged as a genocide.[81]

Schutztruppe military actions in German Southwest Africa and German East Africa, both of which used scorched earth methods, forced entire peoples to the brink of survival, turned survivors into forced labourers, and impoverished them for generations to come. These ways of war were similar to genocide in their intent, execution, and outcomes.

Genocide Is a Particular Kind of War

Genocide channels wartime violence to exterminatory ends. In this sense, genocide is a particular kind of war. State, military, or settler aspirations to purity, hegemony, and security—especially perception of some sort of 'existential threat'—enjoin violence workers to act within a permissive wartime space to carry out genocidal violence. These 'toxification' logics construct entire groups as enemies worthy of destruction, as sub-humans or non-humans unworthy of life except

[79] On 'faminogenic acts', see Alex de Waal, *Mass Starvation: The History and Future of Famine* (Cambridge: Polity, 2018), 94–112. For survivors' recollections and perspectives on German actions during the Maji Maji War, see G. C. K. Gwassa and John Iliffe (eds.), *Maji Maji Research Project* (Dar es Salaam: University College, 1968).

[80] Elisa von Joeden-Forgey, 'Gender and Genocide', in Donald Bloxham and A. Dirk Moses, (eds.), *The Oxford Handbook of Genocide Studies* (Oxford: Oxford University Press, 2011), 78–9. See also Fein, 'Genocide, Terror, Life Integrity, and War Crimes: The Case for Discrimination',101–3.

[81] See also Schaller, 'From Conquest to Genocide', 306–10.

in the most abject conditions, or strictly as sources of unfree labour.[82] 'When armed military force is being extensively used against organized armed enemies', argues Martin Shaw, 'then it is easier for leaders to take the extraordinary, generally illegitimate steps towards also using armed force against social groups as such'.[83] Under these conditions, as Rhiannon Nielsen contends, 'The perpetrator's existence is held as a zero-sum game, wherein it can only be guaranteed at the expense of the victims'.[84]

Counterinsurgency, as a mode of warfare offers clear ways of seeing genocide as a particular kind of warfare. 'Genocides in the modern era', writes Cheng Xu, 'are more likely to be conducted in conjunction with the models of counterinsurgency warfare'.[85] By invoking 'counterinsurgency' as a descriptor, states simultaneously mobilize security-thinking and toxification logic to 'legitimiz[e]' genocide against their enemies.[86] It is not a coincidence that genocidal colonial wars started from the premise that 'insurgents' had to be defeated at all costs.

Counterinsurgency became a vehicle for genocide in decolonized countries as well. The 1994 Rwandan genocide is a case in point. Misguided representations of the Rwandan genocide as an eruption of age-old ethnic hatreds obscure the dynamic counterinsurgency politics that provided ideological scaffolding for genocide. Hutu extremists within the government used a dehumanizing rhetoric of counterinsurgency to cast the Rwandan Patriotic Front (RPF), and by extension all Tutsi, as enemies of the state.[87] In the early 1990s, the RPF's record of cross-border invasions of Rwanda from its base in Uganda featured in Hutu extremist arguments as a rationale for

---

[82] Rhiannon Nielsen, '"Toxification" as a More Precise Early Warning Sign for Genocide than Dehumanization?', *Genocide Studies and Prevention* 9:1 (2015), 83–95. See also Geoffrey B. Robinson, *The Killing Season: A History of the Indonesian Massacres, 1965–66* (Princeton: Princeton University Press, 2018), 17.

[83] Shaw, *War and Genocide*, 44.

[84] Nielsen, 'Toxification', 87.

[85] Xu, 'Draining the Sea', 7. Xu's work 'supplement[s]' Shaw's theory [that genocide occurs in the context of *interstate* war] by proposing that genocides actually more often occur in the context of *intrastate* warfare'.

[86] Ibid., 6. See also Moses, 'Empire, Colony, Genocide', 29.

[87] Xu, 'Draining the Sea', 7.

counterinsurgency.[88] The wider regional context of recurrent patterns of mass political violence in Rwanda and neighbouring Burundi also contributed to Hutu extremists' security logic in 1994. Rwanda was, and remains, a small, tightly controlled state. In 1994 its leaders acted against Tutsis with clear governmental genocidal intent, extrapolating the RPF threat to a more generalized Tutsi threat. Opposed to the multi-partyism that President Habyarimana seemed poised to accept as a result of the Arusha Accords, Hutu extremists with government posts used the downing of President Habyarimana's plane on 6 April 1994 as a pretext to justify launching exterminatory violence, which had been planned at the highest levels well before that date. They seized the opportunity to consolidate power around the genocidal vision of a Rwanda without Tutsis. The genocidaires first murdered all Hutu opposition party members, who the government hardliners perceived as political threats.[89] Over the next three months, Rwandan soldiers, Hutu militia, and civilians murdered up to 800,000 Tutsi. The genocide ended only when the RPF, led by Paul Kagame, occupied the Rwandan capital, Kigali. The genocide, organized by Hutu extremists, carried out by soldiers and ordinary Rwandans, was a war against Rwandan Tutsis and anyone perceived as being allied to the cause of power-sharing.

Genocide also manifested as a particular kind of war in Darfur—a government-directed counterinsurgency that aimed to destroy Darfurian futures. In Khartoum, the al-Bashir government faced an insurgency organized by 'an awkward coalition' of different rebel groups who 'were united by deep resentment at the marginalization of Darfur' within the Sudanese political economy. 'Theirs was not an insurgency born of revolutionary ideals', write Julie Flint and Alex de Waal, 'but rather a last-resort response to the escalating violence of the [militia known as the] Janjawiid and its patrons in Khartoum'.[90] In April 2003, rebels attacked a government airfield at al-Fasher, destroying several military aircraft on the ground. In response,

---

[88] For its part, the RPF sought to force the Hutu-dominated government into a UN-brokered power-sharing arrangement, as laid out in the 1993 Arusha Accords.

[89] Fujii, *Killing Neighbors*, 6–7, 53–6.

[90] Julie Flint and Alex de Waal, *Darfur: A New History of a Long War*, rev. ed. (London: Zed Books, 2008), 115.

Khartoum enlisted *janjawiid* militias to fight a 'counterinsurgency on the cheap'[91] against the Darfur rebels. The government's employment of these militias provided plausible deniability regarding its supporting role in dehumanizing, racist violence against Darfur, part of a much longer history of violence directed against 'non-Arabized Islamic groups' in Sudan's peripheries.[92] At the same time, it gave *janjawiid* militia members ample opportunities to plunder goods and livestock, to rape women, and to force people from their lands.[93] Scorched earth military tactics caused long-term Darfurian suffering and poverty. Fifteen years after the counterinsurgency began, and well after Darfur disappeared from the headlines, Darfurians are still targeted for violence by government forces and their proxies, with the goal of destroying Darfurian life chances.[94] In a region where environmental concerns and scarcity loom large, genocide unfolded as a particular kind of war. Labelled counterinsurgency, it enacted ethnic cleansing.[95]

In counterinsurgency, the lines drawn between those who do violence work and those who become their targets need not correspond to racial, ethnic, or religious differences. Indeed, perpetrators of genocidal violence might draw on any of these factors as they work across different registers. In 1965–6, the Indonesian Army orchestrated the killings of half a million members of the Indonesian Communist Party and other leftist political opponents, and 'another million or so were detained without charge'.[96] In so doing, they

[91] Alex de Waal, 'Counter-Insurgency on the Cheap', *Review of African Political Economy* 31:102 (2004), 716–25.

[92] Salah M. Hassan, 'Naming the Conflict: Darfur and the Crisis of Governance in Sudan', in Salah M. Hassan and Carina E. Ray (eds.), *Darfur and the Crisis of Governance in Sudan: A Critical Reader* (Ithaca: Cornell University Press, 2009), 164.

[93] Abdullahi Osman El-Tom, 'Darfur People: Too Black for the Arab-Islamic Project of Sudan', in Hassan and Ray, *Darfur and the Crisis of Governance in Sudan*, 90–2.

[94] United Nations Security Council, 'African Union-United Nations Hybrid Operation in Darfur: Report of the Secretary-General', 10 April 2019.

[95] 'Erasures' of Rohingya citizenship and homes in Myanmar make a useful comparison to Darfurian experiences. See Ken Maclean, 'The Rohingya Crisis and the Practices of Erasure', *Journal of Genocide Research* 21:1 (2019), 83–95.

[96] Geoffrey B. Robinson, *The Killing Season: A History of the Indonesian Massacres* (Princeton: Princeton University Press, 2018), 3.

destroyed 'the largest nongoverning Communist party in the world', and established an authoritarian state under Suharto that remained in power until 1998.[97] As Jess Melvin has argued, the Indonesian military played the defining role in converting a counterinsurgency operation into a genocide that largely erased all traces of Indonesia's communist past by annihilating any suspected party members. It was, in Melvin's words, 'a campaign intended to secure the entire Indonesian state from the perceived threat of a communist coup'.[98]

In Cambodia, scholars debate whether or not the mass killings that occurred from 1975–9 was politicide or genocide because the Khmer Rouge's strategy cut across a number of organizing features in Cambodian culture.[99] Ethnicity or race were not the key determinants of who became the killers' targets in these examples. Broadening our definitions of who is a people—not only racial/ethnic groups, but political parties, religious groups, etc.—necessarily broadens our definitions of genocide. Similarly, broadening our definitions of genocidal violence can help us to broaden our definitions of war.

Conclusion: Seeing War and Genocide

In 1966, James Baldwin's 'A Report from Occupied Territory' evoked a powerful image with obvious colonial resonances by equating policing in Harlem with occupied territory, in which 'the police are afraid of everything . . . and they are especially afraid of the roofs, which they consider to be guerrilla outposts. This means that the citizens of Harlem who, as we have seen, can come to grief at any hour in the streets, and who are not safe at their windows, are forbidden the very air'.[100] He continues, 'Occupied territory is

---

[97] Ibid.

[98] Jess Melvin, 'How the Military Came to Power', in Saskia E. Wieringa, Jess Melvin, and Annie Pohlmann (eds.), *The International People's Tribunal for 1965 and the Indonesian Genocide* (London: Routledge, 2019), 55. See also Helen Jarvis and Saskia E. Wieringa, 'The Indonesian massacres as Genocide', in ibid., 224–5.

[99] Lisa Pine, *Debating Genocide* (London and New York: Bloomsbury Academic, 2019), 89–102.

[100] James Baldwin, 'A Report from Occupied Territory', *The Nation*, July 11, 1966.

occupied territory, even though it be found in that New World which the Europeans conquered, and it is axiomatic, in occupied territory, that any act of resistance, even though it be executed by a child, be answered at once, and with the full weight of the occupying forces'. Anyone familiar with colonial histories in Africa and elsewhere will easily recognize the similarities between Baldwin's Harlem and the everyday violence meted out by colonial military and police on pretexts that constantly reasserted the state's view of those being policed as subjects, not citizens.[101]

Those typically described as victims of genocide likely have far less difficulty discerning how war and genocide are related than those analysing it from outside.[102] Baldwin commented on this in *The Fire Next Time*:

> White people were, and are, astounded by the holocaust in Germany. They did not know that they could act that way. But I very much doubt whether Black people were astounded—at least, in the same way. For my part, the fate of the Jews, and the world's indifference to it, frightened me very much. I could not but feel, in those sorrowful years, that this human indifference, concerning which I knew so much already, would be my portion on the day that the United States decided to murder its Negroes systematically instead of little by little and catch-as-catch-can.[103]

When people perceive that a state is violating them, they may read these violations as acts of war, whether declared or not, whether recognized as such or not. They see genocidal potential because they are attuned to the ways that state agents empower their violence workers with the language, interpretive and identificatory tools and methods, and weapons that increase the potential for particular kinds

---

[101] For a recent historical extension of Baldwin's ideas, see Simon Balto, *Occupied Territory: Policing Black Chicago from Red Summer to Black Power* (Chapel Hill: University of North Carolina Press, 2019). On 'violence as a social fact', see also Gyanendra Pandey, *Routine Violence: Nations, Fragments, Histories* (Stanford: Stanford University Press, 2006), 3–15. See also Blackhawk, *Violence over the Land*, 9, 15.

[102] Dan Stone, 'The Holocaust and "The Human"', in Richard H. King and Dan Stone (eds.), *Hannah Arendt and the Uses of History: Imperialism, Nation, Race, and Genocide* (New York and Oxford: Berghahn Books, 2008), 238–9.

[103] James Baldwin, *The Fire Next Time* (New York: Vintage Books, 1993), 52–3.

of violence to be enacted against them.[104] And knowing that genocide is a particular kind of war that threatens their erasure, they fight back, flee, hide, or perhaps bide their time, hoping that things will improve, that someone will intervene. This is the next turn scholars must take to more fully account for connections between war and genocide, not just from the standpoint of those who carry out violence, but from below, through the lens of those who imagined themselves as citizens, members of sovereign polities, people who belong, as people worthy of life.

In the end, definitional practices reliant on specific criteria being met before labelling something a genocide or not impede seeing such violence from the perspective of those most likely to experience it. If the notion of 'never again' is to have any meaning in a post-Holocaust world where countless other genocides have occurred, it must be as a way of helping those who are most likely to be targeted in such violence to recognize the patterns that signal processes and pathways to genocide. These patterns often fit within the everyday forms of neglect or quotidian violence that consign certain populations to the worst conditions, invisibilizing their suffering and death. These patterns can include dehumanizing, racializing, or othering language, the expression of security logics casting certain groups as outsiders or threats, or the failure to protect certain populations from harms caused famine, pollution, epidemics, or failing infrastructures. Learning to recognize these patterns hones sensibilities for also recognizing the genocidal potential of any war. Recognition also gives people a chance to muster resources, to protest and enlist allies and accomplices, to escape, and hopefully to survive.[105]

The rhetorical emphasis on interventionism to stop genocides since the Holocaust has not worked. Rather, the usual powerful actors continue to use violence against vulnerable populations with impunity and little fear of opprobrium or meaningful interference from outside.

---

[104] Relatedly, see A. Dirk Moses, 'Genocide and the Terror of History', *Parallax*, 17, 4 (2011), 104.

[105] Victor Klemperer, *I Will Bear Witness 1933–1941: A Diary of the Nazi Years* (New York: The Modern Library, 1999), 120–1, 280–3. Klemperer's diary offers numerous examples of his full awareness of what was happening in Nazi Germany, as well as his efforts to survive.

Seventy years after the UN Convention, with no end in sight to genocidal violence, a shift in perspectives is overdue. It should centre the perspectives of those most likely to die, experience abuse and violation, or lose everything in genocidal wars.[106] This move also holds space for histories of genocidal colonial wars as historical examples that expose the inherent potential for genocide in war, and the interwoven association between the two. In combination, these offer meaningful correctives for disrupting powerful actors' steps towards genocidal violence.

Acknowledgement

I would like to thank Heather Blair, Susan Grayzel, Kate Imy, Manling Luo, Tammy Proctor, Anya Peterson Royce, Melissa Shaw, and Sarah van der Laan for their careful readings and thoughtful comments on previous drafts of this chapter. I am also most grateful to Donald Bloxham and Dirk Moses for their encouragement and suggestions on multiple drafts. I dedicate the chapter to Lee Ann Fujii, wishing she had been here to read it.

Select Bibliography

Baldwin, James, 'A Report from Occupied Territory', *The Nation*, July 11, 1966.

Estes, Nick, *Our History Is the Future: Standing Rock versus the Dakota Access Pipeline, and the Long Tradition of Indigenous Resistance* (London and New York: Verso, 2019).

Hassan, Salah M. and Carina E. Ray (eds.), *Darfur and the Crisis of Governance in Sudan: A Critical Reader* (Ithaca: Cornell University Press, 2009).

Hull, Isabel V., *Absolute Destruction: Military Culture and the Practices of War in Imperial Germany* (Ithaca: Cornell University Press, 2005).

Levene, Mark, *The Crisis of Genocide. Vol 2. Annihilation: The European Rimlands 1939–1953* (Oxford: Oxford University Press, 2014).

Melvin, Jess, *The Army and the Indonesian Massacre: Mechanics of Mass Murder* (London: Routledge, 2018).

---

[106] Rogaia Mustafa Abusharaf, 'Competing Masculinities: Probing Political Disputes as Acts of Violence against Women from Southern Sudan and Darfur', in Hassan and Ray, *Darfur and the Crisis of Governance in Sudan*, 199–212.

Moses, A. Dirk. (ed.), *Empire, Colony, Genocide: Conquest, Occupation, and Subaltern Resistance in World History* (New York: Berghahn Books, 2008).

Shaw, Martin, *War and Genocide: Organized Killing in Modern Society* (Cambridge: Polity Press, 2003).

Straus, Scott, 'The Limits of a Genocide Lens: Violence Against Rwandans in the 1990s', *Journal of Genocide Research* 21:4 (2019), 504–24.

Strozier, Charles B. and Michael Flynn (eds.), *Genocide, War and Human Survival* (London: Rowman and Littlefield, 1996).

9

Genocide and Memory

Dan Stone and Rebecca Jinks

Introduction

We live in a memory-obsessed age. Western culture is suffused with autobiographies, especially with traumatic life narratives about the legacies of abusive childhoods. Tourism consists to a large extent in the consumption of 'heritage' such as castles and stately homes; memorials and museums increasingly dot the landscape; and commemorative events seem to occur with increasing frequency. The history of genocide is also affected by these broad cultural trends; indeed, in some respects it exemplifies them. The perpetration of genocide requires the mobilization of collective memories, as does the commemoration of it. For the individual victims of genocide, traumatic memories cannot be escaped; for societies, genocide has profound effects that are immediately felt and that people are exhorted (and willingly choose) never to forget. 'Dark tourism'—visits to death camps or other sites of mass murder—is fully integrated into the tourist trail.[1] Although thinkers as diverse as Friedrich Nietzsche, Ernest Renan, Paul Ricoeur, and Marc Augé might be right to suggest that forgetting is essential for the health of society, genocide is less amenable to willed oblivion than most events because of the deep wounds it creates; thus, in the memory politics that surround it, genocide can scar societies long before and after its actual occurrence. This chapter shows how genocide is bound up with memory, on an

---

[1] Glenn Hooper and John J. Lennon (eds.), *Dark Tourism: Practice and Interpretation* (London: Routledge, 2016).

individual level of trauma and on a collective level in terms of the creation of stereotypes, prejudice, and post-genocide politics.

Before demonstrating the validity of these claims, it is necessary to say something about 'memory studies', a multidisciplinary and inter-disciplinary field which has expanded rapidly over the last two decades.[2] The basic premise of the study of 'collective memory' is not a quasi-mystical belief in the existence of a social mind, or that societies can be treated as organic wholes (in the manner supposed by many genocide perpetrators); rather, it is the basic claim that, in order to live meaningfully as a human being, that is, in order to have memories (for, as neurologists increasingly show, memory and selfhood are intrinsically linked), one has to exist in a social setting. This claim, which has its origin in the work of French sociologists Emile Durkheim and Maurice Halbwachs, and perhaps reaches its zenith in Ricoeur's last major work, *Memory, History, Forgetting* (2000), overturns the intuitively appealing 'methodological individualism' of much twentieth-century thought, installing in its stead a 'methodological holism'. Whilst groups do not have memories in the neurological sense and thus there is no organic basis to the term 'collective memory', nevertheless, '[c]ollective memories originate from shared communications about the meaning of the past that are anchored in the life-worlds of individuals who partake in the communal life of the respective collective'.[3]

Thus collective memory becomes something that the historian or other scholar can study; memory can be a subject for critical histori-ography in the same way as gender or class. Historians can think theoretically about what collective memory is, how it is constructed and what it excludes, and they can provide detailed case studies, for example, in examining Italians' memories of fascism or the ways in which the My Lai massacre has been domesticated in American collective memory. Most often historians have focused on what Pierre Nora calls '*lieux de mémoire*', sites such as memorials, museums, or significant buildings, showing how a group's (usually a nation's)

---

[2] As evidenced, e.g., by the founding of new journals such as *Memory Studies* (2008), itself both a product and driver of this expansion.

[3] Wulf Kansteiner, 'Finding Meaning in Memory: A Methodological Critique of Collective Memory Studies', *History and Theory* 41 (2002), 188.

self-identity is anchored in these sites of memory. What such sites exclude becomes as relevant for understanding collective memory as the narratives they promote.

This model for studying collective memory has not been without its critics, however.[4] It is too easy to do, they say, because it is focused on material objects or aesthetic representations whose meaning can be shown to change over time as people interact with them differently under changed circumstances. Far more meaningful than studying sites of memory, according to the critics, would be to trace the ways in which conflicts over memory affect social relations. In other words, we need to show how memory is linked with power. Doing so, argues Wulf Kansteiner, would require scholars of memory to delineate more clearly the distinctions between individual and collective memory and to think more about reception than about representation. It would benefit from adopting some of the vocabulary and methodology of media studies, with the result that collective memory would be understood as the result of the interaction of three 'types of historical factors: the intellectual and cultural traditions that frame all our representations of the past, the memory makers who selectively adopt and manipulate these traditions, and the memory consumers who use, ignore, or transform such artefacts according to their own interests'.[5]

More recently, scholars have moved beyond conceiving of memory as anchored in such museums, memorials, and historical representations, and bounded by the borders of the nation-state, as modernity's privileged cultural unit.[6] Instead, memory is now understood to be 'mobile': scholars are paying attention to memory's travels across spatial and community borders, and to the ways in which it is dialogical, comparative, and, in Michael Rothberg's influential rendering,

[4] Alon Confino and Peter Fritzsche (eds.), *The Work of Memory: New Directions in the Study of German Society and Culture* (Urbana: University of Illinois Press, 2002); Alon Confino, *Germany as a Culture of Remembrance: Promises and Limits of Writing History* (Chapel Hill: University of North Carolina Press, 2006); Kansteiner, 'Finding Meaning'.

[5] Kansteiner, 'Finding Meaning', 180.

[6] Lucy Bond, Stef Craps, and Pieter Vermeulen, 'Introduction: Memory on the Move', in Bond, Craps, and Vermeulen (eds.), *Memory Unbound: Tracing the Dynamics of Memory Studies* (New York: Berghahn Books, 2016), 1, 3.

'multidirectional'.[7] Rothberg's work is part of a broader turn to exploring the relationship between memories and representations of the
Holocaust and other genocides and histories of violence.[8] Responding
to a memory framework which often understands memory competi-
tively, as a 'zero sum game'—in other words, the commemoration of
one event 'screens' another—Rothberg suggests we view memory as
'*multidirectional*: as subject to ongoing negotiation, cross-referencing, and
borrowing; as productive and not privative'.[9] Exploring interconnec-
tions across memories of the Holocaust, slavery, and decolonization,
Rothberg argues that such cross-referencing can also be a spur to
empathy and solidarity, and offers 'the possibility of a more just future
of memory'.[10] However, others, most notably Dirk Moses, have demonstrated that comparison can also produce precisely the opposite
effect, 'the terror of history'. 'Instead of tending only in a liberal
direction of transcultural understanding', the Holocaust 'is invoked,
rather, to express the fear of collective destruction: the apocalypse of
genocide'.[11] As Moses notes, everything depends on *how* the Holocaust
is remembered, by whom, when, and under what circumstances. But it
remains the case that, for historians, our material suggests that the use
of memory as a tool of mobilization has been more prevalent, effective,
and dangerous through time.

But for historians memory is more than just a research topic.[12]
Historians are also part of the broader culture, one that already
twenty-five years ago was diagnosed as suffering from a 'surfeit of

---

[7] Bond, Craps, and Vermeulen, *Memory Unbound*; Stef Craps, *Postcolonial Wit-
nessing: Trauma Out of Bounds* (Basingstoke: Palgrave Macmillan, 2013); Michael
Rothberg, *Multidirectional Memory: Remembering the Holocaust in the Age of Decolonization*
(Stanford: Stanford University Press, 2011); Daniel Levy and Natan Sznaider, *The
Holocaust and Memory in the Global Age* (Philadelphia: Temple University Press, 2006).

[8] Rebecca Jinks, *Representing Genocide: The Holocaust as Paradigm?* (London:
Bloomsbury, 2016).

[9] Rothberg, *Multidirectional Memory*, 3.

[10] Ibid., 19. But see also Emma Kuby, *Political Survivors: The Resistance, the Cold
War, and the Fight against Concentration Camps after 1945* (Ithaca: Cornell University
Press, 2019) for a counterargument.

[11] A. Dirk Moses, 'Genocide and the Terror of History', *Parallax* 17:4 (2011), 91.

[12] Kerwin Lee Klein, 'On the Emergence of Memory in Historical Discourse',
Representations 69 (2000), 127–50.

memory'.[13] Critics of memory culture argue that, like 'heritage', memory is exclusionary, reactionary, and nostalgic; at its worst, it can be accused in its quest for authenticity and 're-enchantment' of 'projecting "psychoneurotic jargon" onto the memory of various national or (more often) ethno-racial groups.'[14] Memory is, *in fine*, one of the more dangerous tools of identity politics. Thus, scholars need to consider their own investments in memory politics, especially when writing about subjects like genocide.[15] But finally, memory is inseparable from history, so that even when the current 'memory obsession' has passed, when the piles of confessional literature have been pulped and the commemorative ceremonies are unattended, still, as Ricoeur notes, memory will be the 'bedrock' of history. The fact that people can say that 'this has happened' remains the starting point for historiography.[16] Studying the links between genocide and memory means, then, examining the ways in which collective memories of past humiliations or victories are mobilized in the present, showing how individuals and societies are traumatized by genocide, and analysing the ways in which post-genocidal commemorative practices sustain collective memories. Genocide and memory, then, are inseparable, for reasons of the cultural freight that the term contains as well as, more obviously, the enormity of the crime itself. In what follows, we analyse the nature of this relationship.

Memory as Mobilization

It is tempting, when trying to understand perpetrators of genocide, to assume that they are convinced of their own superiority, that they are the

---

[13] Charles S. Maier, 'A Surfeit of Memory? Reflections on History, Melancholy and Denial', *History & Memory* 5:2 (1993), 136–52.

[14] Klein, 'On the Emergence'.

[15] A. Dirk Moses, 'Paranoia and Partisanship: Genocide Studies, Holocaust Historiography, and the "Apocalyptic Conjuncture"', *The Historical Journal* 54:2 (2011), 553–83.

[16] Paul Ricoeur, *Memory, History, Forgetting* (Chicago: University of Chicago Press, 2004 [orig. French 2000]). See also Dan Stone, 'Beyond the Mnemosyne Institute: The Future of Memory after the Age of Commemoration', in Richard Crownshaw, Jane Kilby, and Anthony Rowland (eds.), *The Future of Memory* (New York: Berghahn Books, 2010), 17–36.

arrogant bearers of an ideology that requires the merciless elimination of the weak. Such rhetoric is not hard to find, especially in colonial settings where the social Darwinist notion of superior races 'superseding' the inferior was common. Yet, in fact, most genocides result from processes of worsening national or imperial crisis that give rise to a feeling of massive insecurity or existential threat among the perpetrators. A curious, paradoxical logic is at work: genocide perpetrators commit the most horrific crimes in the belief—always exaggerated and sometimes outright fantastical—that they are defensive acts to ensure that they will not suffer the same fate.[17] Germans in Southwest Africa (Namibia) 'did not commit massacres in the colonies because they were in a strong position and had the power to decide on life or death of the indigenous population. On the contrary, German settlers felt unsafe and were afraid to lose their existence.'[18] In Rwanda, a history of Hutu-Tutsi conflict from at least 1959 provided the background to genocide. In the Ottoman Empire, small numbers of Armenians joined revolutionary movements that defied the state.[19] Yet in none of these cases was it necessary for the perpetrators to respond by seeking to slaughter the targeted population. What mobilized them to do so, what exacerbated the sense of threat to the point at which genocide became a viable and acceptable option, was fear underpinned by memory: of former oppression or supposed treason. Specifically, collective memories of past suffering are almost always brought to bear on current crises, lending them cultural meaning—the weight of dead ancestors weighing on the minds of the living—and imbuing them with added ferocity.[20] Memory fuels genocide.[21]

---

[17] Moses, 'Genocide and the Terror of History'; Nicholas A. Robins and Adam Jones (eds.), *Genocides by the Oppressed: Subaltern Genocide in Theory and Practice* (Bloomington: Indiana University Press, 2009).

[18] Dominik J. Schaller, 'From Conquest to Genocide: Colonial Rule in German Southwest Africa and German East Africa', in A. Dirk Moses (ed.), *Empire, Colony, Genocide: Conquest, Occupation, and Subaltern Resistance in World History* (New York: Berghahn Books, 2008), 311.

[19] Donald Bloxham, *The Great Game of Genocide: Imperialism, Nationalism and the Destruction of the Ottoman Armenians* (Oxford: Oxford University Press, 2005).

[20] Abdelwahab El-Affendi, *Genocidal Nightmares: Narratives of Insecurity and the Logic of Mass Atrocities* (New York: Bloomsbury, 2014).

[21] See Mark Levene, *Genocide in the Age of the Nation State*. vol. i: *The Meaning of Genocide* (London: I. B. Tauris, 2005), 196–202.

Stalin's Soviet Union and Pol Pot's Cambodia both illustrate the point. In the former, the construction of the 'Kulak', which began with Stolypin's reforms before 1917, revived fears of starvation and social conflict. Belief that peasants were hoarding food, which would lead to death on a massive scale for urban dwellers, then permitted massive oppression.[22] And in the latter, Khmer Rouge support was massively boosted by the effects of American bombing in the early 1970s. The response to this attack does not explain the ferocity of the 'auto-genocide' between 1975 and 1979, but memories of French colonial wars, Prince Norodom Sihanouk's contempt for the majority rural population, and the age-old fear of the Vietnamese certainly drove many ordinary Cambodians into the arms of the Khmer Rouge, as did the regime's revival of the grandeur of the Angkorian dynasty. As Ben Kiernan notes, 'The total reshaping of Cambodia under Pol Pot may be said to demonstrate the power of a myth'.[23]

The Rwandan example is equally full of such fears and fantasies, based on the memory of Hutu-Tutsi conflict from at least the Hutu Revolution of 1959 if not from the period of colonial rule (first German, then Belgian) from the late nineteenth century. Tutsi refugees and their children actively kept alive the memory of the land they had left (like Hutu refugees from Burundi in Tanzania),[24] so that even those young members of the Rwandan Patriotic Front (RPF) who had been born in Uganda and had never seen Rwanda felt that they were 'returning home' in 1994. And the memory of the colonial period, in

[22] Nicolas Werth, 'The Crimes of the Stalin Regime: Outline for an Inventory and Classification', in Dan Stone (ed.), *The Historiography of Genocide* (Basingstoke: Palgrave Macmillan, 2008), 400–19.

[23] Ben Kiernan, 'Myth, Nationalism and Genocide', *Journal of Genocide Research* 3:2 (2001), 190. See also Ben Kiernan, 'Serial Colonialism and Genocide in Nineteenth-Century Cambodia', in Moses (ed.), *Empire, Colony, Genocide*, 205–28; Alexander Laban Hinton, 'Oppression and Vengeance in the Cambodian Geno-cide', in Robins and Jones (eds.), *Genocides by the Oppressed*, 84–102; David P. Chandler, 'Seeing Red: Perceptions of Cambodian History in Democratic Kampuchea', in David Chandler and Ben Kiernan (eds.), *Revolution and Its Aftermath in Kampuchea: Eight Essays* (New Haven: Yale University Southeast Asia Studies, 1983), 34–56.

[24] Liisa Malkki, *Purity and Exile: Violence, Memory and National Cosmology among Hutu Refugees in Tanzania* (Chicago: University of Chicago Press, 1995).

which minority Tutsi domination was established according to the warped racial logic of the colonizers, was mobilized by Hutu extremists in the run-up to the genocide, especially as the framework for peace established by the Arusha Accords started collapsing.[25] Here the point about memory not as an organic phenomenon but as a key component of political power is especially clear. For although there had always been tensions between Hutus and Tutsis in Rwanda since the colonial period, when the Belgian authorities institutionalized the distinction as 'racial',[26] there was nothing like a permanent state of war between the two 'communities', which were, after the post-revolutionary violence of the early 1960s, in fact thoroughly mixed. Only with the threat of war did Hutu extremists revitalize the memory of pre-1959 Rwandan society, dominated by the Tutsi minority, and whip up fear among the Hutu population that they should eliminate the Tutsis because otherwise this same fate would be reserved for them. Indeed, as Scott Straus has shown, the speed with which certain parts of the country threw themselves into participating in genocide was determined less by the reception of infamous propaganda such as the 'Hutu Ten Commandments', *Kangura* magazine or Radio Télévision Libres des Milles Collines, than affinity to the ruling Mouvement républicain national pour la démocratie et le développement (MRND), proximity to the front line, and fear of the approaching RPF.[27] And, indeed, the RPF has made equally effective use of collective memories of expulsion and exile, with violent results both during and after the genocide. Since the RPF took power, the government has come under increasing scrutiny by Western scholars who have grown suspicious of its 'harmonising perspective on pre-colonial society and history'. The instrumentalization of Rwandan memories

[25] E.g. Nigel Eltringham, '"Invaders Who Have Stolen the Country": The Hamitic Hypothesis, Race and the Rwandan Genocide', *Social Identities* 12:4 (2006), 425–46; Christopher C. Taylor, *Sacrifice as Terror: The Rwandan Genocide of 1994* (Oxford: Berg, 1994); René Lemarchand, 'Exclusion, Marginalization and Political Mobilization: The Road to Hell in the Great Lakes', *University of Copenhagen Centre of African Studies Occasional Paper* (March 2000).

[26] Mahmood Mamdani, *When Victims Become Killers: Colonialism, Nativism, and the Genocide in Rwanda* (Princeton: Princeton University Press, 2001).

[27] Scott Straus, *The Order of Genocide: Race, Power, and War in Rwanda* (Ithaca: Cornell University Press, 2006).

of both the pre-colonial period and the 1994 genocide—for example, by labelling all Hutu refugees as genocidaires or by employing guilt discourses in the international arena—not only maintains RPF power but 'perpetuates violence in the Great Lakes'.[28]

Perhaps the most infamous example of such memory mobilization is the speech given by Slobodan Milošević in 1989 at the site of the Battle of Kosovo Polje that took place 600 years earlier on 28 June 1389. That battle (and that date—also the day of Gavrilo Princip's shooting of Archduke Franz Ferdinand in 1914) is ingrained into Serbian memory as a moment of military defeat at the hands of the Turks, but a moment of moral victory, on the basis of Knez Lazar choosing a heavenly instead of an earthly kingdom for the Serbs. As well as confirming the Serb nation's place in the divine realm, the myth established the continuity of the Serb nation across the centuries and confirmed Serbia's right to its ancestral lands in Kosovo.[29] It was also the source of the 'betrayal syndrome'—Serb allegations that Muslims in Yugoslavia are 'that part of themselves which betrayed the "faith of their forefathers"'.[30] Milošević's speech is regularly cited as one of the key moments in his rise to power, and the use of the legend of the battle a central component in his ethno-nationalist arsenal and in the building of a nationalist consensus in Serbia. Although its significance can be overstated, this manipulation of Serbian national memory—which of course required grassroots activity to operationalize it, not Milošević alone—is key to understanding the 'ethnic cleansing' that accompanied the Yugoslav wars of the 1990s and, especially, the violent efforts to expel ethnic Albanians

---

[28] Johan Pottier, *Re-Imagining Rwanda: Conflict, Survival and Disinformation in the Late Twentieth Century* (Cambridge: Cambridge University Press, 2002), 130. See also Scott Straus and Lars Waldorf, *Remaking Rwanda: State Building and Human Rights after Mass Violence* (Madison: University of Wisconsin Press, 2011); Eric Stover and Harvey M. Weinstein (eds.), *My Neighbor, My Enemy: Justice and Community in the Aftermath of Mass Atrocity* (Cambridge: Cambridge University Press, 2004).

[29] Florian Bieber, 'Nationalist Mobilization and Stories of Serb Suffering: The Kosovo Myth from 600th Anniversary to the Present', *Rethinking History* 6:1 (2002), 95–110; Jasna Dragović-Soso, *'Saviours of the Nation': Serbia's Intellectual Opposition and the Revival of Nationalism* (London: C. Hurst, 2002).

[30] Milica Bakić-Hayden, 'Nesting Orientalisms: The Case of Former Yugoslavia', *Slavic Review* 54:4 (1995), 927.

from Kosovo at a point when Serbia was already isolated as a pariah state in the eyes of the 'international community'. Extremists prevailed over moderates in Serbia because they persuaded a large enough constituency that 'the powerful can fear the weak'.[31]

More important even than the myth of Kosovo, which represents Serbian 'deep memory', was the memory of what had happened in the Second World War. In the 1990s, the self-identification of Serbian and Croatian paramilitaries as Chetniks and Ustaše respectively was a conscious echo of the war, when 'Independent Croatia'—in reality, a Nazi puppet state under the leadership of the clerico-fascist collaborator Ante Pavelić—was responsible for the murder of tens of thousands of Serbs, Jews, and Romanies. No serious historian doubts that Serbs were subjected to a genocidal onslaught under the rule of Nazi-protected Croatia, but the manipulation of the figures of the dead in the 1980s and 1990s was a major contributor to the worsening of relations between the two major components of the Yugoslav federation. Croatia's neo-fascist president, Franjo Tuđman, was not only a Holocaust denier but a belittler of Serb suffering during the Second World War, and Serbian historians and politicians regularly exaggerated the numbers killed at Jasenovac and elsewhere in order to spread fear throughout the Serbian population (especially outside of the borders of Serbia) as Yugoslavia was breaking apart. A figure of 700,000 Serb deaths at Jasenovac was commonly heard in the 1980s, when the true figure is likely to have been about 100,000.[32]

---

[31] Anthony Oberschall, 'The Manipulation of Ethnicity: From Ethnic Cooperation to Violence and War in Yugoslavia', *Ethnic and Racial Studies* 23:6 (2000), 982–1001.

[32] Tea Sindbaek, *Useable History? Representations of Yugoslavia's Difficult Past from 1945 to 2002* (Aarhus: Aarhus University Press, 2012); Robert M. Hayden, 'Mass Killings and Images of Genocide in Bosnia, 1941–5 and 1992–5', in Dan Stone (ed.), *The Historiography of Genocide*, 487–516; Robert M. Hayden, 'Recounting the Dead: The Rediscovery and Redefinition of Wartime Massacres in Late- and Post-Communist Yugoslavia', in Ruby S. Watson (ed.), *Memory, Opposition and History under State Socialism* (Santa Fe: School of American Research Press, 1994), 167–84; Tomislav Dulić, *Utopias of Nation: Local Mass Killings in Bosnia and Herzegovina, 1941–42* (Uppsala: Uppsala University Press, 2005); Paul B. Miller, 'Contested Memories: The Bosnian Genocide in Serb and Muslim Minds', *Journal of Genocide Research* 8:3 (2006), 311–24. On the figures from the 1990s, see Ewa Tabeau and

This strategy was highly effective, as fear of becoming victims of genocide divided previously mixed communities into ethnically separate groups: 'Everyone was traumatized by all the talk of World War Two atrocities', wrote Bogdan Denitch, 'even those who had seemed immune to nationalism'.[33]

The Holocaust can also to some extent be seen through this lens. Dirk Moses argues that the Holocaust should be understood using a framework in which genocide is seen as a combination of colonial expansion, security fears, and subaltern revenge. Hitler drew on the overseas colonial experience, especially in India and North America, for inspiration for his own vision of a colonized Europe. The treatment of Ukrainians, Poles, and other conquered nations certainly conforms to this colonial pattern, in which the 'natives' were to become a reservoir of slave labour. And the murder of the Jews, according to Moses, was in part a subaltern genocide, through which Hitler aimed to 'emancipate' Germany from perceived 'foreign occupation', that is, Jewish rule. Thus, whilst Slavic populations were regarded as *Untermenschen* (sub-humans), suitable for enslavement, the Jews were a source of fear, for they sought to take over the world, and their elimination was a project of 'national liberation'.[34] Genocide, in Moses' formulation, 'is as much an act of security as it is racial hatred'.[35] It is worth noting that this stress on Nazi fears of Jews—as opposed to the standard narrative that stresses Nazi racial theory and the need to rid the world of inferior 'non-Aryans'—provides common ground between scholars who incorporate the Holocaust into the comparative genocide framework, and those who argue that the racial paradigm at the heart of the Nazi *Weltanschauung* ultimately owed less

---

Jakub Bijak, 'War-Related Deaths in the 1992–1995 Armed Conflicts in Bosnia and Herzegovina: A Critique of Previous Estimates and Recent Results', *European Journal of Population* 21 (2005), 187–215.

[33] Bogdan Denitch, *Ethnic Nationalism* (Minneapolis: University of Minnesota Press, 1996), 81, cited in Oberschall, 'The Manipulation', 990.

[34] A. Dirk Moses, 'Empire, Colony, Genocide: Keywords and the Philosophy of History', in Moses (ed.), *Empire, Colony, Genocide*, 34–40.

[35] A. Dirk Moses, 'Moving the Genocide Debate Beyond the History Wars', *Australian Journal of Politics and History* 54:2 (2008), 264.

to race science than to a paranoid political conspiracy theory. This view suggests that the Nazis were not so much driven by their sense of superiority as by their fear of the power of 'the Jew'. Hence the lengths to which Goebbels went in his propaganda output to convince the German public that '[t]he Jews are guilty of everything!'.[36] The source of this sense of existential threat was the 'stab-in-the-back' legend from 1918, the belief that Germany lost the Great War because the Jews had betrayed the country. Michael Geyer notes that '[t]he rhetoric of *Endkampf* [final battle] found its most potent enemy in the figure of the Jew'.[37] Indeed, the feeding through of the memory of 1918 into Nazi ideology is a textbook example of the power of traumatic memory, of what Mark Levene calls 'the perpetrator's "never again" syndrome'. 'They should not have staged 9 November 1918 with impunity', fumed Hitler to the Czech foreign minister in 1939, 'That day shall be avenged... The Jews shall be annihilated in our land.'[38]

Post-Genocidal Traumatic Memory

What happens after genocide? When communities are devastated, often all that is left is memory, and that a 'memory shot through with holes'.[39] Thus survivors turn inwards, and focus on themselves and the need for familial and community repair.[40] This process is intrinsically related to memory, in the production of memorial books and monuments, and, in interacting with the wider world, in attempts to bring

[36] See Jeffrey Herf, *The Jewish Enemy: Nazi Propaganda During World War II and the Holocaust* (Cambridge, MA: Belknap Press of Harvard University Press, 2006). Goebbels cited at 209. See also Moses, 'Paranoia and Partisanship'; Doris L. Bergen, 'Instrumentalization of *Volksdeutschen* in German Propaganda in 1939: Replacing/Erasing Poles, Jews, and Other Victims', *German Studies Review* 31:3 (2008), 447–70 for an example of the manipulation of fears of German victimization at the hands of Poles.

[37] Michael Geyer, '*Endkampf* 1918 and 1945: German Nationalism, Annihilation, and Self-Destruction', in Alf Lüdtke and Bernd Weisbrod (eds.), *No Man's Land of Violence: Extreme Wars in the Twentieth Century* (Göttingen: Wallstein, 2006), 47.

[38] Levene, *The Meaning of Genocide*, 197.

[39] Henri Raczymow, 'Memory Shot Through With Holes', *Yale French Studies* 85 (1994), 98–105.

[40] Devon E. Hinton and Alexander L. Hinton (eds.), *Genocide and Mass Violence: Memory, Symptom, and Recovery* (Cambridge: Cambridge University Press, 2015).

what happened to general notice and to bring perpetrators to justice. If collective memory is essential for mobilizing perpetrators, it also underpins attempts to commemorate genocide in its immediate aftermath and to advocate on behalf of survivors in their quest for justice. But this, too, is a contested process: the 'truth' of genocide 'often becomes a power-laden tool over which politicians, activists, and the international community wrestle by asserting and contesting representations cobbled together from the often fragmented and clashing memories of survivors, perpetrators, witnesses, and bystanders'.[41] In the more extreme cases, memory ensnares such groups; for example, 'Turkish denial traps both Turks and Armenians, reproducing the cycles of violence in different ways: Turks steadily refuse to remember that past, and Armenians continually refuse to forget it'.[42]

A large literature now exists on reparations, compensation, restitution, war crimes trials, truth commissions, and the developing international law on genocide since the founding of the International Criminal Court (ICC) in 1999. In numerous contexts, from Guatemala to Poland, national commissions of inquiry have been set up to inquire into genocidal pasts. Questions of restitution, and the link between property and memory—and, especially in settler-colonial contexts, between land and memory—are a window into memory politics, and provide a link between issues of memory that are victim community-focused and those that are aimed at the wider world.[43] Perhaps post-genocide trials represent the purest form of the latter.

[41] Alexander Laban Hinton and Kevin Lewis O'Neill, 'Genocide, Truth, Memory, and Representation: An Introduction', in Hinton and O'Neill (eds.), *Genocide: Truth, Memory, and Representation* (Durham, NC: Duke University Press, 2009), 5.

[42] Fatma Müge Göçek, *Denial of Violence: Ottoman Past, Turkish Present and Collective Violence against the Armenians, 1789–2009* (Oxford: Oxford University Press, 2015), 3.

[43] Dan Diner and Gotthard Wunberg (eds.), *Restitution and Memory: Material Restoration in Europe* (New York: Berghahn Books, 2007); Martin Dean, *Robbing the Jews: The Confiscation of Jewish Property in the Holocaust, 1933–1945* (Cambridge: Cambridge University Press, 2008); Uğur Ümit Üngör and Mehmet Polatel, *Confiscation and Destruction: The Young Turk Seizure of Armenian Property* (London: Continuum, 2011); Jeff Benvenuto, Andrew Woolford, and Alexander Laban Hinton, 'Introduction', in Benvenuto, Woolford, and Hinton (eds.), *Colonial Genocide in Indigenous North America* (Durham, NC: Duke University Press, 2014), 9; Damien Short, 'Australia: A Continuing Genocide?', *Journal of Genocide Research* 12:1 (2010), 53–5.

The memory of Nuremberg informs the currently developing international law on genocide and human rights,[44] and issues of compen-
satory and/or corrective justice, as well as penal/retributive justice,
are in evidence in different sorts of trials, depending on whether these
deal with reparations or punishment. As work on the International
Criminal Tribunal for the former Yugoslavia (ICTY), International
Criminal Tribunal for Rwanda (ICTR), and Extraordinary Chambers in the Courts of Cambodia (ECCC) is showing, the significance of
post-genocide trials for memory work is not to be underestimated.[45]
Even though it is widely acknowledged that the punishment in such
cases can never fit the crime—'The Nazi crimes, it seems to me,
explode the limits of the law; and that is precisely what constitutes
their monstrousness'[46]—the impact of such trials explains why they
have been avoided in so many instances, from France to Cambodia,
by the use of delaying tactics. Numerous scholars identify shortcomings in the United Nations Genocide Convention, and some assert
that these shortcomings have negative consequences for the establishment of collective memories of genocide;[47] but there is a good reason
why the authorities often resist and place obstacles in the way of post-
genocide trials.

When memory is the subject, the focus of attention is usually on
commemorative practices, monuments, and museums. An enormous

[44] William A. Schabas, *The UN International Criminal Tribunals: The Former Yugoslavia, Rwanda and Sierra Leone* (Cambridge: Cambridge University Press, 2006),
esp. 3–46; Donald Bloxham, *Genocide on Trial: War Crimes Trials and the Formation of
Holocaust History and Memory* (Oxford: Oxford University Press, 2001).

[45] See e.g. Stover and Weinstein (eds.), *My Neighbour, My Enemy*; James Gow,
Rachel Kerr, and Zoran Pajić (eds.), *Prosecuting War Crimes: Lessons and Legacies of the
International Criminal Tribunal for the Former Yugoslavia* (Abingdon: Routledge, 2013);
Timothy Longman, *Memory and Justice in Post-Genocide Rwanda* (Cambridge: Cam-
bridge University Press, 2017); Alexander Laban Hinton, *The Justice Facade: Trials
of Transition in Cambodia* (Oxford: Oxford University Press, 2018).

[46] Hannah Arendt to Karl Jaspers, 17 August 1946, in *Arendt/Jaspers Correspond-
ence 1926–1969*, ed. Lotte Kohler and Hans Saner (San Diego: Harcourt Brace,
1992), 54.

[47] E.g. Caroline Fournet, *The Crime of Destruction and the Law of Genocide: Their
Impact on Collective Memory* (Aldershot: Ashgate, 2007); Gerry Simpson, *Law, War and
Crime: War Crimes Trials and the Reinvention of International Law* (Cambridge: Polity,
2007).

body of research now exists on Holocaust memorials and museums, of which there are many throughout the world.[48] But it is not only the Holocaust that provides material to test James E. Young's claim that monuments propagate an 'illusion of common memory'. The desire to memorialize traumatic events such as the Holocaust 'may actually spring from an opposite and equal desire to forget them', since the assumption that the monument is always there tends to encourage a lack of engagement with the issues.[49] A casual stroll through any major city, most of whose monuments remain unnoticed and, for the inhabitants, unidentifiable, suggests that Young has a point.

Apart from the question of whether genocide memorials too readily take their cue from representations of the Holocaust,[50] it is worth considering what forms of memory genocide memorials and museums are meant to encourage. In Rwanda, the graphic display of the bones of the dead (contrary to burial customs) at Rwanda's national genocide memorials generates a 'traumatic silence' amongst visitors.[51] This memorial strategy, as Jens Meierhenrich has noted, exemplifies the Rwandan government's 'exercise of power over memory', and 'seems to have served, more often than not, the purpose of legitimating authoritarian rule rather than honouring the genocide dead'.[52] While many local *lieux de mémoire* are left to fade, the display of the bones and bodies of the dead—either sorted into rows of femurs, tibias, and skulls, or left 'as they fell'—'justify a repressive government by presenting a spectre of past violence as a permanent future possibility, [and] also serve as an instrument of repression'.[53] In Cambodia, the Tuol Sleng Museum of Genocidal Crimes and the Choeung Ek 'killing fields' site serve a similar function. They also aim to preserve the memory of genocide, but do so by shocking visitors (mostly

[48] Dan Stone, 'Memory, Memorials and Museums', in Stone (ed.), *The Historiography of the Holocaust* (Basingstoke: Palgrave Macmillan, 2004), 508–32.

[49] James E. Young, *The Texture of Memory: Holocaust Memorials and Meaning* (New Haven: Yale University Press, 1993), 6–7.

[50] Jinks, *Representing Genocide*.

[51] Sara Guyer, 'Rwanda's Bones', *boundary 2*, 36:3 (2009), 162.

[52] Jens Meierhenrich, 'Topographies of Forgetting and Remembering: The Transformation of *Lieux de Mémoire* in Rwanda', in Straus and Waldorf (eds.), *Remaking Rwanda*, 292.

[53] Guyer, 'Rwanda's Bones', 161.

Western tourists), partly by deliberately borrowing a Holocaust-inspired form of representation, and partly by instilling a new national narrative.[54] The sheer mass of bones in these monuments provokes the shock and horror that are appropriate responses to genocide, but are ineffective in producing the kind of engaged responses that move beyond the platitudes of 'never again'.[55] Their anonymity means that they also recapitulate the logic of genocide: the reduction of individual human beings to representatives of a (perpetrator-defined) group. Hence the importance of local memorials and commemorative festivals in Cambodia.[56] And hence the great significance of naming in general, as seen in many memorial practices, from the post-Holocaust *yizker-bikher* (memorial books) to the recovery of names in Spain's *Todos los nombres* project.[57]

Remembering genocide, however, is only one side of the coin of responding to such traumatic events. The other is willed amnesia. Especially in instances where former perpetrators and surviving victims have to live together in close proximity, closing off memory, or at least trying to do so, is a meaningful way of dealing with the past. In Rwanda, for example, what is striking about Susanne Buckley-Zistel's interviews with people from across the country's diverse population is that, whilst they often referred to the 1994 genocide, 'the causes of the genocide and the decades of tension between Hutu and Tutsi were ignored'.[58] Precisely the years of tension from 1959 onwards that saw the mobilization of memory in the early 1990s were the years that had

[54] Judy Ledgerwood, 'The Cambodian Tuol Sleng Museum of Genocidal Crimes: National Narrative', in David E. Lorey and Willian H. Beezley (eds.), *Genocide, Collective Violence, and Popular Memory: The Politics of Remembrance in the Twentieth Century* (Wilmington: Scholarly Resources, 2002), 103–22; Brigitte Sion, 'Conflicting Sites of Memory in Post-Genocide Cambodia', *Humanity* 2:1 (2011), 1–21; Paul Williams, 'Witnessing Genocide: Vigilance and Remembrance at Tuol Sleng and Choeung Ek', *Holocaust and Genocide Studies* 18:4 (2004), 234–54.

[55] Jinks, *Representing Genocide*, 220–3; Rachel Hughes, 'Dutiful Tourism: Encountering the Cambodian Genocide', *Asia Pacific Viewpoint* 49:3 (2008), 318–30.

[56] Rachel Hughes, 'Memory and Sovereignty in Post-1979 Cambodia: Choeung Ek and Local Genocide Memorials', in Susan E. Cook (ed.), *Genocide in Cambodia and Rwanda: New Perspectives* (New Brunswick: Transaction, 2006), 257–80.

[57] Guyer, 'Rwanda's Bones'.

[58] Susanne Buckley-Zistel, 'Remembering to Forget: Chosen Amnesia as a Strategy for Local Coexistence in Post-Genocide Rwanda', *Africa* 76:2 (2006), 131.

to be 'forgotten' (that is to say, left undiscussed), rather than the events of the genocide itself. Gacaca trials can address issues of who did what in the context of the genocide, but leave the underlying causes unaddressed. The Rwandan government's 'national unity' policy and its associated rigid management of memory—via a binarized construction of victim/Tutsi and perpetrator/Hutu, which marginalizes many of those who were the victims of genocide but do not fit within these two distinct categories (e.g. Hutu widows)—only amplifies this silence.[59] In the Former Yugoslavia, as Ljiljana Radonić argues, war memories—of both the Second World War and the 1990s wars—pervade the still-radicalized atmosphere. Serbs, Croats, and Bosniaks each construct hegemonic narratives of victimhood, and—in an example of competitive rather than cosmopolitan 'Holocaust comparison'—'often tend to conceive of themselves as the new Jews'.[60] These highly politicized memories prove an obstacle to transitioning 'from a negative to a positive peace'.[61] Nevertheless, Cornelia Sorabji has shown that while memories of traumatic events continue 'to affect the social fabric', possibly sustaining the sort of hostility that fuelled conflict in the first place, individuals often 'manage' their own memories differently.[62] Sorabji correctly notes that the risk of analysing memory as a carrier of conflict is that it serves to perpetuate 'ancient hatreds' style arguments, which suggest that war in the Balkans is a more or less natural condition. It is important, then, to situate individuals and their memories—'real' or 'transmitted'—into the context of the politics of memory, that is, the broader framework of competing

[59] Jennie E. Burnet, 'Whose Genocide? Whose Truth? Representations of Victim and Perpetrator in Rwanda', in Hinton and O'Neill (eds.), *Genocide*, 80–110. See also Straus and Waldorf (eds.), *Remaking Rwanda*.

[60] Ljiljana Radonić, 'From "Double Genocide" to "the New Jews": Holocaust, Genocide and Mass Violence in Post-Communist Memorial Museums', *Journal of Genocide Research* 20:4 (2018), 527–8.

[61] Jelena Subotić, 'Political Memory as an Obstacle to Justice in Serbia, Croatia, and Bosnia-Herzegovina', in Martina Fischer and Olivera Simić (eds.), *Transitional Justice and Reconciliation: Lessons from the Balkans* (London: Routledge, 2015), 121–38.

[62] Cornelia Sorabji, 'Managing Memories in Post-War Sarajevo: Individuals, Bad Memories, and New Wars', *Journal of the Royal Anthropological Institute*, NS, 12 (2006), 1–18.

narratives at group or state level that seek to 'channel' people's memories in certain ways, and to leave room for 'individual memory management and change down the generations'. One should not assume 'that human minds are endlessly manipulable and that schooling or the broadcasting of nationalistic commemorative ceremonies can fundamentally alter personal memories of strongly emotional, life-changing events such as violent bereavement'.[63]

Of course, one of the characteristics of traumatic memory is that it cannot be suppressed at will. It is by its very nature a memory that returns unexpectedly and uncontrollably to haunt individual victims and post-genocide societies. There is no need for memories of genocide to be 'recovered'—in the dubious manner of childhood abuse cases of the 1980s—since it has never gone away in the first place. Many scholars are now rightly critical of the view, fashionable in the 1990s especially in literary studies, that 'traumatic memory' is a widely applicable concept. The idea that whole societies can be traumatized has been subjected to serious criticism, so that what we are generally left with is a more or less appropriate metaphor, not a concept that carries any of the precise, clinical meaning that it does when applied to individuals (when used carefully, and not just in the vernacular, as in 'what a traumatic day that was'). As Kansteiner notes, 'none of the existing concepts of Holocaust trauma is well suited to explain the effects of Holocaust representations on individuals or collectives who encounter the Final Solution only as a media event for educational or entertainment purposes'.[64] Still, in the case of societies that have experienced genocide, we are facing a situation where the concept of traumatic memory, if it has any use at all, is about as applicable as one can expect. This is why we noted at the outset that genocide is less amenable to willed amnesia than other events. What one actually sees, for example, in the cases of Bosnia or Rwanda mentioned above, is a form of repression, rather than a 'healthy forgetting' in the manner of

---

[63] Sorabji, 'Managing Memories', 2.

[64] Wulf Kansteiner, 'Testing the Limits of Trauma: The Long-Term Psychological Effects of the Holocaust on Individuals and Collectives', *History of the Human Sciences* 17:2–3 (2004), 97; Wulf Kansteiner, 'Genealogy of a Category Mistake: A Critical Intellectual History of the Cultural Trauma Metaphor', *Rethinking History* 8:2 (2004), 193–221.

Nietzsche. And what is repressed sooner or later returns, as we currently see the memory of the post-Civil War 'repression'—a somewhat coy term for what some historians actually consider a genocidal onslaught—of the Francoists' enemies in Spain.[65] The continuing tensions and conflict in south-east Europe and the Great Lakes region indicate that the politics of post-genocidal memories are matters of life and death.

Commemoration and Memory Conflicts

In February 2008, Kevin Rudd, the new Australian Prime Minister, made a decisive break with the politics of John Howard's conservative administration by making a public apology to the country's indigenous people for the suffering endured by the 'stolen children' and their families. This policy, which began in the early twentieth century and lasted until the 1960s, removed 'half-caste' children from Aboriginal communities, bringing them up in separated institutions. Until the 1940s the approach was one of biological absorption, or 'breeding out the black', which aimed to prevent white Australia from being threatened—so the fear went—by 'a large black population which may drive out the white'.[66] But child removal continued for several decades, devastating Aboriginal communities and leading the authors of the 1997 *Bringing Them Home* report to argue that the policy constituted genocide under Article IIe of the UNGC. Whether or not this was an appropriate designation is in this context not the point (Rudd, incidentally, denies that it was genocide), so much as the fact that the subsequent furore revealed the way in which controversy about genocidal origins haunts 'national memory' generations after the cessation of frontier conflict.

---

[65] Helen Graham, *The War and its Shadow: Spain's Civil War in Europe's Long Twentieth Century* (Eastbourne: Sussex Academic Press, 2012).

[66] Quoted in Robert Manne, 'Aboriginal Child Removal and the Question of Genocide, 1900–1940', in A. Dirk Moses (ed.), *Genocide and Settler Society: Frontier Violence and Stolen Indigenous Children in Australian History* (New York: Berghahn Books, 2004), 229, 237; Anna Haebich, *Broken Circles: Fragmenting Indigenous Families, 1800–2000* (Fremantle: Fremantle Arts Centre, 2000).

The perpetration of genocide requires the mobilization of memory, but post-genocidal conflicts over memory, especially national memory, reveal another aspect of the question: memory can intervene in national politics in unexpected ways and present challenges to cherished national narratives. The issue here is not a 'zero-sum' competition for space in the memorysphere, *pace* Rothberg—it is about the attempted *rewriting* of national memory. This is particularly true of settler societies, and is best illustrated by the Australian case. With the emergence of what its opponents pejoratively called 'black armband history', debates over Australian history overshadowed contemporary political debates concerning how best to deal with troubled Aboriginal communities. Conservative historians, most notably Keith Windschuttle, charged 'politically correct' historians with failing to appreciate the true nature of frontier conflict (where, they say, mutual incomprehension rather than genocidal intent was at work), and also with deliberately exaggerating the numbers of Aborigines killed in massacres.[67] The 'history wars' that followed the publication of Windschuttle's revisionist book have been described as an 'Australian *Historikerstreit*', a designation that is revealing, since the 1980s' West German debate about the uniqueness of the Holocaust broke no new historical ground but was fundamental to the self-image of the Federal Republic. The challenge to the Australian story of mates pulling together to create the 'lucky country' did not sit well with conservative cultural politics, which was not open to the fact that historians of early Australia were not arguing that the colonization of Australia was the same as the Holocaust, only that similarities in the perpetrators' discourses of race and security in both cases ought to offer food for thought, particularly where current-day policies towards Aborigines are concerned.[68] But whilst debate raged in Australia—unlike in

[67] Keith Windschuttle, *The Fabrication of Aboriginal History* (Sydney: Macleay Press, 2002).
[68] Moses, 'Moving the Genocide Debate', 254–5. See also Patrick Brantlinger, ' "Black Armband" versus "White Blindfold" History in Australia', *Victorian Studies* 46:4 (2004), 655–74; Neil Levi, ' "No Sensible Comparison"? The Place of the Holocaust in Australia's History Wars', *History & Memory* 19:1 (2007), 124–56; Andrew G. Bonnell and Martin Crotty, 'Australia's History under Howard, 1996–2007', *Annals of the American Academy of Political and Social Science* 617 (2008), 149–65.

Germany—as to whether the country should be understood as a 'post-genocidal society', the fact that the colonization process was 'objectively lethal' for the Aborigines continued to be overlooked.[69] Irrespective of the statistics and other facts being debated by historians (and here the comparison with the *Historikerstreit* is unconvincing, for in West Germany no historians questioned whether genocide had occurred), the bigger point is that Australian collective memory was being deconstructed and reconstructed anew or, for conservative historians, being undermined by subversives bent on ridiculing national heritage.

Even long after genocide has taken place, memory wars can erupt when group narratives are felt to be under threat. The history of nation-building is inseparable from the 'memories' that nations create, in the shape of the narratives or monuments they construct. Indeed, collective memory does not emerge after the process has come to an end but is an essential part of the process whereby a group constitutes itself as a group; as Jens Bartelson notes, 'the coincidence of state and nation that we normally take to be the very culmination of a successful process of state formation had virtually been *remembered* into existence'.[70] The motives of memory, as James Young reminds us, are never pure.[71]

It is hardly surprising, then, that especially in societies founded on colonial settlement, challenges to positive national narratives are considered problematic. In the US, the genocide question is still almost wholly ignored, even by prominent scholars of genocide; in Canada, limited national debate over the Residential Schools has been guided by a Truth and Reconciliation Commission, but settler colonial crimes committed in the pursuit of 'civilizing' the 'Canadian wilderness' are often erased, and indigenous peoples are often

---

[69] A. Dirk Moses, 'An Antipodean Genocide? The Origins of the Genocidal Moment in the Colonization of Australia', *Journal of Genocide Research* 2:1 (2000), 89–106.

[70] Jens Bartelson, 'We Could Remember it for You Wholesale: Myths, Monuments and the Constitution of National Memories', in Duncan Bell (ed.), *Memory, Trauma and World Politics: Reflections on the Relationship Between Past and Present* (Basingstoke: Palgrave Macmillan, 2006), 51.

[71] Young, *The Texture of Memory*, 2.

instructed to 'just get over it'; in Israel, Holocaust memory continues to poison relations with Palestinians.[72] And such contestation over the meaning of the past is not limited to settler-colonial societies: after 1990, Eastern European countries fought 'memory wars' over the meaning of the Second World War II and the Holocaust, especially as they prepared to join the European Union (EU), which had its own homogenizing narrative of that past;[73] Turkish denial of the Armenian genocide remains vociferous. At the root of this denial is a defence of the Turkish national historical narrative of the Republic's glorious birth out of its independence struggle—and also its fear that recognizing this genocide might open up other minority 'issues' (especially regarding the Kurds and Cyprus), and lead to the fragmentation of Turkish lands, in a repeat of the dissolution of the Ottoman Empire. In this sense, recognizing Turkish state violence against its minorities—past and present—becomes an existential question.[74] Thus, while memory may be mobile, transnational, transgenerational, and transcultural, national renderings of memory still seem to produce the most potent conflict. Such conflicts are potentially destabilizing and certainly have the power to inspire not only a cosmopolitan culture of human rights but also new outbursts of resentment and revanchism.

Conclusion

In a key article on the historical study of memory, Alon Confino asks: 'if the study of memory focuses creatively on how people construct a past through a process of appropriation and contestation, is the real

---

[72] Benjamin Madley, 'Reexamining the American Genocide Debate: Meaning, Historiography, and New Methods', *American Historical Review* 120:1 (2015), 98–139; Tricia Logan, 'National Memory and Museums: Remembering Settler Colonial Genocide of Indigenous Peoples in Canada', in Nigel Eltringham and Pam Maclean (eds.), *Remembering Genocide* (London: Routledge, 2014); Moses, 'Genocide and the Terror of History'.

[73] Maria Mälksoo, 'The Memory Politics of Becoming European: The East European Subalterns and the Collective Memory of Europe', *European Journal of International Relations* 15:4 (2009), 653–80.

[74] Göçek, *Denial of Violence*.

problem not, perhaps, that people construct the past by using the term "memory" at all?'.[75] There is, in other words, a danger of studying a phenomenon ('memory') by taking it as its own explanation. This problem, however, is not merely a methodological one of memory studies but a reflection of the complex place that 'memory' holds in contemporary societies. For memory is not simply synonymous with the way in which the past is represented in the present; it is itself constitutive of the present. Memory and identity go hand in hand.

Thus, irrespective of methodological problems, issues connected with memory will continue to resonate. Exclusivist, exclusionary memories remain powerful in many contexts; the generation of genocidal ideologies through the manipulation of memory is as much a possibility as it ever was. Indeed, memory wars by no means guarantee a peaceful resolution or mutually agreeable arbitration between competing versions of the past. As Peter Fritzsche notes, the reason that national memories 'remain so resonant' is 'not because they are more true, but because the narratives of collective guilt and collective victimization that they generate have the effect of recognizing and commemorating individual suffering in socially meaningful, if tendentious, ways'.[76] For this reason, the study of memory cannot be avoided or swept aside. Despite the risks of perpetuating old divisions or reopening unhealed wounds, grappling with memory, especially after traumatic events like genocide, remains essential in order to remind the victims that they are not the worthless human beings that their tormentors have portrayed them as. For nothing is more human, and thus more geared towards the generation of meaning where meaning is otherwise absent (or at least to 'keeping watch over absent meaning'[77]), than the broad spectrum of practices that come under the heading of 'memory'.

[75] Alon Confino, 'Collective Memory and Cultural History: Problems of Method', *American Historical Review* 102:5 (1997), 1403.

[76] Peter Fritzsche, 'The Case of Modern Memory', *Journal of Modern History* 73:1 (2001), 117.

[77] Maurice Blanchot, *The Writing of the Disaster* (Lincoln: University of Nebraska Press, 1986), 42.

Acknowledgement

Our thanks to Donald Bloxham and Dirk Moses for their comments on earlier versions of this chapter.

Selected Bibliography

Barayón, Ramon Sender, *A Death in Zamora* (San Francisco: Calm Unity Press, 2003).

Bizot, François, *The Gate* (London: Harvill Press, 2003).

Confino, Alon, 'Telling about Germany: Narratives of Memory and Culture', *Journal of Modern History* 76:2 (2004), 389–416.

Gigliotti, Simone, *The Memorialization of Genocide* (Abingdon: Routledge, 2016).

Moradi, Fazil, Ralph Buchenhorst, and Maria Six-Hohenbalken (eds.), *Memory and Genocide: On What Remains and the Possibility of Representation* (Abingdon: Routledge, 2017).

Radonić, Ljiljana (ed.), 'The Holocaust/Genocide Template in Eastern Europe', Special issue of the *Journal of Genocide Research* 20:4 (2018).

Ricoeur, Paul, *Memory, History, Forgetting* (Chicago/London: University of Chicago Press, 2004).

Rothenberg, Daniel (ed.), *Memory of Silence: The Guatemalan Truth Commission Report* (Basingstoke: Palgrave Macmillan, 2012).

Stone, Dan, *The Holocaust, Fascism and Memory: Essays in the History of Ideas* (Basingstoke: Palgrave Macmillan, 2013).

10

Genocide and Military Intervention

Alex J. Bellamy and Stephen McLoughlin

Introduction

The commission of genocide and mass atrocities has provoked calls for military intervention by external actors since the nineteenth century.[1] From the 1820s to the 1870s, groups of activists collectively known as 'atrocitarians' agitated for armed intervention to protect Christians in the Greek, Syrian, and Bulgarian lands of the Ottoman Empire. At century's end, the US invaded Cuba partly in response to calls from notable figures, including former President Theodore Roosevelt, that it should act to put an end to Spanish atrocities there.[2] In the twentieth century, the Armenian genocide, Holocaust, and more recent genocides in Bosnia and Rwanda all elicited widespread agitation in favour of armed intervention. The present century is no different, with activists maintaining that those with the power to do so should have intervened forcibly in Darfur and Iraq/Syria, amongst others, to protect civilian populations from their tormentors. In 2005, two centuries of political agitation produced a landmark commitment from the world's governments when they unanimously declared their responsibility to protect populations from genocide and to take 'timely

---

[1] See Gary J. Bass, *Freedom's Battle: The Origins of Humanitarian Intervention* (London: Alfred Knopf, 2008).

[2] Ernest R. May, *Imperial Democracy: The Emergence of America as a Great Power* (New York: Imprint Publications, 1961), 127.

and decisive' action in cases where a state manifestly fails in its responsibility to protect.[3]

Historically, once started, genocides tend to end either with the military defeat of the perpetrators or the suppression (though not necessarily the annihilation) of the victim groups.[4] Only military force can directly prevent genocidal killing, stand between perpetrators and their intended victims, and protect the delivery of life-saving aid. But its use entails risks for all parties and does not necessarily resolve the underlying conflict. Its impact is difficult to predict and force might sometimes inflame rather than improve situations. Properly used, force can offer physical protection to populations in immediate danger. But it cannot compel the parties to build sustainable peace, rebuild shattered governments, economies, and societies, protect populations in the long term, or provide comprehensive security. Moreover, there is a real danger that a generalized right to intervene for humanitarian purposes could be abused, such as Russia's use of the 'Responsibility to Protect' as justification for its 2008 invasion of Georgia, and the use of humanitarian rhetoric to justify the 2003 invasion of Iraq.[5] Then there is the additional hazard that promises of intervention might encourage acts of rebellion that elicit genocidal responses.[6]

[3] For accounts of the emergence of the Responsibility to Protect principle see Gareth Evans, *The Responsibility to Protect: Ending Mass Atrocity Crimes Once and for All* (Washington: The Brookings Institution, 2008), and Alex J. Bellamy, *Responsibility to Protect: The Global Effort to End Mass Atrocities* (Cambridge: Polity, 2009).

[4] The question of how genocides end remains relatively understudied. In 2006, the Social Science Research Council organized an insightful forum on this question. Available at: https://items.ssrc.org/category/how-genocides-end/

[5] The misuse of humanitarian arguments in the Georgia case have been detailed in Alex J. Bellamy and Stephen McLoughlin, 'Humanitarian Intervention', in Alan Collins (ed.), *Security Studies* (Oxford: Oxford University Press, 2019), and in the Iraq case in Alex J. Bellamy, 'Ethics and Intervention: The "Humanitarian Exception", and the Problem of Abuse in the Case of Iraq', *Journal of Peace Research* 41:2 (2004), 131–47.

[6] A 'moral hazard' documented by Alan J. Kuperman, 'Humanitarian Hazard: Revising the Doctrine of Intervention', *Harvard International Review* 26:1 (2004), 64–8, and Alan J. Kuperman, 'The Moral Hazard of Humanitarian Intervention: Lessons from the Balkans', *International Studies Quarterly* 52:1 (2008), 49–80.

What is more, by the time external military forces can be deployed and the agents of genocide defeated, the death toll amongst the victim group is likely to be staggeringly high. Although his analysis may be considered overly pessimistic, Alan Kuperman's sober assessment of what intervention could have achieved in Rwanda provides a cautionary tale for would-be humanitarian warriors. Kuperman maintained that, had the US speedily and successfully deployed forces to Rwanda in 1994 once it became known that genocide was under way, the total number of lives saved would have been around 'only' 125,000 of the approximately 500,000–800,000 victims of the genocide.[7]

In short, military intervention does not address why genocides happen in the first place and provides only a short-term palliative at best. Finally, it is important that we not allow a preoccupation with intervention to obscure the manner in which hegemonic powers, conceptions of statehood, and governing economic arrangements can sustain the preconditions for genocide.

The purpose of this chapter is to examine the role that military intervention can play in ending genocide and the political, moral, and legal debates that surround it. It proceeds in three parts. The first section briefly examines how genocides have ended since the beginning of the twentieth century, and explores the place of military intervention by external powers. The second section examines whether there is a moral and/or legal duty to intervene to end genocide. In the third section, we consider the reasons why states intervene only infrequently to put an end to genocide despite their rhetorical commitments.

Intervention and the Ending of Genocide

To what extent has military intervention brought genocide to an end? Table 10.1 sets out—in necessarily rudimentary form—how some of

---

[7] The precise death toll of the genocide is contested and estimates vary according to the data sources, timescales and method of counting used. Although some analysts—Kuperman included—estimate the death toll to be significantly lower than 800,000, most studies put the toll somewhere around that figure. See Linda Melvern, *Conspiracy to Murder: The Rwandan Genocide* (London: Verso, 2006).

Table 10.1. Commonly Accepted Genocides Since 1900 and How They Ended[8]

Date	Where	Ending
1904–5	German South West Africa (killing of Herero)	Decimation and 'pacification' of targeted group
1915–18	Ottoman Empire (forced deportation and killing of Armenians)	Largely successful 'cleansing' of Anatolia. Ottoman defeat in the First World War
1935–9	Ethiopia (Italy annihilation of Ethiopians as reprisal— envisaged 'Ethiopia without Ethiopians')	Decimation and pacification of targeted groups
1937–9	USSR (great purge of *kulaks* and others)	Decimation and pacification of targeted groups
1937–45	East Asia (Japanese destruction of Chinese in Manchuria, 'rape of Nanking', and genocidal atrocities in the Philippines and elsewhere)	Defeat of Japanese in the Second World War
1941–5	Nazi occupied Europe (Jewish Holocaust)	Defeat of Nazis in the Second World War
1965–6	Indonesia (massacre of ethnic Chinese and suspected communists)	Suppression of ethnic Chinese and elimination of communists as a political force
1967–70	Nigeria (Biafra) (genocidal killing in support of Federal forces in civil war)	Suppression of Biafran rebels and government victory in civil war
1971	Bangladesh ('cleansing' of Hindus by West Pakistan government)	Intervention by India

[8] Based on information in de Waal and Conley-Zilkic, 'Reflections'; Adam Jones, *Genocide: A Comprehensive Introduction* (London: Routledge, 2017); Ben Kiernan, *Blood and Soil: A World History of Genocide and Extermination from Sparta to Darfur* (New Haven: Yale University Press, 2008); Crisis Group, 'A New Dimension of Violence in Myanmar's Rakhine State', *International Crisis Group*, Briefing no. 154/Asia (24 January 2019), https://www.crisisgroup.org/asia/south-east-asia/myanmar/b154-new-dimension-violence-myanmars-rakhine-state.

1972	Burundi (elimination of Hutus)	Suppression of Hutus, especially educated class
1975–9	Cambodia (Khmer Rouge)	Intervention by Vietnam
1981–3	Guatemala (killing of 'communists' especially targeting five Maya groups)	Decimation and pacification of targeted group
1992	Sudan (Nuba mountains) (Jihad, mass killing and forced relocation of Nuba people with genocidal intent)	Local resistance and disagreement within government of Sudan
1992–5	Bosnia ((i) general—mass killing of Bosnian Muslims mainly be Bosnian Serbs but also by Bosnian Croats (ii) genocide at Srebrenica—killing of males by Bosnian Serbs)	(i) peace settlement coerced by combination of NATO and Croat-Muslim forces; (ii) male population largely exterminated
1994	Rwanda (killing of Tutsi and Hutu moderates by Hutu militia supported by government)	Defeat of militia and government forces by Rwandan Patriotic Front (RPF)
2003–8	Sudan—Darfur (killing and forced displacement of various African groups by government backed militias)	Decimation and forced removal of targeted group lead to reduction of violence
2014–19	Iraq and Syria (killing, forced displacement of the Yazidis by Islamic State)	Islamic State defeated by international coalition and Kurdish armed groups
2016–	Rakhine State, Myanmar (killing and forced displacement of Rohingya)	Myanmar depopulated of Rohingya. Rohingya population displaced into Bangladesh

the most commonly accepted cases of genocide since 1900 have come to an end and reveals three important insights. First, with only two partial exceptions, once begun, genocidal killing ends in only one of two ways—by perpetrators deciding that they have successfully completed their objectives, or their military defeat. The partial exceptions are the Nuba Mountains and Bosnia cases. In the Nuba Mountains case, local resistance slowed the pace of killing and relocation, and divisions within the government brought about its end.[9] In the Bosnia case, a political settlement (the 'Dayton Accords') rather than the military defeat of the Bosnian Serbs ended the violence, although the Bosnian Serb leadership was coerced into accepting the accords by a combination of NATO air strikes and ground attacks (Operation 'Deliberate Force') and, more importantly, military advances by the Bosnian-Croat alliance forged and armed by the US. The single largest act of genocide in Bosnia—the 1995 killing of 7,600 men and boys sheltering in Srebrenica—succeeded in its immediate aim of eradicating the Muslim males of that town.[10] To this day, Srebrenica remains an almost exclusively Serb town, an ethnic reality forged by genocide. However appealing, non-military measures such as economic and political sanctions, arms embargoes, inducements, 'naming and shaming,' diplomacy, and threat of legal punishment have not, historically, sufficed to bring genocide to an end.

Despite the outpouring of academic literature on the subject and much political angst at the United Nations (UN) and elsewhere, external intervention to end genocide remains the exception rather than the norm. Of the eighteen cases identified in Table 10.1, nine ended more or less successfully for the perpetrators and a further two (Armenia and Bosnia-Srebrenica) ended badly for the perpetrators but not before they had achieved core goals ('cleansing' of Anatolia and Srebrenica). Of the eight genocides that did not end on the perpetrators' own terms, three endings were related to their military defeat in campaigns that were not directly related to the genocides (the defeat of the Ottoman Empire, Germany, and Japan in the First and Second World Wars), one was ended by the perpetrators' defeat by local actors (Rwanda), and another by a combination of local and external actors (Bosnia). Across all the cases, local resistance played a significant part in ending three episodes (Nuba, Rwanda, Bosnia). Only three episodes were ended by external military intervention specifically aimed at defeating the perpetrators of genocide (Bangladesh, Cambodia, and the Yazidis). Somewhat counterintuitively, two of these three interventions were conducted unilaterally by post-colonial

---

[9] De Waal and Conley-Zilkic, 'Reflections', 5.

[10] Jan Willem Honig and Norbert Both, *Srebrenica: Record of a War Crime* (London: Penguin, 1996).

(not Western) states that were not primarily motivated by humanitarian concerns.[11] The third involved an international coalition marshalled by the US and supported by the state that hosted the genocide (Iraq). Thus, although the West is commonly identified as the principal advocate of humanitarian intervention, in fact Western military activism to end genocide is very rare. There has been much less actual external military intervention to end genocide than there has been talk about such intervention.

Although the broader literature on humanitarian intervention often suggests that interventions are not tantamount to war and involve a variety of different military tasks—sometimes labelled 'military expedients', such as protecting safe areas, humanitarian convoys, no-fly zones, etc.[12]—it seems clear that, on the whole, external intervention to end genocide requires the military defeat of the perpetrators. In other words, whatever may be required by other forms of external engagement in armed conflict, such as peace operations, military intervention to end genocide is identical in form to warfare and has the same objective, namely the military suppression of the enemy.

A Duty to Intervene?

Is there a duty to intervene to 'save strangers' from genocide?[13] We argue that there is a clear moral duty to intervene in circumstances where intervention is thought likely to do more good than harm. There is also evidence of an emerging—but much less well established—legal duty. Both ideas, however, remain deeply controversial principally because armed intervention by external actors is rarely disinterested, leading some to fear that the duty to intervene can be a thinly veiled justification for a coercive form of Western

---

[11] As Wheeler points out, both interventions were primarily conceived and justified in terms of self-defence. See Nicholas J. Wheeler, *Saving Strangers: Humanitarian Intervention in International Society* (Oxford: Oxford University Press, 2000), 55–110.

[12] John G. Heidenrich, *How to Prevent Genocide: A Guide for Policymakers, Scholars and Concerned Citizens* (Westport: Praeger, 2001), 163. Also see Bass, *Freedom's Battle*.

[13] To use the phrase coined by Nicholas J. Wheeler.

hegemony or neo-imperialism that supports the very global system that nourishes the preconditions for genocide.

Usually associated with liberalism, cosmopolitanism, and the Christian Just War tradition, the case for intervention is typically premised on the idea that external actors have a *duty* as well as a *right* to intervene to halt genocide.[14] For advocates of this position, all humans have certain fundamental rights—chief among them being the right not to be arbitrarily killed—and sovereign rights are conditional on the fulfilment of the state's responsibility to protect populations under its care. When states fail in their duties towards their citizens, they lose their right to non-interference.[15] There are a variety of ways of arriving at this conclusion. Some liberal cosmopolitans draw on the work of the German philosopher Immanuel Kant to insist that all individuals have certain fundamental rights that deserve protection.[16] Others follow John Stuart Mill in thinking about possible exceptions to the basic principle of non-interference.[17] Other advocates of the Just War tradition ground their arguments in Christian theology.[18] Still others argue that today's globalized world is so integrated that massive human rights violations in one part of the world have an effect on every other part. This social interconnectedness, they maintain, creates moral obligations.[19] One of the leading contemporary proponents of this view is former British Prime Minister, Tony Blair. Shortly after NATO began its 1999 intervention in Kosovo, he gave a

[14] For an excellent account of antecedent thought see Stefano and Jennifer Welsh (eds.), *Just and Unjust Military Interventions: European Thinkers from Vitoria to Mill* (Cambridge: Cambridge University Press, 2013).

[15] Fernando R. Tesón, 'The Liberal Case for Humanitarian Intervention', in J. L. Holzgrefe and Robert O. Keohane (eds.), *Humanitarian Intervention: Ethical, Legal and Political Dilemmas* (Cambridge: Cambridge University Press 2003), 93. The principle of non-interference is discussed in more detail below.

[16] Simon Caney, 'Human Rights and the Rights of States: Terry Nardin on Non-Intervention', *International Political Science Review* 18:1 (1997), 34.

[17] Michael W. Doyle, *The Question of Intervention: John Stuart Mill and the Responsibility to Protect* (New Haven: Yale University Press, 2015).

[18] Paul Ramsey, *The Just War: Force and Political Responsibility* (Lanham: Rowman and Littlefield, 2002), 20.

[19] The idea that interconnectedness creates *moral* responsibilities is eloquently set out by Martha C. Nussbaum, *The Cosmopolitan Tradition: A Noble but Flawed Ideal* (Cambridge, MA: Belknap Press of Harvard University Press, 2019).

landmark speech setting out his 'doctrine of the international community'. Blair maintained that globalization was changing the world in ways that rendered traditional views of sovereignty anachronistic.[20]

A further line of argument is to point to the fact that states have already agreed to certain minimum standards of behaviour and that military intervention to end genocide is not about imposing the will of a few Western states upon the many, but about protecting and enforcing the collective will of international society. Advocates of this position argue that there is a customary right (but not duty) of intervention to put an end to genocide and mass atrocities.[21] They maintain that there is agreement in international society that genocide constitutes a grave wrong warranting external intervention.[22] From this perspective, state practice since the end of the Cold War suggests the emergence of a customary right of humanitarian intervention.[23] In particular, they point to the justifications offered to defend the American-, French-, and British-led intervention in Northern Iraq in 1991 to support their case. In that instance, the British argued that they were upholding customary international law, France invoked a customary 'right' of intervention, and the US noted a 're-balancing of the claims of sovereignty and those of extreme humanitarian need'.[24]

According to this perspective, the movement towards acceptance of a customary right of humanitarian intervention was reinforced by state practice after Northern Iraq. For example, throughout the UN Security Council's deliberations about how to respond to Rwanda in 1994, no state argued that either the ban on the use of force (Article 2 [4] of the UN Charter) or the non-interference rule (Article 2[7] of the Charter) should prohibit armed intervention to halt the bloodshed,

[20] Tony Blair, 'Doctrine of the International Community', speech to the Economic Club of Chicago, Hilton Hotel, Chicago, 22 April 1999.

[21] Wheeler, *Saving Strangers,* 14.

[22] See Anthony C. Arend and Robert J. Beck, *International Law and the Use of Force: Beyond the UN Charter Paradigm* (London and New York: Routledge, 1993), Jack Donnelly, *International Human Rights*, 2nd ed. (Boulder: Westview, 1988), and Tesón, 'The Liberal Case'.

[23] See Wheeler, *Saving Strangers* and Martha Finnemore, *The Purpose of Intervention: Changing Beliefs About the Use of Force* (Ithaca: Cornell University Press, 2003).

[24] Adam Roberts, 'Humanitarian War: Military Intervention and Human Rights', *International Affairs* 69:3 (1993), 436–7.

suggesting that such intervention would have been legitimate in that case. What stood in the way of intervention in Rwanda was the fact that no government wanted to risk the lives of its own soldiers to save Africans (see below). Throughout the 1990s, the Security Council expanded its interpretation of 'international peace and security' and authorized interventions to protect civilians in safe areas (Bosnia), maintain law and order and protect aid supplies (Somalia), and restore an elected government toppled by a coup (Haiti). These cases prompted Thomas Weiss to argue that 'the notion that human beings matter more than sovereignty radiated brightly, albeit briefly, across the international political horizon of the 1990s'.[25] Progress did not stop at the turn of the century. Since 2000, the Security Council has mandated peacekeepers to protect civilians under threat in Sierra Leone, the Democratic Republic of Congo, Burundi, Côte d'Ivoire, Liberia, Darfur, South Sudan, Mali, and the Central African Republic though it has usually insisted on receiving the consent of the host government.[26]

All this suggests that there is a growing international consensus around a moral duty to intervene to put an end to massive human suffering. However, there are also grounds for thinking that there is an emerging legal responsibility to do so as well, derived from a combination of the 'Responsibility to Protect' principle and a recent ruling of the International Court of Justice (ICJ). Although it might be premature to speak of a specific legal obligation to intervene militarily, the emergence of such a duty is important because it places legal obligations on states and creates the potential for redress if those obligations are not satisfied.

---

[25] Weiss, 'The Sunset of Humanitarian Intervention', 135.

[26] See Paul D. Williams with Alex J. Bellamy, *Understanding Peacekeeping*, 3rd ed. (Cambridge: Polity, 2009), Victoria K. Holt and Tobias C. Berkman, *The Impossible Mandate? Military Preparedness, the Responsibility to Protect and Modern Peace Operations* (Washington: The Henry L. Stimson Centre, 2006), Lise Morje Howard, *UN Peacekeeping in Civil Wars* (Cambridge: Cambridge University Press, 2008), and Lise Morje Howard, *Power in Peacekeeping* (Cambridge: Cambridge University Press, 2019).

In 2000, the Canadian government created the International Commission on Intervention and State Sovereignty (ICISS) to develop a way of reconciling sovereignty and human rights. The Commission's report, released in late 2001, was premised on the notion that the principle of non-interference 'yields to the responsibility to protect' when states are unwilling or unable to protect their citizens from grave harm.[27] Influenced by Annan and Deng, the ICISS argued that the 'Responsibility to Protect' entailed responsibilities to prevent and react to massive human suffering and help rebuild states and societies afterwards. Of the three responsibilities, the Commission identified the 'responsibility to prevent' as the single most important. In relation to the use of force for humanitarian purposes, the Commission proposed the adoption of criteria to guide decision-makers. Drawing from the Just War tradition, the Commission's proposed criteria included 'just cause thresholds' (large-scale loss of life or ethnic cleansing, actual or apprehended) and 'precautionary principles' (right intention, last resort, proportional means, and reasonable prospects).[28]

In 2005, the 'Responsibility to Protect' was transformed from a concept advanced by a Commission of high-profile figures to an international principle unanimously endorsed by world leaders. At the 2005 World Summit summoned to consider a UN reform package, world leaders adopted a declaration affirming the Responsibility to Protect, which was subsequently reaffirmed by the UN Security Council in 2006. According to the UN Secretary-General, Ban Ki-moon, the 'Responsibility to Protect' principle agreed to by world leaders rests on three pillars. First, the responsibility of the state to protect its own populations from genocide, war crimes, ethnic cleansing, and crimes against humanity. Second, the international community's duty to assist states in meeting these obligations. Third, the international community's responsibility to respond in a timely and decisive manner when a state is manifestly failing to protect its population, using Chapters VI (peaceful means), VII (coercive means

---

[27] International Commission on Intervention and State Sovereignty (ICISS), *The Responsibility to Protect* (Ottawa: IDRC, 2001), xi.

[28] ICISS, *Responsibility to Protect*, xi.

authorized by the UN Security Council), and VIII (regional arrangements) of the UN Charter.[29]

The 2005 declaration established a politically potent principle based on unanimous consensus produced by one of the largest gatherings of heads of state ever seen.[30] It is important to stress the unanimity of consensus among member states. Indeed, two traditional sceptics about this line of thinking, China and Russia, actually reaffirmed their commitment to the 'Responsibility to Protect' principle in Security Council Resolution 1674 (2006).[31] Moreover, by referring to Chapter VII of the UN Charter, world leaders specifically recognized the need to consider the use of force to protect populations from genocide. This of course does not mean that governments will agree about the most appropriate and effective form of engagement with specific crises, but the principle helps define the parameters and at least means that they can no longer avoid public consideration of engagement. In 2011, neither China nor Russia exercised their veto in two Security Council resolutions that invoked the Responsibility to Protect while authorizing the use of force against governments that were killing their own people. Resolution 1973 authorized 'all necessary measures ... to protect civilians' under attack by the Libyan government.[32] This precipitated NATO-led strikes on Libyan forces, that eventually led to the overthrow of Muammar Gaddafi. Likewise, in relation to Côte d'Ivoire, Resolution 1975 authorized 'all necessary means ... to protect civilians under imminent threat ...'.[33] This led to UN forces, in partnership with French forces, apprehending former President Laurent Gbagbo, and allowing the legitimately elected President, Alassane Ouattara to resume power. Though neither of these cases involved genocide per se, they did point towards new practices of intervention in response to mass atrocities.

[29] Ban Ki-moon, 'Responsible Sovereigns', address of the Secretary-General, SG/SM/11701, 15 July 2008, and Edward C. Luck, 'The United Nations and the Responsibility to Protect', *Stanley Foundation Policy Analysis Brief*, August 2008.
[30] Luck, 'The United Nations', 3.
[31] On China's position on the Responsibility to Protect see Sarah Teitt, 'China and the Responsibility to Protect', *Global Responsibility to Protect* 1:2 (2009), 208–36.
[32] S/RES/1973 (2011).
[33] S/RES/1975 (2011).

It is well known that the 1948 Genocide Convention not only prohibits genocide but establishes a duty to prevent and punish it (Article 1). This duty to prevent genocide is widely understood to be a principle of customary international law.[34] However, it was never clear whether this general duty amounted to a legal obligation to intervene to halt specific genocides. Although some legal scholars have argued that Article 1 imposes a duty on the UN and its member states to act (including through military intervention) wherever a genocide takes place,[35] the majority view seemed to support US Secretary of State Colin Powell's assertion that the Convention's language did not impose such a wide-ranging obligation.[36] However, important new light was shed on this issue by the ICJ's 2007 ruling in the *Bosnia and Herzegovina v. Serbia and Montenegro* case.

The Court found that Serbia was not guilty of genocide but had violated its Article 1 obligation to prevent and punish the crime of genocide. The ICJ found that, whilst states are not obliged to succeed in their efforts to prevent genocide, they 'must employ all means which are reasonably available to them to do so'.[37] The ruling confirmed that responsibility for prevention is not confined to local parties to violence. State-parties with the information and capacity to influence events also have responsibilities. Given that the Security Council has particular responsibility for international peace and security, unique authority which gives it the capacity to influence events

---

[34] William Schabas, *Genocide in International Law: The Crime of Crimes* (Cambridge: Cambridge University Press, 2000), 500.

[35] Stephen J. Toope, 'Does International Law Impose a Duty upon the UN to Prevent Genocide?', *McGill Law Journal* 46:1 (2000), 187–94.

[36] Jerry Fowler, e.g., argued that 'the language of the [Genocide] Convention does not provide any indication that such an extensive obligation was contemplated. Indeed it would be quite bizarre to think that the drafters intended in 1948 to make intervention in the internal affairs of other states obligatory'. Jerry Fowler, 'A New Chapter of Irony: The Legal Definition of Genocide and the Implications of Powell's Determination', in Samuel Totten and Eric Markusen (eds.), *Genocide in Darfur: Investigating the Atrocities in the Sudan* (London and New York: Routledge, 2006), 131.

[37] In Marko Milanovic, 'State Responsibility for Genocide: A Follow-Up', *European Journal of International Law* 18:4 (2007), 686.

wherever it deems fit to do so, and access to information not available to most individual states, it is clear that this ruling clarifies the specific responsibilities of the Council. As was argued by the former UN High Commissioner for Human Rights, Louise Arbour, the ruling—especially when taken in conjunction with the 'Responsibility to Protect' principle—imposes specific responsibilities on the members of the UN Security Council, and the permanent members especially.[38] The UN Security Council has the legal authority to authorize armed intervention whenever it identifies a threat to international peace and security. Moreover, as the world's leading military powers, permanent members of the Security Council have the military capacity to intervene to halt genocide. Thus armed with both the collective authority to intervene and—between them—the capacity to do so, it could be argued that armed intervention to halt genocide falls well within the scope of 'reasonably available' measures for permanent members of the Security Council.

None of this resolves difficult questions about the most appropriate and effective response to specific cases of genocide and mass atrocities. It remains the case that the idea that there might be a right or duty to intervene is controversial. Opponents—including several states in the Global South—maintain that international order and the preservation of core values such as the right to self-determination requires something approximating an absolute ban on the use of force outside the two parameters set out by the UN Charter—Security Council authorization (Chapter VII) and self-defence (Article 51)—and that the Security Council should interpret its remit narrowly.[39] The starting point for this position is the assumption that international society comprises a plurality of diverse communities each with different ideas about the best way to live. According to this view, international society is based on rules—the UN Charter's rules on the use of force first among them—that permit these communities to coexist relatively

---

[38] Arbour, 'The Responsibility to Protect'.

[39] For a good exposition of this position, linking it to the views of several Third World governments, see Mohammed Ayoob, 'Third World Perspectives on Humanitarian Intervention and International Administration', *Global Governance* 10:1 (2004), 99–118.

peacefully.[40] In a world characterized by radical disagreements about how societies should govern themselves, proponents of this view hold that a right and duty of humanitarian intervention would create disorder, as states would wage wars to protect and violently export their own cultural preferences. What is more, a right of intervention would open the door to potential abuse. Historically, states have sometimes 'abused' humanitarian justifications to legitimize wars that were anything but humanitarian. It was precisely because of the fear that states would exploit any loophole in the ban on the use of force that the delegates who wrote the UN Charter issued a comprehensive ban with only the two limited exceptions: force used in self-defence and under the authority of the Security Council.[41] In addition to the problem of abuse, many post-colonial states continue to oppose humanitarian intervention because they consider it a dangerous affront to another core principle, self-determination. They worry that a duty to intervene would grant a licence for the great powers to interfere in their domestic affairs, undermining their right to self-government.[42]

Although these are powerful arguments which should temper enthusiasm for and analysis of armed intervention, it is important to avoid the belief that the duty to intervene is an agenda that is exclusively, or even primarily, concerned with imposing Western values on the rest. On the one hand, those who caution against intervention as a matter of principle should be mindful of the evidence about how genocides end. On the other hand, it is important to not assume that the post-colonial world speaks as one on this issue. There are good grounds for thinking that there is global consensus that intervention, properly authorized, can be a legitimate response to genocide and mass atrocities when done properly and in the right circumstances. Nine years before NATO intervened in Kosovo without the authority of the Security Council, a group of West African states (ECOWAS) did likewise in Liberia. Four years before the

---

[40] A position set out and defended at length by Richard H. Jackson, *The Global Covenant: Human Conduct in a World of States* (Oxford: Oxford University Press, 2002).

[41] An argument put forth in detail by Simon Chesterman, *Just War or Just Peace? Humanitarian Intervention in International Law* (Oxford: Oxford University Press, 2001).

[42] A position set out by Ayoob, 'Third World Perspectives'.

adoption of the Responsibility to Protect principle by world leaders, members of the African Union gave the regional institution a right to intervene in response to serious humanitarian emergencies.[43]

A more recent criticism—arising largely in response to concerns regarding the use of force in Libya—relates to regime change. On 17 March 2011, the UN Security Council issued Resolution 1973, authorizing all means necessary to protect civilians in Libya, as well as establishing a no-fly zone over the country, and setting up an arms embargo. This was the first time the use of force was authorized without the consent of a sitting government. A NATO-led operation commenced air strikes that targeted Libya's military. These strikes prevented the Libyan government's attack on Benghazi, and eventually led to the rebels gaining the upper hand in the civil war. Following the NATO-led intervention in Libya, which preceded the overthrow of Gaddafi, Security Council members, China, Brazil, and South Africa stressed that the protection of civilians should never veil agendas that included regime change. In other words, regime change and human protection should never be conflated.[44] Valid as this criticism is, it is often difficult to disentangle human protection from regime change. It is difficult to imagine how else, other than regime change, Cambodians could have been saved from the Khmer Rouge, or Tutsis from the government-supported *Interahamwe*, or Ugandans from Idi Amin. Once such perpetrators have committed to genocidal violence to achieve their goals, there is scant evidence to suggest they could be persuaded to change course. While protecting civilians should never be used as an excuse to enact regime change, sometimes regime change is necessary to stop genocidal killing. Moreover, there are ways to allay these concerns. Military intervention should always have the right authority—according to international law, a Security Council mandate. Prevention should always be the first priority, with the use of force only considered once non-coercive options have been exhausted. The intention of intervening actors should be interrogated to ensure that what they say they intend to do aligns with what we

---

[43] See Paul D. Williams, 'From Non-Interference to Non-Indifference: The Origins and Development of the African Union's Security Culture', *African Affairs* 106:423 (2007), 253–79.

[44] See S/PV.6531, 10 May 2011.

know about the situation at hand. Strategies chosen should never compromise the goal of civilian protection, and there must be a commitment to rebuild afterwards.

Despite the controversy around regime change, the Libya intervention did prevent a potential massacre in Benghazi, thus fulfilling its mandate to protect civilians. Critics, of course, question how real the threat was and suggest that Libyan forces did not pose an imminent threat to Benghazi's civilians.[45] We can never know for sure, of course, and this is one of the structural challenges confronting atrocity prevention: act precipitately and it is impossible to judge whether civilian lives were saved; waiting for certainty involves standing aside until atrocities are committed. This is the 'double-bind' of humanitarian intervention described by Cecilia Jacob.[46] Although critics claim that NATO-led intervention pushed the country into instability and war that continues to this day, it must be stressed that the civil war in Libya had already erupted prior to the authorization of Resolution 1973. Had the resolution not have been authorized, the civil war would have continued. Conjectures that the intervention extended the duration and lethality of violence are just that, conjectures. The civil wars that continue to rage in Syria and Yemen provide some insight into the extent to which the war in Libya may have likely continued and spread. However bad the situation in Libya, the extent of blood-letting there is far lower than in Syria and Yemen where there has been no humanitarian intervention. But what matters is what decision-makers believed at the time, and it is clear that on balance they believed that there was a real threat of massacre in Benghazi.[47] The threat was sufficiently strong that even Russia and China were prepared to acquiesce in the armed intervention, and South Africa and Nigeria were prepared to support it.

---

[45] E.g. Alan Kuperman, 'A Model Humanitarian Intervention? Reassessing NATO's Libya Campaign', *International Security* 38:1 (2013), 105–36.

[46] Cecilia Jacob, 'Transcending the Double-Bind of Humanitarian Intervention: The Costs of Action and Inaction', *Journal of Genocide Research* 21:1 (2019), 108–13.

[47] Frederic Wehrey, *The Burning Shores: Inside the Battle for the New Libya* (New York: Farar, Straus, and Giroux, 2018), 38–44.

There is no doubt that Libya's current political situation remains highly unstable, with no central government and a breakdown in the provision of public services. Yet, this was not an inevitable consequence of intervention.[48] A large and sustained peacekeeping effort following the NATO operation might have prevented, or in the very least limited the fragmentation of authority in the country. Such a move was proposed at the time, but it was emphatically rejected by the National Transitional Council.[49]

Another concern is that military interventions are always tainted by power politics because an intervener's motives are never wholly humanitarian.[50] Indeed, critics often see malign self-interest and great power conspiracy lurking behind every intervention.[51] Wil Verwey defined humanitarian intervention as 'the threat or use of force . . . *for the sole purpose* of preventing or putting a halt to a serious violation of human rights'. He argued that there had never been genuine humanitarian interventions because prior interventions had almost always been motivated by non-humanitarian concerns. Such interventions could not be considered humanitarian or 'disinterested' and were therefore illegitimate.[52]

Although this line of thinking points to some important concerns, there are at least three problems. First, there are good reasons to

---

[48] A point emphasized by both Wehrey, who says that the turmoil of post-intervention Libya was 'not preordained', Wehrey, *Burning Shores*, 5–6 and Chivvis, who argues that a limited intervention was always likely to deliver limited results. Christopher S. Chivvis, *Toppling Qaddafi: Libya and the Limits of Liberal Intervention* (Cambridge: Cambridge University Press, 2014).

[49] Alex J. Bellamy and Stephen McLoughlin, *Rethinking Humanitarian Intervention* (Basingstoke: Palgrave Macmillan, 2018), 111.

[50] See Rajan Menon, *The Conceit of Humanitarian Intervention* (Oxford: Oxford University Press, 2016), 76.

[51] See e.g. suggestions that the 2011 intervention in Libya was inspired by French interests in selling arms, Frank Ledwidge, 'The Strong Do What They Can, the Weak Suffer as They Must: The Reality of Humanitarian Intervention', *Journal of Genocide Research* 21:1 (2019), 99.

[52] Wil Verwey, 'The Legality of Humanitarian Intervention after the Cold War', in Elizabeth G. Ferris (ed.), *A Challenge to Intervene: A New Role for the United Nations?* (Uppsala: Life and Peace Institute, 1992), 12–36, and Bhikhu Parekh, 'Rethinking Humanitarian Intervention', *International Political Science Review* 18:1 (1997), 55–74.

suggest that states will not risk the lives of their own citizens in order to save the lives of others. As Donald Bloxham has persuasively argued, 'humanitarian intervention tends to occur only when the cause overlaps with the material interests of those intervening'.[53] By insisting that interveners be guided by purely humanitarian motives, the bar is placed so high that no military action could realistically pass the test, even though in some cases only military measures will remedy human suffering. From this perspective, it was entirely correct for the West not to intervene in Armenia, Rwanda, Srebrenica, and Darfur because they could not have done so in a disinterested fashion.

Second, motives and purposes are subjective and can be easily disguised by clever political leaders. Making motives the sole criterion of legitimacy is problematic, therefore, because it is very difficult for them to be properly assessed, especially without the help of considerable hindsight. Finally, focusing solely on what motivates an action tells us little about its consequences. Contra those that demand purely humanitarian motives, a self-interested intervention that ends a genocide (e.g. Vietnam in Cambodia) is surely preferable to a disinterested intervention that ultimately fails (e.g. the US in Somalia). Indeed, it is usually the presence of a degree of self-interest that makes states prepared to sacrifice the lives of their citizens to save foreigners from peril.

A more sophisticated position is put forward by Nicholas Wheeler. The starting point is the idea that humans, much less states, are never prompted to act by a single motive. Wheeler therefore argues that whilst motives are important they should not be the 'threshold' consideration. That is, actions that produce humanitarian good should not be condemned because they are not inspired by humanitarian motives. The key test should be that the means chosen by the intervener must not undermine the positive humanitarian outcome.[54] Thus, Vietnam's self-interested intervention in Cambodia should be applauded because the non-humanitarian motives did not undermine the humanitarian goal of removing the Khmer Rouge from power. By contrast, because the French government was primarily motivated by

[53] Donald Bloxham, 'Genocide: Can We Learn from History?', *BBC History Magazine*, January 2007, 48.
[54] Wheeler, *Saving Strangers*, 33–4.

a concern to protect Hutu allies and Francophones in Rwanda, rather than a desire to end the Rwandan genocide, it chose a strategy that did relatively little to protect the genocide's victims. In that case, non-humanitarian motives undermined potential humanitarian outcomes. According to Wheeler's schema this should render the French intervention (*Operation Turquoise*) illegitimate.[55] This more sophisticated approach allows us to factor the important concerns expressed by Verwey into our assessment of intervention while acknowledging that states usually have mixed motives.

Inhibitors to Intervention

Why, when there is so much agreement about the necessity of preventing and ending genocide, are states so reluctant to intervene militarily? This section examines three of the most often cited reasons for the failure to intervene—international law, political will, and prudential considerations.

International law

Questions about intervention tend to be framed around an enduring struggle between sovereignty and human rights. By this account, sovereignty refers to the rights that states enjoy to territorial integrity, political independence, and non-intervention. Where sovereign states are either unwilling or unable to protect the fundamental freedoms of their citizens, sovereignty and human rights come into conflict. This tension is evident in the UN Charter. Whilst calling for cooperation to reaffirm faith in fundamental human rights, the Charter (Article 2(4)) outlaws war as an instrument of policy with only two exceptions (each state's inherent right to self-defence [Article 51] and collective measures authorized by the UN Security Council [Chapter VII]) and affirms the principle of non-interference [Article 2(7)]) by prohibiting the UN from interfering 'in matters essentially within the domestic jurisdiction of states'. These legal rights, it is often argued, constitute a powerful barrier to intervention, and it has proven very difficult to

---

[55] See ibid., chs. 3 and 7.

build sufficient consensus in the UN Security Council to persuade it to authorize intervention against a full-functioning state guilty of perpetrating genocide or mass atrocities. For example, in a March 2005 Security Council debate on whether to refer alleged crimes in Darfur to the International Criminal Court (ICC), the US representative explained that country's abstention by arguing that the Court 'strikes at the essence of the nature of sovereignty'.[56]

States that act without the authority of the Security Council can pay a very high price. For example, in 1979, when Vietnam invaded Cambodia and ousted the murderous Khmer Rouge regime, responsible for the death of some two million Cambodians, it was condemned for violating Cambodian sovereignty. China's representative at the UN described Vietnam's act as a 'great mockery of and insult to the United Nations and its member states' and sponsored a resolution condemning Vietnam's 'aggression'. The US agreed.[57] France argued that 'the notion that because a regime is detestable foreign intervention is justified and forcible overthrow is legitimate is extremely dangerous. That could ultimately jeopardize the very maintenance of law and order.'[58]

However, there are grounds for doubting the extent to which international law actually is a barrier to intervention. Simon Chesterman has demonstrated that sovereignty has not in fact inhibited unilateral or collective intervention to uphold human rights in other countries. In response to arguments that intervention could be promoted by relaxing the prohibition on the use of force, Chesterman argued that: 'implicit in many of the arguments for a right of humanitarian intervention is the suggestion that the present normative order is preventing interventions that should take place. This is simply not true. Interventions do not take place because states do not want them to take place.'[59] Ultimately, it was not primarily concerns about sovereignty that prevented timely intervention in Rwanda, but rather the basic political fact that no state wanted to risk its own troops to save strangers from genocide (see below).

[56] S/PV.5158, 31 March 2005, 12.
[57] Cited in Wheeler, *Saving Strangers*, 90–1.
[58] Cited in Chesterman, *Just War or Just Peace?*, 80.
[59] Ibid., 231.

What, though, of Vietnam's invasion of Cambodia? Was it not the case that Vietnam paid a heavy political and economic price because it was seen as violating Cambodia's sovereignty? This position certainly has merit but needs to be viewed alongside two other considerations. First, Vietnam was not principally motivated by humanitarian concerns and nor did it justify its invasion as a humanitarian intervention. Second, and perhaps more importantly, we need to take the arguments levelled against Vietnam with a pinch of Cold War salt. Whilst not denying the fact that many states, particularly some members of the Non-Aligned Movement, opposed Vietnam on principled grounds, political considerations played an important part in shaping the way that international society reacted to the intervention.[60] In the same year as Vietnam's invasion of Cambodia, Tanzania—a highly regarded state with a well-respected President, Julius Nyerere—invaded Uganda and deposed Idi Amin with barely a ripple of condemnation.[61]

Either way, it is clear that contemporary international law does not enable the forging of consensus on collective action to end genocide beyond provisions on Security Council authorization. This is where recent developments such as the Responsibility to Protect principle and *Bosnia v. Serbia* ruling, which seek to change the relationship between sovereignty, the responsibilities of states, and the place of non-interference, might have a positive effect.

Political will

Following on from Chesterman's insight that interventions do not happen primarily because states do not want them to happen, the second major inhibitor of armed intervention is political will. Political will works in two ways to inhibit the chances of intervention to end genocide. The first, and least discussed, is the presence of prevailing interest. In other words, it is not just that powerful states lack the will to take risks to save strangers, but that their pursuit of their own

[60] Wheeler, *Saving Strangers*, 78–110.

[61] On this see Grant Evans and Kelvin Rowley, *Red Brotherhood at War: Vietnam, Cambodia and Laos since 1975*, 2nd ed. (London: Verso, 1990).

interests leads them to support or shield the perpetrators. The link between China's (and to a lesser extent, Russia's) obstinate support for the government of Sudan and its interest in Sudanese oil and arms sales is well known.[62] Russia's close relations with Syria also inhibited a collective Security Council response as the civil war there escalated in 2011 and 2012.[63] But the West has also often put its own interests ahead of the protection of populations from genocide. During the Cold War, the US supplied arms to the Indonesian government as its army fuelled the massacre of more than 600,000 alleged communists in 1965–6 and the UK sold it fighter jets as East Timor was brutally repressed. The US and UK helped arm and train the Khmer Rouge in the art of laying land-mines after its defeat by Vietnam. In the early 1980s the US supported, funded, and armed the genocidal regime in Guatemala. Motivated mainly by its interest in preserving its influence in former colonial territories, France funded and armed the Hutu government in Rwanda and supplied a substantial portion of the guns and machetes that made mass killing possible.[64] All of the permanent members of the Security Council, which has a special responsibility to protect populations from genocide, have therefore been implicated in genocide through their support for the perpetrators in the past half-century. Sometimes, therefore, political will prompts great powers to actively protect or assist perpetrators, presenting a major obstacle to the goal of ending genocide. The permanent members of the Security Council would therefore do well to begin their engagement with the

[62] For instance, 'China and Darfur: The Genocide Olympics?', *Washington Post*, 14 December 2006, A30.

[63] Jess Gifkins, 'Briefing: The UN Security Council Divided: Syria in Crisis', *Global Responsibility to Protect* 4 (2012), 381–2.

[64] On the US and Indonesia, see Yves Beigbeder, *International Justice Against Impunity: Progress and New Challenges* (The Hague: Martinus Nijhoff, 2005), 17–18. On US support for Guatemala's genocidal regime see the report of the UN-administered Historical Clarification Commission, *Memory of Silence: Report of the Commission for Historical Clarification: Conclusions and Recommendations*, http://shr.aaas. org/guatemala/ceh/report/english/toc.html; On British support for the Khmer Rouge, see Tom Fawthrop and Helen Jarvis, *Getting Away with Genocide: Elusive Justice and the Khmer Rouge Tribunal* (Sydney: University of New South Wales Press, 2005), 68–9. On France and Rwanda, see Daniela Kroslak, *The French Betrayal of Rwanda* (London: Hurst, 2007).

ending of genocide by desisting from actively supporting its perpetrators.

The second, and more commonly discussed, aspect of political will relates to the idea that states consider themselves to be responsible first and foremost for the wellbeing of their own citizens and are reluctant to spend tax money and risk the lives of their soldiers in order to save strangers from genocide in other countries. The effects of this lack of will were demonstrated in detail by the 1999 Report of the Independent Inquiry into the UN's failure to prevent and then halt the Rwanda genocide of 1994.[65] The report opened with a damning but general criticism, insisting that the Rwanda genocide resulted from the failure of the whole UN system.[66] The lack of resources and will was manifested in the UN mission deployed in Rwanda (UNAMIR) not being adequately 'planned, dimensioned, deployed or instructed' in a way that would have 'provided for a proactive and assertive role' in the face of the deteriorating situation in Rwanda.[67] The mission was smaller than recommended by the UN secretariat, slow to deploy owing to the reluctance of states to contribute troops, debilitated by administrative difficulties, and when troops did arrive they were generally inadequately trained and equipped.[68]

The Inquiry concluded, therefore, that the UN's failure in Rwanda was largely created by a critical disjuncture—endemic in many UN operations at the time[69]—between the tasks given to peacekeepers and their conceptual and material tools. For largely political reasons the United Nations Assistance Mission in Rwanda (UNAMIR) was conceived as a small, cheap, and consent-dependent operation despite evidence at the time that this would be inadequate. In a tragic coincidence of history, UNAMIR's mandate came onto the Security Council's agenda just one week after the killing of American peacekeepers in Somalia in the infamous 'Black Hawk down' incident. The

---

[65] This discussion draws on Bellamy and Williams, *Understanding Peacekeeping*, ch. 5.

[66] Independent Commission, *Report of the Independent Inquiry into the Actions of the United Nations During the 1994 Genocide in Rwanda*, 12 December 1999, 1.

[67] Independent Commission, *Report*, 2.

[68] Ibid.

[69] See Part 3 of Bellamy and Williams, *Understanding Peacekeeping*.

US was understandably in no mood to consider supporting the dispatch of more peacekeepers to Africa and insisted that any force sent to Rwanda be limited in size and dependent on the consent of the parties.

Even when the political will is found to reach consensus on the use of force—as happened in Libya in 2011—the coalescence of forces that enabled the Security Council to act was highly unusual and unlikely to be repeated. The growing threat against civilians in the city of Benghazi was very clear; Gaddafi's international standing was poor; and regional actors—particularly through the appeals of the League of Arab States (LAS)—called for immediate action to mitigate the threat.[70]

Prudential considerations

Even when states have genuine moral concerns about the commission of genocide in foreign countries, prudential considerations or competing priorities may augur against armed intervention. The first prudential inhibitor to intervention is the calculation that intervention might do more harm than good. Prominent human rights nongovernmental organization (NGO), the International Crisis Group, and individuals such as Gareth Evans and Francis Deng all argued against military intervention in Darfur on the grounds that it would be counter-productive, and indeed exacerbate the violence. They were supported in this view by a leading commentator on African affairs, Alex de Waal, whose own position on intervention changed between 2004 and 2006. Initially, de Waal argued that foreign troops could make a 'formidable difference' to the lives of Darfuri civilians.[71] However, the negotiators failed to persuade all but one of the rebel groups to sign the Darfur Peace Agreement. The experience of coming 'agonisingly close' to a political settlement and the further

[70] Alex J. Bellamy and Paul Williams, 'The New Politics of Protection? Côte d'Ivoire, Libya and the Responsibility to Protect', *International Affairs* 87:4 (2011), 825.

[71] Alex de Waal, 'Darfur's Deep Grievances Defy all Hopes for an Easy Solution', *The Observer*, 25 July 2004, http://www.guardian.co.uk/society/2004/jul/25/internationalaidanddevelopment.voluntarysector.

complication of the situation on the ground no doubt contributed to de Waal's change of heart on the potential for military intervention to make a 'formidable difference'. In 2006, he argued that without the consent of the Sudanese government and the majority of the Darfurian population, 'UN troops will not only fail but will make the plight of Darfurians even worse'.[72]

This is the sort of difficult dilemma that well-intentioned policy-makers must find answers to in the midst of the genocidal storm. Francis Deng, a well-respected diplomat and the UN's Special Representative on Internal Displacement for over a decade, supported de Waal's 2006 opinion. Non-consensual intervention, he concluded, would 'complicate and aggravate' the crisis by increasing the level of violence and undermining the potential for cooperation with the Sudanese government.[73]

There was also a concern that a possible military intervention in Syria—following the descent into civil war in 2011—would have done more harm than good. While the Security Council faced other obstacles to consensus in response to growing atrocities there, there were strong arguments at the time that authorizing a no-fly zone or another form of military response would have provoked 'a wider regional conflagration'.[74] Implementing a no-fly zone in Syria for the purposes of inhibiting the Syrian military's capacity to launch attacks on population zones would have entailed an operation of such scale that no member of NATO—or any other state—was prepared to commit to.[75] Other options—such as deploying ground forces or establishing safe zones risked the strong possibility that such a force would have been entrenched in the conflict, further escalating fight that was

[72] Alex de Waal, 'The Book Was Closed Too Soon on Peace in Darfur', *The Guardian*, 29 September 2006, http://www.guardian.co.uk/commentisfree/2006/sep/29/comment.sudan.

[73] E/CN.4/2005/8, 27 September 2004, paras. 22, 26, and 36.

[74] Justin Morris, 'Libya and Syria: R2P and the Spectre of the Swinging Pendulum', *International Affairs* 85:5 (2013), 1276.

[75] James Joyner, 'Why NATO Won't Intervene in Syria', *Atlantic Council*, 6 June 2013, https://www.atlanticcouncil.org/blogs/new-atlanticist/syrian-supernova; see also Jason Ralph, Jack Holland, and Kalina Zhekova, 'Before the Vote. UK Foreign Policy Discourse on Syria 2011–2013', *Review of International Studies* 43:5 (2017), 875–97.

already underway.[76] Moreover, while the League of Arab States suspended Syria's membership in November 2011, and called for the Security Council to authorize a range of non-coercive measures in response to the conflict, measures were vetoed by Russia and China during the drafting process in the following months.[77] Thus, calls for military action were few and far between.

There are clearly difficult choices that policymakers confront when weighing up whether to commit troops to an intervention. When coupled with either countervailing interests or an absence of national interests and the danger of sustaining casualties, it is not hard to see why the uncertainty of success in any complex operation to combat genocide tends to produce scepticism about the merits of intervention. In addition to these considerations, we need to bear in mind that policymakers often have to balance competing priorities.

None of this is meant to justify inaction in the face of genocide but it goes some way towards explaining why it is that governments usually choose to stand aside when there is such a clear moral imperative to intervene to put an end to genocides once begun. It also helps to illuminate the difficult choices that policymakers confront.

Conclusion

Typically, genocide ends with either the suppression and/or destruction of the victim group or with the military defeat of the perpetrators. Only very rarely are those military defeats affected by the intervention of external powers spurred primarily by the intention to put an end to genocide. Indeed, only twice in the past century have states intervened to put an end of genocide, and in both cases the interveners had decidedly mixed motives. The problem, then, is not that there is too much humanitarian intervention in times of putative genocide, but that there is far too little. International society's default response to genocide is to stand aside and hope that the blood-letting comes to an end incidentally. This is at least partly because the often much greater costs of inaction are rarely stacked up alongside the

---

[76] Harlan Ullman, 'Syrian Supernova?' *Atlantic Council*, 30 May 2013, https://www.atlanticcouncil.org/blogs/new-atlanticist/syrian-supernova.

[77] Gifkins, 'Briefing', 385.

all-too-obvious costs of action.[78] This is despite the emergence of a clear moral, political—and some would say legal—responsibility to take timely and decisive action to put an end to genocide. It is, of course, correct to argue that the responsibility to protect populations from genocide does not create a duty of armed intervention in every case but we know that once genocide has begun, only the choice of the perpetrators or their military defeat is likely to bring it to an end. We should acknowledge, however, that decisions to intervene are fraught with difficulties. Military intervention is legally problematic, especially when there is no consensus in the Security Council. States, especially democratic states, are understandably reluctant to sacrifice their citizens in order to save foreigners in peril. Policymakers therefore need to make difficult calculations about the prospective costs and benefits of armed intervention in a context of radical uncertainty. And, of course, there is no guarantee that intervention will succeed in saving lives.

No amount of institutional reform and rhetorical finessing can get around the fact that armed intervention to end genocide requires leaders who are prepared to pay the political costs of failure. These decisions will always be taken on an ad hoc and case-by-case basis and will always involve mixed motives, require difficult judgements and a degree of risk taking. Because intervention to end genocide is so necessary and yet so rare, we commentators might help by worrying less about the damage done to international order by armed intervention against tyrants and more about the damage done to really existing human beings when international society stands aside. Clearly, non-violent prevention is much better than cure but, ultimately, we must face the fact that once genocide has begun only war on the perpetrators will bring it to a premature end. That said, it is rare for the requisite political will and prudential considerations to align in such a way that makes military intervention both possible and feasible. The business of human protection involves a broad spectrum of preventive and reactive strategies, most of which are non-coercive in character. At the very least, this starts with a commitment not to assist the perpetrators, even when material or strategic interests would seem to demand such support.

---

[78] Jennifer Welsh, 'A Scattergun Attack on Humanitarian Intervention', *Journal of Genocide Research* 21:1 (2019), 119.

Select Bibliography

Bass, Gary J., *Freedom's Battle: The Origins of Humanitarian Intervention* (London: Alfred Knopf, 2008).

Chesterman, Simon, *Just War or Just Peace? Humanitarian Intervention in International Law* (Oxford: Oxford University Press, 2001).

Doyle, Michael W., *The Question of Intervention: John Stuart Mill and the Responsibility to Protect* (New Haven: Yale University Press, 2015).

Evans, Gareth, *The Responsibility to Protect: Ending Mass Atrocity Crimes Once and for All* (Washington: The Brookings Institution, 2008).

Jones, Adam, *Genocide: A Comprehensive Introduction* (London: Routledge, 2017).

Kiernan, Ben, *Blood and Soil: A World History of Genocide and Extermination from Sparta to Darfur* (New Haven: Yale University Press, 2008).

Melvern, Linda, *Conspiracy to Murder: The Rwandan Genocide* (London: Verso, 2006).

Menon, Rajan, *The Conceit of Humanitarian Intervention* (Oxford: Oxford University Press, 2016).

Recchia, Stefano and Jennifer Welsh (eds.), *Just and Unjust Military Interventions: European Thinkers from Vitoria to Mill* (Cambridge: Cambridge University Press, 2013).

Wheeler, Nicholas J., *Saving Strangers: Humanitarian Intervention in International Society* (Oxford: Oxford University Press, 2000).

11

Genocide and the Politics
of Punishment

Donald Bloxham and Devin O. Pendas

Introduction

Alongside military and diplomatic intervention, as well as economic
sanctions, criminal trials have become the international community's
instrument of choice for reckoning with genocide and crimes against
humanity. While the other responses tend in one way or another to be
interventionist, seeking to halt genocide as it is occurring, what we
term the legalist paradigm of response to genocide is generally retrospective in orientation, seeking to punish acts that have already taken
place. Although the initiation of legal proceedings has recently developed interventionist aspects that will be examined towards the end of
this chapter, the basic fact remains that law punishes past acts, rather
than intervening in ongoing ones. Why has this preference for punishment arisen, what is it intended to achieve, and does it achieve it?

The preference does not arise, as some of the advocates of international legalism would maintain, as a way of depoliticizing the
response to genocide. All law is in some respects political, but legal
cases that adjudicate political conflicts are especially so.[1] International
criminal law is different than its municipal counterpart, in that there is

---

[1] For a typology of political trials, see Jens Meierhenrich and Devin O. Pendas,
'"The Justice of My Cause Is Clear, but There's Politics to Fear": Political Trials in
Theory and History', in Meierhenrich and Pendas (eds.), *Political Trials in Theory and
History* (Cambridge: Cambridge University Press, 2016), 1–64.

no clear sovereign, capable of either legislation or enforcement. International criminal legal norms develop through multilateral negotiations, which preserve 'opt-out' provisions for sovereign nations who decline to join. International criminal law has thus far struggled to impose itself on most unwilling nations. Unsurprisingly, the states most likely to exempt themselves from the jurisdiction of international criminal law are the great powers whose military and diplomatic muscle would be required for robust enforcement. The US's 'unsigning' of the Rome Statue of the International Criminal Court in 2002 is only the most notorious example of this.

Therefore, international criminal law remains a political instrument and a relatively inexpensive one at that. In both economic and political terms, international criminal trials require only limited expenditures of financial or human capital. Accordingly, trials tend to be highly disposable—all the more so because they take place, if they take place, after the fact. As for what international criminal law can be expected to achieve, there are a number of potential justifications: retribution, various modalities of prevention, and historical-cum-political pedagogy. This chapter will argue that few of these things are achieved by international law. Retribution offers cold comfort, at best. The historical pedagogy in criminal trials has proven itself problematic more often than not, although the broader moral lessons proffered by such trials can have a meaningful impact on political culture. It is also true that in very specific circumstances, there may be reasons to believe that the threat of prosecution may hinder ongoing atrocities. Yet just as often, there is the risk that the demands of justice—the indictment of key political actors—conflicts with the diplomatic negotiations necessary to bring peace and, hence, an end to atrocities.

Instead, we argue that law's crucial contribution is articulating a normative consensus that mobilizes *political* pressure for compliance. As a mechanism for articulating norms and forging consensus, the new international legalism offers a chance—albeit a modest one—to shift patterns of behaviour and place limited checks on the free hand of international power. But this is an ongoing political battle, one that can never be resolved by the simple establishment of international courts, conventions and case-law, nor any of the other trappings of law. Whatever the aspirations of its jurist cheerleaders, international law will never be analogous to domestic law. *International legalism remains contiguous with international politics.*

Law's role as a continuation of politics by other means brings with it a downside. It is one thing to recognize that law cannot be dissociated from politics, but quite another to suggest that it can operate in similarly elastic ways without bringing into question the legitimacy of its role. Precisely because legal responses to genocide are a form of politics, they are both readily manipulable for strategic ends and highly dependent upon the constellation of global political forces at any given moment. Allegations of human rights violations or genocide can be instrumentalized to stigmatize political opponents, as exemplified by Colombia's 2008 attempt to have Venezuelan President Hugo Chavez indicted at the International Criminal Court (ICC) for genocide for his support of the Revolutionary Armed Forces of Colombia (FARC) guerrilla movement in Colombia. Alternatively, international legalism can be used to validate military interventions where politically convenient, and in other cases to substitute for intervention when such action would not be politically convenient. And on some of those occasions when the institutions of law play an interventionist role in ongoing atrocities, that is, at the point at which they are most pointedly political agents, they put themselves in a position to which they are least tactically suited: see the discussion of Sudan below. Finally, international trials often simply provide a venue for the articulation of competing accounts of mass atrocities which cannot themselves be resolved in the courtroom, what Gerry Simpson has referred to as the 'proceduralized clash of competing ideologies'.[2]

Prior to the concluding section, which tries to establish an overall balance as to what can be expected from legalist responses to mass atrocity, this chapter is divided into three roughly chronological sections, each dealing with an important stage in the chequered history of the legalist paradigm. Despite the real innovations of the nineteenth century, we take the Nuremberg Trials as our starting point because the legal developments of the immediate postwar period served as the crucible for most subsequent developments in

---

[2] Gerry Simpson, *Law, War and Crime* (Cambridge: Cambridge University Press, 2007), 13.

international legalism. Almost as soon as the Nuremberg model was developed and implemented in new legal instruments like the 1948 United Nations Convention on the Prevention and Punishment of Genocide, its efficacy was undermined by the global Cold War, which thus marks the second phase of our analysis. The third phase deals with the re-emergence of the legalist paradigm in the first decade after the end of the Cold War. International legal codes saw significant growth in this period, new international criminal courts, both ad hoc and, from 2002, permanent, came into being and major trials for genocide, war crimes, and crimes against humanity were conducted. The New World Order proclaimed by the first President Bush was implicitly a juridified one, in which legal norms would be universally applied through international institutions. The wave of utopian expectations surrounding these developments obscured the ongoing reality of power politics. The US's reaction to September 11, 2001, its mounting opposition to the ICC, and its unilateral invasion of Iraq, demonstrated that the limits of the legalist paradigm had not by any means been overcome. Indeed, the problems besetting the paradigm are intrinsic to the nature of an international political system based on nation-state sovereignty and influenced by 'great power' agendas backed by the use of military violence. The Cold War, with all its hot wars and 'interventions', was only a particularly pointed illustration of the primacy of the political order over the legal.

The Paradigm Established: The Postwar Moment

In January 1942, the governments in exile of the occupied countries of Europe declared that among the principal aims of the Second World War should be 'the punishment, through the channel of organized justice, of those guilty and responsible for these crimes [by Nazi Germany], whether they have ordered them, or in any way participated in them'.[3] In October 1943, the Big Three Allies followed suit, proclaiming that any German soldiers or Nazi party members guilty of 'atrocities, massacres and executions' would be 'sent back to the

---

[3] Arieh J. Kochavi, *Prelude to Nuremberg: Allied War Crimes Policy and the Question of Punishment* (Chapel Hill: University of North Carolina Press, 1998), 20.

countries in which their abominable deeds were done in order that they may be judged and punished according to the laws of these liberated countries'.[4] Those perpetrators whose crimes were without clear 'geographical localization' were to be punished by a subsequent 'joint decision of the government of the Allies'.

With this, the Allies declared that justice, as much as peace or renewed international stability would be an essential goal of postwar policy. There had of course been similar declarations in the First World War, culminating in the disastrous trials of German war criminals at Leipzig and of Ottoman ones at Constantinople. What distinguished the declarations of the Second World War from their counterparts in the First was that this time, the Allies actually implemented their promises. Indeed, the chief lesson of the First World War for the architects of the post-Second World War international legal regime was that it was unwise to leave the punishment of war criminals to their own states. There were two distinct and not entirely consonant principles at work in the Allied response to this insight. First, there was the territoriality principle articulated in the Moscow Declaration, under which Nazi criminals would be punished by states representing their victims. The second, not yet clear in the Moscow Declaration, was an internationalist principle, according to which some wartime criminals, the political leadership in particular, were in effect too big to be left to national courts. It was the Americans in particular who, in the closing stages of the war, came to embrace the idea of an international trial for the major war criminals.[5] The reasons for this preference were both those of principle, a moral opposition to the major alternative of summary executions, and political. Roosevelt's advisers wanted to ensure broad public backing for their postwar policies and hoped a major trial would drum up support, both domestic and international, for a new, multilateral structure of global stability.

---

[4] *A Decade of American Foreign Policy: Basic Documents, 1941–49* (Washington, DC: Government Printing Office, 1950), 13.

[5] For the full story, see Kochavi, *Prelude.* Although for reasons of their own, the Soviets were also interested in an international trial for major Nazi criminals. See Francine Hirsch, 'The Soviets at Nuremberg: International Law, Propaganda, and the Making of the Postwar Order', *American Historical Review* 113/3 (June 2008), 701–30.

Consequently, the International Military Tribunal (IMT) at Nuremberg and its sister Tribunal in Tokyo were intended from the start to be only one element in a much broader effort at legal prosecution. Indeed, although Nuremberg's fame, both at the time and subsequently, has overshadowed the other trials for Nazi atrocities, the IMT was truly a drop in the ocean, quantitatively speaking. According to the latest estimates, more than 95,000 Germans and Austrians were convicted for wartime crimes throughout Europe.[6] Of these, nineteen were convicted by the IMT.

Nonetheless, it is the IMT and to a lesser extent, the twelve so-called successor trials conducted by the American Military Tribunals, likewise at Nuremberg, that form the model for the subsequent development of the international legalist paradigm of genocide. In part, this is for statutory reasons. The London Charter, authorizing the IMT, criminalized three categories of offences. The least innovative of these, and hence the least controversial, was war crimes, namely, 'violations of the laws or customs of war'.[7] 'Crimes against peace' criminalized wars of aggression or in violation of international treaties. Although this was the crucial charge in the minds of the Americans at the time, it has been the one with the least subsequent international legal resonance. Finally, and in this context most importantly, the London Charter criminalized 'crimes against humanity'. These included the mass murder and persecution of civilians, as well as 'persecutions on political, racial, or religious grounds'.[8] War crimes and crimes against humanity both penalized the killing of civilians, the crucial difference being whether the victims and the perpetrators were of the same or different nationalities, and the connection to military operations and military occupation. Crimes against humanity, unlike war crimes, could be perpetrated against a state's own citizens. Furthermore, persecutions were criminalized, 'whether or not in violation

---

[6] Norbert Frei, 'Nach der Tat: Die Ahndung deutscher Kriegs- und NS-Verbrechen in Europa—eine Bilanz' in Frei (ed.), *Transnationale Vergangenheitspolitik* (Göttingen: Wallstein, 2006), 32. The figures here only include convictions in Germany (East and West) through 1959.

[7] International Military Tribunal, *Trial of the Major War Criminals before the International Military Tribunal*, (Nuremberg: IMT, 1947), vol. 1, 11.

[8] Ibid.

of domestic law of the country where perpetrated'. Thus, the London Charter for the first time prioritized international over domestic law and the sanctity of national sovereignty was, in principle at least, subordinated to international jurisdiction.

While the term genocide was used in the IMT indictment and in those of several of the successor trials to describe the criminal acts in question, it was not one of the criminal charges articulated in the London Charter. No Nazi criminals were ever convicted of genocide as such. Although war crimes and crimes against humanity between them cover most of the actions constituting genocide, the specificity of that crime as it was articulated by Raphael Lemkin and subsequently codified in the Genocide Convention was not formally part of the Nuremberg model. Lemkin's central insight was that certain atrocities targeted individuals as bearers of largely non-negotiable identities, that it was the groups themselves, rather than the individual victims, who were the real targets of the perpetrators. This view was to a degree implicit in the concept of persecution contained in crimes against humanity but Lemkin, who disliked the concept of crimes against humanity, wanted to go further and provide protection, not just to an amorphous humanity, but to the identifiable groups actually persecuted in the world. This notion, that certain kinds of human groups—those based on presumably 'fixed' identities—required special legal protection in a dangerous world, led to the first and most dramatic expansion of the Nuremberg model with the UN Genocide Convention of 1948.

In December 1946, the first session of the UN General Assembly passed a genocide resolution, GA Resolution 96 (I), at the behest of Cuba, India, and Panama.[9] It affirmed the criminal character of genocide and urged states to criminalize it under domestic law. As a non-binding resolution, it also called on the United Nations (UN) to study the feasibility of a more potent genocide convention. The Economic and Social Council of the UN and the Sixth (Legal) Committee wrote and debated various drafts of a genocide convention throughout 1947 and 1948, before finally passing the Convention in

---

[9] William A. Schabas, *Genocide in International Law: The Crime of Crimes* (Cambridge: Cambridge University Press, 2000), 42–47, 51–81.

December 1948. There was a good deal of bureaucratic back-and-forth in the legislative history of the Genocide Convention. This had little to do with bureaucratic inertia. It was easy (and cheap) to morally abhor genocide, as in the Genocide Resolution. Doing something about it invariably came with political costs attached. The most obvious and important of these was that formally criminalizing genocide in an international convention would inevitably entail at least nominal restrictions on the behaviour of states and potentially provide a pretext for international interference in domestic affairs. The potential for such intervention was deliberately and tightly limited by the UN Charter (the foundation stone of the postwar political order) which was a 'Westphalian document par excellence', stressing the central significance of the sovereign state as the fundamental building-block of the international system.[10] Rhetoric aside, the architecture of that system as a whole was primarily structured towards prohibiting inter-state warfare and the transgression of inter-state boundaries, and was much less concerned with crimes committed within established state borders. Indeed, as had been the case in the interwar period and the nineteenth century, it was in certain circumstances simply preferable for internal population groups like Turkey's Kurds, or other potential secessionists, to be violently repressed in the interests of maintaining borders arrived at through earlier warfare.[11] A genocide convention threatened to undermine this carefully constructed edifice of postwar stability by introducing a countervailing principle of humanitarian intervention.

There was also the related question of jurisdiction. If genocide was a crime of state, who could prosecute it? As many would argue in the subsequent debates, only an international criminal court was likely to have the independence necessary to sit in judgment on such crimes. Yet a permanent court laying claim to a superordinate international jurisdiction proved to be an intolerable threat to national sovereignty for a great many UN delegates. Nuremberg was one thing, since it was an ad hoc tribunal with jurisdiction exclusively over Nazi crimes.

[10] Kalevi J. Holsti, *The State, War, and the State of War* (Cambridge: Cambridge University Press, 1996), 189.

[11] Donald Bloxham, *The Great Game of Genocide* (Oxford: Oxford University Press, 2005), ch. 1 and the second 'interlude'.

A standing court was a different matter entirely. Finally, there was the simple fact that a convention would require a careful and authoritative definition of genocide. This could either narrow or expand the meaning of what was already becoming a particularly potent term of moral and political opprobrium. There were costs to either approach.

In order to get the Genocide Convention passed at all, several compromises were necessary which rendered the document virtually inert from the very start.[12] The first and most important compromise concerned jurisdiction. The initial secretariat draft of the Genocide Convention contained as an appendix two draft statutes for a permanent international criminal court, one with restricted jurisdiction over genocide alone, another with expansive jurisdiction over international crimes to be defined by the International Law Commission. The guiding assumption, even if it was not made explicit in the Convention, was that genocide was essentially a state crime and therefore required international jurisdiction if there was to be any hope of prosecution. The French delegate to the Sixth (Legal) Committee strongly supported this notion. 'Genocide was committed only through the criminal intervention of public authorities; that was what distinguished it from murder pure and simple. The purpose of the convention which the Committee was drawing up was not to punish individual murders, but to ensure the prevention and punishment of crimes committed by rulers.'[13] Hence, it was imperative, he concluded, to establish an international criminal court forthwith. The French support for linking the Genocide Convention to the formation of an international court proved to be the minority position, however.

The Venezuelan representative on the Sixth Committee, for instance, warned that 'the institution of international criminal jurisdiction could only lead to unfortunate results, in view of the existing world situation. Friction might be created which could disturb the peace among nations. The establishment of international penal jurisdiction should be reserved for the future when international relations

---

[12] Devin O. Pendas, 'Towards World Law: The Failure of the Legalist Paradigm of War, 1945–1980', in Stefan-Ludwig Hoffmann (ed.), *Human Rights in the Twentieth Century: Concepts and Conflicts* (Cambridge: Cambridge University Press, 2011).

[13] UN Doc. A/C.6/SR 97, 373.

would be more favorable to such an institution.'[14] The Polish delegate concurred, saying that he could on no account 'sacrifice questions of principle' concerning the sanctity of national sovereignty. The Americans and the British, meanwhile, crafted a compromise that prevented the issue of an international court from torpedoing the negotiations altogether. At US initiative, Article VI of the final Convention left open the possibility that in future, an international criminal court might have jurisdiction over genocide, while the British inserted into Article IX an option to have the existing International Court of Justice adjudicate inter-state disputes over the interpretation of the Convention. This was enough to satisfy supporters of international jurisdiction without alienating the advocates of national sovereignty.

The price was rather high, though. Article VI of the final Convention states that perpetrators of genocide 'shall be tried by a competent tribunal of the state in the territory of which the act was committed'.[15] This harkened back to the territoriality principle of the Moscow Declaration. For genocides committed by foreign invaders, this meant that military defeat would have to precede any attempt at justice. And for internecine genocides, it suggested that as long as the genocidal regime remained in place, there could be no possibility whatsoever of an actual prosecution for genocide. Regime change and military defeat would be a prerequisite for the prosecution of genocide. Given regime change and victory in war, any trial would not threaten the inter-state order because the perpetrators would already have been defeated and the erstwhile perpetrator state would be ruled by a new regime; absent regime change, both state and regime would remain untouched—all of this is the obverse side of the achievement of individualizing responsibility for state atrocity under international law (the state itself remains unprosecuted). The Genocide Convention was therefore effectively stillborn. It is hardly surprising that the first successful prosecution of genocide did not occur until the Akayesu case before the International Criminal Tribunal for Rwanda (ICTR) in 1998, and then not under the Genocide Convention but under the Statute for the ICTR. The Nuremberg breakthrough, according to

---

[14] UN Doc. A/C.6/SR 130.
[15] Schabas, *Genocide*, 566.

which international law would trump domestic law (in limited circum-stances), proved to be less a general principle than a short-term expedient.

The Disappearance of the Paradigm: The Cold War

Nothing better illustrated the transitory nature of 'Nuremberg' than the collapse of the Nuremberg edifice in the 1950s. A growing German opposition to the Allied trial and occupation regimes found a condu-cive environment with the onset of the Cold War. The need to placate German national sentiment amid the burgeoning political conflict with the USSR led first to the ending of the war crimes trials pro-grammes in all Western occupation zones in the late 1940s, in the context of a general easing of occupation policy. Alongside unease in some quarters of the American occupation regime about perceived unfairness in the early war crimes trials, this led to a series of 'sentence reviews' which ultimately developed the simple aim of releasing all war criminals, most of them prematurely.[16] The final four war crim-inals in US custody were released by 1958. Jails in the erstwhile British zone of Germany were empty by 1957.[17] Among those released after serving only a few years of life sentences and commuted death sen-tences were some of the worst Nazi offenders, including commanders of the *Einsatzgruppen* (SS killing squads) and senior members of the concentration camp hierarchy. Rejection of the legal validity of the trials was subtly built in to Articles 6 and 7 of the 1952 Bonn Treaty ending the Allied occupation statute.[18]

Treatments of the Nuremberg Trials by legal scholars have gener-ally been silent on the collapse of the legal machinery, focusing instead on the achievements of the courtroom itself, and the legacies created

---

[16] Donald Bloxham, *Genocide on Trial: War Crimes Trials and the Formation of Holocaust History and Memory* (Oxford: Oxford University Press, 2001), ch. 4; Peter Maguire, *Law and War: An American Story* (New York: Columbia University Press, 2001). For an account emphasizing internal American concerns about the fairness of the Nuremberg trials in particular, see Robert Hutchinson, *After Nuremberg: Nazi War Criminals and Clemency, 1949–1958* (New Haven: Yale University Press, forthcoming).

[17] Bloxham, *Genocide on Trial*, ch. 4; Maguire, *Law and War*, chs. 5–6.

[18] Maguire, *Law and War*, 237–9, 256.

in law. Yet divorcing the German trials from any broader political context is to undermine one of the most important rationales for trial in the first place. That rationale, to paraphrase US chief prosecutor Robert Jackson's opening address before the IMT, was to impose the rule of law on naked power relations. In other words, the collapse of 'Nuremberg' in the 1950s (along with that of the IMT for the Far East) illustrates that law may influence the exercise of might but the process also works in reverse. The particular problem with the Nuremberg case is that much of its importance rested on the fact that it brought a major world power to book, but the enduring geopolitical significance of Germany (and Japan) effectively placed a limit on the extent of this reckoning.

Scholarly silence on the releases of the 1950s may be legitimate for a narrow legal approach that is only interested in legal instruments, institutions, and precedents, and can leap across time, like a frog jumping from one water-lily to the next, landing selectively on those moments where the law does seem to come into its own.[19] According to that depiction, which mirrors some of the more teleological scholarship on the emergence of human rights, the Cold War can be seen as a simple hiatus, an aberration in the development of worldwide democracy and international law; with the end of the Cold War, the time of genuine sovereign accountability has now arrived, and we can just pick up where Nuremberg left off. As Geoffrey Robertson puts it on the concluding page of what is otherwise a measured assessment of the progress of humanitarian law: '[A]lthough the twenty-first century will have its share of despots, they will be fewer and in the absence of the Cold War, they will not have superpower support. There will no longer be any need to say, as FDR said of Grandfather Somoza, "he may be a son of a bitch, but he's our son of a bitch." '[20]

The alternative view, grounded in an appreciation of the political context so often missing from the work of legal scholars, is to see the Cold War as a pointed illustration of some of the potentialities of 'our'

---

[19] See e.g. Gary Jonathan Bass, *Stay the Hand of Vengeance: The Politics of War Crimes Tribunals* (Princeton: Princeton University Press, 2000).

[20] Geoffrey Robertson, *Crimes Against Humanity: The Struggle for Global Justice* (New York: The New Press, 1999), 387.

(Western) political-ethical system.[21] The Cold War also illustrated how far legal and humanitarian language could be abused by strategic interest. Atrocities and aggressive wars were perpetrated by both sides and their proxies, while the rhetoric of international law and human rights was frequently used as a weapon to stigmatize the other side for things that one's own side was also doing, in a manner that disillusioned both former Nuremberg lawyers and historians of the trial.[22] Invocation of the Genocide Convention in the third quarter of the twentieth century over cases like Nigeria (Biafra) and East Pakistan (Bangladesh) only served to underline the irrelevance of the document as a concrete ground for political action, much like the rights declarations of the same period.[23] The UN Security Council was divided among its permanent members into capitalists and communists (neither 'side' internally harmonious) while, in the General Assembly and among the temporary members of the Security Council, the situation was complicated by the representatives of a growing number of often non-aligned post-colonial states in Africa and Asia as UN membership nearly tripled from 1945 to 1975. Some of these states provided the battlegrounds for the indirect warfare of the first and second worlds, and provided most of the death toll of the Cold War. Other states were courted by the major protagonists in the economic-political-cultural contest, and thus gained temporary influence. Still others even succeeded in limited ways in using the UN to press their own agendas against Security Council states, as Algeria did with France.[24] Almost none was prepared to compromise its hard-won post-colonial independence by supporting potentially intrusive human rights regimes or general principles of 'humanitarian intervention'. Indeed,

---

[21] Wolfgang Kaleck, *Mit zweierlei Maß. Der Westen und das Völkerstrafrecht* (Berlin: Wagenach, 2012).

[22] Telford Taylor, *Nuremberg and Vietnam: An American Tragedy* (New York: Bantam, 1971); Eugene Davidson, *The Nuremberg Fallacy* (Columbia: University of Missouri Press, 1973).

[23] On Pakistan, A. Dirk Moses, 'The United Nations and the Failure to Prosecute: The Case of East Pakistan, 1971–1974', in Hoffmann (ed.), *Human Rights in the Twentieth Century*, 258–82.

[24] Matthew Connelly, *A Diplomatic Revolution: Algeria's Fight for Independence and the Origins of the Post-Cold War Era* (Oxford: Oxford University Press, 2003).

one could with some justification view this as the major achievement of the non-aligned movement.

The record of the Cold War shows how dangerous it is to extrapolate to general trends from brief moments of 'legalist' triumph such as the year 1945. The legal optimism greeting the end of the Second World War was repeated at the end of the Cold War; with the benefit of historical perspective we should be equally wary of succumbing to the temptations of that optimism. The end of the Cold War left the most important 'vanquished' protagonist—what became the Russian Federation—untouchable in terms of accountability for crimes committed by the Soviet regime. Even in its weakened state, Russia remained too powerful for foreign powers to contemplate even retroactive interference in its 'domestic' affairs. If anything, the domestic appetite for a reckoning was even less. There was no question under any circumstances of bringing the Cold War victor to book for its earlier crimes—and insofar as any of the US's former Latin American allies addressed the abuses of their former right-wing dictatorships, this was generally done outside the courtroom through truth and reconciliation processes, and in ways that limited any threat to the socio-economic order that the dictators had put in place.[25] When criminal law was used in post-authoritarian Latin America, as in for instance Argentina, it was carefully calibrated so as to not disturb the fragile balance of domestic power and risk renewed violence.[26] While these South American trials have been lauded as the starting point for a 'justice cascade', it is important to remember that the balance of power in Latin America remains precarious.[27] Jorge Julio López, a key witness in the 2006 trial of Argentine police official Miguel Etchecolatz for crimes committed during the 'Dirty War', disappeared shortly after the trial, almost certainly murdered. No one has

---

[25] Lawrence Weschler, *A Miracle, a Universe: Settling Accounts with Torturers* (Chicago: University of Chicago Press 1998) and more generally, Robert I. Rotberg and Dennis Thompson (eds.), *Truth v. Justice: The Morality of Truth Commissions* (Princeton: Princeton University Press, 2000).

[26] Carlos Santiago Nino, *Radical Evil on Trial* (New Haven: Yale University Press 1996).

[27] Kathryn Sikkink, *The Justice Cascade: How Human Rights Prosecutions are Changing World Politics* (New York: W.W. Norton, 2011).

ever been held accountable for his disappearance. If there has been a modest 'end to impunity' in Latin America, this has hardly been cost-free. Nor is there reason to think that a return to authoritarian rule is impossible. In the sense of taming power, therefore, the legal developments after the Cold War are actually less impressive than the temporary achievements of Nuremberg. Yet it was precisely Nuremberg, alongside the Genocide Convention, that was invoked in the 1990s. With the end of communism in Eastern Europe, it became possible to talk more realistically—however temporarily—about a single world order with a single set of governing frameworks. Alongside the vanguard organizations of free market capitalism in the first instance and the apostles of parliamentary democracies in the second, Western jurists could make their mark on shaping the norms of that order, and they were hurried into action by the ethnic cleansing and mass murder attendant upon the dissolution of the former Yugoslavia.

The Paradigm Reasserted

The unanticipated collapse of the Soviet Empire in 1989 and the ensuing end to the Cold War brought with it sweeping, if short-lived hopes for a peaceful, stable 'New World Order', in which the entire world increasingly came to resemble the US and history itself came to an end as the great ideological struggles of the past gave way to a universal consumer democracy. Of course history did not end in 1989. Nor did the New World Order prove to be anything like as peaceful and stable as its proponents anticipated. Indeed, the collapse of the Cold War order brought with it outbreaks of large-scale violence in unanticipated places, including Europe itself with the break-up of Yugoslavia in the 1990s. In the absence of great power rivalries, much of the violence of the post-Cold War period operated below the level of geopolitical concern for the major international actors. Secretary of State James Baker's notorious comment that the US had no dog in the fight between Croatia and Serbia can be taken as indicative. Baker was only more blunt, not more callous than his many counterparts in the US and Europe—though the calculus about intervention changed for many parties as the realization dawned that the Yugoslav conflict had the potential for wider destabilization, leading the Clinton administration to change course and initiate an American-led, NATO bombing campaign against Bosnian-Serb forces starting in August 1995.

Given the lack of traditional great power 'interests' in many of the world's new conflict zones, interventions, even of the cynical proxy war variety typical of the Cold War, were hard to justify.[28] At the same time, however, the near universal mediatization of the world meant that these conflicts were often difficult for politicians simply to ignore. If action was not necessarily called for, pseudo-action was. It is in this context that one must understand how the return of history after 1989 brought with it what Norbert Frei has called the 'return of law'.[29] International criminal tribunals, with their promise of retrospective punishment for mass atrocity, were ideally suited to providing the semblance of action while diffusing pressure to undertake more substantive interventionist measures. The initial impetus for the formation of the International Criminal Tribunal for the former Yugoslavia (ICTY) came, after all, not from the members of the UN Security Council but from Human Rights Watch.[30] In the face of such pressure from below, it was largely what Pierre Hazan called the 'opportunistic steeplechase between France and the United States' that eventually led to the creation of the ICTY, as each tried to claim moral leadership while avoiding military action. That the ICTY was intended to be weak is apparent in the complete lack of resources placed at its disposal initially. That in the end the tribunal was not quite so impotent as its creators originally planned was due largely to the political skills of its first two chief prosecutors, Richard Goldstone and Louise Arbour.[31] Goldstone, though not so effective a prosecutor as his successors, was politically skilled and was able to mobilize

[28] David Rieff, *Slaughterhouse: Bosnia and the Failure of the West* (New York: Touchstone, 1995); Philip Gourevitch, *We Wish to Inform You that Tomorrow We Will Be Killed with Our Families: Stories from Rwanda* (New York: Picador, 1998).

[29] Norbert Frei, 'Die Rückkehr des Rechts: Justiz und Zeitgeschichte nach dem Holocaust—eine Zwischenbilanz', in Arnd Bauerkämper, Martin Sabrow, and Bernd Stöver (eds.), *Doppelte Zeitgeschichte: Deutsch-deutsche Beziehungen, 1945–1990* (Bonn: Dietz, 1998).

[30] Pierre Hazan, *Justice in a Time of War: The True Story behind the International Criminal Tribunal for the Former Yugoslavia* (College Station: Texas A&M, 2004), 14.

[31] John Hagan, *Justice in the Balkans: Prosecuting War Crimes in the Hague Tribunal* (Chicago: University of Chicago Press, 2003).

private resources to get the tribunal up and running. Arbour forged an effective prosecutorial strategy that led to actual trials. By indicting Slobodan Milošević in May 1999 for his ongoing crimes in Kosovo, she interjected the tribunal directly into the political process in the Balkans, which at once made it more directly relevant than it might otherwise have been and raised questions about the appropriate domain of international legal institutions (on which see the discussion below about Sudan).

Nonetheless, two points are worth stressing about the two ad hoc UN tribunals of the 1990s, the ICTY and its sister tribunal for Rwanda, the ICTR. The first is that neither seems to have done much to prevent the violence under their jurisdiction. The ICTR was not even created until after the Rwandan genocide had concluded. And while Arbour's indictment of Milošević during the Kosovo conflict may have made the tribunal an actor in the political process, it did not prevent the atrocities in Kosovo from continuing. The second point concerns the independence of the courts. Obviously, as ad hoc tribunals, like the Nuremberg Trials, the ICTY and the ICTR were created with deliberately restricted jurisdictions. This in itself limited their remit considerably and kept them to a degree under the political control of their sponsors on the UN Security Council. If the tribunals, especially the ICTY, nonetheless achieved greater independence than their sponsors envisaged, this ought not to blind us to the ultimate limits the tribunals faced. After all, they remained dependent on state actors, the Americans in particular, for intelligence resources, as well as on UN troops for the enforcement of their arrest warrants. The real boundaries of this independence revealed themselves in the ICTY's investigation of NATO for war crimes during the air war in Kosovo. The simple fact that the ICTY investigated these at all was, in Louise Arbour's words, 'staggering' for the NATO powers.[32] Whatever the merits of the case, though, it can hardly be surprising that the ICTY found that NATO had committed no war crimes. NATO spokesperson Jamie Shea had reminded the prosecutor's office, 'Don't bite the hand that feeds you . . . The people of NATO are the ones who apprehend the war criminals indicted by

[32] Hazan, *Justice in a Time of War*, 130.

the Tribunal . . . We all want to see war criminals judged and I am certain that, when Prosecutor Arbour returns to Kosovo and sees the facts, she will indict the Yugoslav nationals, and no other nationality.'[33] This was exactly what happened under Arbour's successor, Carla Del Ponte.

The ad hoc tribunals of the 1990s were thus ambiguous institutions. On the one hand, there can be no doubt that many of the men and women working for these tribunals were passionate in their pursuit of justice. Nor can there be much doubt that those convicted by the ICTY and the ICTR richly deserved their punishment and that it is preferable to see such criminals punished rather than left free. However, the inflated promises made on behalf of these tribunals that henceforth, war criminals and genocidaires would, in the words of Boutros Boutros-Ghali, 'know the sanction of international law' proved, predictably, to be hyperbolic. Moreover, the fiasco of the Milošević trial, which dragged on for years before terminating with the former dictator's death in prison, has revealed an unavoidable tension between the hyper-careful concern for due process embodied in the ad hoc tribunals and the moral and political requirements of swift and efficacious justice.

The changed atmosphere of the 1990s also gave a renewed impulse to an older idea: the establishment of an international criminal court to work alongside the International Court of Justice established in 1945. The International Criminal Court (ICC) came into effect in 2002, and its jurisdiction and functions are based on the Rome Statute of 1998. The ICC operates on the principle of complementarity with domestic courts: it will only concern itself with the prosecution of cases in which the state concerned is unable or unwilling to prosecute its citizens for breaches of international law. Like the ad hoc tribunals, the ICC's mandate was to consider genocide, crimes against humanity, and war crimes.[34] As of July 2018, it can also exercise jurisdiction

---

[33] Ibid., 132.

[34] On the institutional background, M. Cherif Bassiouni, 'The Permanent International Criminal Court', in Mark Lattimer and Philippe Sands (eds.), *Justice for Crimes Against Humanity* (Oxford: Hart Publishing, 2007), 173–211.

over the crime of aggression.[35] This concept had been seen by the Nuremberg lawgivers as their most important legacy.[36] Of course, the ICC has no jurisdiction over acts of aggression committed by non-party states (e.g. Russia, China, the US, Israel, Iran, India, Pakistan) and even state parties have the option of simply declaring themselves exempt from the court's jurisdiction in matters concerning aggression. In other words, very many of the states on the planet with the capacity to commit a meaningful act of aggression are immune from ICC prosecution. *De facto* enforceability is another thing again, given the age-old use of aggressive warfare by the most powerful states, and the equally venerable tradition of states finding 'self-defensive' pretexts for warmongering, though the latter is a matter for the inside of the courtroom rather than a question of whether anyone gets to the courtroom in the first place.

A particularly important aspect of the ICC, like the ad hoc tribunals, is its genuinely international constitution. On the whole, one cannot talk about 'victor's justice' in prosecution in the way that applied in the Nuremberg era—though voices from the African Union might have a point about the Libya case's smacking of colonial justice. Important elements implicit in the accusation of victor's justice persist, however. In particular, genuinely neutral enforcement will be difficult to achieve. The ICC by definition will depend on the cooperation of powerful states to enforce its decisions, making it difficult to imagine how it could ever enforce its will upon those states. This problem, already foreshadowed in the ICTY's ruling on the NATO bombing of Kosovo, is unlikely to go away any time soon.

Even though it is not itself an ad hoc tribunal, with all the limitations on jurisdiction thereby implied, the ICC cannot escape its subordination to the existing global power structure. The ICC's remit is limited to states that have ratified and acceded to the Rome Statute or to acts by non-signatory states committed on the territory of

---

[35] Assembly of State Parties Resolution, 14 December 2017, http://www.ejiltalk.org/wp-content/uploads/2017/12/ICC-ASP-16-L10-ENG-CoA-resolution-14Dec17-1130.pdf.

[36] Jonathan Bush, '"The Supreme...Crime" and Its Origins: The Lost Legislative History of the Crime of Aggressive War', *Columbia Law Review* 102 (December 2002), 2324–401.

state parties. The only exceptions are for cases brought to the court's attention by the UN Security Council under Article VII of the UN Charter, concerning acts likely to disturb the peace internationally. Yet the three most politically and militarily powerful states with crucial permanent membership of the Security Council—the US, China, and Russia—are not Rome signatories. (The US has also signed bilateral immunity agreements with around 100 states, including Rome signatories, to keep American nationals from the court's jurisdiction.) The three states are largely exempt from the court's scrutiny, and are in the best imaginable position to keep their allies, whether or not they are Rome signatories, out of the court's reach.

The recent decision by the ICC appeals court to allow an investigation of possible US war crimes in Afghanistan to proceed will test the ability of the ICC to act against the wishes of a major power. The-then US Secretary of State Mike Pompeo's reply that 'We will take all necessary measures to protect our citizens from this renegade, unlawful, so-called court', does not seem to bode well, however.[37] The Americans had already revoked the visa of the ICC's chief prosecutor, and the US government will presumably put enormous pressure on other states not to cooperate with the investigation. Indeed, Secretary Pompeo already promised as much in 2019. 'These visa restrictions will not be the end of our efforts. We are prepared to take additional steps, including economic sanctions if the I.C.C. does not change its course.'[38] It certainly seems likely that the already substantial hostility to the ICC by successive American governments will only increase as a result of this investigation, with uncertain consequences.

Given that the Security Council's approval will often be necessary to enforce arrest warrants against ICC indictees, there is yet further scope for the Security Council to undermine the ICC. The extent to which the ICC, more specifically the Office of the Prosecutor (OTP), can enforce its will in the pursuit of politically significant suspects will

---

[37] Elian Peltier and Fatima Faizi, 'ICC Allows Afghan War Crimes Inquiry to Proceed, Angering U.S.', *New York Times*, 5 March 2020, https://www.nytimes.com/2020/03/05/world/europe/afghanistan-war-crimes-icc.html.

[38] Marlise Simons and Megan Specia, 'U.S. Revokes Visa of I.C.C. Prosecutor Pursuing Afghan War Crimes', *New York Times*, 5 April 2019, https://www.nytimes.com/2019/04/05/world/europe/us-icc-prosecutor-afghanistan.html

in turn influence the seriousness with which the court is taken by the many signatory states, states which might also have to lend their troops to Security Council-mandated operations in pursuit of suspects.[39]

The practical constraints on the ICC help explain why the majority of cases it has pursued, and all that have so far reached the prosecution stage, stem from a part of the world with relatively little global power: Africa. It has been suggested, against a backdrop of longstanding self-interested Western intervention in Africa, that the cases concerning the Central African Republic, the Democratic Republic of Congo (DRC), Uganda, Côte d'Ivoire, Mali, Kenya, Sudan, and Libya are illustrations of neo-imperial victimization. This interpretation does not quite fit the facts, though the historical context makes the concern absolutely understandable. The first five cases on this list were referred to the ICC by the states themselves, each of which is party to the Rome Statute. At least two of those cases were motivated by purely domestic considerations, as states tried to delegitimize local opponents by accusing them of crimes similar to those also committed by state authorities. The Sudanese and Libyan cases were Security Council referrals against non-signatory states.[40] (Only the Kenyan case was initiated by the OTP on its own initiative—*proprio motu*—under Article 15 Rome Statute powers, and tellingly in that instance lack of Kenyan official cooperation in evidence provision, plus intimidation and even murder of witnesses, proved an insuperable obstacle to trial.) The

---

[39] On the credibility problems for the ICC, see Phil Clark, 'Ocampo's Darfur Strategy Depends on Congo', *Oxford Transitional Justice Research Working Paper Series*, 20 August 2008, http://www.csls.ox.ac.uk/otjr.php.

[40] For a relevant exchange of views, with extensive bibliographical references, see https://iccforum.com/africa. See also Louisa Lombard, 'Justice for Whom? The ICC in the Central African Republic', on the SSRC Blogs, http://www.ssrc.org/blogs/darfur. For a defence of the ICC against the neo-imperialism charges, but one that does not address the concerns raised in this chapter, see Max du Plessis, 'The International Criminal Court and its Work in Africa: Confronting the Myths', Institute for Strategic Studies paper 173 (November 2008)—also see p. 11 on DRC's and Uganda's attempt to use the court for political ends. More extensively on the question of selective prosecution of parties, Mark Kersten, *Justice in Conflict: The Effect of the International Criminal Court's Interventions on Ending Wars and Building Peace* (Oxford: Oxford University Press, 2016), ch. 8.

African *marginality* that accounts for the heavy concentration of ICC effort there also helps to explain why no greater international political and military investment was made to halt some of the crimes now under investigation while they were in progress.

At the same time, we need to take note of the way in which the ICC has blurred the distinction between the realm of intervention and that of punishment. This blurring is a step beyond the situation in Rwanda and, in the first instance, Yugoslavia, when legal proceedings were instituted in the midst of ongoing atrocity, not as a complement to interventionist action, but as a substitute for such action.[41] The interventionist agenda presents the ICC at its most explicitly political. Before asking conceptual questions as to the appropriateness of a judicial body playing such a role, we will consider how effective this agenda—call it intervention on the cheap—has been in practice.

In some instances intervention in the form of the threat of indictments does seem to have made a contribution to the reduction of violence and/or to rendering violence less likely.[42] In Côte d'Ivoire, incendiary broadcasts on state media attacking those citizens and

---

[41] Rachel Kerr, 'The Road from Dayton to Brussels? The International Criminal Tribunal for the Former Yugoslavia and the Politics of War Crimes in Bosnia', *European Security* 14:3 (2005), 319–37, here 325, and the material cited there in n. 41.

[42] The literature emphasizing the effectiveness of the ICC includes the following: Payam Akhavan, 'Are International Criminal Tribunals a Disincentive to Peace?', *Human Rights Quarterly* 31 (2009), 624–54, though alongside much less qualified assertions Akhavan also writes, 'it is difficult to ascertain the exact impact of the credible threat of ICC intervention' (640). On the basis of modelling Michael Gilligan, 'Is Enforcement Necessary for Effectiveness? A Model of the International Criminal Regime', *International Organization* 60:4 (2016), 935–67, argues that the ICC may have some deterrent effect 'at the margins'. James Meernik, 'The International Criminal Court and the Deterrence of Human Rights Atrocities', *Civil Wars* 17:3 (2015), 318–39 makes a statistical case for some ICC deterrent effect but there is a circular quality to his argument that 'for the ICC to have a positive impact on human rights states must be committed to the rule of law domestically and must take steps internationally to support the ICC', and 'the potentially positive impact of the ICC on human rights abuses is contingent upon the willingness of states to make manifest their commitment to the rule of law both domestically and internationally' (quotes at 324 and 325). This is akin to saying that the threat of prosecution deters criminality, but only among people who are not inclined to commit crimes in the first place. Catherine Gegout argues, unexceptionably, that 'in the larger international context, the contribution of the ICC

immigrants labelled as 'non-Ivorians' and also attacking the French as 'imperialists', were curbed in November 2004. One obvious reason for the change was the threat of referral to the ICC of government members by the UN Special Advisor on the Prevention of Genocide, Juan Méndez. Around that same time (15 November), the UN Security Council adopted Resolution 1572 demanding that the Ivorian government 'stop all radio and television broad-casting inciting hatred, intolerance and violence'. Of course resolutions and intimations of legal proceedings did not exhaust the context for Ivorian compliance. Another part of the context was that the UN pronouncements came on the heels of an attack (on 6 November) by the Ivorian army on French troops already in this former French colony; French forces had responded by destroying the entirety of the small Ivorian air force. That French action in turn led to attacks on French citizens and properties, which clearly influenced the UN resolution and a simultaneous arms embargo, which was the clearest expression of 'hard' power to complement the softer power of the legal threat.[43] It should also be pointed out that a threatened referral to the ICC carries considerably more weight when backed by a Security Council Resolution than it does when it is simply an independent investigation by the ICC prosecutor's office on its own initiative.

---

to international justice and peace depends on its institutional power and the support it receives from states, on its own impartial work, and on the way it is perceived by potential criminals and victims in the world': Gegout, 'The International Criminal Court: Limits, Potential and Conditions for the Promotion of Justice and Peace', *Third World Quarterly* 34:5 (2013), 800–18 (quote from abstract). Courtney Hillebrecht argues in relation to Libya since 2011 that 'the ICC's involvement in conflict does have a dampening effect on the level of mass atrocities committed': Hillebrecht, 'The Deterrent Effects of the International Criminal Court: Evidence from Libya', *International Interactions* 42:4 (2016), 616–43 (quote from abstract). Focusing not just on the deterrent effect of possible imprisonment but of reputational and other 'audience costs' (domestically and internationally), Benjamin J. Appel argues for an ICC deterrent effect amongst Rome signatory states as far as human rights abuse generally is concerned: Appel, 'In the Shadow of the International Criminal Court: Does the ICC Deter Human Rights Violations', *Journal of Conflict Resolution* 62:1 (2018), 3–28.

[43] Akhavan, 'Are International Criminal Tribunals a Disincentive to Peace?', 636–41.

Of another case, that of the rebel Lord's Resistance Army (LRA) in Uganda, Payam Akhavan writes that amid 'a complex range of factors, there is a noticeable link between the ICC's exercise of jurisdiction over the case and the LRA's demise'. Shortly after Uganda referred the LRA to the ICC for investigation in 2003—and the issue of timing noted by Akhavan is telling—the Sudanese regime significantly reduced its military assistance to the LRA, which presumably reflects Khartoum's desire to protect its reputation and distance itself from the LRA. The longer-term context is that the government of Sudan had agreed to a cease-fire with the Sudan People's Liberation Army (SPLA) in Southern Sudan at the end of 2002, and had signed a security agreement in September 2003. This gave Khartoum important strategic reasons to reduce support for the LRA.[44] So while we may reasonably conclude that the indictment induced some changes in Sudan's behaviour, it is unknowable how much difference—if any—an indictment alone would have made absent the wider strategic situation. Put differently, we are dealing with a conjunction of causes: the relevant policy shift would probably not have happened—or not happened at that time, or in that way—without the indictment element of the conjunction, but on its own the indictment might not have changed anything.

A third example is Kenya. Against the backdrop of violence that brought at least 1,000 deaths after the 2007 elections, the fact of ICC indictments against some elite actors and the threat of same against others *may* have helped to ensure that the 2013 elections were conducted more peacefully.[45] That said, one of the ironic outcomes of the ICC arrest warrants against President Uhuru Kenyata and opposition leader William Ruto was that the two then made a coalition of strange bedfellows based on a shared desire to avoid ICC prosecution. The simple fact is that in 2013, the two figures most likely to organize and initiate elector violence were on the same side in opposition to the ICC. This is, at best, an ironic and unintended kind of ICC 'deterrence'. Moreover, other factors loom equally large in the reduction of violence. Citizens monitoring groups mobilized around the election

---

[44] Ibid., 641–3, quote at 643; Appel, 'In the Shadow of the International Criminal Court', 10.

[45] Appel, 'In the Shadow of the International Criminal Court', 11–12.

(the most famous being Ushahidi, a web-based, crowd-sourced election monitoring site/app). Then there was the unanimous opposition to further electoral violence on the part of business financiers whose support the political parties needed to function.

Even these modest deterrent effects on the part of the ICC are by no means guaranteed. As always, so much depends on context.[46] A number of studies have concluded, based on both empirical data and projections of political calculus, that ICC indictments can make regime and rebellion leaders involved in mass crimes more reluctant to come to peace terms, and more determined to hold onto power, which can prolong the suffering for the populations under their sway. Equally, forces fighting against those whose representatives have been indicted may, feeling vindicated and supported by an international body, extend their military efforts and therefore themselves prolong conflicts that might otherwise more swiftly have reached a negotiated settlement.[47] In such connections we may contemplate aspects of the case of Sudan's Omar al-Bashir, perhaps the most celebrated ICC indictment because it was the first directed at a sitting head of state.

As predicted by observers at the time, Bashir's indictment in 2009 for crimes in the Darfur region had deleterious effects on the situation in Darfur.[48] One immediate result was sharply intensified Sudanese obstruction and intimidation of UN-African Union Mission in Darfur

[46] On the spectrum of outcomes, i.e. the highly contextual impact of ICC involvement, see Kersten, *Justice in Conflict.*

[47] Nick Grono and Adam O'Brien, 'Justice in Conflict? The ICC and Peace Processes', in Nicholas Waddell and Phil Clark (eds.), *Courting Conflict? Justice, Peace and the ICC in Africa* (London: Royal African Society, 2008), 13–20; Monika Nalepa and Emilia Powell, 'The Role of Domestic Opposition and International Justice Regimes in Peaceful Transitions of Power', *Journal of Conflict Resolution* 60:7 (2016), 1191–218; Kurt Mills, 'R2P and the ICC: At Odds or in Sync?', *Criminal Law Forum* 26 (2015): 73–99; Allard Duursma and Tanja R. Müller, 'The ICC Indictment Against Al-Bashir and Its Repercussions for Peacekeeping and Humanitarian Operations in Darfur', *Third World Quarterly*, 40:5 (2019), 890–907.

[48] On debates and predictions around the time of the indictment, see Chidi Odinkalu, 'What if Ocampo Indicts Bashir? 2'; Alex de Waal, 'Africa's Challenge to the ICC'; Heather Adams, 'Putting the Cart Before the Horse', all on SSRC Blogs, http://www.ssrc.org/blogs/darfur; Stephen Oola, 'Bashir and the ICC: The Aura or Audition of International Justice in Africa', *Oxford Transitional Justice Research Working Paper Series*, 15 October 2008, http://www.csls.ox.ac.uk/otjr.php.

(UNAMID) peacekeepers and aid workers as a backlash against representatives of the international community, which was perceived to be taking a more confrontational line against Sudan at a time of sensitive diplomatic negotiations. Amongst other things, Khartoum made the link between the ICC indictment and the international community because UNAMID was, as its name suggests, a partly UN organization, and the UN Security Council had referred the Bashir case to the ICC—the first such referral it had made. Immediately after the announcement that an arrest warrant had been issued for Bashir in March 2009, Khartoum expelled thirteen international non-governmental organizations (NGOs) and hindered the operations of UN refugee workers, on suspicion that these people had provided the ICC with information on regime crimes. The total number of staff working for aid agencies in refugee camps and elsewhere had been 16,250 at the beginning of March; by the end of the month it had decreased to 9,750 with negative consequences for aid distribution, and thus increased mortality. More than one million people were left without access to water, food, and health care. This was only the most dramatic part of the squeeze on international agencies.[49]

The other issue for Sudan was that Bashir was facing election in 2010 and was seriously considering stepping down and handing power over to a trusted successor. However, he did not trust anyone enough to protect him from the ICC, and so he stepped up his efforts to rig the election to get the necessary majority. The electoral system required that he get 50 per cent+1 on the first round to avoid a runoff. Since it was certain that he would *not* receive any votes from the 25 per cent of the electorate in southern Sudan, he needed a supermajority in the north. This required extra efforts on his part to rig the election,

---

On such issues generally, Steven R. Ratner and Jason S. Abrams, *Accountability for Human Rights Atrocities in International Law* (Oxford: Oxford University Press, 2001), 224–5. For more recent assessments on the 'justice versus peace' debate, see Kersten, Justice in Conflict and 'International Criminal Court Cases in Africa: Status and Policy Issues' *Congressional Research Service*, 22 July 2011, 28–30.

[49] Duursma and Tanja R. Müller, 'The ICC Indictment Against Al- Bashir', with statistics at 898–9 and Akhavan, 'Are International Criminal Tribunals a Disincentive to Peace?', 648.

though he was aided by the disarray and incompetence of the political opposition. As a result, not only did he win re-election, but his party swept the slate. The only safe place in Sudan for Bashir was in the presidential palace. It seems quite plausible that the ICC indictment was a spur to keeping Bashir in power nine years longer than he would have been otherwise.

The major question for the OTP, in cases where it is not prepared to wait until after the conclusion of a conflict to indict a political actor, is whether individuals should be pursued irrespective of political consequences ('let justice be done though the heavens fall'), or if pursuit should be suspended if the political consequences of continuing are deemed too great. In the first instance the hope for justice—and in many cases it can only be a hope, given that the OTP relies on the coercive power of other parties for enforcement—will come at the cost of possibly prolonging and even intensifying suffering. This is basically the 'justice versus peace' dilemma. In the second instance the court itself may come to be seen as a potentially disposable tool, the requisites of justice negotiable, meaning that 'justice' is assimilated to the very 'politics as usual' that it was supposed to modify. Further, malefactors may extend conflicts in the hope of gaining something tantamount to amnesty, so this route is not guaranteed to bring swifter peace either. All such considerations are grist to the debate as to whether ICC intervention was appropriate during the conflict in the first place. There is also the possibility that the indictment remains live which, while constituting an ongoing threat to the perpetrator in principle, can, depending on outcome, also simply become an ongoing reminder of the court's inability to bring a key player to justice. In cases where an indictment remains active after the end of a conflict, by contrast, there is a possibility that at least some perpetrators will face the court. At the time of writing, in later 2020, this seems to be what is happening with Bashir. In February 2020, Sudan announced that it would cooperate with the ICC and allow Bashir to 'appear' before the court.[50] This ambiguous wording may suggest that

[50] 'Omer al-Bashir: Sudan agrees Ex-President Must Face ICC', BBC, February 11, 2020, https://www.bbc.com/news/world-africa-51462613.

Sudan is angling for a trial in Khartoum rather than The Hague.[51] After years in which dozens of countries, including Rome signatories, hosted Bashir, and ICC referrals of host states to the UN Security Council elicited little action, things may change.[52] It is, of course, still possible the generals on Sudan's Sovereign Council may change their minds, depending on how negotiations with the ICC play out. (They will almost certainly want to prevent an overly broad investigation into Sudanese military actions.) It is also worth noting that in this case, the apparent willingness of Khartoum to allow the ICC to prosecute Bashir was a concession to the rebels in peace negotiations. It follows Bashir's fall from power for largely domestic reasons, and his prior conviction by Sudanese courts for domestic crimes. By this point, Bashir is simply a bargaining chip to be sacrificed as needed. In this case, regime change—a political process—has proven to be a precondition for (possible) international justice.

Conclusion: A Balance

Criminal trials are intended to punish crime. Such punishment has classically been justified in one of three ways, as retribution, as a means for preventing the perpetrator from committing similar crimes again in future, and as a way of deterring other potential offenders from engaging in similar crimes themselves. In addition, trials for genocide and crimes against humanity have often been justified as forms of political and historical pedagogy.[53] In this final section we assess how far, if at all, these expectations are met in the legal reckoning with genocide.

Retribution, as articulated most clearly by Immanuel Kant, argues that one punishes the criminal in order to restore the moral balance

---

[51] Justin Lynch, 'Will Sudan's Bashir be Handed to the ICC at Last?' *Foreign Policy*, 12 February 2020, https://foreignpolicy.com/2020/02/12/sudan-omar-al-bashir-icc-darfur/.

[52] Tom White, 'States "failing to seize Sudan's dictator despite genocide charge"', *The Observer* 21 October 2018; and http://www.coalitionfortheicc.org/cases/omar-albashir

[53] Mark Osiel, *Mass Atrocity, Collective Memory, and the Law* (New Brunswick: Transaction 1997).

his or her crime has upset. Punishment is retribution, meted out by a court, according to a 'principle of equality' so that 'whatever undeserved evil you inflict upon another within the people, that you inflict upon yourself'.[54] Proportionality is the key element in this analysis. There are two problems with retributive justice as applied to genocide. First, retribution is an inherently individualizing approach to punishment. Yet genocide and crimes against humanity are, by their nature, systematic, mass crimes in which individual perpetrators operate within broad institutional or social frameworks. Consequently, the individualized moral claim at the heart of retributive justice tends to miss its mark. Second, it is difficult to conceive of a proportional retribution for genocide. After all, the most one can do is execute an individual perpetrator, which is hardly proportional to the thousands of murders for which he or she may be responsible.

At the same time, a principle requiring violence on the scale of the original genocide would, assuming a mismatch between the numbers of perpetrators and victims in that genocide, violate the principle of individual guilt at the heart of Kant's concept.

Special prevention assumes that one punishes a criminal in order to prevent recidivism. Given that genocide and crimes against humanity are invariably political crimes, the risk of recidivism by individual perpetrators would depend entirely on political circumstances. Eliminate the conditions (the perpetrator regime, e.g., or the context of civil war) and one eliminates the chance of recidivism. Under such circumstances, there would be no need to punish individual perpetrators at all according to the special prevention rationale.

It has been claimed, in a variant of the special prevention argument, that indicting leaders for crimes still in progress might deter them from continuing to commit such offences. We have seen some modest evidence to support this contention in individual cases of atrocity or other infringements of international criminal law. But as we have shown, there is also evidence that indictments frequently have no impact. Moreover, some indictments might actually prove to be counterproductive, spurring leaders to greater efforts to complete

---

[54] Immanuel Kant, *The Metaphysics of Morals* (Cambridge: Cambridge University Press, 1996), 105.

their genocide, since they no longer have anything to lose, as was arguably the case with Milošević, or more generally to cling tenaciously to their positions of power and thwart the peace that might bring political transition and render them vulnerable, as was the case with Bashir.

Reflection on the modified special prevention claim leads us to argue that while supporting the *norms* embodied in international law is important (see below), expecting too much from the *institutions* of international law is a potentially dangerous self-deceit, one encouraged by the bold claims made by prominent observers of and participants in the ad hoc tribunals and the ICC. When the institutions of law encroach onto the domain of active intervention in ongoing conflicts involving genocide or crimes against humanity, they can introduce an inflexible element into a situation in which diplomatic flexibility is of the essence or, alternatively, they can become politicized in such a way and to such an extent that they lose legitimacy as an instrument of justice, rather than politics. Law courts are *part* of the means of negotiating the *aftermath* of crises. Law talk should not claim more than law can achieve in the very messy and quintessentially pragmatic, compromise-ridden world of conflict resolution and regime transition.

General prevention seems in many ways to be the most plausible explanation for why we should punish genocidaires. The claim is that punishing perpetrators deters future genocides. It is hard to know how to test this proposition robustly in its own general terms because it 'is measured by what does not happen'.[55] Cases in which it might have had purchase can be paired off with cases in which it does not seem to have obtained. The Serbian state, for instance, committed crimes against humanity in Kosovo long after the establishment of the ICTY to address a different set of crimes earlier; mass criminality has continued in the DRC despite the ICC's prosecution of certain parties to previous atrocities.

Theoretical reflection shows why general deterrence might not be effective in cases of genocide. Deterrence works, to the extent that it does, by raising the potential cost to the criminal of his or her crime,

[55] Akhavan, 'Are International Criminal Tribunals a Disincentive to Peace?', 636.

such that the anticipated benefit is no longer worth the risk involved.[56] Yet in some instances, genocide is arguably, in Weberian terms, a value rational act, not an instrumentally rational one.[57] This means that certain questions of costs and benefits are explicitly excluded from consideration. What matters is the normative consistency of the act, not its anticipated success or failure. Consequently, raising the costs of acting in the given manner can have no impact whatsoever. In other cases, genocide can be triggered by a heightened sense of crisis and a paranoid evaluation of the threat posed by the victim group. In this situation, the cost of the failure to act, that is, to commit genocide, is perceived by the perpetrating regime to be infinitely higher than any punishment that might be imposed in the event of failure and defeat. Besides, the sheer historical inconsistency of punishment for genocide removes the most important precondition for deterrence in many regions of the world and even within states in which some perpetrators are brought to book: relative certainty of punishment.[58] The effectiveness of deterrence depends heavily on convincing perpetrators they are in fact quite likely to face punishment. If they are reasonably confident they can get away with their crimes, the threat of even draconian punishment will have little impact. In any given genocide, perpetrators often number in the tens or even hundreds of thousands, while—apart from the exceptional case of Rwanda with its *gacaca* trials, which happen to serve the political interests of the Kagame regime[59]—the numbers convicted remain at best in the hundreds or thousands; and, of course there are many genocides where none of the

[56] John J. Donohue and Justin Wolfers, 'Uses and Abuses of Empirical Evidence in the Death Penalty Debate', *Stanford Law Review* 58 (December 2005), 791–846 and Richard Berk, 'New Claims about Execution and General Deterrence: Déjà vu All over Again' *Journal of Empirical Legal Studies* 2 (July 2005), 303–30.

[57] Max Weber, *Economy and Society: An Outline of Interpretive Sociology* (Berkeley: University of California Press, 1968), Vol. 1, 24–6.

[58] William C. Bailey, J. David Martin, and Louis N. Gray, 'Crime and Deterrence: A Correlation Analysis', *Journal of Research in Crime and Deliquency* 11 (1974), 124–43. Erling Eide in cooperation with Jorgen Aasness and Terje Skjerp, *Economics of Crime: Deterrence and the Rational Offender* (Amsterdam: North-Holland, 1994).

[59] Jens Meierhenrich, *The Violence of Law: The Formation and Deformation of Gacaca Courts in Rwanda, 1994–2012* (Cambridge: Cambridge University Press, forthcoming); perhaps to be read alongside Meierhenrich, *Lawfare: A Genealogy* (Cambridge:

perpetrators are ever brought to trial.[60] So the risk of any given perpetrator being punished for genocide remains low, and the deterrence effect of prosecutions consequently limited.

The determination of which genocides, crimes against humanity, or war crimes are prosecuted and which are not is largely a political and geopolitical one, as the proliferation of ICC cases against politically relatively marginal states in Africa shows. Elsewhere, given great power support for many genocidal regimes over the past fifty years, there can be a direct continuity between the political context which led to genocide and the subsequent impunity for genocidaires themselves, as was, for instance, the case in Cambodia for many years. The case of Kenya illustrates how even a relatively weak state can, with the 'right' arrangement of internal forces, frustrate the ICC in the prosecution of its politicians; and alongside Sudan, Burundi has prevented ICC investigators from entering the country. (Insofar as the ICC has a deterrent effect, one imagines that such instances weaken it.) It seems highly unlikely, therefore, that there will be any indictments successfully brought to court against alleged perpetrators from, say, the US, or any of its close strategic allies, as former Secretary of State Pompeo made clear in response to the recent ICC investigation of alleged US war crimes in Afghanistan. Absurd as it may seem, the American President even has congressional authorization to invade the Netherlands to rescue any Americans charged at the Hague should this become necessary.

Ours is not a purely materialist or realpolitik-driven interpretation of international law. Underlying structural factors of the international political economy and geopolitical strategy *do* obviously come strongly into play in decisions as to who reaches trial, but the constitutions of internationally-mandated courts, and the procedures in individual

---

Cambridge University Press, 2019). See also Lars Waldorf, 'Local Transitional Justice', in Olivera Simic (ed.), *Introduction to Transitional Justice* (London: Palgrave, 2017), 157–76.

[60] On the failure of expectations that ICC indictments would prompt complementary domestic trials, see the examination of the cases of Sudan and Uganda in Sarah Nouwen, *Complementarity in the Line of Fire: The Catalysing Effect of the International Criminal Court in Uganda and Sudan* (Cambridge: Cambridge University Press, 2013).

court cases, are generally not functions of those structural factors. Otherwise, legal legitimacy would be totally lost, as happened in the case of the American-dominated trial of Saddam Hussein, assiduously hived-off from the control of the UN. That such legal legitimacy has been maintained in the eyes of many observers, including the present authors, is a credit to the committed individuals and organizations involved in such institutions as the ICTY, the ICTR, and the ICC. It is also a testament to the existence of an organized international value community of some sort beyond the international power system constituted by the world's most powerful states and multinational corporations. To what extent this legal community can prevail over the system in cases where their interests are antipathetic remains—to take the most optimistic assessment—an open question. But that it can articulate norms that can be used as a foundation for political opposition to mass violence is beyond question.

Even in conflicts that have been subject to adjudication, the problems of equitable prosecution have been enormous, in particular as a result of the post-genocidal power relations, both domestic and international. Cases where atrocities have been committed by all sides to a conflict, however unevenly, are particularly difficult in this regard. There may be prosecutions in which not all parties to a conflict involving multilateral atrocities are prosecuted, as in Rwanda or Uganda, and even—despite the extensive efforts of the ICC—the DRC.[61] Alternatively, different problems may arise as for instance with the ICTY's genuine efforts at proportionality in prosecution. The evidence seems to indicate that the ICTY's efforts have succeeded mainly in generating broad resentment against the court, with all ethnic parties feeling that the court is biased against them and overly lenient towards their adversaries.[62] And as Rachel Kerr's contribution

[61] Lombard, 'Justice for Whom?'; Lisa Clifford, 'ICC risks Losing the Plot in Congo', Institute for War and Peace Reporting Comment, 21 November 2008, http:// www.iwpr.net.
[62] Eric Stover and Harvey M. Weinstein (eds.), *My Neighbor, My Enemy: Justice And Community in the Aftermath of Mass Atrocity* (Cambridge: Cambridge University Press, 2004); A. Uzelac, 'Hague Prosecutors Rest Their Case', *Institute for War and Peace Reporting* (27 December 2004); relatedly, Human Rights Watch, 'Justice at Risk: War Crimes Trials in Croatia, Bosnia and Herzegovina, and Serbia and

to this volume mentions, in findings published in 2016, about what can only be interpreted as a case of wilful blindness in the name of collective self-exculpation, only 20 per cent of the Bosnian Serb population believed that any crime at all was committed in Srebrenica in July 1995.

The Srebrenica example brings us to the next point, that trials have sometimes been justified for their purported value as sites of historical and political pedagogy, particularly in the context of so-called democratic transitions. Unlike the other justifications, which tend to amalgamate trials for mass atrocity to ordinary criminal law, this argument highlights the specificity of such trials as elements in transitional justice. The argument is that such trials can be effective means for establishing the history of past atrocities and creating a constructive sensitivity towards the past as well as delegitimizing the erstwhile perpetrator regime. While it is true that criminal prosecution can be highly effective at gathering evidence, it is less effective at marshalling this evidence to construct a coherent and accurate narrative. All too often, the history lessons taught by criminal trials are distorted and misleading.[63] This is not due to any malice or incompetence on the part of the court but rather a result of the quite distinct methods and objectives of judges and historians.[64] Trials are not designed so much

Montenegro', *Human Rights Watch*, 16:7 (2004), 1–31; James Meernik, 'Justice or Peace: How the International Criminal Tribunal Affects Societal Peace in Bosnia', *Journal of Peace Research* 42 (2005), 271–90; Rachel Kerr, 'Lost in Translation: Perceptions of the Legacy of the ICTY in Former Yugoslavia', in J. Gow, R. Kerr, and Z. Paji (eds.), *Prosecuting War Crimes: Lessons and Legacies of the International Criminal Tribunal for the former Yugoslavia* (London: Routledge, 2014), 103–15. For reception problems related to the ICTR, see S. Kendall and S. Nouwen, 'Speaking of Legacy: Toward an Ethos of Modesty at the International Criminal Tribunal for Rwanda', *American Journal of International Law*, 110:2 (2016), 212–32.

[63] Devin O. Pendas, *The Frankfurt Auschwitz Trial, 1963–1965: Genocide, History and the Limits of the Law* (Cambridge: Cambridge University Press, 2005); Bloxham, *Genocide on Trial*.

[64] Carlo Ginzburg, *The Judge and the Historian: Marginal Notes on a Late-Twentieth-Century Miscarriage of Justice* (London: Verso, 1999) and Norbert Frei, Dirk van Laak, and Michael Stolleis (eds.), *Geschichte vor Gericht: Historiker, Richter und die Suche nach Gerechtigkeit* (Munich: Beck, 2000).

to ascertain what happened and why, as to determine who is to blame. By definition, trials are less interested in historical processes than they are in concrete manifestations of criminal intent; their goal is to establish individual guilt, not historical causation, and while these need not be entirely separate things, the overlap is very far from complete. As a consequence of this necessary focus on the individual in the dock, the remainder of the perpetrator polity can, with some justification, feel themselves exculpated. Unintentionally, then, such trials frequently end up serving as alibis for that majority of perpetrators and bystanders who are not prosecuted.[65] Trials thus manifest an irreconcilable tension between any general pedagogical impulse and the individuating character of criminal justice.

However, even if trials unavoidably tend to teach inadequate history lessons, this in itself does not mean that they cannot contribute to transitional justice. The form may be more important than the content. Mark Osiel contends that criminal trials are especially effective venues for 'stimulat[ing] public discussion in ways that foster the liberal virtues of toleration, moderation, and civil respect'.[66] Because such trials operate under the ground rules of liberal legalism (individual culpability, due process, fair defence, etc.), they perforce validate a pluralistic debate about the meaning of past atrocities, what Osiel terms 'civil dissensus'. According to this view, the benefit of the politico-legal system facilitating such a pluralism of views and the testing of one against the other, without imposing either in an authoritarian or unquestioning fashion, would become increasingly self-evident. As a consequence, the population will then come to embrace a liberal democratic polity.

While theoretically appealing, the empirical evidence hardly supports this hypothesis, as the highly partisan responses to the ICTY show. Osiel's problem is ultimately one of scale. Such trials are unlikely to have this kind of liberalizing impact within post-conflict

---

[65] For an argument that the American-led military tribunals at Nuremberg were reasonably successful in generating collective, structural accounts of Nazi criminality, and thus avoided this problem, see Kim Christian Priemel, *The Betrayal: The Nuremberg Trials and German Divergence* (Oxford: Oxford University Press, 2016).

[66] Osiel, *Mass Atrocity*, 2.

societies themselves, where they will if anything tend to harden, rather than ameliorate, the boundaries between conflicting parties. Indeed, the exculpatory capacity of such trials for the unindicted can actually reinforce the sense of victimization, even among groups associated with the perpetrators (as e.g. in Serbia or postwar Japan and Germany).

If the conclusions thus far are somewhat deflationary, it is important to recognize the ways in which the cup of international justice is, if not half-full, at least not entirely empty. International law, precisely because it is *not* analogous to municipal law can play an important political role, even when it fails as deterrence, or indeed, by and large fails to hold perpetrators accountable at all. Even with the increasing promulgation of multilateral treaties codifying international criminal and humanitarian law, much of the work of international legalism remains symbolic. It articulates customary norms, which can serve as the basis of a *political* critique of atrocities and aggression. This in turn can on occasion help to mobilize the international community for action.

Above all, prosecuting genocide and crimes against humanity is a statement of principle, an act of symbolic disapproval on the part of the international community. This may have limited significance for the parties to specific conflicts but it is important to the international community itself. It is an aspirational statement about what we hope the international community can become. To remain silent in the face of genocide would be to tacitly approve it, as is all too often the case at the moment. By extension, prosecuting genocide can be a useful instrument for forging an emerging consensus regarding international norms. The very force of the label 'genocide' as a mobilization slogan and condemnation illustrates, if only in the vigorous efforts of states like Turkey and Sudan to avoid its application, that the language of values can have real currency in the global arena. Trials are a prominent way of posing in insistent terms the question of what is right and they offer answers, however modest, which can be incorporated into international political conversations. Such an emergent consensus can be discerned, again in a modest way, in the relatively wide adoption of the Rome Statute of the ICC, keeping in mind again that the most important international powers have thus far refused to join the court. Still, that so many countries are now ready to adopt a standing international court, when a few short decades ago almost none were, is a sign of at least limited progress.

Of course, the legalist paradigm is all too easily subject to manipulation. This is why it is important for genuinely independent NGOs, media outlets, and ordinary citizens to monitor the use and abuse of international legal norms as well as the transgression of the norms themselves. In other words, focus needs not just to be on those who have actually committed genocide and related crimes but on the wider forces that enable such crimes and provide many of their perpetrators with effective immunity. International criminal law is too important to be left to lawyers alone, whose claims to embody a universal class of disinterested humanitarians evinces an all too obvious partiality. The same obviously goes for politicians. The norms expressed through international criminal law must be continually reaffirmed by an emerging global civil society, the inchoate and fragile international value community that nevertheless offers the most realistic hope we have for a somewhat more humane future.

Acknowledgement

We are indebted to Alex DeWaal for reading sections of this chapter. He made many useful suggestions that we incorporated at a number of points but his advice was especially important in the discussions of Kenya and Sudan; indeed in those parts we have incorporated verbatim or almost verbatim a number of sentences from his feedback.

Select Bibliography

Bloxham, Donald, *Genocide on Trial: War Crimes Trials and the Formation of Holocaust History and Memory* (Oxford: Oxford University Press, 2001).

Cooper, John, *Raphael Lemkin and the Struggle for the Genocide Convention* (Basingstoke: Palgrave MacMillan, 2008).

Earl, Hilary, *The Nuremberg SS-Einsatzgruppen Trial, 1945–1958: Atrocity, Law, and History* (Cambridge: Cambridge University Press, 2009).

Hagan, John, *Justice in the Balkans: Prosecuting War Crimes in the Hague Tribunal* (Chicago: University of Chicago Press, 2003).

Hazan, Pierre, *Justice in a Time of War: The True Story behind the International Criminal Tribunal for the Former Yugoslavia* (College Station: Texas A&M, 2004).

Maguire, Peter, *Law and War: An American Story* (New York: Columbia University Press, 2001).

Osiel, Mark, *Mass Atrocity, Collective Memory, and the Law* (New Brunswick: Transaction 1997).

Pendas, Devin, *The Frankfurt Auschwitz Trial, 1963–1965: Genocide, History and the Limits of the Law* (Cambridge: Cambridge University Press, 2005).

Pendas, Devin, *Democracy, Nazi Trials and Transitional Justice in Germany, 1945–1950* (Cambridge: Cambridge University Press, 2020).

Schabas, William A., *Genocide in International Law: The Crime of Crimes* (Cambridge: Cambridge University Press, 2000).

Simpson, Gerry, *Law, War and Crime* (Cambridge: Cambridge University Press, 2007).

12

Genocide and the Limits
of Transitional Justice

Rachel Kerr

Introduction

Transitional Justice scholarship and practice has focused for many years on responding to atrocity crimes, including war crimes, crimes against humanity, and genocide, but there has been little discussion of the particular challenges of responding to genocide. There has been a tendency in discussions of transitional justice to conflate genocide with the other atrocity crimes, or even with the broader category of human rights abuses, rather than interrogate it on its own.[1] But genocide creates particular problems for transitional justice. The challenges of responding to genocide highlight all of the broader, and well-rehearsed difficulties of dealing with atrocity, but genocide, as the 'crime of crimes', carries with it a host of additional legal and political baggage that sets in stark relief the limits of transitional justice.

This chapter asks what happens when transitional justice tries to reckon with such an extraordinary crime. Donald Bloxham and Devin Pendas' chapter in this volume addresses the development of genocide as an international crime, its adjudication in international courts, and the legal and political challenges inherent in its prosecution. But as

---

[1] Martha Minow, e.g., talks of mass murders, torture, mass violence, and massacres, any and all of which may or may not have constituted genocide in particular contexts. Martha Minow, *Between Vengeance and Forgiveness: Facing History After Genocide and Mass Violence* (Boston: Beacon Press, 1998).

they argue, international criminal law is too important to be left to lawyers alone.[2] Trials may well be a necessary response to genocide, but they are seldom sufficient. Carlos Nino was worried about the capacity of criminal justice to respond to the 'radical evil' of human rights abuses in his native Argentina; how much more concerned would he be about the capacity of criminal justice to respond to the even more radical evil of genocide? Trials matter, but so does what occurs around them, directly and indirectly. Contending with genocide is not only a problem of law, but also one of politics, culture, and society. This chapter interrogates how mechanisms of transitional justice—trials, truth commissions, memorialization, and reparations—have grappled with genocide. A key concern is recognition. Why does it matter, and to whom, whether or not a particular situation is officially deemed to be genocide, whether by a court, a commission, a government, or a museum? What's in a name?

The chapter begins with a brief overview of the history and evolution of transitional justice as a field of study and practice and then moves on to discuss the ways in which some of the different transitional justice approaches, including trials, truth commissions, reparations, and memorialization, have been applied and with what effects. The chapter focuses on a handful of cases in which some form of transitional justice mechanism was applied, and a legal determination of genocide was made or contested (chiefly, Bosnia, Rwanda, Cambodia, and Guatemala). Of course, leaving out other potential cases is not meant to imply that other instances of atrocity—including the many discussed in this volume—were not in fact genocide, nor does it mean that some other form of reckoning that might be categorized under the umbrella of transitional justice did not occur.

What Is Transitional Justice?

The term Transitional Justice was first coined in the context of discussions about the possibility of justice and accountability in the transitions from authoritarian to democratic rule in South America in

---

[2] See Chapter 11, 'Genocide and the Politics of Punishment' by Donald Bloxham and Devin O. Pendas.

the late 1980s to early 1990s.[3] Its first outing was in Argentina, where a delicate balance was sought between the interests of peace and stability and those of justice. The military junta, which seized power in 1977 and fought a 'Dirty War' against its opponents on the left, fell in December 1983. After the fall of the junta, there were calls for those responsible for the thousands of 'disappeared' and other human rights abuses to be held accountable, and the new President Raúl Alfonsín passed a law initiating legal proceedings against nine military officers. At the same time, there was a need to know what had happened to so many people. Alfonsín created a truth commission (*Comisión Nacional sobre la Desaparción de Personas*, CONADEP) to collect testimony to establish what had happened to the disappeared. The report of the truth commission, *Nunca Màs* (Never Again), documented the cases of over 9,000 people disappeared, presumed dead.

Trials of the junta commenced in 1985, but were halted just the next year, in 1986, in the face of opposition by the military and other supporters of the former regime, who continued to hold considerable power. Between 1989 and 1990, President Carlos Menem pardoned all those who had already been convicted. Many, including the Mothers of the Plaza de Mayo (*Las Madres de la Plaza de Mayo*), a group of women whose children had disappeared, who had campaigned long and hard for justice, felt cheated. For others, however, it was an illustration of the compromises necessary to achieve peaceful transition. Meanwhile, in Chile, the removal of General Augusto Pinochet in 1990 involved a series of compromises, and the amnesty law he had passed earlier to protect himself and members of the regime was upheld. At the same time, a National Commission on Truth and Reconciliation was established but, unlike in Argentina, the commission in Chile was not mandated to collate evidence for prosecution, but rather to recommend reparations to victims.[4] Transitional justice was the term used to describe both the normative drive

---

[3] For discussion of the origins and evolution of transitional justice, see Paige Arthur, 'How "Transitions"' Reshaped Human Rights: A Conceptual History of Transitional Justice', *Human Rights Quarterly* 31:2 (2009), 321–67; and Ruti G. Teitel, 'Transitional Justice Genealogy', *Harvard Human Rights Journal* 16 (2003), 69–94.

[4] Michael Newman, *Transitional Justice* (Cambridge: Polity Press, 2019), 6.

for justice and accountability and the pragmatic compromises that ensued in the context of fragile political transitions.

Since then, transitional justice has significantly broadened its scope in terms of both the type of *transition* and the form of *justice*. Originally conceived of in the context of transitions to democracy from authoritarianism, it was applied in the context of transition from communist rule in Eastern Europe and from Apartheid in South Africa. Then, from the mid-1990s onwards, it was increasingly applied as part of a 'toolkit' of measures in transitions from war to peace, that is, in the context of post-conflict peacebuilding.[5] Ruti Teitel describes this as Phase 3 of transitional Justice's genealogy, with Phase 1 being the post-Second World War trials, and Phase 2 being the transitions to democracy in Latin America.[6] Expectations of the role that transitional justice could play in transition also grew; it was expected to foster societal transformation through adoption of human rights standards and rule of law. As such, it was inextricably linked to goals and practices of liberal peacebuilding, and subject to the same critiques that it was a form of Western imperialism—a 'global project'—imposed top-down and not sensitive enough to local context and political realities.[7]

The demand for justice in transitional justice was originally tied to criminal trials as mechanisms for accountability and redress and there remains a dominant legalist tendency in much transitional justice scholarship. But there is also a recognition that transitional justice is not 'ordinary justice' in the sense we might understand it in relation to domestic criminal trials, but 'extraordinary' because it was applied in extraordinary circumstances.[8] It therefore allows for alternative approaches to, and conceptions of 'justice' extending beyond criminal justice processes, to non-judicial mechanisms such as truth (and reconciliation) commissions, reparations, memorialization, reform of the

[5] Chandra Lekha Sriram, 'Justice as Peace? Liberal Peacebuilding and Strategies of Transitional Justice', *Global Society*, 21:4 (2007), 579–91.

[6] Ruti Teitel, *Transitional Justice* (New York: Oxford University Press, 2000).

[7] Rosemary Nagy, 'Transitional Justice as Global Project: Critical Reflections', *Third World Quarterly* 29:2 (2008), 275–89.

[8] Teitel, *Transitional Justice*.

security and justice sectors, and even education.[9] Building on Teitel's genealogy, what we might term Phase 4 is the notion of 'transformative justice', building on ideas of justice as reparative, rather than retributive or restorative, a form of social repair, focused on the collective, not the individual.[10]

Transitional justice is also now concerned not only with legacies of gross human rights violations within a single country, but with atrocity crimes, including genocide, crimes against humanity, and war crimes committed in the context of international and non-international armed conflict. Put in the broadest possible terms, transitional justice involves a wide range of approaches to the challenges of contending with the past. The United Nations (UN) defines transitional justice as the 'full range of processes and mechanisms associated with a society's attempts to come to terms with a legacy of large-scale past abuses, in order to ensure accountability, serve justice and achieve reconciliation'. As this indicates, it also boasts a diverse set of highly ambitious, normative, and highly contested goals, including peace, justice, truth reconciliation, deterrence, democracy, and rule of law, some of which may be, as Bronwyn Leebaw incisively pointed out, 'irreconcilable' with one another.[11]

The International Centre for Transitional Justice (ICTJ), a prominent non-governmental organization (NGO) in the field, sets out the various means through which it is supposed to achieve these goals, namely: establishing accountable institutions and restoring confidence in them; ensuring access to justice for the most vulnerable; ensuring that women and marginalized groups play an effective role; ensuring respect for the rule of law, facilitating peace processes, and fostering conflict resolution; establishing a basis to address the underlying causes of conflict and marginalization; and advancing the cause of

[9] Elisabeth Cole, 'Transitional Justice and the Reform of History Education', *International Journal of Transitional Justice* 1:1 (2007), 115–37.

[10] See Wendy Lambourne, 'Transitional Justice and Peacebuilding after Mass Violence', *International Journal of Transitional Justice*, 3:1 (2009), 28–48; and Rama Mani, 'Dilemmas of Expanding Transitional Justice, or Forging the Nexus between Transitional Justice and Development', *International Journal of Transitional Justice*, 2:3 (2008), 253–65.

[11] Bronwyn Leebaw, 'The Irreconcilable Goals of Transitional Justice', *Human Rights Quarterly*, 30:1 (2008), 95–118.

reconciliation.[12] The ICTJ concludes: 'The aims of transitional justice will vary depending on the context but these features are constant: the recognition of the dignity of individuals, the redress and acknowledgment of violations; and the aim to prevent them happening again.' The key is to find a balance, between vengeance and forgiveness,[13] between legalism and pragmatism,[14] and between law and politics in the context of a very messy reality. As such, we also need to calibrate expectations and be modest. Transitional justice is, as Martha Minow observed, 'a fractured mediation on the incompleteness and inadequacy of each possible response to collective atrocity'.[15]

Transitional Justice and Genocide

Transitional justice has occasionally grappled directly with the challenge of contending with genocide, but it has also largely tended to blur the distinction between it and other atrocity crimes, so it is difficult to disaggregate transitional justice and genocide per se. Not least because the legal definition is relatively narrow, and historians and social scientists might well apply a different set of criteria, so that just because an event or set of events has not been legally adjudicated as genocide, it does not mean that we should not recognize it as such. The exception of course is Rwanda, where there is a clear legal consensus that genocide did occur. Hence, Phil Clark and Zachary Kaufman's volume was safely named *After Genocide*.[16] In contrast, Adam Smith's volume of the same name discusses Rwanda, Bosnia, and Sierra Leone.[17] In the latter country, the civil war undoubtedly involved widespread and heinous atrocity crimes, but these did not

---

[12] Available at https://www.ictj.org/about/transitional-justice.

[13] Minow, *Between Vengeance and Forgiveness*.

[14] Jack Snyder and Leslie Vinjamuri, 'Trials and Errors: Principle and Pragmatism in Strategies of International Justice', *International Security*, 28:3 (2004), 5–44.

[15] Minow, *Between Vengeance and Forgiveness*.

[16] Phil Clark and Zachary D. Kaufman, *After Genocide: Transitional Justice, Post-Conflict Reconstruction and Reconciliation in Rwanda And Beyond* (New York: Columbia University Press, 2009).

[17] Adam Smith, *After Genocide: Bringing the Devil to Justice* (New York: Prometheus Books, 2009).

meet the legal definition of genocide. Similarly, Alex Hinton and
Kevin O'Neill's edited volume has genocide in the title[18] but, as
Eugenia Zorbas points out in her review of the work, it includes
cases that may or may not have been, legally speaking, genocide,
such as Nigeria, Indonesia, and East Timor.[19] We can question how
much this matters and a recurring theme addressed in this volume is
the problem of definitionalism.[20] If we exclude those cases from
consideration that do not conform to an 'ideal type', or have not
been officially designated genocide by lawyers or jurists, we risk
missing a great deal.

Indeed, there are specific ways in which the limits of the legal
definition of genocide set out in the 1948 Convention on the Prevention and Punishment of the Crime of Genocide (Genocide Convention) have affected the impact of transitional justice mechanisms. This
is perhaps most evident in criminal proceedings, where in order to
secure a conviction, the prosecution must prove beyond reasonable
doubt not only the factual elements of the crime, but also the mental
element (*mens rea*). So, it is not enough to prove that one of the
enumerated acts has been committed against a member or members
of a group (killing, causing serious bodily or mental harm, inflicting
conditions of life calculated to bring about its physical destruction,
imposing measures to prevent births and forcibly transferring children), it must also be proven that this was done with the specific intent
of destroying it.[21] There are also defined limits on the type of group
that has protection under the Genocide Convention, which is confined to national, racial, ethnic, or religious groups. It is a very high
bar, and one that has infrequently been crossed.

However, there are other conceptions of genocide that are relevant
to transitional justice, beyond the legal terminology that established it

[18] Alexander Laban Hinton and Kevin Lewis O'Neill (eds.), *Genocide: Truth, Memory, and Representation* (Durham, NC: Duke University Press, 2009).

[19] Eugenia Zorbas, [review] '*After Genocide: Transitional Justice, Post-Conflict Recon-struction, and Reconciliation in Rwanda and Beyond*, Phil Clark and Zachary D. Kaufman (eds); *Genocide: Truth, Memory, and Representation*, Alexander Laban Hinton and Kevin Lewis O'Neill (eds)', *International Journal of Transitional Justice*, 4:2 (2010), 290–5.

[20] See discussion in the Introduction to this volume.

[21] As the jurisprudence of the International Criminal Tribunals (ICTs) for the Former Yugoslavia and Rwanda have demonstrated, intent can be inferred.

as an international crime in the Genocide Convention. On one hand, there are efforts to expand its legal meaning. One such example is the term 'cultural genocide', invoked by the Canadian Truth and Recon-ciliation Commission in 2015 to describe the policy of removing indigenous children from their families and communities to be 'edu-cated' (read assimilated) in Indian residential schools.[22] The survivors of residential schools celebrated this application of genocide as appro-priate recognition of the suffering endured by indigenous communi-ties. But it also carried with it considerable disquiet, exacerbated in 2019, when the Report of the National Inquiry into Missing and Murdered Indigenous Women and Girls, *Reclaiming Power and Place*, described the 'persistent and deliberate human and Indigenous rights violations and abuses [which are] the root cause behind Canada's staggering rates of violence against Indigenous women, girls and 2SLGBTQQIA people' amounted to 'a race-based genocide of Indigenous Peoples, including First Nations, Inuit and Metis'.[23] The storm of controversy over the use of the term genocide risked over-shadowing and distracting from the reality of continuing oppression and inequality.[24] Even in the cases discussed later in this chapter, of Bosnia, Rwanda, Cambodia, and Guatemala, where a legal ruling of genocide was made, the precise details and scope was contested, and this contestation has impacted on the range of judicial and non-judicial mechanisms to address its legacy.

Trial and Punishment

Genocide was not prosecuted at Nuremberg because it was not an international crime when the London Agreement which provided the

[22] Available at http://www.trc.ca/about-us.html.
[23] *Reclaiming Power and Place: The Final Report of the National Inquiry into Missing and Murdered Indigenous Women and Girls*, 31 May 2019, https://www.mmiwg-ffada.ca/final-report/.
[24] Payam Akhavan, 'Cultural Genocide: When We Debate Words, We Delay Healing', *The Globe and Mail*, 10 February 2016, https://www.theglobeandmail.com/opinion/cultural-genocide-when-we-debate-words-we-delay-healing/article28681535/. See also Umut Özsu, 'Genocide as Fact and Form', *Journal of Genocide Research*, published online 24 October 2019, DOI: 10.1080/14623528.2019.1682283.

jurisdictional basis for the Nuremberg trials, was made (although it should be noted that the status of crimes against peace and crimes against humanity were also far from settled). Nonetheless, genocide would perhaps have been stretching the law beyond breaking point. The main focus of the trial of the major German war criminals at Nuremberg was not, as is often imagined, Nazi crimes of genocide, or even predominantly crimes against humanity, but rather crimes against peace and war crimes.

Raphael Lemkin, having failed to have genocide included at Nuremberg, turned his attention to ensuring that in the future it could be deployed in international criminal proceedings.[25] The Genocide Convention for the Prevention and Punishment of the Crime of Genocide established genocide as an international crime, and thus one for which states might assert universal jurisdiction. Very few trials followed, although, notably, in 1946, two years before the Genocide Convention was adopted, a Polish court sentenced Gauleiter Arthur Geiser to death for war crimes. Mark Drumbl, in his close study of the trial, argues that the Geiser prosecution and judgment, whilst not explicitly including genocide as a crime, nevertheless incorporated Raphael Lemkin's understanding of and approach to genocide within the charge of 'exceeding the rights accorded to the occupying authority by international law'.[26] The trial of Adolf Eichmann in 1961 stands out the most, however, which also had the effect of reverse engineering perceptions of Nuremberg in the popular imagination. As Lawrence Douglas has argued, the Eichmann trial, with its clear focus on crimes against the Jewish people, shifted popular perceptions of the Nuremberg trial from being primarily about Nazi crimes of aggression to being primarily about the Holocaust.[27]

[25] See Chapter 1, 'Fit for Purpose? The Concept of Genocide and Civilian Destruction' by A. Dirk Moses. See also Philippe Sands, *East West Street* (London: Weidenfield & Nicolson, 2017).

[26] Mark Drumbl, ' "Germans are the Lords and Poles are the Servants": The Trial of Arthur Geiser in Poland, 1946', in Kevin Jon Heller and Gerry Simpson (eds.), *The Hidden Histories of War Crimes Trials* (Oxford: Oxford University Press, 2013).

[27] Lawrence Douglas, 'Film as Witness: Screening Nazi Concentration Camps before the Nuremberg Tribunal', *Yale Law Journal* 10:(2 (1995), 449–81.

Major changes in international politics resulted from the end of the Cold War; among them a renewed impetus to accountability for genocide, alongside other core atrocity crimes. Adam Jones points out the irony that the International Criminal Tribunal for the former Yugoslavia (ICTY) was created to deflect accusations of Western complacency in the face of genocide in Bosnia.[28] The irony was compounded in 1994, when the international community created a second ad hoc International Criminal Tribunal for Rwanda (ICTR), following even more abject and catastrophic failure to prevent genocide there, when in a matter of 100 days, around 800,000 Tutsi were murdered, along with Hutu 'conspirators'. A further irony is that the very institutions established to provide a judicial response to genocide have laid bare the inadequacy of the law to respond.

That is not to say that they did not have some impact. Indeed, the judicial record of both tribunals was impressive. When it closed its doors in 2017, the ICTY had concluded proceedings for all 161 of its accused. Among its indictees were those at the highest levels of political and military responsibility, including the Bosnian Serb political and military leaders, Radovan Karadžić and Ratko Mladić, and the former Serbian President Slobodan Milošević. Its cases reflected the broad sweep of crimes, targeting all groups, and addressing the most notorious examples of ethnic cleansing and genocide. The ICTR meanwhile indicted ninety-three individuals and concluded proceedings against just eighty of them.

Together, the ICTY and ICTR contributed more to the prosecution of genocide and the application of the Genocide Convention than anything else since it was adopted. The ICTY severed any connection between genocide (and crimes against humanity) and armed conflict, meaning that it was no longer necessary to prove a nexus with armed conflict, whether international or non-international, and genocide. Second, they contributed to the elucidation of what constituted a victim group under the Convention. The ICTR established that groups did not necessarily have to self-identify or have objective markers of a particular national, ethnic, racial, or religious group,

---

[28] Adam Jones, *Genocide: A Comprehensive Introduction*, 1st ed. (London: Routledge, 2006), 1366.

but that belonging to such a group could be imputed—that is, the key determining factor was whether the perpetrator identified the victim as a member of such a group. Both tribunals also made significant rulings on rape and sexual assault. Specifically in relation to genocide, the ICTR, in its first case, defined rape as a form of genocide as a result of both causing serious bodily or mental harm and of preventing births within the group.[29] The ICTR made the first conviction for genocide of a head of state, and extended the boundaries of criminal responsibility for genocide to incitement in the 'Media case'.[30]

But there have been shortcomings as well, and a significant gap between the tribunals' self-proclaimed achievements and their impact on the constituencies they were supposed to serve in the Former Yugoslavia and Rwanda. On the one hand, the high cost and slow pace of proceedings at both tribunals and the relatively small number of perpetrators brought to account was a source of irritation. Both tribunals were also accused of being too remote—based in The Hague, Netherlands, and Arusha, Tanzania, rather than in the countries in which the crimes were committed. They were also remote in terms of communication—they did not make a concerted effort to engage through outreach until a few years into their mandates. The criticism of 'distant justice' is one that is echoed in relation to the permanent International Criminal Court (ICC) as well.[31]

The failure to engage was partly the fault of the tribunals, but also the fault of highly divisive political discourse, which meant that the proceedings, mediated by politics and a politicized media, were 'lost in translation'.[32] In Former Yugoslavia, while some small signs of progress existed, narratives of denial and victimhood remained deeply entrenched and attitudes and perceptions of the tribunal in the region remained largely negative.[33] In 2016, Marko Milanović concluded his

[29] AKAYESU, Jean Paul (ICTR-96-4).

[30] *Nahimana et al.* (Media case) (ICTR-99-52).

[31] Phil Clark, *Distant Justice: The Impact of the International Criminal Court on African Politics* (Cambridge: Cambridge University Press, 2018).

[32] Rachel Kerr, 'Lost in Translation: Perceptions of the Legacy of the ICTY in Former Yugoslavia', in James Gow, Rachel Kerr, and Zoran Pajič (eds.), *Prosecuting War Crimes: Lessons and Legacies of the International Criminal Tribunal for the former Yugoslavia* (London: Routledge, 2014).

[33] Ibid.

'anticipatory' post-mortem of the ICTY with the finding that 'denialism and revisionism are rampant in the former Yugoslavia. Twenty years on, barely one-fifth of the Bosnian Serb population believed that *any* crime (let alone genocide) happened in Srebrenica, while two-fifths said that they never even heard of any such crime.'[34]

For victims, the ICTY has also been a disappointment in many regards. First of all, the tribunal spent a lot of time at the outset focused on 'small fry', only getting to those higher up the chain of responsibility later on. The trial of Serbian President Slobodan Milošević appeared to a be a turning point, but expectations that he would be punished were dashed when he died before the judgment was issued. We will never know whether the Trial Chamber would have convicted Milošević for genocide, for which he was indicted. The Bosnian Serb military and political leaders, Ratko Mladić and Radovan Karadžić, were convicted for genocide, but as with other rulings at the ICTY, only in relation to Srebrenica, where over 8,000 Bosnian Muslim men and boys were killed in a matter of days in July 1995. Charges of genocide relating to other areas of Bosnia and Herzegovina (especially Prijedor, in North-West Bosnia, the site of the most notorious detention centres) have been routinely quashed. This has been a source of considerable upset among victims in Bosnia, reaffirming the sense among Bosnian Muslims that the tribunal is not 'for them'.[35]

The failure of the ICTY to convict individuals for genocide outside Srebrenica compounded the disappointment of the International Court of Justice (ICJ)'s ruling on genocide in Bosnia. In 1993, the government of Bosnia and Herzegovina filed a complaint at the ICTY against the then Federal Republic of Yugoslavia claiming that Serbia and Montenegro had violated Articles 1–4 of the Genocide Convention. In 2006, the ICJ finally issued its ruling, that while the killings

[34] Marko Milanović, 'The Impact of the ICTY on the Former Yugoslavia: An Anticipatory Postmortem.' *American Journal of International Law* 110:2 (2016), 233–59.
[35] Refik Hodžić, 'Accepting A Difficult Truth: ICTY Is Not Our Court', Balkan Transitional Justice, 9 March 2013, https://balkaninsight.com/2013/03/06/accepting-a-difficult-truth-icty-is-not-our-court/.

elsewhere in Bosnia were quite possibly war crimes and crimes against humanity, only the mass murders in Srebrenica in 1995 constituted genocide. In doing so, the ICJ set a very high threshold for 'intent'.[36]

In Rwanda, meanwhile, whilst there was much less legal argument over whether or not the crimes were genocide, there was a mismatch between domestic and international justice in dealing with it. The ICTR, 500 miles away in Arusha, Tanzania was seen as biased and remote from the concerns of ordinary Rwandans and their demands for justice. Notably, it was not even supported by the government of Rwanda, which had originally requested that a tribunal be established by the Security Council, but then objected to the form it took. The opposition of the government was reflected also in the population: after the acquittal of two suspects in the Cyangagu case in 2004, thousands of people protested against the 'revisionist' tribunal and 'useless' United Nations.[37] For the tribunal however, its primary audience did not seem to be Rwandans, but the international community.[38] Meanwhile, national trials were trying to deal with the thousands of suspects held in Rwandan jails for years, and community-based *gacaca* courts were established to help deal with the backlog. There was a perceived inequality because domestic courts could apply the death penalty whereas the ICTR could not, and generally dealt with people with higher levels of responsibility.

In Cambodia, the task of prosecuting individuals for genocide fell to the Extraordinary Chambers in the Courts of Cambodia (ECCC). The ECCC was essentially an 'internationalized' domestic court, created in 2005, following a long and tortuous negotiation between the government of Cambodia, the US, and the UN. It was mandated to try those most responsible for the death of an estimated 1.7 million Cambodians as a result of starvation, torture, execution, and forced labour inflicted by the Khmer Rouge regime from 1975–9. Pol Pot,

---

[36] Vojan Dimitrijević and Marko Milanović, 'The Strange Story of the Bosnian Genocide Case', *Leiden Journal of International Law*, 21:1 (2008), 65–94.

[37] Adam Smith, *After Genocide*, 88.

[38] Sara Kendall and Sarah M. H. Nouwen, 'Speaking of Legacy: Toward an Ethos of Modesty at the International Criminal Tribunal for Rwanda', *American Journal of International Law*, 110:2 (2016), 212–32.

the leader of the Khmer Rouge, had already been convicted in absentia by a People's Revolutionary Tribunal.

The ECCC took a long time to begin work and was beset with problems. In the end, it seems likely that only prosecute a very small handful of those responsible for the genocide. It had five cases on its docket, with nine accused, but only three have been convicted and the ECCC had cost $21.4 million by the end of 2019.[39] The first conviction to be handed down was of former prison guard 'Comrade Duch' (Kain Guek Eav), who was sentenced to life imprisonment in 2010 for ordering the torture and murder of over 12,000 men, women, and children at the notorious Tuol Sleng (S-21) prison (Case 001).[40] Case 002 against Nuon Chea, Khieu Samphan, Ieng Sary, and Ieng Thirith included charges of genocide against Vietnamese and Cham minorities, forced marriages and rape, internal purges, the persecution of Buddhists, forced labour in work camps, and cooperatives and crimes committed at security centres (Case 002/02). Ieng Sary died during the trial and Ieng Thirith was found to be unfit to stand trial and died soon after. Nuon Chea and Khieu Samphan were both convicted and sentenced to life imprisonment in 2018. By focusing on the persecution of minority ethnic and racial groups, the ECCC worked within a narrow reading of the Convention, rather than trying to expand the categories of victim groups to include political groups. This meant that genocide was not charged in respect of the majority of killings, which were of ethnic Khmers who perished as a result of the massive experiment in socio-economic reorganization and associated purges. Julie Bernath finds this problematic, as it had the effect of creating a hierarchy of victims, with victims of genocide elevated above the rest, and it

---

[39] ECCC at a glance, https://www.eccc.gov.kh/sites/default/files/publica tions/ECCC%20AT%20THE%20GLANCE%20JULY%202019%20%20latest %20version%204.pdf.

[40] For analysis of the Duch trial, see Alex Hintion, *Man or Monster: The Trial of a Khmer Rouge Torturer* (Durham, NC: Durham University Press, 2016). See also the author's epilogue, which continues the dialogue with Hannah Arendt's study of the trial of Adolf Eichmann, *Eichmann in Jerusalem: A Report on the Banality of Evil*: (New York: Penguin, 1964): Alexander Laban Hinton, 'Postscript—Man or Monster?', *Journal of Genocide Research*, 20:1 (2018), 181–92.

differed starkly from the socio-political understanding of what happened under the Khmer Rouge as genocide.[41]

Ultimately, notwithstanding the myriad other problems associated with international justice, criminal trials must fall short when it comes to genocide because the nature of the crime they seek to address is beyond the capacity of the court to address. As Julie Mertus put it, reflecting on the ICTY, 'No charges can be filed for the destruction of souls, the loss of childhood and the breaking of dreams'.[42] Second, criminal trials are flawed repositories for history lessons. And, as Hannah Arendt famously observed in her study of the trial of Adolf Eichmann in Jerusalem in 1961, evil can be revealed at trial to be more 'banal' than expected. For Arendt, Eichmann resisted characterization as a radical anti-semite, or a 'dangerous and sadistic personality'. Rather, he appeared to be 'an average, "normal" person, neither feeble-minded nor indoctrinated nor cynical', but nevertheless someone capable of sending millions to their death 'with great zeal and meticulous care', and 'perfectly incapable of telling right from wrong'.[43] This tells us something about the capacity of so-called 'ordinary men' (and women) to commit extraordinary crimes.[44] But it also reveals the incapacity of the law to address the extraordinary, and the extent to which it might be inappropriate to expect it to do so. Alexander Hinton echoes this sentiment in his study of the Duch trial, where he was left with a haunting sense of an evil not properly reckoned with precisely because it was a product of absence of conviction—a 'banality of everyday thought'.[45]

---

[41] Julie Bernath, 'The Politics of Difference in Transitional Justice: Genocide and the Construction of Victimhood at the Khmer Rouge Tribunal', *Journal of Intervention and Statebuilding*, 12:3 2018), 367–84.

[42] Julie Mertus, 'Only a War Crimes Tribunal: Triumph of the International Community, Pain of Survivors', in Belinda Cooper (ed.), *War Crimes: The Legacy of Nuremberg* (New York: TV Books, 1999), cited in Pierre Hazan, *Judging War, Judging History: Beyond Truth and Reconciliation* (Stanford: Stanford University Press, 2007), 3.

[43] Hannah Arendt, 'Eichmann in Jerusalem I', *The New Yorker*, 8 February 1963, https://www.newyorker.com/magazine/1963/02/16/eichmann-in-jerusalem-i.

[44] Christopher Browning, *Ordinary Men: Reserve Police Battalion 101 and the Final Solution in Poland* (New York: HarperCollins, 1992).

[45] Hinton, 'Postscript', 185.

Alternatives to Prosecution

Given the shortcomings of criminal justice, whether domestic or international, in responding to the needs of post-genocide societies, are any of the other remedies in the transitional justice medicine box any more useful? Some form of truth commission is often posited as an alternative to criminal justice, and in recent years, 'traditional', 'informal', 'local,' or 'indigenous' approaches to justice, healing, and reconciliation have also sometimes been advocated as a tool for addressing past atrocity.

In his 2004 report on the *Rule of Law and Transitional Justice in Conflict and Post-Conflict Societies*, the UN Secretary-General advised that 'due regard must be given to indigenous and informal traditions for administering justice or settling disputes'. These come in a wide range of forms and can include both retributive and restorative justice elements. Critically, they are seen as desirable because they better reflect local cultures, values, and norms. But they also fall subject to criticisms that they are not always consistent with human rights standards (a particular concern has been raised in relation to gender discrimination) international law, or with domestic legal systems for that matter.

In Rwanda, *gacaca* courts (*iniko gacaca*) were based on the traditional *gacaca* dispute resolution mechanism normally employed to settle familial and community disputes. As discussed above, because of the large numbers of defendants awaiting trial in domestic courts, the government of Rwanda turned to *gacaca* courts to deal with crimes related to the 1994 genocide. Between 2005, when *gacaca* started to function, to 2012, when they ended, they had processed 1.8 million cases involving over a million suspects, of which a third of the cases dealt with genocide.[46] *Gacaca* were harshly criticized for violating not only international, but also Rwandan domestic legal standards for fair trials, for amounting to little more than 'victor's justice', and for imposing collective guilt on the Hutu population as nearly all suspects were Hutu.[47] As Nicola Palmer also details, there were also bureaucratic and paradigmatic conflicts between the ICTR, the national

---

[46] Lars Waldorf, 'Local Transitional Justice', in Olivera Simic (ed.), *Introduction to Transitional Justice* (London: Palgrave, 2017) 166.

[47] Ibid, 166–7.

courts, and the *gacaca* courts.[48] Lars Waldorf argues that because of these shortcomings, *gacaca* failed to bring reconciliation—he points to the fact that most survivors received no restitution or compensation, and over 70 per cent of survivors *and* prisoners felt that it had aggravated not alleviated tensions.[49] In contrast, Phil Clark argued that, notwithstanding their flaws, *gacaca* delivered tangible benefits, and were important for creating space for dialogue and reconciliation.[50]

Other states have established investigatory commissions of different sorts. Often called 'truth commissions' or 'commissions of inquiry', the precedent for these was established in the context of transitions from authoritarian to democratic rule in Latin America in the late 1980s and early 1990s (Argentina and Chile, discussed above, as well as El Salvador and Guatemala). Often, they have involved some form of conditional amnesty. Perhaps the most famous example is the South African Truth and Reconciliation Commission, established in 1994 in the context of the transition from Apartheid to democracy. Truth commissions have seldom been tasked with examining genocide, however. Priscilla Hayner's survey of forty truth commissions includes only two cases in which genocide has been found or invoked: Guatemala and Canada.[51]

Guatemala presents an interesting case study of a transitional justice process that involved a truth commission (Commission for Historical Clarification), amnesty, reparations, and eventually criminal trials as the country tried to grapple with the legacy of the civil war, in which the Mayan people had been subjected to a 'scorched earth' campaign, resulting in killings and disappearances of up to 70,000 Mayan people.[52] In 2013, the former leader of the military regime, General Efrain Rios Montt, had the dubious distinction of

---

[48] Nicola Palmer, *Courts in Conflict: Interpreting the Layers of Justice in Post-Genocide Rwanda* (Oxford: Oxford University Press, 2015).

[49] Waldorf, 'Local Transitional Justice', 167.

[50] Phil Clark, *The Gacaca Courts: Post-Genocide Justice and Reconciliation in Rwanda* (Cambridge: Cambridge University Press, 2010).

[51] Priscilla Hayner, *Unspeakable Truths: Transitional Justice and the Challenge of Truth Commissions*, 2nd ed. (New York: Routledge, 2011). Somewhat oddly, genocide is not even included in the book's Index.

[52] Andrew D. Reiter, 'Measuring Success or Failure', in Simic (ed.), *Introduction to Transitional Justice*.

being the first former head of state to be convicted of genocide in his own country (the ruling was later overturned on procedural grounds). A new trial was started in 2017, but Montt died before the verdict could be given. It did, however, spark anew debate about responsibility for genocide in which Guatemalan society was separated into two factions: those who recognized the genocide and those who denied it.[53] Lisa Laplante concluded that the impact of this was huge: '[T]he trial of Ríos Montt thus required the country to contemplate a more horrific truth that went beyond excesses or rogue soldiers, and instead face the grim reality of a premeditated attempt to eliminate a segment of their society.'[54]

Another mechanism for responding to atrocity is reparations. Whilst in some cases, they can be tied to international institutions (the ICC has a reparations programme administered by the Victims' Fund, for example), responsibility for enacting and administering both falls primarily on the state concerned. Reparations seek to recognize and address the harms suffered by victims of atrocity crimes. They can take the form of financial or in-kind compensation for losses suffered, or they can be more programmatic and future oriented, including, for example, rehabilitation programmes, social services such as health care or education, and symbolic measures such as formal apologies, art projects, or public commemorations, which tend to be more future-oriented whereas compensation involves making amends for the past. In Cambodia, the ECCC ordered symbolic and collective reparations in the court's first conviction for crimes against humanity.

An important form of symbolic reparation is memorialization. Memorials and memorialization have been around for a long time; it is only more recently that they have been analysed as modes of contending with the past and included in the lexicon of transitional justice. Memorialization is essentially about remembrance, *lest we forget*. It can take the form of public memorials, national days, monuments, and sculptures, but it can also include museums, public art exhibitions, theatre, music, and literature, and even spontaneous,

---

[53] Lisa J. Laplante, 'Memory Battles: Guatemala's Public Debates and the Genocide Trial of Jose Efrain Rios Montt', *Quinnipiac Law Review*, 32:3 (2014), 621–73.

[54] Ibid., 649.

temporary memorials, such as murals, marches, and installations. Judy Barsalou distinguishes between three types of memorial: at the site of atrocity, sites constructed elsewhere, and activities, such as peace marches or commemorations.[55]

The impetus for these types of responses stems from the realization of what was lost. Genocidal campaigns have often not stopped at the physical elimination of the group, but also sought to destroy its culture, and the dignity of its members. Commemorating victims and reasserting culture can therefore be powerful responses. In cases of genocide, where the horror is almost unimaginable, memorials seek to relay the enormity of the crime. The aesthetics are remarkably similar—in Rwanda, piles of skulls and human remains invoke the memory of the Cambodian killing fields. The Potočari Memorial in Srebrenica was constructed in the face of Bosnian Serb opposition to remember the more than 8,000 men and boys killed by Bosnian Serb forces in 1995. As discussed above, the events of July 1995 in Srebrenica is the only instance of 'ethnic cleansing' that has been legally and officially recognized as genocide. The Potočari Memorial as a result attracts much more attention and is afforded greater significance than other memorials to victims elsewhere in Bosnia. Inaugurated in 2003, it is the site of remembrance services and reburials, and a 'peace march' each year on the anniversary of the beginning of the attack on the Srebrenica 'safe area'. The memorial is based just outside the town of Srebrenica, at the former Potočari battery factory, which was used as a base by the Dutch battalion, and was where many had fled to safety, tragically denied. Dutch forces stood by as Bosnian Serb forces separated men and boys from their families and carried out executions. Most of the killings took place in Potočari, or in the woods around as men and boys fled. In the old factory building, which was used as a holding cell in July 1995, there is a Memorial Room. Outside, there is a cemetery and a Memorial Wall, where the names of victims are inscribed.

List of names or walls of photographs is another common motif, reproduced at the Kigali Memorial Center in Rwanda or the Tuol

---

[55] Judy M. Barsalou, 'Reflecting the Fractured Past: Memorialisation, Transitional Justice and the Role of Outsiders', in Susanne Buckley-Zistel and Stefanie Schafer (eds.), *Memorials in Times of Transition* (London: Intersentia, 2014).

Sleng Genocide Museum in Cambodia.[56] The process of naming victims is to individualize the numbers and restore some dignity to them. Others opt for more conceptual representations, such as the Memorial to the Murdered Jews in Europe in Berlin, which consists of 2,711 concrete blocks arranged in rows in a square in the centre of the city. This is in stark contrast to older memorials, which tended towards solid plinths or depictions of heroic figures, and reflects a shift in memorial culture from commemorating war heroes in the traditional sense, to remembering its victims.[57]

Memorials can also be sites of remembrance for otherwise marginalized victims, for example, the memorial to the homosexuals persecuted by the Nazi regime which now sits in the Tiergarten in the middle of Berlin.[58] And they can be powerful sites of contestation and resistance. The postwar politics of ethnic cleansing in Prijedor is a case in point. The blocking of a memorial for the 102 children (not only Bosniak, but also including Serb and Croat victims) killed in Prijedor in 1992 encapsulated the culture of division and denial that is still very current in Republika Srpska.[59] Official monuments celebrating the so-called Serbian 'war for defense and freedom' was coupled with inadequate representation of the suffering of other people, a lack of support for victims searching for missing persons.[60] In 2013, associations of victims' families and camp survivors launched 'White Armband Day', which is marked every 30 May, with a gathering of victims' families and activists in Prijedor's main square, who lay 102 roses bearing the names of the killed children in the main square, in place of a permanent memorial.[61] That there is still denial of the systematic expulsion and extermination of 3,173 Bosnian Muslims

---

[56] Susanne Buckley-Zistel and Annika Björkdahl, 'Memorials and Transitional Justice', in Simic (ed.), *Introduction to Transitional Justice*, 252.

[57] Ibid., 253, 264.

[58] Ibid.

[59] Refik Hodžić, 'Flowers in the Square', in International Center for Transitional Justice, https://www.ictj.org/sites/default/files/subsites/flowers-square-prijedor/.

[60] Haris Subašić and Nerzuk Ćurak, 'History, the ICTY's Record and the Bosnian Serb Culture of Denial', in Gow, Kerr, and Pajič (eds.), *Prosecuting War Crimes*.

[61] Hodžić, 'Flowers in the Square'.

and Bosnian Croats from the region rankles, as does the situation in which, whilst the facts have been established and convictions secured for war crimes and crimes against humanity, the acts of torture, rape, murder, etc. have not been legally determined to be acts of genocide.

Conclusion

Hannah Arendt contended that in the face of genocide, we 'are unable to forgive what [we] cannot punish and [we] are unable to punish what has turned out to be unforgivable'.[62] As Martha Minow shows, even if she was right, the range of responses that societies have made indicate that there is a shared feeling that it would be wrong to do nothing. Transitional justice alone is clearly inadequate to the task of social transformation or individual healing, but it may be able to bring some form of repair and to create space for dialogue. Contending with genocide shares the common challenges of contending with other atrocity crimes, but also has the added complication of the baggage associated with a determination of genocide which, when withheld, can exacerbate the sense of disappointment in transitional justice mechanisms that might anyway be felt. Whilst there are important reasons for holding on to the special status of genocide as capturing the more heinous crime of targeting people for something they cannot choose, there is also a danger in giving too much weight to its status, creating a hierarchy of victims.

Ultimately, whilst there are shortcomings in transitional justice and its ability to deal with genocide, this is hardly surprising. Nor is it surprising that in very different contexts, different conclusions about the impact of transitional justice might be drawn. It is not simply a case of allowing time for people and societies to 'heal'; different types of intervention elicit different results. And contending with the past is, as the term suggests, highly contentious. It involves dilemmas around whether to draw a line under the past, forgive and forget, or continue to dredge it up and revisit it in different ways. It also highlights competing narratives and 'memory wars', as well as potentially unleashing a competition for victimhood, in which a legal

---

[62] Minow, *Between Vengeance and Forgiveness*, 4.

determination of genocide can play a powerful role. Moreover, it is a long-term political process, played out in the arenas of law, society, and culture. As David Forsythe points out, Turkish acceptance of responsibility for the Armenian genocide, or even recognition that it was genocide, has yet to materialize, 100 years later.[63] Until politics can catch up, perhaps justice—however inadequate, and in whatever form it is enacted—can nevertheless 'do something' in the face of genocide.

Select Bibliography

Buckley-Zistel, Suzanne and Stefanie Schafer, *Memorials in Times of Transition* (London: Intersentia, 2014).

Clark, Phil and Zachary D. Kaufman, *After Genocide: Transitional Justice, Post-Conflict Reconstruction and Reconciliation in Rwanda And Beyond* (New York: Columbia University Press, 2009).

Hayner, Priscilla, *Unspeakable Truths: Transitional Justice and the Challenge of Truth Commissions*, 2nd ed. (New York: Routledge, 2011).

Hinton, Alex, *Transitional Justice Global Mechanisms and Local Realities After Genocide and Mass Violence* (New Brunswick: Rutgers University Press, 2010).

Lehrer, Erica, Cynthia Milton, and Monica Patterson, *Curating Difficult Knowledge: Violent Pasts in Public Places* (London: Palgrave, 2011).

Minow, Martha, *Between Vengeance and Forgiveness: Facing History After Genocide and Mass Violence* (Boston: Beacon Press, 1998).

Palmer, Nicola, *Courts In Conflict: Interpreting the Layers of Justice in Post-Genocide Rwanda* (Oxford: Oxford University Press, 2015).

Shaw, Martin, *What is Genocide?* (Cambridge: Polity, 2007).

Simic, Olivera (ed.), *An Introduction to Transitional Justice* (London: Routledge, 2017).

---

[63] David Forsythe, 'Human Rights and Mass Atrocities: Revisiting Transitional Justice', *International Studies Review*, 13:1 (2016), 93.

13

From Past to Future

*Prospects for Genocide and its Avoidance
in the Twenty-First Century*

Mark Levene

Introduction

> Severe problems of overpopulation, environmental impact,
> and climate change cannot persist indefinitely: sooner or
> later they are likely to resolve themselves, whether in the
> manner of Rwanda or in some other manner not of our
> devising, if we don't succeed in solving them by our own
> actions.[1]

How should we understand the wellsprings of genocide? The above
statement could be read either as a list of potential ingredients, or a
line of explanatory inquiry at marked variance with nearly all standard treatments of our subject. Indeed, from Lemkin onwards, most
genocide scholars have been at pains to distance the phenomenon, at
least in its contemporary guise, from any explanation of a generalizing
kind. To travel down that road would be to diffuse 'genocide' into
something wholly more amorphous. Even insofar as it is clearly a
matter of violence, inclusion of any particular case-history *as* genocide

---

[1] Jared Diamond, *Collapse: How Societies Choose to Fail or Survive* (London: Penguin, 2005), 328.

rests on the fulfilment of criteria that mark it as *only* belonging to that special category of violence. Thus to speak of an event as genocide is almost *ipso facto* to repudiate the possibility that it might have been shaped or determined by factors or circumstances associated with the politics, economics, social, or cultural behaviour of dominant international society. On the contrary, genocide is almost always assumed to mark a radical rupture with, or from, its norms. It is aberrant; abnormal; the outcome of sad, malfunctioning polities, usually led by seriously mad or bad leaders.

Here I propose an alternative approach, briefly stated, as dependent on underlying but systemic *preconditions* broadly common to crises of state and out of which genocide has regularly emanated. Their historical roots are in some respects quite straightforward. The avant-garde model of the coherent nation-state developed in a limited number of early modern polities in Western Europe and then north America in tandem with efforts to achieve the maximization of their resource potential—human, biotic, and material—as determined by the needs of an almost perpetual military competition or actual warfare between these polities. It was no accident that the states that were most successful in this competition were not only the most technologically innovative but also the most predatory in their efforts to develop and utilize their respective resource-bases for the capital accumulation necessary in turn to feed that technological advance. Asset-stripping corporate capitalism, state formation—or reformulation, and military revolution, though coming through various, often unrelated pathways, thus coalesced in the late eighteenth-century West as a potent nexus of all three. The paradigm also necessarily carried its own dynamic logic, the shorthand for which we might read in social Darwinian terms not so much as the survival of the fittest but rather the survival of the *fastest*.

Thus, we have the protean beginnings of what one historian has dubbed the 'Great Acceleration'[2] towards the contemporary globalized political economy. To make good, or perhaps more soberly put, simply to stay afloat in a world as determined by the new Western

---

[2] J. R. McNeill, 'Social, Economic and Political Forces in Environmental Change: Decadal Scale (1900 to 2000)', in Robert Constanza et al. (eds.), *Sustainability or Collapse, An Integrated History and Future of People on Earth* (Cambridge, MA: Dahlem University Press, 2007), 301–29.

dispensation, required emulation of its practice. The alternative was to go under, that is, to be colonized. Even with the later shift after 1945, to the post-colonial framework in which all formerly Western colonized zones nominally became sovereign and independent entities, the urge to hothouse, preferably industrial, development became the *sine qua non* of each and every one, to the point where 'advocacy of anything short of maximum economic growth came to seem a form of lunacy or treason'.[3] This did not fundamentally shift the balance of geopolitical and economic power away from the metropoli, at least not until quite recently. On the contrary, it simply intensified the urge of more self-consciously aware and resentful latecomer states within the periphery and semi-periphery to seek their own shortcuts to catch up.

In an earlier piece exploring the likely contours of violence in the near-future of our contemporary world, I proposed a three-tier schema with some passing reference to this model as proffered by Immanuel Wallerstein.[4] A first tier consisted of wealthy first world countries (the 'liberal West') closely approximating what under the era of bi-polarity was also referred to as the 'free world.' A second tier was made up of the vast majority of modern nation-states, not only those in the former Soviet bloc but polities in all hemispheres who continued to see themselves as bona fide players in the international system competition for position and power. A third tier was posited as more notional than real. Nevertheless, it was based on the argument that some of the very poorest, weakest, and most underdeveloped countries who had entered into forced-pace, usually state-driven modernization to meet the institutional demands of the system, were already so broken by the challenge that it was only a matter of time and/or the termination of tier one ('international') aid before they ceased to operate as *effective*, infrastructurally cohesive states

---

[3] Ibid., 302.

[4] See Immanuel Wallerstein, *The Capitalist World-Economy* (Cambridge: Cambridge University Press, 1979), and Immanuel Wallerstein, *The Modern World System*, 3 vols. (San Diego and New York: Academic Press, 1974–1988) , for the Wallersteinian system. Also Mark Levene, *Genocide in the Age of the Nation State, vol. 1: The Meaning of Genocide* (London and New York: I.B. Tauris, 2005), ch. 3, for a fuller rendition of the argument herein.

altogether. Suggested candidates for this unfortunate grouping included 'much, if not all, of sub-Saharan Africa, as well as possibly large chunks of Central Asia'.[5]

The further implication of this schema was that potential trajectories, patterns, and ultimately forms of violence were specific to each tier. In tier one, for instance, it was posited that while these state-societies were directly or indirectly responsible, or at least complicit for much of the conflict or threat of conflict, including genocide in the world at large, they were largely insulated themselves from suffering extreme, mass violence within their own domestic contexts. In tier three, by contrast, the actuality or likelihood of violence was endemic and rampant, yet, paradoxically, with insufficient in the way of state authority to scotch or at least put a brake on its widespread but diffused prevalence and persistence.

It was thus in tier two that that the *preconditions* of modern genocide were at their greatest: on the grounds that it was precisely in these states that the driving forces associated with the developmentalist imperatives of the system were at their most intense and urgent. However, as this tier two grouping ranged from large, relatively strong states such as China or Russia at one end, to small, relatively weak ones such as Rwanda and Burundi, at the other, Wallerstein's distinction between semi-periphery and periphery proved ultimately less apposite to the argument than understanding the crises of states out of which the actual *conditions* for genocide emanated. If, however, the overriding implication of the 1999 article was that both the preconditions and conditions of modern genocide remained closely intertwined with the very driving forces, not to say building blocks of our contemporary global system, some ten years on, the purpose of this chapter is to reconsider the argument in the light of environmental evidence which now puts the long-term sustainability of the entirety of the international system in serious doubt.

It has been known for some decades that the scope, scale, and relentlessly accelerating pace of developmentalism are entirely out of

[5] Mark Levene, 'Connecting Threads: Rwanda, the Holocaust and the Pattern of Contemporary Genocide', in Roger W. Smith (ed.), *Genocide: Essays Toward Understanding, Early Warning and Prevention* (Williamsburg, VA: Association of Genocide Scholars

synch with the carrying capacity of the planet.[6] Now, with the full effects of that developmentalism self-evident in terms of the knock-on consequences of greenhouse gas emissions (ghg) on the biosphere, one might even propose that the appropriate question is not so much about whether there will be future genocide but whether there will be future generations of *homo sapiens* upon this planet at all.[7]

If this on its own might be grounds for deciding that the study of our subject is facing redundancy, we have already hinted at why ongoing predictive analysis could be of value to the greater cause of humanity's survival. If the growing scope, scale, and frequency of genocidal events in the most recent centennial sequence is itself an indicator of the cul-de-sac nature of systemic drives towards the unattainable, we might expect the acceleration of those drives set against increasing environmental blockages—not least global warming—to be an equally strong indicator of where we are more generally heading. By the same token, if the scale of biospheric breakdown actually begins to unravel the statist project, then we might expect to see the specific path of genocide radically diffuse or possibly metamorphose into *other* forms of violence.

To be sure, making prognostications about the future is to enter onto dangerous terrain. That said, developing scenarios for future climate change impacts as set against different levels of ghg emissions has become practically a staple of climate and earth science modelling. What is needed now, however, is a broader contextualization of genocidal potentialities that take into account the genuine environmental, including climatic factors.

We have sought to develop this analysis—albeit only in the most-sparse outline—by offering two new routes into the future. Both are necessarily grounded in realities of the present. Both hold fast to the three-tier approach. However, if the earlier exposition might be

[6] Donatella Meadows et al., *The Limits to Growth* (New York: Universe, 1972), for the classic study.

[7] See WWF report, *Climate Change, Faster, Stronger, Sooner* (London: WWF, 2008),. http://www.wwf.org.uk/research_centre/index.cfm%3FuNewsID%3D2289. Also David Wasdell, 'Radiative Forcing & Climate Sensitivity'; Tällberg Consensus Project: 'The Tipping Points We Cannot Cross: Defining the Boundary Conditions for Planetary Sustainability,'', 25–26 June 2008, http://www.jimhadams.com/eco/RadiativeForcingEd3.doc.

characterized as one of 'business as usual', that is, in which genocide continues to be a symptom of systemic dysfunctionality but in which political and economic factors are assumed to be paramount, what we seek to do in our additional Scenario 1 is work up the argument by suggesting how a world of resource scarcity, set against systemic demands on the one hand, population pressures on the other, are becoming destabilizing forces in their own right. Our forecast, as previously, implies that genocide could be one of *several* possible outcomes in terms of extreme, mass violence. Indeed, our focus on the Great Lakes region of Central Africa, more especially the eastern Congo, contains within it the proposition that tier three conditions are particularly indicative of what we describe as post-genocidal conflict.

Does this mean paradoxically, that genocide *qua* genocide could be on the wane? As a prelude to Scenario 2—in which we introduce the true elephant into the room: anthropogenic climate change—we offer the briefest of commentaries on the case the Chittagong Hill Tracts (CHT). This is a region where environmental breakdown, while intermeshed with other more standard factors, can already be seen to be symptomatic of a descent into genocidal conflict. The key point about the pursuit of this theme in Scenario 2, however is that the disruptive potential of climate change, whether writ-small in terms of the single state, or writ-large in terms of the international system, is entirely exponential. All the more reason why it cannot be ignored by genocide scholars, nor anybody else. Whether climate change will simply be a 'threat multiplier' to already existing conflicts—as security analysts now repeatedly tout[8]—or *the* key factor in a civilizational collapse, only time will tell. In our concluding remarks, we briefly iterate the current direction of flow towards ever greater violence, as a consequence of the perpetuation and/or intensification of present conditions. Gazing into this crystal ball, however, will not clarify whether genocide will, or will not be a major facet of this ravaged landscape. It will simply confirm the urgent necessity for a paradigmatic shift in our relationship not only to each other but to our precious planet if we are to avoid not simply genocide but *omnicide*.

[8] CNA, *National Security and the Threat of Climate Change* (Alexandria, VA: CNA Corporation, 2007), http://www.securityandclimate.cna.org/.

Scenario 1: Business as Usual as Set Against the Carrying Capacity of the Planet

Back in 1972, a small team of far-sighted, US-based systems analysts, produced a report for the Club of Rome on future prospects for humanity. They did so by extrapolating available data, particularly on industrialization, food production, pollution, and demographic patterns, as set against the carrying resource capacity of the planet. Their conclusion was stark: exponential growth would lead to eco-logical overshoot, the consequence of which would be 'a rather sudden and uncontrollable decline' within a timeframe of 100 years. *Limits to Growth* was a landmark event and so duly received a barrage of criticism from mainstream policymakers and academics.[9] More than thirty years on, however, leading scientific report after report corroborates the fundamental contours of the team's findings. The Millennium Ecosystem Assessment in 2005 for instance, concluded:

> Over the past fifty years, human beings have changed ecosystems more rapidly and extensively than in any comparable period of time in human history, primarily to meet rapidly growing demands for fresh-water, timber, fiber, and fuel. This has resulted in a substantial and largely irreversible loss in the diversity of life on Earth.[10]

More recently, in late 2007, a report from the UN Environment Program, represented simply one more authoritative voice iterating that the planet's water, land, air, plants, animals, and fish stocks were all in 'inexorable decline'.[11] Meanwhile, a new generation of 'eco-logical footprint' scientists are setting out with a degree of mathemat-ical precision the gap between the current demands of the human *Oikumene* and the limits of planetary supply. One leading figure, for instance, calculates that while in practice the earth can offer 1.8

---

[9] See Dennis L. Meadows, 'Evaluating Past Forecasts, Reflections on One Critique of Tthe Limits to Growth', in Constanza, *Sustainability*, 399–415, for a more recent assessment.

[10] Millennium Ecosystem Assessment (MEA) 2005, extract reprinted in Nathan. J. Mantua, 'A Decadal Chronology of 20th[th] Century Changes in Earth's Natural Systems', in Constanza, *Sustainability*, 292.

[11] See John Vidal, 'Global Food Crisis Looms as Climate Change and Fuel Shortages Bite', *Guardian*, 3 November 2007.

hectares of cropland, pasture, forest, and fishing ground to each of us, what we are on average consuming amounts to 2.2. hectares. More sobering still, the Earth's ability to regenerate its resources is taking some fifteen months against what we are using up in twelve. Again, the picture is abundantly clear: our current globalized political economy as it developed out of a particular but relatively recent historical trajectory is radically at odds with nature's bounty with the consequence that 'overshoot will ultimately liquidate the planet's ecological assets'.[12]

The 64,000 dollar question for us is what does all this mean in terms of human, more exactly social and political, consequences? It should not be rocket science to deduce that as environmental stress on the human condition sets in and, with it, loss of control over what previously had been assumed to be normal and predictable, something—or *things*—will have to give, with likely violent repercussions. But that still poses the questions of where, when, and how? This, however, hardly needs to be a matter of future forecasting. If the scientific pronouncements are correct, then there should be enough evidence in the recent or present-day record to confirm the relationship between environmental pressures and forms of conflict.

However, while the relationship between third world population increase and environmental stress is the standard point of access into this subject, the greatest destroyers of planetary resource in overall global terms are not the poor at all, but the rich. The average Briton burns up more fossil fuels in a day than a Tanzanian family uses in an entire year. Indeed, if we were to make further striking comparisons, if everyone's ecological footprint were European we would need 2.1 planet Earths to sustain us, while if we all followed the US lead, we would need nearly five.[13] But if more needs to be said below about the *localized* causes of extreme violence, including genocide in third world—again both poor tier two and tier three—countries, let us

---

[12] Mathis Wackernagel, quoted in Fred Pearce, *Confessions of an Eco-Sinner, Travels to Find Where My Stuff Comes From* (London: Eden Project Books, 2008), 315.

[13] Johann Hari, 'Don't Call Iit Climate Change—iIt's Chaos', *Independent*, 15 November 2005; 'World Economy Giving Less to Poorest in Spite of Global Poverty Campaign Says New Research', 23 January 2006,. http://www.neweconomics,org/gen/news.growthisntworking.

just for one moment run with the implications of still hegemonic tier one efforts to continue a maximized control of third world mineral and energy supply against the backdrop of an increasingly undisputed resource scarcity. Here, for instance, is a report extract from defence analysts working under the British Ministry of Defence on a possible near-future scenario for Africa:

> Climate change and HIV/AIDS, scarcity of food and water and regional conflict could lead to Africa becoming a failed continent, where even large, currently self-sustaining states become chaotic. Outside engagement and intervention would effectively be limited to a small number of well-defended entry points and corridors, which would provide access to raw materials essential to the global economy. Nations or corporations wishing to trade with Africa would increasingly be required to provide security for their nationals and the necessary support to sustain critical areas of access and security.[14]

What is particularly valuable about this assessment is its remarkably frank and, one might add, naked assertion of the primacy of the national interest. Africa matters because it has mineral as well as fossil-fuel resources. The bottom line, hence, is that in conditions of instability, Britain must exert maximum political-cum-military leverage to recover these for herself, and by implication, prevent other 'unfriendly' predators, from squeezing her out. The language is redolent of the nineteenth-century scramble for Africa, some of the consequences of which *were* genocidal. More to the point, if this can be taken to be the genuine bottom line of ongoing British foreign policy,[15] it casts a disturbing commentary on African conflicts in which resource issues have played a prominent role.

Take the most obvious and glaring example; the ongoing conflict in eastern Democratic Republic of Congo (DRC), more exactly centred on Ituri and North and South Kivu. The immediate trigger to destabilization was the political crisis, culminating in the 1994 genocide, in

---

[14] From DCDC (Development, Concepts, and Doctrines Centre, MOD) 'Strategic Trends, 2030', quoted in Nick Mabey, *Delivering Climate Security, International Security Responses to a Climate Changed World*, Whitehall Papers, 69 (London: Royal United Services Institute, 2008), 31.

[15] See Mark Curtis, *Web of Deceit, Britain's Real Role in the World* (London: Vintage, 2003), esp. ch.apter 10, for the necessary confirmation.

neighbouring Rwanda. Massacre-led intervention in DRC's east, by the new Rwandese Patriotic Front (RPF) government, initially against the fleeing Hutu militias, quickly catalyzed a much wider set of military interventions involving half a dozen additional African states. The primary goad to each was not geostrategic but venal, that is, to use the opportunity of DRC's internal breakdown to maximize their own access to, and exploitation of, its mineral and natural largesse. They did so either by seeking concessions from the failing Kinshasa government (Mobutu, then Kabila) in return for military support; in the case of Uganda and Rwanda by a degree of direct intervention, though more especially in the east, where the competition was greatest, through the military backing of what became a multiplicity of warlord-led militias.[16]

So far, one might ask, what has any of this to do with Western involvement or complicity? The answer is that we are speaking here about a range of resources, including copper, cobalt, cassiterite (tin oxide) gold, and diamonds, whose value to their African interlopers only existed if they could be traded for foreign currency, in other words through purchasing intermediaries who were willing not to ask difficult questions about the minerals' sourcing. This, we must remember, against a late-1990s surge of market price as industrial demand for minerals in leading developed countries—including now India and China—began rapidly to outstrip supply. In eastern Congo, the interrelationship between these diverse factors and the potential for an exponential violence began to hinge on the mineral compound, coltan. The compound includes the precious metal tantalum much in demand as a conductor in hi-tech communications and aerospace industries (in other words primarily for military purposes), but also for making capacitors in a range of electric devices—computers, play stations, digital computers, and especially mobile phones. Eighty per cent of the world's reserves of coltan are located in the Kivus. The Rwandan and Ugandan interlopers in DRC, acting through their local proxies, thus happened to be sitting on a mineral whose market value, in direct response to a rapid global take-off in mobile phone

---

[16] See Thomas Turner, *The Congo Wars, Conflict, Myth and Reality* (London and New York: Zed Books, 2007), for background.

demand, went through the roof in a matter of months, from $65 in late 1999, to $530 in mid-December 2001.[17]

We can rather too well state what happened to the region as a consequence. The traditional, actually thriving pastoral-cum-agricultural economy collapsed as all able-bodied men and boys scrambled to participate in constructing do-it-yourself, ramshackle, inherently dangerous as well highly toxic mines, in addition to the ones already overrun by the warlords. There was a growing incidence of congenital deformities and respiratory problems as a result but with no health care for the population to fall back on—no administration of course existing to pump mine revenues back into social infrastructure—mortality from these illnesses rapidly accelerated. But then, disease-related mortality increased across the board, as coltan dependency linked to military competition for its control made rapid inroads into the social cohesion and survivability of the region. With male employment (including forced labour) all coltan-related—mostly in the mines or the various militias numbering an estimated 200,000 combatants—young women and children were sucked into this burgeoning *alternative* economy primarily as prostitutes. The statement is shocking but only set against non-governmental organization (NGO) estimates that 30 per cent of the region's children were also succumbing to severe malnutrition; while a staggering 50 per cent of the region's population overall had been displaced.[18] Here, then, was a society literally spiralling out of control, where not only was HIV/Aids rife but previously contained diseases including whooping cough, measles, even bubonic plague, part and parcel of an ever-increasing cycle of degradation, starvation, and of course, atrocity. Indeed, this was exactly the sort of 'in the midst of Africa' breakdown that our British defence analysts had warned against, the critical caveat being that lack

[17] See Mikolo Sofia and Dominic Johnson, 'The Coltan Phenomenon', Pole Institute/CREDAP report, January 2002, http://www.odi.org.uk/HPG/papers/bkground_drc.pdf/; Pearce, *Confessions*, 273–5, for additional background.

[18] Amnesty International, 'Democratic Republic of Congo "Our brothers who help kill us"—economic exploitation and human rights abuses in the east', AI INDEX AFR62/010. 2003 1 April 2003; Oxfam, 'No End in Sight: The Hhuman Ttragedy of the Conflict in the Democratic Republic of Congo', August 2001. http://www.oxfam.org.uk/resources/policy/conflict_disasters/downloads/bp12_drc.rtf.

of food and environmental stress were hardly a consequence of (a localized) resource scarcity but rather of the exact opposite.

All of this, of course, was entirely illegitimate to the United Nations (UN) eyes which, having set up a panel of experts to investigate the illegal exploitation of DRC's natural resources, demanded a moratorium on their trade.[19] How, then, did countries such as the UK respond? By duly ignoring or circumventing the UN's panel request to investigate the eighteen British registered businesses held to be 'deliberately or through negligence' among the eighty-five named Western companies helping to prolong the conflict through their economic involvement.[20] Nor did the UK freeze its substantial aid programmes to Uganda and Rwanda. Why should it do so when Kigali and Kampala's foreign accounts were duly audited as clean?

If, then, this is an example of the practice of business of usual it has to be firmly set against the carrying capacity of the planet, though now repeatedly involving tier one states in major resource conflicts. The DRC may illustrate an example where they have done so at second hand, but also underscores how conflict of this type carries substantial economic gains which, consciously, or unconsciously, are accepted by policymakers as overriding the third world human cost.[21] More cynically, one might propose that because most of these conflicts do not fall within a rubric of genocide, Western governments are all the better positioned to eschew responsibility for them.

None of this should greatly surprise. A rising but resource-challenged China was perfectly willing to give its full backing to the Sudanese government in the late 1990s as the latter focused its efforts on recovering control of major oil fields in its long-standing genocidal war against the secessionists in southern Sudan—this, of course, before the present climate-related conflict in Darfur. The US equally provided covert counterinsurgency support to ensure the Nigerian

[19] UN Panel of Experts, *Illegal Exploitation of Natural Resources and Other Forms of Wealth of the DRC* (New York:; United Nations, 2001).

[20] Terry Slavin, 'DTI Failing to Act on Africa's Dirtiest War', *Guardian*, 6 February 2005.

[21] See David Keen, *The Economic Functions of Violence in Civil Wars*, Adelphi Papers 319 (Oxford: Oxford University Press, and International Institute for Strategic Studies, 1998), for further development of the argument.

government maintained firmer control of its oil-rich delta region.[22] In democratic countries, such as Britain, the intermeshing of relationships between private military companies (PMCs) such as Executive Outcomes UK and the Canadian-owned Heritage Oil (the latter the concessionary in a huge but highly dubious 3.1 million hectares stakeout of Ituri), is known to those with a specialist watching brief but not something anybody is going to contest in a court of law.[23] Where tier one states can leave corporate business to sort out their camouflaged, old-style mercantilist methods of access to tier three African resource wealth, or that elsewhere, they will.

Of course, not all contemporary resource conflicts can be so easily packaged in this corporatized way. Across the DRC border in Rwanda, recent studies have suggested that behind the overt Tutsi-Hutu ethnic-cum-political conflict was a neo-Malthusian style crisis founded on the country's rapidly burgeoning rural population as set against a rapidly diminishing ecological resource base.[24] Thus, the intense competition for land in Rwanda in the decades up to 1994 not only produced tensions between land-owning 'haves' and 'have nots', they also drove the marginalized latter increasingly up the slopes of Rwanda's famous hillsides. The further up they went the more they cut down the remaining forest, the greater the erosion they caused. By 1990, an estimated 8,000 hectares per year 'enough to annually feed about 40,00 people' was being washed down the country's slopes. Arguably even worse, the rate at which the forest was being cut down and consumed for fuel was outstripping its ability to regenerate itself

[22] See Doug Stokes, 'Blood for Oil? Global Capital, Counter-Insurgency and the Dual Logic of American Energy Security', *Review of International Studies* 33 (2007), 245–64.

[23] Duncan Campbell: 'Making a Killing: Marketing the New Dogs of War', 11 July 2008, http://www.craigmurray.org.uk/archives/2008/07/duncan_cam pbell.html for the PMC: Heritage connect and, by extension, the wider world of corporate business.

[24] Catherine Andre and Jean-Philippe Platteau, 'Land Relations Under Unbearable Stress: Rwanda Caught in the Malthusian Ttrap', *Journal of Economic Behaviour and Organisation* 34 (1998), 1–47; Robert M. McNab and Abdul Latif Mohamed, 'Human Capital, Natural Resources Scarcity and the Rwandan Ggenocide,'', *Small Wars and Insurgencies* 17:3 (2006), 311–32. Also Diamond, *Collapse*, chap. 10, 'Malthus in Africa: Rwanda's Genocide'.

by a factor of well beyond two to one. In turn, that meant the peasants fell back on straw and other crop residues for fuel, depriving the soil of its normal nutrient cycle.[25] When it came to the crunch in 1994, they were communes where there was intense grassroots bloodletting, yet few or no Tutsi among the victims.

There is, however, a point of interconnectedness between the deforestation that occurred over a period of decades in Rwanda and what happened more rapidly to much vaster stretches of DRC, as a result of foreign government, especially Ugandan and Zimbabwean military-cum-corporate concessions, at the height of the Congo conflict.[26] Indeed, in overarching terms, these might be seen as two sides of the same coin, one localized and demotically driven, the other venal and corporate, yet both of which, through the asset-stripping of one of the planet's basic ecological reserves are contributing to a planetary backlash that could well herald what some have already dubbed 'an anthropocene extinction event'.[27] After all, while on the one hand, tropical forests offer a major CO_2 bio-sink mitigating the effect of anthropogenic climate change, on the other, the ongoing and accelerating rate of their loss is estimated to be causing between a fifth and a quarter of current global carbon emissions.[28] Somewhere, in all this, are the people, both indigenous and incomer, who live in and depend on the tropical forest. It is no coincidence that some of the most intense conflicts of the here and now are between those seeking to maximize its dead-end exploitation and commodification for quick monetary gain and those who depend upon its *sustainability* for their livelihoods and wellbeing. Often lethal struggles between state-backed

[25] James Gasana, '"Remember Rwanda?": People and Population Pressures report, 6 January 2003', http://www.peopleandplanet.net/doc.php%3Fid%3D1780/.

[26] UN Panel, 'Illegal Exploitation', 11–13; Ssee also Patrick Alley, 'Branching Out, Zimbabwe's Resource Colonialism in DRC' (London: Global Witness, August 2001), http://www.globalwitness.org/.

[27] See David Wasdell, 'Beyond the Tipping Point: Positive Feedback and the Acceleration of Climate Change', http://www.meridian.org.uk/Resources/Global%20Dynamics/TippingPoint/index.htm.

[28] See both World Rainforest Movement (WRM) http://www.fern.org/pages/about/wrm.html/ and Biofuelwatch, http://www.biofuelwatch.org.uk/background.php for regular up dated information and articles on this theme.

corporations and diminishing tribal groups over land and water rights have been part and parcel of conflict in the Amazon basin for decades, particularly in recent years over clearances to make way for export-orientated soya bean production. There are similar processes unfolding in India and Borneo.[29]

But do any of these instances of what are often disparagingly referred to as 'low-level' violence amount to genocide? And do they serve in any sense as indicators for how climate change per se might impact on much broader elements of the world's populations who are not arboreal but agricultural, or urban? There is one case, however, where recent historic experience combines with latent conditions of the present to offer a potentially valuable insight into what could be an aspect of all our futures: mass genocidal displacement.

From Past to Future: The Case of the Chittagong Hill Tracts

During the late 1970s and 1980s, efforts by the newly formed state of Bangladesh to comprehensively integrate, consolidate, and develop its sylvan eastern hill region led to the intensification of an already long-sustained campaign of military-led terror and violence against its then estimated 700,000 indigenous peoples, collectively known as the *jumma*. Some NGOs, as well as expert researchers, considered these, and indeed the wider sequence of events in the CHT, as genocide.[30] My own 1999 study was slightly more circumspect, pointing less to

---

[29] OECD Development Centre Working Paper 233, 'Land, Violent Conflict and Development (Paris: OECD, 2004); Melanie Jarman, *Climate Change* (London: Pluto Press, 2007), 121; 'Indian Maoist Violence', *Reuters*, 27 August 2008, http://www.alertnet.org/db/crisisprofiles/IN_MAO.htm%3Fv%3Din_detail. Also Forest Peoples Programme, http://www.forestpeoples.org/ for regular updates.

[30] See *The Chittagong Hill Tracts, Militarisation, Ooppression and the Hill Tribes* (London: Anti-Slavery Society, 1984); '*Life Is Not Ours'; Land And Human Rights in the CHT, Bangladesh* (Copenhagen and Amsterdam: Chittagong Hill Tracts Commission, 1991); *Genocide in Bangladesh, Survival International Review* 43 (London: Survival International, 1984); Wolfgang Mey, 'Genocide in Bangladesh: The CHT Case', paper for 7th European Conference on Modern South Asian Studies, 7–11 July 1981 (unpublished). Amnesty by contrast is one NGO which was notable for not articulating the conflict as genocide per se. *Bangladesh, Unlawful Killings and Torture in the Chittagong Hill Tracts* (London: Amnesty International, 1986).

any given moment of mass annihilation and more to an ongoing campaign of mass human rights violations, including some thirteen major massacres in the period 1980– to 1993, described as elements of a 'creeping genocide'.[31] A quantitative survey of the fatalities from the conflict has never been conducted. Nevertheless, it is also clear that the violence reached its high-point in the early 1980s when the then dictatorship of General Ershad initiated a full-scale military campaign against a growing native insurgency. There were clearly some similarities here with contemporaneous events in the Guatemala highlands, though a slightly closer parallel might be drawn with the Indonesian military campaigns in Irian Jaya and East Timor. As in the latter cases, Dhaka's aim was to eliminate by force the native resistance in order to clear the CHT 'frontier' for mass migration and settlement—in its case, of Bengali peasant plains farmers, into the highlands valleys.[32] With the natives duly subjugated and ultimately swamped by the incomers, the state could then get on with its more focused, primary agenda, the maximization of the region's perceived resource potential: its timber, water supply, mineral and most of all, its believed oil and gas reserves, for state-corporate development.

In all this we may note close parallels with our wider picture of forcing factors for violence in the contemporary world. As with Rwanda, demographic pressures in an appallingly poor, 'underdeveloped' third world, agricultural economy were well-noted in the 1970s and 1980s by Western donor communities. With the Bangladeshi population already at that stage rising fast from around 40 million in the 1950s to its present 141 million—with some estimates suggesting further exponential increase to 340 million before stabilization—here was a country whose size was equivalent to Nicaragua yet whose demographic weight made it the eighth largest in the world.[33] Moreover, with 80 per cent of that population living in conditions of absolute poverty all policy-makers, whether within the state, or

---

[31] Mark Levene, 'The Chittagong Hill Tracts: A Case Study in the Political Economy of "Creeping" Genocide', *Third World Quarterly* 20:2 (1999), 339–69.

[32] Bernard Nietschmann, 'Indonesia: Bangladesh, Disguised Invasions of Indigenous Nations, Third World Colonial Expansion', *Fourth World Journal* 1:2 (1985), 96–7.

[33] Levene, 'Chittagong Hill Tracts', 347.

among first world aid providers, were agreed that only radical, remedial action could lift the people's prospects and in the process prevent massive social unrest. Development of an international market-orientated textile industry employing mass cheap labour, much of it emanating from a degraded countryside, was part and parcel of Bangladesh's masterplan to keep afloat in a globalized economy, if only in order to service the country's enormous and growing external debt. An extreme case of social Darwinism in practice—what has been dubbed 'the race to the bottom'—such efforts to earn foreign currency and so avoid the country from falling out of its already weak tier two status altogether have, however, failed to transcend the underlying limiting factors.

Bangladesh, at heart, is a great riverine delta region seeping into the Bay of Bengal. Historically, the source of its fertility and with it of its great human fecundity, both elements now represent a trap for Bangladesh's inhabitants. It is the delta's ecological fragility, as evident in the increasing severity of monsoon-driven cyclones, on the one hand, the intensity of riverine erosion from up-river Himalayan deforestation and glacial retreat, on the other, which are the immediate causes of this encroaching catastrophe.[34] Back in the 1970s and 1980s, nobody in Bangladesh properly understood that global warming was the key amplifier and accelerator to these processes. Or that year on year, decade on decade, this situation could only get worse, not least from sea-level rises which would lead inexorably to deltaic flooding and ultimately complete inundation. Factor in the rather larger rises in global temperature than that which had been previously adduced by the Intergovernmental Panel on Climate Change (IPCC) and figures of a over 70 million Bangladeshis permanently displaced from their domicile have become common currency.[35]

Yet in one sense, state and donor policy-making was already fixated on the problem of a displaced population more than a generation ago. And as nobody in positions of power either inside or outside the country was prepared to grapple with the fundamental social issue

[34] See Abdul M. Hafiz and Nahid Islam, 'Environmental degradation and intra/interstate conflicts in Bangladesh', Environment and Conflicts Project, (ENCOP), Zurich and Bern, Occasional Paper No. 6, May 1993.

[35] Mabey, *Delivering*, 85.

at stake—namely, the tightening *zamindari* (landowner) grip over an increasingly indebted peasant class, and, as a consequence, the former's consolidation and aggrandizement of their own landholdings, at the expense of the latter—the focus on some sort of partial internal population transfer founded on the supposedly almost people-free 9nine per cent of the country which was the CHT, had a certain logical ring to it. CHT's existence within Bangladesh may have been something of a political accident, emanating from the rushed nature of the 1947 partition of British India into India and Pakistan but it was also clearly an undisputed part of the latter's sovereign territory. In international eyes, therefore, Bangladesh was free to legitimately 'develop' the region as it chose. The country has already suffered mass trauma and bloodshed in its 1971 secession from Pakistan. No aid donor was going 'to endanger the survival of millions of Bangladeshis just for the sake of the hill tribes—who are 0.5 per cent of our population'.' So stated an official Dhaka spokesperson, in 1994.[36] In principle, he was correct. Dhaka in the late 1970s and early 1980s received foreign assistance and funding for its migration programme; foreign consultancies were engaged to offer advice on how to diversify a return from the region's forest potential, Western counter-insurgency experts too, were soon on hand to assist in stamping out the *jumma* insurgency.[37]

The outcome was genocide or, if not that, something very close to it. Ershad's settlement programme found itself stymied by ferocious resistance from the armed wing of the *jumma*'s chief political movement, the JSS: clearly the notion of CHT as practically people-less was false. In response, the military ratcheted up not only its own anti-*jumma* terror campaign but also organized Muslim radicals among the settlers into paramilitary units to do the same. As a consequence, the ethno-religious elements of the conflict as one between majority Muslim Bengalis and minority tribal Buddhists and animists became much more pronounced. The region itself descended into chaos. Tens of thousands of *jumma* who were not immediate partiesy to the conflict, or who had survived being incarcerated into military-run strategic

[36] Quoted in Tim McGirk, 'Fear-Filled Return Home for Exiles', *Independent*, 25 February 1994.
[37] Levene, 'Chittagong Hill Tracts,'', 354–6.

hamlets, fled; at least 40,000 of them across the border into India. But if the indigenous population of CHT had now become largely a displaced one, so too, from a different angle, were the some four to six hundred thousands settlers who found themselves unable to adapt their traditional plains husbandry to entirely different conditions. In the process, they further undermined the once traditional swidden (slash and burn) agriculture which had sustained the *jumma* habitat for centuries[38] and so confirmed the settlers' utter dependency on the military in order to be protected and fed.

Again we can see standard 'business as usual' elements at work but one we now have no choice but to set against an entirely new and exponential order of stress provided by anthropogenic climate change. In this context, the question one must starkly pose can only be: 'if the delta is inundated within the next century, as the climate science now seems to consider *inevitable*, where will its people go?'. The issue is hardly an academic one: whole areas of the cyclone-buffeted Sundarbans are already disappearing very fast, leaving the country's capital ever-more heaving with the inflow of environmental refugees. But then the crisis is more than simply an internal one. India, already chastened by previous experiences of millions of refugees fleeing from Bangladesh—not to say its own ongoing internal sequence of climate-related disasters—is busily constructing a more than 2000- mile long fence along the international border. The signal to Dhaka is blunt: its future travails will not be Delhi's responsibility.[39] In such circumstances, is it entirely absurd to imagine a last, mad, desperate struggle for Bangladesh's survival played out between the embattled military custodians of Dhaka's residual, sinking state and its equally embattled hill peoples?

[38] See Kabita Chakma and Glen Hill, 'Thwarting the Indigenous Custodians of Biodiversity', in Philip Gain (ed.), *Bangladesh: Land, Forest and Forest People*, (Dhaka: Society for Environment and Human Development, 1995), 123–37.

[39] See 'Time runs out for islanders on global warming's front line', *Observer*, 30 March 30 2008; also http://www.independent.co.uk/news/world/asia/special-report-bangladesh-is-set-to-disappear-under-the-waves-by-the-end-of-the-century-850,938.html.

Scenario 2: Business as Usual Overwhelmed by Global Warming

To raise such scenarios seems grotesque where not gratuitously apocalyptic. One can try and temper them with the argument that Bangladesh's situation is a unique one,[40] that its particular circumstances are unlikely to be replicated elsewhere, or alternatively, that global warming is not as dire as many of the climate scientists are predicting.

This author, however, would argue that on both counts the contrary is true. The cumulative radicalization of Bangladesh's woes currently in train are no more, nor less, than a harbinger of the wider global crisis. All the evidence, moreover, is stacking up to suggest earlier climate predictions radically underestimated the rate at which CO_2 is building up in the atmosphere, leading to much more serious earth system feedbacks and hence producing much steeper as well as more imminent average temperature rises than previously thought possible. What the particular circumstances of Bangladesh-CHT provide is insight into how an interaction between rapid climate change and the vagaries of *political* geography could lead to contours of extreme, including genocidal violence along *two* possibly parallel trajectories. In the first, states will practice triage against those parts of its citizen or subject population considered least savable or, more cynically put, most superfluous. The specific conditions of climate catastrophe, however, raise the possibility of exclusion from a universe of obligation being practisced *across* borders, and even applying to whole populations of perhaps, *once* sovereign states. In contemporary international law, a polity must have a defined territory to exist as a state and so enter into relations with other states.[41] The case of an increasingly submerged Bangladesh thus poses questions not only about what leverage its twilight leadership might have within the world community but also what status its surviving citizens would enjoy as fleeing for safety they are confronted with the reality of

---

[40] See Astri Suhrke, 'Environmental Degradation, Migration and the Potential for Violent Conflicts,',' in Nils Petter Gleditsch et al. (eds.), *Conflict and the Environment* (Dordrecht: Kluwer Academic, 1997), 257.

[41] Mabey, *Delivering*, 87; Helen Fein, 'Genocide: A Sociological Perspective', *Current Sociology*, 38:1 (1990), 1–126 for more on the universe of obligation concept as a tool of genocide studies.

India's fence. In these circumstances, the possibility of genocide, whether at first or second remove, becomes a function of a still extant state repudiating any notion of obligation to those from a neigbouring one who *ipso facto* have become stateless.

Climate change realities in fact are pushing all manner of states towards radical measures designed to deny entry to those so dispossessed. Indeed, it would appear to be the richest amongst such states who are most exercised about the environmental refugee 'threat'. In a recent climate change war game, for instance, conducted under the auspices of the Centre for New American Security (CNAS), game players placed migration-prevention as the number one priority in any long-term framework agreement on climate change, with an emphasis on the repatriation of climate refugees to their country of origin as the necessary outcome. The proposed agreement stated non-coercive repatriation as the 'preferred' method towards this purpose, though one might be inclined to ask how exactly that would be accomplished for peoples from low-lying Pacific island nations such as Tuvalu or Kiribati who are already threatened with early inundation?[42] In fact, the implied policy recommendations offered in the CNAS game are consistent with the general thrust of US 'security' thinking dating back at least to the 2004 Pentagon-commissioned report on 'abrupt' climate change. Then, as now, the whole emphasis has been not on humanitarian assistance to states or societies reeling from climate catastrophe but rather on shoring up 'fortress America' against waves of anticipated environmental refugees. Behind such thinking too, are major Department of Defense research and development (R&D) programmes whose purpose is to develop a range of hi-tech weapon systems designed to interdict and immobilize 'perimeter' intruders. Proclaimed to be non-lethal, what damage such tazers, projectiles, 'calmative' chemicals, as well as heat and noise weapons would actually do to masses of human beings in the event of a major 'emergency' is entirely uncharted territory.[43]

[42] CNAS, Climate Change Wargame', 28–30 July 2008, http://www/cnas. org/ClimateWarGame/. Thanks to Marc Hudson for alerting me to this exercise.

[43] See Dave Webb, 'Thinking the Worst, The Pentagon Report'; Steve Wright, 'Preparing for Mass Refugee Flows, the Corporate-Military Sector,'', respectively chapters. 2 and 3 of David Cromwell and Mark Levene (eds.) *Surviving Climate Change, The Struggle to Avert Global Catastrophe* (London: Pluto Press, 2007).

The Oxford Research Group has aptly described this sort of thinking as that of a 'control paradigm' or more exactly 'liddism': a situation where leading states, instead of attempting to address the causes of the problem of which they, as major carbon emitters are at the root, instead place their emphasis on preserving the status quo, primarily through military means.[44] Liddism, as policy, is clearly both illogical and redundant. It cannot resolve the problem because the climate change threat embraces all humanity and so can only be mitigated by an international cooperation aimed at an overall planetary reduction of ghg emissions to zero, in an already carbon-saturated atmosphere. Nor can liddism hope to save the rich fossil-fuel dependent economies themselves, through some sort of security isolation in the shorter- term, not least as their heavily populated but low-lying or deltaic metropolitan regions are swept by an increasing frequency of climate-driven storm surge and or, flooding, in part as a consequence of polar ice-melt.[45]

Again as a further empirical example of what this may actually mean, consider at the other end of the spectrum conflict-ridden Central Asia, most obviously Afghanistan. At the time when this chapter was being drafted in late October 2008, the Royal United Services Institute (RUSI) announced that eight million people in that country could now be threatened with winter-time starvation, as much as a consequence of global warming-induced drought and soaring world food prices as due to the ongoing Taliban insurgency. With the retreat of Himalayan glaciers and hence the further deterioration of already stressed irrigation systems in a region hugely dependent on the careful husbanding of exactly this limited, or seasonal water resource, complete societal breakdown *is* conceivable.[46] Numerous expert studies have considered how governments in

---

[44] Chris Abbott, Paul Rogers, and John Sloboda, *Global Responses to Global Threats, Sustainable Security for the 21st Century* (Oxford: Oxford Research Group, 2007), 28.

[45] See IPPC 4th assessment report (AR4), 2007, http://www.ipcc.ch/ipccreports/ar4-syr.htm, 10, for examples of anticipated regional impacts.

[46] 'Afghanistan, Preventing an Approaching Crisis', RUSI briefing note, 31, 31October 2008, http://www.rusi.org/downloads/assets/RUSIAfghanBriefing Notepdf.pdf/. Also Stephan Harrison, 'Climate Change, Future Conflict and the Role of Climate Science', *Royal United Services Institute Journal*, 150:6 (2005), 18–23.

environmentally challenged parts of the world, when combined with demographic pressures and weak undeveloped economies, are the most likely to default on delivery of basic services to their populations and so most likely to pay the price through increased militancy (jihadist or otherwise), insurgency, and warlordism.[47] But what we are contemplating here are countries that have not simply 'failed' per se in the Western lexicon of what constitutes 'success' and failure but ones that may actually 'disappear' off the modern sovereign state map altogether. After all, great civilizations of the past, famously along the Silk Route, did exactly this as the wells and oases dried up and the raiders closed in.[48] The question for us is what happens—as in past times, happened—to the peoples of these polities in the face of such calamities? Left to their own devices do they, for instance, fight it out among themselves in some Hobbesian zero-sum game, as the food and water resource itself diminishes to zero? This would be a truly *post*-genocidal landscape in which atrocity is not simply the norm as perpetuated by the simple conditions of extreme scarcity but one in which, without the state or even outside agencies to offer a calculus as to the political purposefulness of violence, no one single group of actors can be blamed, let alone held to account, for the resulting carnage.

For the substantial (tier two) bloc of states, in other words those who seek to stay afloat as coherent political entities above this fray, the climate change threat operates in *political* terms from two pincer-like directions. In the first, there is the straightforward fear of being 'swamped' by environmental refugees from a neighbouring state or states which have already fallen into the lower tier three category, or may soon do so. In the second, the threat operates on the level of finding oneself unable to resist other wealthier, more powerful and militarily stronger—though not necessarily tier one—states,

[47] See amongst others, Colin H. Kahl, *States, Scarcity, Civil strife in the Developing World* (Princeton: Princeton University Press, 2006); James D. Fearon and David . D. Laitin, 'Ethnicity, Insurgency, Civil War', *American Political Science Review* 97:1 (2003), 75–90; Jon Barnett and W. Neil Adger, 'Climate Change, Human Security, and Violent Conflict', *Political Geography* 26 (2007), 639–55.

[48] See Rob Johnson, 'Climate Change, Resources and Future War: The Case of Central Asia', in Mark Levene, Rob Johnson, and Penny Roberts (eds.), *History at the End of the World? History, Climate Change and the Possibility of Closure* (Penrith: Humanities E-Books, 2009).

interfering with or directly appropriating one's own scarce resources, most obviously food, water, as well as energy supply. The anxiety of having to navigate between these twin Scylla and Charybodis—like perils, moreover, will be exacerbated for each state's elite by a historic sense of mission to carry their country forward to ever higher levels of preferably carbon-fuelled, industrially- based development in order to meet the needs of a fiercely competitive global market. Climate change, of course, contradicts this aspiration foursquare. But it does so not simply through its range of growing physical stresses but in the psycho-cultural burden it imposes on those who have imbibed nothing other than a *telos* of development.

A world replete with nuclear weapons, moreover, could turn a struggle for diminishing resources into an altogether more deadly encounter involving whole national populations. In normal conditions, leading tier two players, including Russia, China, and India might be looking forward to a political ascendancy on the world stage without recourse to inter-state conflict let alone use of their nuclear arsenals. But then how are they likely to respond to conditions in which collapsing neighbours might use the threat of military force, including, where those states have their own nuclear weapons, to punch their way out of encroaching turmoil? Ecological fragility could be the final straw for an already embattled, increasingly lawless, indeed fragmenting Pakistan which, nevertheless, still retains its nuclear wherewithal. By the same token, how is a clearly tier one, nuclear-armed Israel set amongst altogether more precarious, yet hostile tier two Middle Eastern neighbours likely to react to a sustained regional water crisis? Or is it, actually, the other way round: an Israel which has most to fear not least from the Palestinians of the occupied territories as perhaps, they make one final, desperate subaltern attempt to redress the ecological as well as political balance?

Finally, though, where do the leading tier one states fit into this darkening scene? Expert Western opinion generally grafts a map of already existing global economic poverty onto any forward-looking plot of vulnerability to climate conflict.[49] Yet the very fact that a very

---

[49] See Dan Smith and Janani Vivekananda, *A Climate of Conflict: The Links between Climate Change, Peace, and War* (London: International Alert, 2007), 18–19.

poor country like Ivory Coast, for instance, has taken in so many environmental refugees could equally indicate that the less 'developed' a state or society, the more resilient it is to the most serious environmental or socio-economic challenges, man or nature can throw at it.[50] At least populations in such countries (whether urban or rural) have direct relationships with land and water, however degraded those basic elements have become. By contrast, it is in rich tier one countries where such relationships are at their most tenuous and where, arguably, fears of mass refugee 'invasions' are also at their most intense. It is a truism that hierarchic, complex, city-centered societies are only three or four meals away from anarchy. Catastrophic breakdown in other words, is quite conceivable in the face of some all-embracing crisis, not least given these societies' absolute dependency on thin, often distant supply lines to provide basic services, including water, food, heat, and light.[51] In circumstances in which standard front-line public services find themselves overwhelmed or unable to cope, populations will not only be unable to meet their own basic physical needs but also be seriously psychologically disturbed by the realities confronting them. It is in exactly such emergency conditions that elites of tier one state might become the most obvious candidates to make responses which in normal times would be deemed not only unthinkable but unforgivable.

Conclusion

In the course of this chapter, we seem to have come a long way from Lemkin or of his vision of how genocide, through international law, might one day be ultimately removed from the actions of human states and societies. Lemkin's purport was not only entirely honourable but was passionately fought for, largely single-handedly. To cut across this

[50] Mabey, *Delivering*, 119. See also 'Climate Change and Displacement,'', *Forced Migration Review* 31 (October 2008), for the current debate on third world responses to environmental refugees compared with other migration and/or displacement factors.

[51] See Deborah MacKenzie, 'The End of Civilisation', and MacKenzie, 'Are We Doomed?,'', *New Scientist*, 5 April 2008; Joseph A. Tainter, *The Collapse of Complex Societies* (Cambridge: Cambridge University Press, 1988), for the wider argument.

aspiration with not only an entirely more dystopian forecast but one which in key respects questions the long-term value of the term 'genocide' itself, seems both churlish and contradictory. Lemkin's law attempted to achieve not simply clarity on the subject but in the process a mechanism for making things better. By contrast, we have argued that without a firm grip on the understanding of the driving forces which determine the wider formation and organization of our present international system, implementation of the Convention will not only remain piecemeal and inadequate but will be rapidly overtaken by forces which render its fragile efficacy null and void.

There is something more which needs to be said here. While we are now standing at the apex of a particular human trajectory, at the same time, we also possess sufficient analytical tools and material evidence to survey the *entire* landscape of human history and experience which *preceded* it. Throughout the historical record, the struggle for human existence carried with it, repeated proclivities towards *strages gentium*. What is distinct about this potentially final global epoch is that the disparity between the material overreach and the limits of the planetary carrying capacity are taking us all—tier one included—into a *totalizing* mode of exterminatory behaviour. If one is thus looking for aone single prediction it is this: it will be mass self-violence, not climate change per se which will take us over the abyss.

What is the antidote? On one level, it is a terribly simple one. Arnold Toynbee—that same great if now much forgotten historian of civilizsation—who also had so much of prescient value to say on the subject of genocide—put it aptly just before his death. Our mission must be to seek not 'a material mastery' over the non-human environment, but for 'a spiritual mastery' over ourselves.[52] As for Mahatma Gandhi, that apostle, as well as arguably greatest exponent of nonviolence of recent times, he put the case even more tersely on behalf of the peoples of this overcrowded planet: there is 'enough for everybody's need but not for everybody's greed'.[53]

---

[52] Arnold Toynbee, *Mankind and Mother Earth: A Narrative History of the World* (New York and Oxford: Oxford University Press, 1976), 18.

[53] Quoted in M. S. Dadage, 'Science and Spirituality,", http://www.mkgandhi.org/articles/sci.%20and%20sprituality.htm. Significantly this translates exactly into Aubrey Meyer's visionary yet scientific Contraction and

In short, for those who would seek to avoid genocide in the twenty-first century, the task cannot somehow be reduced to Lemkin's law. The phenomenon cannot be contained within this box: it is too fundamental a by-product of a more general dysfunction, not to say, even as it transmutes into persistent post-genocide, a key indicator of a more all-encompassing Nemesis. To arrest the encroaching inevitability of this trajectory will require, amongst other things, a thoroughly post-Lemkian effort to recognize the false chimera of the globalizsing project and with it the *necessity* for a sufficiency and sustainability upon which the term *oikonomia*—economy—was originally founded. Such an approach will be geared towards the values of human scale and with it of an entirely gentler and certainly more heterarchic social and communal empowerment.

Coda

Ten years on from the original writing of this chapter, the recognition of where we have arrived at in species terms seems finally, if vastly belatedly, to be seeping through into public consciousness. The plethora of scientific reports on the destruction of a planetary bio-diversity upon which we all fundamentally depend have become too pervasive and all-encompassing for any but the most obdurately and willfully denialist to ignore.[54] With the Bulletin of Atomic Scientists' Doomsday Clock now symbolically poised at a mere two minutes to midnight, the threat of mass biological extinction added to that of nuclear obliteration has impelled hundreds of thousands of young and not so young grass-roots activists around the world to take to the streets to

---

Convergence proposition for how humankind might still tackle climate change. See Aubrey Meyer, 'The Case for Contraction and Convergence,'', in Cromwell and Levene, *Surviving*, 29–56.

[54] Sandra Diaz et al., United Nations Intergovernmental Science-Policy Platform on Biodiversity and Ecosystem Services (IPBES) global assessment report, 6 May 2019, ipbes.net/for the most wide-ranging recent meta-analysis. For a much-noted report on catastrophic insect decline see also Francisco Sanchez-Bayo et al., 'Worldwide Decline of the Entomofauna: A Review of its Drivers', *Biological Conservation*, 232 (April 2019), 8–27.

demand radical action on anthropogenic climate change.[55] Whether after decades of inertia, governments—and corporate business—will heed this call in what has been described as 'a closing window of opportunity' remains open to question.[56] Even so, at the time of writing there appears just the glimmer of hope that advanced (and hence the most materialist and consumer-driven) societies might begin to move beyond tinkering with the problem to a concerted effort to reduce dependence on fossil- fuels and towards an essentially renewables-based carbon neutral economy.

Unfortunately, any notion that a series of technological fixes, however beneficial, will of themselves release the world from ongoing environmental breakdown, including radically oscillating temperatures, polar and glacial ice melt, sea- level rise and consequent coastal inundation, cyclone havoc, flood, and, at the other end of the spectrum, drought, wholesale forest-fire destruction, and accelerating desertification, are belied by the earth science facts. The climatic impacts that we are experiencing today are the time-lag effect of accumulated carbon dioxide concentrations in the atmosphere from several decades ago. In other words, waking up to a perpetual climate emergency in relation to this chapter's human focus narrows down to the diminishing carrying capacity—or if one prefers parametric conditions—of the planet. At a minimum one might suggest that translates for *homo sapiens*' populations into clean drinking water, healthy soils upon which to grow edible plants, or, in the absence of terra firma, sea or lake-borne biota, plus materials and fuel for shelter and warmth against the elements.[57] And where those parametric conditions no longer pertain or can sustain such populations, they will—where they can—do precisely the same as other species in order

[55] Bulletin of the Atomic Scientists, http://thebulletin.org/. For growing grassroots mobilizsation against climate breakdown, see notably Extinction Rebellion, http://rebellion.earth/.

[56] Laurie Laybourn-Langton et al., 'This is a Crisis: Facing up to the Age of Environmental Breakdown', IPPR report. February 2019, https://www.ippr.org/files/2019-02/risk-and-environmentfeb19.pdf.

[57] Xiaoxin Wang, et al., 'Climate Change of 4C Global Warming above Preindustrial Levels', *Advances in Atmospheric Sciences* 35:7 (July 2019), 757–70, for the most recent meta-analysis, confirming the likelihood of 4C warming by 2084. See also Jason Kottke's speculative *New Scientist* 2009 map, https://kottke.org/18/

to survive. They will move. This destabilizing variable underscores the yawning contradiction between a globalizsed yet territorially boun-darizsed modernity and the reality of biospheric collapse. In turn, this sets the most likely, globally endemic contours for future, genocidal conflict, that is,i.e. between those dispossessed of a home and those still in possession.

At this present time, the involuntary flight of peoples—the figure currently stands at one every two seconds—not necessarily for envir-onmental reasons but increasingly so, has led either to large-scale internal displacement within state boundaries, thus putting vast stress on political systems whose ability to provide basic services to its citizenry is already at breaking point, or movement beyond those borders. The largest movements of both kinds overwhelmingly are in the very poorest third world countries where environmental break-down interacts with war, civil strife, and glaring social injustice.[58] What is becoming ever more apparent, however, is that movements of the dispossessed and traumatized are beginning to impact heavily on wealthy or wealthier countries who until recently imagined them-selves largely immune from both climate change crisis and mass refugee flows. An event such as the genocide-precipitated mass flight of over 720,000 Rohingya from Myanmar from August 2017 was thus perceived in the West as at several degrees removed from themselves. Yet the civil war turmoil in Syria beginning a few years earlier and the subsequent flight of over a million seeking asylum in the European Union (EU)—though this actually only a fraction of the displaced total—proved critical in polarizsing EU inhabitants for or against Middle Eastern, Asian, and African refugees, whether Muslim or otherwise.[59]

02/a-map-of-the-world-after-four-degrees-of-warming/ for the likely remaining food growing zones under these conditions, primarily in high northern latitudes and western Antarctica.

[58] 'UNHCR: Figures at a Glance', https://www.unhcr.org/uk/figures-at-a-glance.html.

[59] Ibid.; Phillip Connor, 'Where Syrian Refugees Have Settled Worldwide', Pew Research Center, 29 January 2018, https://www.pewresearch.org/fact-tank/2018/01/29/where-displaced-syrians-have-resettled/.

The populist backlash in favour of a supposed national integrity and a perceived cultural homogeneity highlights a potential scenario of things to come as many millions more refugees flee poor, ravaged, environmentally exhausted, or indeed territorially diminished third world lands to the relative safety of rich yet still temperate refugia. Except for precisely the reasons explicit in this survey, the opportunity to do so will either narrow or close entirely as these states or state agglomerations' security apparatuses throw up yet more barbed wire, lethal perimeters, and buffer zones to deny the world's 'have nots' ingress. Indeed, on present evidence one can almost infer a hierarchy of behavioural response, the richer a country is, or alternatively perceives its entitlement to be, the more jealously it reinforces its borders to preserve its sacrosanct 'way of life', while on the receiving end the more obvious a refugee's racial, ethno-religious, cultural, and linguistic difference, the more probable her or his exclusion. And as the climate noose tightens the populist clamour to remove those who arrived before the drawbridge was pulled tight will also grow, to which a vast no man's land of Zbasyn-like makeshift camps to which thousands of Jews eructed from Germany yet disallowed entry into Poland found themselves dumped in 1938, offers just one bitter contemplation.

Yet this could well be the dystopian world of the near future, even while founded on a key 'normative' legacy of the recent past at the very core of Lemkin's urgent exertions for the establishment of a universal Genocide Convention: the nation-state. It has been both corner stone and building block of the international political system for over 100a hundred years, indeed the notion of each and every state's sovereign right to do as it pleases within its territorial compass goes back to Westphalian origins. For Lemkin, however, the modern nation-state's supposed benignity to its citizens was found wanting at the first hurdle in its relationship to those communal groupings who failed to fit the elite vision of precisely that endowment of citizenship. To be sure, as other genocide scholars have also inferred, citizenship confers political and welfare rights on those embraced in its universe of obligation.[60] But to be excluded from that universe, and thus to be

---

[60] Samuel A. Moyn, 'The Universal Declaration of Human Rights of 1948 in the History of Cosmopolitanism', *Critical Inquiry* 40:4 (2014), 365–84.

deprived of some or all of the rights owed to the recognized social majority, renders the individual or communal outsider not just worthless in the eyes of the polity and its law but dangerously exposed to its wrath.

One might argue that in today's world it is not so much 'the racial, religious, ethnic and national' per se who suffer the full brunt of this exposure so much as those groups—culturally different as they obviously are—whose socio-economic practice is at odds with the developmental demands of an obsolete modernity. 4Fourth world peoples, nomads, marginal subsistence farmers, and fishermen, plus historic outsiders, such as Romani, remain the obvious candidates for such obloquy and potential erasure.[61] Yet if this *was* the diminishing margins of a 'world we have lost', heading towards some supposedly inexorable globalization, in the now clearly demarcated age of the anthropocene and thus of mass human displacement, it is, as Hannah Arendt argued long ago, the condition of statelessness which is the rock upon which shatters any concept of universal human rights by way of a state-given citizenship.[62] Indeed, if in this 'now' world of emergent biospheric breakdown any of us could become environmental refugees and so, *apatrides*, the gulf between territorially-endowed citizens and the denationalized rest offers an invitation to flag-waving chauvinists, racists, and xenophobes throughout all hemispheres to do their worst.

There is an alternative. It is to reject human worth founded on a narrow claim of *sacro egoismo* and with it the justification of a territorial state of siege against the 'barbarians at the gate'—in other words, the fear of the hordes of dispossessed who might envelop us—and to replace it with a renewed quest not for our citizenship but for our common humanity. This would hardly be to negate the rights of group heterogeneity. It was a desire to celebrate the ethnographic diversity of the human condition, which as Dirk Moses demonstrated in the very first chapter of the *Oxford Handbook on Genocide Research*

---

[61] Mark Levene and Daniele Conversi, 'Subsistence Societies, Globalisation, Climate Change and Genocide: Discourses of Vulnerability and Resilience', *International Journal of Human Rights* 18:3 (2014), 279–95.

[62] Hannah Arendt, *The Origins of Totalitarianism* (New York: Harcourt Books, 1994 [1951]), 278–300.

in 2010, impelled Lemkin towards a juridical mechanism for its protection.[63] The fork in the historical road did not arise through human difference but the opposite, the urge to make everyone nationally *the same*. And it should not be too difficult to see how this political building block of an environmentally predatory, destructive, and thus self-destructive globalizsation has brought us and, with us, the rest of the living world, to the existential precipice upon which we now stand. Perhaps we may yet overcome the crisis. But it might be worth finishing with the words of one notably far-sighted environmentalist, Alistair McIntosh:

> The question of whether technology, politics and economic muscle can sort the problem is the small question. The big question is about sorting the human condition. It is the question of how we can deepen our humanity to cope with possible waves of war, famine, disease and refugees without such outer wounds festering to inner destruction.[64]

Select Bibliography

Abbott, Chris, Paul Rogers, and John Sloboda, *Global Responses to Global Threats: Sustainable Security for the 21st Century* (Oxford: Oxford Research Group, 2007).

Cromwell, David, and Mark Levene (eds.), *Surviving Climate Change, The Struggle to Avert Global Catastrophe* (London: Pluto Press, 2007).

Davis, Mike, *Late Victorian Holocausts, El Nino Famines and the Making of the Third World* (London and New York: Verso, 2001).

Diamond, Jared, *Collapse: How Societies Choose to Fail or Survive* (London: Penguin, 2005).

Levene, Mark, *Genocide in the Age of the Nation State, vol. 1: The Meaning of Genocide, vol 2: The Rise of the West and the Coming of Genocide* (London and New York: I.B. Tauris, 2005).

Meadows, Donatella, et al., *The Limits to Growth* (New York: Universe, 1972).

Smith, Dan, and Janani Vivekananda, *A Climate of Conflict: The Llinks between Climate Change, Peace And War* (London: International Alert, 2007).

Tainter, Joseph A., *The Collapse of Complex Societies* (Cambridge: Cambridge University Press, 1988).

---

[63] A. Dirk Moses, 'Raphael Lemkin, Culture and the Concept of Genocide', in Donald Bloxham and A. Dirk Moses (eds.), *The Oxford Handbook of Genocide Studies* (Oxford: Oxford University Press, 2010), 22–5.

[64] Alastair McIntosh, *Hell and High Water: Climate Change, Hope and the Human Condition* (Edinburgh: Birlinn, 2008), 191.

Wallerstein, Immanuel, *The Modern World System*, 3 vols. (San Diego and New York, Academic Press Inc.,1974–1988).

Wasdell, David, 'Radiative Forcing & Climate Sensitivity', Tällberg Consensus Project, 'The Tipping Points we cannot cross: Defining the Boundary Conditions for Planetary Sustainability', 25–26 June 2008, http://www.jimhadams.com/eco/RadiativeForcingEd3.doc.

Index